Bord Fáilte
Irish Tourist Board

Ireland Guide

Bord Fáilte
Irish Tourist Board

Ireland Guide

THOMAS DUNNE BOOKS
ST. MARTIN'S GRIFFIN
New York

THOMAS DUNNE BOOKS.
An imprint of St. Martin's Press.

BORD FAILTE IRELAND GUIDE.
Copyright © 2001 by Bord Fáilte – Irish Tourist Board.
All rights reserved.

Printed in Spain by Mateu Cromo.

For information, address St. Martin's Press, 175 Fifth Avenue, New York, N.Y. 10010.

ISBN 0-312-27048-8

First published in Ireland by Gill & Macmillan Ltd.

Fourth U.S. Edition

10 9 8 7 6 5 4 3 2 1

Based on the Ordnance Survey
by permission of the Government (Permit No. 7050)

ACKNOWLEDGMENTS

The producers wish to acknowledge the dedication and commitment of the following contributors to this book:

PRODUCERS
Language & Publishing Partners International
65 Abberley, Killiney, Co. Dublin. Ireland.
Tel: 00 353 1 282 7866. Fax: 00 353 1 272 0227
E-mail: langpp@iol.ie

MANAGING EDITOR
Anna Bruning White

REGIONAL EDITOR
Birgit Roth

PUBLICATION CO-ORDINATOR
Marie Therese Naismith

DESIGN & LAYOUT
Norrie

AUTHORS (THE REGIONS)
Michael Beausang
Germaine Dalton
Lloyd Gorman
Alisha McGivern

FEATURES
Michael Beausang
Gerry Boland
Nicholas Furlong
Lloyd Gorman
Richard Killeen
Tom Mooney

REPRO
The Type Bureau

PHOTOGRAPHY
Bord Fáilte Photographic Library
Shannon Development Photographic Library
Northern Ireland Tourist Board Photographic Library
Language & Publishing Partners International Photographic Library
Gill & Macmillan Photographic Library

ILLUSTRATIONS
Fiona Arnold

MAPS
Courtesy of Ordnance Survey, Ireland.

We would like to express our deep gratitude to Bord Fáilte for their invaluable help and courtesy, particularly to John Rafferty and Frances Downey, Direct Marketing, Print and Distribution Department, and to Derek Cullen of the Photographic Unit who supplied the majority of photographs in this book.

Contents

How to Use this Guide
Information for the Visitor

Welcome   1

THE REGIONS

Bord Fáilte
Irish Tourist Board

FEATURES

HISTORY

CULTURE

LIFE AND LEISURE

ECONOMY AND ENVIRONMENT

How to Use this Guide

As well as being an authoritative and informative source of information, the Ireland Guide is designed for ease of use, and we hope it will ultimately become a tool that will help you carve out a memorable visit. This user-friendly approach is reflected in the layout and structure of the guide.

The country is divided into seven main regions:

- **The East**
- **The Midlands**
- **The Shannon Region**
- **The South**
- **The West**
- **The North-West**
- **Northern Ireland**

The east region, for example, consists of Counties Louth and Meath, Dublin, Kildare and Wicklow, and Wexford and Waterford. Rather than a straightforward county-by-county breakdown, this format brings together those counties that are clustered together in close geographical proximity. Within this framework the cities of Dublin and Belfast are examined through their own regional profiles, in acknowledgement of their individual historical, economic and sociological importance.

Each region begins with an artist's impression of the area, incorporating the most important and distinctive sites as well as geographical features.

A general introduction to the region presents the defining historical and geographical characteristics of that area, giving a flavour of its unique culture and life. Each region is then further divided into sub-regions, also shown on the artist's map at the beginning of each chapter, and finally into local areas, i.e. counties. Again the introductory passages attempt to give a flavour of the uniqueness of each region and are strongly influenced by the individual authors, who offer their own thoughts and commentaries.

Suggested touring routes provide a carefully calculated passage through each region. These routes take in the most scenic areas and the most significant historical sites as well as curious or worthwhile byways off the beaten track that merit attention. All touring routes are complemented by a full-page picture and are therefore easy to find when leafing through the book.

Interspersed throughout the book, feature articles examine various aspects of Irish life that provide an insight into Ireland's past and facets of this modern and contemporary nation.

Each local area profile concludes with a box of suggestions for 'Must see' and 'All-weather options'. The former allows the reader to see at a glance what are the major attractions or points of interest in an area, while the latter provides an alternative against the distinct likelihood of the Irish climate living up to its reputation.

Quality photographs combined with detailed and up-to-date Ordnance Survey maps enhance the visual quality of this guide, helping the traveller to find and identify individual sites and to plan excursions.

A detailed index at the back of the book allows the reader to pinpoint information at a glance. In some instances, for example where a town or historic site exists in the hinterland of two regions, it will be featured twice. In these instances the index is especially helpful.

Accommodation details, admission charges, opening times for visitor attractions have not been included, as Bord Fáilte (the Irish Tourist Board) offers up-to-the-minute and seasonal information about all of the above (see Ireland's Reservation Service advert on page 301).

Each region is colour-coded by means of a bar on the top of every page for quick and convenient reference.

MEDIA

There are numerous newspapers in Ireland, the main national dailies being the *Irish Times,* the *Irish Independent,* and the *Examiner.* There are numerous radio stations, the national station being RTE (FM, 88.2–90.0; MW, 567); there is also an Irish-language radio station, Raidió na Gaeltachta (FM, 92.6–94.4). The national television stations are RTE1, Network 2, TV3, and TG4 (in Irish), with British stations (BBC, ITV, and Channel 4) being widely available, and satellite sources transmitting Continental European stations also occasionally available.

TELEPHONE

Public telephone kiosks will be found throughout Ireland, and telephoning is also possible in pubs, hotels, and many shops. Telephone cards are widely available (from post offices and most newspaper shops), and in larger towns a number of telephone kiosks have recently been opened from where you can phone abroad at greatly reduced rates. The international access code is **00** followed by the country code (see the first part of the telephone directory). For telephone enquiries dial **1190**, for Britain **1197**, and other countries **1198**. For operator assistance dial **10** (in Northern Ireland, **100**).

POST

Standard letters and postcards to anywhere in Europe require a 32p stamp. Stamps are generally available only from post offices, which are open Monday–Friday, 9:00–17:30, and Saturday, 9:00–13:00. British rates and British stamps apply in Northern Ireland.

ILLNESS AND EMERGENCY

Visitors from EU countries have a right to free medical and hospital treatment and should procure form E111 from their national health authorities before travelling. The emergency telephone number in Ireland is **999**.

EMBASSIES

British Embassy, 31 Merrion Road, Dublin 4; telephone (01) 2695211. American Embassy, 42 Elgin Road, Dublin 4; telephone (01) 6688777. Australian Embassy, Wilton Terrace, Dublin 2; telephone (01) 6761517. Canadian Embassy, 65 St Stephen's Green, Dublin 2; telephone (01) 4781988.

New Zealand Embassy, New Zealand House, Haymarket, London SW1 4QT, England; telephone 0044 171 9308422.

TRAIN AND BUS SERVICES

Ireland possesses a basic rail network, linking most of the larger towns, but has little apart from that, except for the DART, the Dublin electrified suburban rail system. For information on connections, telephone (01) 8366222. Bus connections are much more numerous, linking not only the main towns but also villages and even remote areas. These buses are operated by the national bus service, Bus Éireann, and in Northern Ireland by Ulsterbus, though the principal routes are now also covered by private operators. The central bus depot in Dublin for mainline buses is Busáras, Store Street, Dublin 1; telephone (01) 8366111. 'Rambler' tickets allow full use of bus services in the Republic; the 'Emerald Card' ticket allows unrestricted travel by bus and rail throughout the country. The 'Eurorail' pass also covers all national bus and rail services in the Republic, as well as the ferries from Le Havre and Cherbourg to Rosslare and Cork. For information on rail services in Northern Ireland contact Victoria Railway Station, Belfast, telephone (0232) 230310, and for bus services contact Ulsterbus, Belfast, telephone (0232) 333000. Guided bus tours are available from all larger towns, as multi-day tours or as single-day or half-day excursions. For further information on bus tours, contact the local tourist office.

RULES OF THE ROAD

Road traffic in Ireland drives on the left, and the wearing of seat belts is compulsory. As the sign system is being 'Europeanised', there is at present a mixture of signs, some giving distances in miles and others in kilometres. All main roads are now signposted in kilometres in the Republic, while in Northern Ireland all signs are in miles. Speed limit signs are all in miles. The maximum speed on trunk roads is 60 miles per hour (96 km/h) and in built-up areas 30 miles per hour (48 km/h), unless otherwise specified. The maximum permitted speed on motorways is 70 miles per hour (112 km/h).

Distances in Ireland are deceptive, not least because of the quality of the roads; always allow twice as long as you would calculate (you will average about 45 miles an hour on most roads and as little as 30 miles an hour on some western coastal roads). Car hire is widely available, with a surcharge for automatic cars.

CRIME

Though Ireland still has the lowest crime rate in the European Union, petty crime is a problem in cities, and violent crime is on the increase. Be careful with handbags, and don't leave valuables in cars. The emergency number for Garda or RUC assistance is **999**. There is a special and very conscientious Victim Support service in the Republic for tourists, which will help with anything from crime to problems with credit cards; it can be contacted at (01) 4785295.

Welcome

Ireland in the year 2000 is at an exciting juncture in its development. This is because of the complex mixture of contemporary Irish life, rapid change, a young, vibrant population, an enthusiastic mental opening to the world set against a conscious retention of older values, relentless patriotism, and a continued love for language, word play, talk, and the 'social scene'.

Travellers to Ireland have traditionally enthused about the friendliness of its people, their spirited character and almost Mediterranean *joie de vivre*, the extraordinary literary heritage, and the stunning natural beauty of its landscapes and coasts. Little has changed in this, with one exception: visitors now also regularly refer to the vitality, youth and sheer trendiness of Irish society.

The tourism market in Ireland has also changed dramatically in recent years. Mass tourism is giving way to a flow of discerning tourists, often here for a second or third time, who are keen to explore new and hidden aspects of the country. The internal market has also expanded rapidly. More Irish people with expendable income are now eager to discover new corners of their own country. The Irish tourism industry has responded to these dramatic changes and provides the visitor with a modern tourism infrastructure.

It is the purpose of this book to provide you with reliable, up-to-date information researched and compiled by a team of local authors who, with their intimate knowledge, passion, and critical insights, provide the reader with the ultimate guide to Ireland in a compact and readable style. Whether you have Irish blood or not, whether this is your first visit or your umpteenth, we hope that within these pages you will discover what it is that makes Ireland special. There is much in this book on the natural beauties of Ireland, on its astonishing human-made artefacts, on the multitude of leisure activities available to the visitor, and all the information you will need for your Irish holiday.

The *Ireland Guide* explores the realities and myths of the 'Emerald Isle', the 'Celtic Tiger', the 'Literary Giant', and the 'Green, Clean Emotional Paradise'. We hope this latest edition of the *Ireland Guide* will be a good-natured companion as you discover (or rediscover) the charms of this fascinating country. Most of all, we hope you will be captivated by that love of place, the passion for the peculiar, which is universal in Ireland.

Anna Brüning White

ANNA BRÜNING WHITE
MANAGING EDITOR

The East

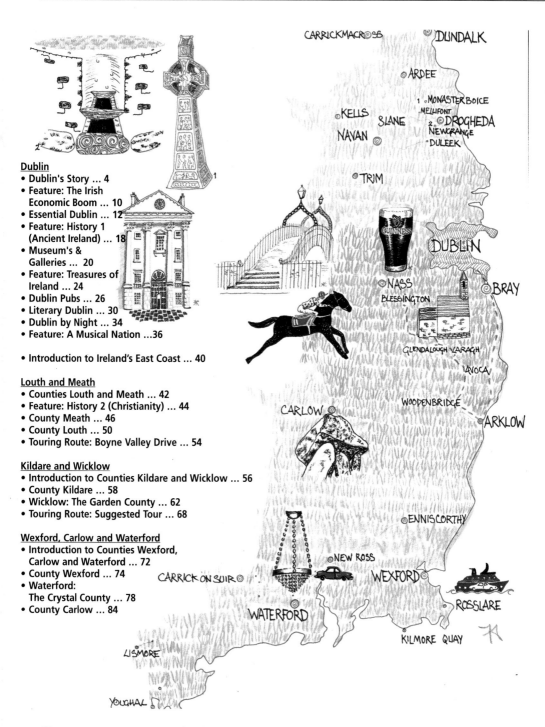

Georgian Dublin,
Upper Mount Street.

Dublin's Story

View of River Liffey by night.

To *Brendan Behan,* Dublin was 'the largest village in Europe'. For *James Joyce* it was the city that would help him understand all the other cities of the world. They may both have been right. It is a parochial city with global dimensions and a place of contradiction, change, and complexity.

Some six thousand years before the Vikings landed on the banks of the River Liffey in the year 837, the land on which Dublin stands was thinly populated by Mesolithic hunter-gatherers and later by Neolithic (New Stone Age) farmers. It was not until the arrival of the Celts about the year 700 BC that a more sophisticated life-style and culture developed. Christianity had

come to Ireland through contact with Roman Britain, and this was consolidated following the arrival of *St Patrick* about the year 461. The Norse or Scandinavians are mostly thought of as marauding warriors, but they were even more successful as traders, and their presence placed Ireland at the heart of a network stretching from the south of Spain to Scandinavia and from Greenland to Russia. However, they were not welcome visitors and were resisted by the indigenous Celts. At the Battle of Dublin in the year 919 (fought upstream of the present site of Heuston Station), the king of Tara was slain and his forces scattered by the Danes. It was not until 1014, at the Battle of

4

Clontarf, that *Brian Bórú* levelled the score. But the vanquished Vikings remained in Dublin, and it is from the date of their arrival that Dublin charts its development as a city.

The Normans arrived in Ireland at the request of the deposed High King of Ireland, *Diarmaid Mac Murchú*, who was usurped by *Ruairí Ó Conchúir* in 1166. In his bid to regain the title, Mac Murchú sought the help of King Henry II of England, who despatched 200 knights and 1,000 soldiers in 1169. This force was led by the ambitious Norman *Richard de Clare* ('Strongbow'), who married Mac Murchú's daughter, *Aoife*, thus securing his position in Ireland. With the death of the Irish lord in 1171, Henry II feared Strongbow's intentions to gain authority over the whole country. He set sail for Ireland with a massive army in the hope of dissuading the Irish chieftains from offering resistance.

The show of force worked, and during a four-month stay he changed the political landscape of the country for ever. A temporary palace was built to establish his presence and authority, Strongbow was granted the province of Leinster, and Dublin's first charter was granted to the city of Bristol, with *Hugh de Lacy* appointed its first governor. This event would irrevocably shape the future of Dublin and the country as a whole. The Machiavellian tactic of 'might is right' adopted by Henry II typified the long history of British control over Ireland, ironically begun by an internal conflict between two feuding Irish chieftains, which would continue until independence in 1922.

With the struggle for power complete, Henry wanted to ensure future compliance in the outpost. The city was fortified against outside attack, the foundations of Christ Church Cathedral were laid in 1172, and Dublin Castle, the permanent centre of British power, was built between 1204 and 1224. The pace of development quickened. Outside the city walls St Patrick's Church, built in honour of Ireland's patron saint, was granted cathedral status, and the 'Liberties' became a prominent area. The walled city comprised an area of 44 acres; and apart from the danger of attack, its citizens were constantly on their guard against the threat of fire, a serious hazard in a town consisting mostly of wooden houses, and of disease, such as the Black Death (bubonic plague), which decimated the city's population in 1348.

Dublin in the 16th and 17th centuries

Ireland's distance from the centre of power in London ensured that insurrection was always a distinct possibility for the English Crown. In 1534 *'Silken' Thomas Fitzgerald's* attempted uprising was rigorously quelled by the then King of England, *Henry VIII*. Just three years later, Henry's self-serving Act of Supremacy not only made him head of the Church but King of Ireland as well. The newly appointed Protestant king attempted to suppress all aspects of Irish culture, including religion and language. His successor, *Queen Elizabeth I* (1558–1603), carried on with the colonisation of the country with great gusto, going as far as to adopt 'ethnic cleansing' tactics. The land, property and privileges of those not loyal to the throne were taken from them and given to English subjects who were willing to move to Ireland and live here. Dublin was already under the administrative and military aegis of the Castle, yet Elizabeth felt that more could be done to impose English control over the city. In 1592 she founded Trinity College, for the purpose of 'the planting of learning, the increasing of civility, and the establishing of true religion within the realm.'

Oliver Cromwell began his ruthless and murderous conquest of Ireland from Dublin and was responsible for the deaths of thousands of men, women, and children. The actions of the English monarchy and military had over time established Dublin and its environs as the 'land of peace', commonly known as the 'Pale'; beyond this territory the promise of government was less secure.

Dublin in the 18th century

As the capital city of an English dominion, Dublin began to grow in stature. In 1600 the population was estimated to be 10,000—

much smaller than that of York, Bristol, Norwich, Edinburgh, or London. A century later it had jumped to 60,000, and by 1800 Dublin was the second-largest city in Ireland or Britain and a major European urban centre. This was the beginning of a golden age for the city. The population had trebled, and the city contained many magnificent public buildings that were unequalled in Europe. The arts flourished in this prosperous environment. *George Frederic Handel* staged the world premiere of his oratorio *Messiah* in the Old Musick Hall (now demolished) in Fishamble Street in 1742. It was during this era too that *Jonathan Swift* (1667–1734), Dean of St Patrick's Cathedral, wrote *Gulliver's Travels*.

Queen Elizabeth's legacy of investment in the education of the Protestant classes was paying dividends. They formed a new ascendancy that was confidently replacing the ancient Catholic aristocracy, both Irish and Old English, who were finding it increasingly difficult to hold their ground.

Large, elegant and elaborately decorated houses were built north and south of the River Liffey, and roads were widened and improved, while bridge-building made movement within the city easier. At a political level the Irish Parliament, in its purpose-built College Green building, persuaded the British Parliament to declare the executive and judicial independence of Ireland in 1782. Approaching the turn of the century there was little to suggest that the days of wealth and success for Dublin were in fact numbered.

In 1801, when the Act of Union came into effect, Ireland was governed directly from London. The act operated to the detriment of the city and the country. The Protestant aristocracy fled the city, and with them they took its social, cultural and economic life force. The 1798 rising had failed to overthrow English control and had strengthened the resolve of the authorities to keep a tight reign over the country.

Dublin slid into decline and its population grew wretchedly poor, living in crowded tenement buildings that were once the homes of the wealthy classes.

The Great Famine forced a million people to emigrate, while another million died of hunger and malnutrition. The disaster forced thousands into Dublin in the hope of escape. They found little solace in the workhouses of the time, and thousands died of disease as well as hunger. These conditions marked a nadir from which it would take Dublin another hundred years to recover, whereas just a century previously it had been noted for its wealth and elegance.

Not surprisingly, it was about this time that a new trend in Irish politics was emerging. Two leaders in particular tried to better the conditions of victimised Catholic tenants and the country as a whole.

Daniel O'Connell (1775–1847) earned the name 'the Liberator' for his political championing of Catholic rights in the exclusively Protestant English Parliament. Having won the right for Catholics to sit in Parliament, he went on in 1843 to choose Clontarf, the site of Brian Bórú's famous victory, as the rallying point for his most important mass meeting in his next campaign. He never obtained repeal of the Union, but his achievements earned him an eternal place in Dublin's main street, now named after him, and a monument and grave in Glasnevin Cemetery.

Charles Stewart Parnell (1846–91) brought the country close to the gates of home rule yet failed to open them. Parnell's era was accompanied by intense activity in the form of the Gaelic Athletic Association (GAA), founded in 1894, and the Gaelic League (1893). The literary renaissance lead to the foundation of the Abbey Theatre and a new generation of Irish writers. If these movements reflected a new confidence in Irish identity, they had other, far-reaching repercussions. *Arthur Griffith*, a Dublin printer, founded the *United Irishman*, which represented the views of Sinn Féin, a party that had sought an independent parliament in Dublin and was central to the emerging nationalist consciousness. But cultural awareness did little to improve the lot of the unskilled workers in Dublin, who laboured and lived in some of the worst conditions in Europe. The trade unionist *James Larkin*, or 'Big Jim', as he was affectionately called, organised the workers and championed their rights. Larkin inspired such fear in employers that they ordered their workers to sign a declaration that they would not join his union, the Irish Transport and General Workers' Union. This led to the bitter 'lock-out', which lasted from August 1913 to February 1914 and saw the city brought to a standstill. In the end the employers won the campaign and the workers went back to work, but the crisis forced a new era in industrial relations in the city and country. A statue of Larkin by *Oisín Kelly* stands in the middle of O'Connell Street in tribute to his memory. It depicts him in full oratorical flow and as a man of passion. When he died, in January 1947, he was remembered by the poet Patrick Kavanagh and Dublin dramatist Seán O'Casey, who are quoted on the statue's base. Larkin's fundamental message also appears on the plinth: 'The great appear great because we are on our knees. Let us arise.'

The Easter Rising of 1916 began and finished in Dublin. From a military point of view it was badly conceived, yet it profoundly affected public opinion. Initial contempt for the Irish Volunteers and the destruction the rising caused was quickly replaced by general admiration in response to the harsh reaction of the British government. The subsequent War of Independence and Civil War had their roots in both these events and ensured Dublin a continued role in the course of Irish history.

The new Dublin

The next epoch through which Dublin passes will be dictated in commercial and cultural terms. The Government is striving to establish Dublin as the 'e-commerce' hub of Europe. Ireland is the second-largest exporter of software in the world, and some 1,400 'blue chip' international companies are established here. The International Financial Services Centre, founded in 1987, has already established Dublin as a world-class banking centre, and further banking and commercial developments are planned to extend this success story.

The Dublin–London air route is the

General Post Office (GPO) in O'Connell Street.

The East

Bistro, Castle Market, Dublin.

fourth-busiest in the world, and the country's economic success is now a model for other governments hoping to improve their economies.

The pedestal of cultural achievement created by Dublin writers such as *James Joyce* and *Samuel Beckett* is now shared by a new generation of artists. Dublin groups like *U2* and *Boyzone* have become the most successful bands in music history and ensure the city and country a positive international standing with legions of young people who may otherwise never think of visiting Ireland.

The ramifications of a rapid transition to prosperity can also be negative. It is little more than a decade since Ireland was in recession; and while aspects of the economy and society have prospered, the shortcomings are most evident in Dublin.

Inroads have been made into unemployment figures, but the level of long-term unemployment remains high. Petty crime has dropped, yet it is something visitor and local need to be aware of at all times. House prices have increased dramatically, beyond the reach of most ordinary people, and traffic congestion is rampant on the capital's streets. Once a nation with a tradition of emigration, Ireland is now itself the recipient of an influx of immigrants attracted to a rich country and the hope of a better life. The homeless and street beggars are at odds with a population that is more affluent than ever.

Roddy Doyle's comment in the film version of his novel *The Commitments* that 'the Dubs are the blacks of Ireland and north-siders are the blacks of Dublin' reveals a deep, often bitter division that dissects the

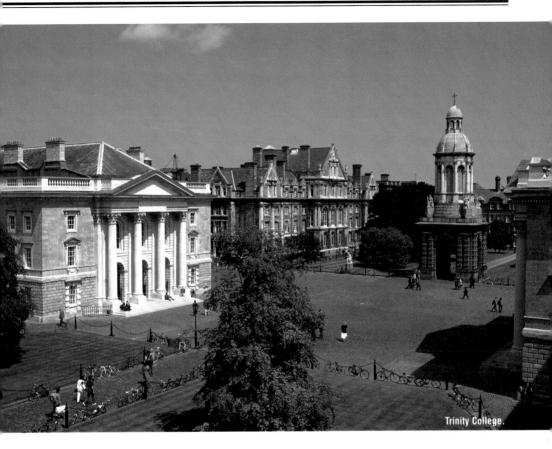

Trinity College.

population of this city of contradictions. The difference in atmosphere is noticeable as soon as one crosses the Liffey in either direction. Yet the notion that the south side is the richer and more pleasant half of the city belies many of the fine qualities and places that influence the identity of the north side.

Despite its shortcomings, Dublin is a city that appeals to the senses. It has an air of history that is tangible and a cultural legacy that will enchant the intellect. Buskers are a common aspect of the streetscape around Dublin, the music varying from classical and traditional Irish to pop and jazz. The distinctive odours of coffee from the world-famous Bewley's cafés and the characteristic fumes of the Guinness brewery combine to give the city its individual fragrance, which you will not find anywhere else in Ireland.

Over the ages Dubliners have come to terms with new if not necessarily invading races that made the city their home. Adept at cultural change, the indigenous population now shares the capital with short-term and long-term visitors from every corner of the world. This trend, combined with the fact that Irish people are now travelling more and experiencing new ways of life, is changing attitudes towards the city from the inside out. Juice bars and a café culture have found a regular niche for a taste-thirsty population, and the concept of sitting outside with an espresso, which would have been almost alien just a few years ago, is now common practice. These changes are being carried through by a new breed of Dubliners who are typically young, confident and educated and believe their city is as important as Paris, London, or New York.

The Irish Economic Boom

Young schoolgirls.

The Irish economy is radically different in structure from that of any other European country: over 70 per cent of industry in Ireland is foreign-owned, and over 65 per cent of domestic product is exported. The Republic has only 3.8 million inhabitants, but Irish agriculture, which now accounts for less than a tenth of all exports, produces enough food for 13 million people.

In the last thirty years the country has undergone a radical and profound transformation. From a poor economy with a backward industrial base exporting largely unprocessed agricultural produce to Britain, it has now emerged as a modern industrialised society specialising in high-tech engineering, pharmaceuticals and an ultra-modern food-processing industry, and exporting throughout the world. The economy has sustained an extraordinary average annual growth of over 8 per cent since 1994—the highest in the European Union—with cumulative growth of over 50 per cent. It was this performance that prompted a leading British journal, the

Economist, to coin the term 'Celtic Tiger' in 1996.

This success story is recent. From independence, the Irish state was trapped in a cycle of unemployment and emigration that reached a desperate low point in the 1950s. The opening up of the post-war world allowed a dramatic change of policy. Encouraged by tax incentives and eager to gain a foothold in Europe, many American and other multinational corporations established a production base in Ireland. In the 1960s, Ireland experienced its first economic boom since independence.

Membership of the European Union since 1973 has led to a clearing out of old industries, and this brought rising unemployment. But it ended dependence on the British market and allowed the new foreign-owned industries of the 1960s to thrive. Present Irish economic success is due to a complex mixture of tax incentives, emigration demographics, and the fact that Ireland is a largely English-speaking country with little industrial history.

The end of mass emigration in the 1970s left Ireland with one of the youngest populations in Europe, with 50 per cent under the age of thirty. This is a well-educated population, as Irish parents have always insisted on their children being educated in preparation for possible emigration. Irish education has a good reputation, and foreign firms eagerly come to Ireland to recruit young graduates for technical jobs abroad. This is also why firms, particularly high-tech companies, are eager to open branches here. The lack of ingrained industrial traditions also means that the economy and work force are flexible, and this has greatly facilitated the rapid development of a high-tech industrial base.

Many of the firms attracted to Ireland in the past have since moved on to cheaper production bases elsewhere, especially companies producing hardware products, such as Digital Equipment and Packard. Ireland being an island, the large transport costs in exporting heavy goods remains a disadvantage for exporters. As opposed to this, micro-electronics and software products have negligible export costs: millions of microchips fit on a single aeroplane. The state pays for education and training, and charges low capital taxes, and therefore the cost structure for such firms remains attractive. Today many world leaders, such as Apple, Intel, and Analog Devices, as well as many software corporations, maintain their European base in Ireland. Over 90 per cent of high-tech production is exported, and Ireland is now the second-largest exporter of software in the world, after the United States. Other production sectors of importance are multinational pharmaceutical companies and modern co-operatively owned food-processing industries, again producing largely for export.

There are disadvantages to the huge industrial development of recent years. The young 'bulge' in the population is passing, and this will not be the great advantage it was previously. Environmental problems have followed industrialisation, and are gaining in political importance. The new industries require a high level of skill, and there is a declining demand for low-skilled workers.

Despite the fact that a net 1,000 additional jobs are being created per month, therefore, there is now an acute skills shortage. Unemployment has fallen from 19 per cent in 1989 to 6 per cent in 1999. Over half this figure relates to low-skilled long-term unemployed, who live in concentrated areas of severe deprivation. In Dublin alone a further 13,000 people are on special schemes and training courses for the long-term unemployed.

Will the boom last? While growth is expected to slow down, not least because of labour shortages, economists are unanimous that it will continue until 2010 at least. The dependence on exports and the high rate of foreign investment also make the economy particularly sensitive to a recession in the United States. But again, ten years ago no economist predicted the boom or indeed any change in the despondent state of the Irish economy.

Essential Dublin

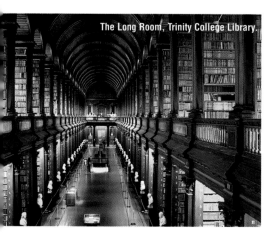

The Long Room, Trinity College Library.

For many of the millions of visitors who arrive in Ireland each year, Dublin is their first point of contact. A small city by comparison with the rest of Europe's capitals, many of its sights can be found within walking distance of each other.

Trinity College

Founded in 1592 by Queen Elizabeth I, this is the oldest university in Ireland. Situated in the heart of the city, the college grounds were at the time of building outside the original walled city, on a site that used to suffer from flooding when the Liffey was at high tide. Today the only flood that threatens to engulf the college is that of curious tourists and its own student population and staff. Close to ten thousand people work and study in Trinity, but many times that number congregate in the college grounds. As you walk through the front entrance of the college you will enter the cobbled quadrangle of Parliament Square, which faces directly onto the Campanile. This curious hollow tower is perhaps the most-photographed feature in Trinity, if not Dublin. However, it is not the most remarkable item on the agenda. This honour must fall to the **Book of Kells**, an 8th-century illuminated manuscript containing the four Gospels written in Latin, decorated

with many colourful and intricate designs. The Book of Kells is one of many interesting artefacts on display, which include the **Book of Durrow** and the **Book of Armagh**—both as old as the Book of Kells—and a mediaeval harp that is the model for the state emblem.

If you are impressed by the Book of Kells you will certainly enjoy the Library's **Long Room**. Two hundred feet in length, capped by a barrel-vaulted oak ceiling installed in 1859, it houses 200,000 of Ireland's most important books, manuscripts, and historical documents.

Bank of Ireland

Directly across the street from Trinity College lies the **Parliament House**, now occupied by the Bank of Ireland. The curved façade of this building, erected between 1729 and 1739, once stood in alliance with Trinity to dominate every other structure in the city. Designed by *Edward Lovett Pearce*, it was later extended. The additions to the east and west of the original portico were designed by the prolific architects *James Gandon* and *Robert Parke*, respectively. It was the first purpose-built parliament building in Europe containing a two-chamber legislature.

The Irish Parliament was abolished after the passing of the Act of Union in 1800, and the Bank of Ireland purchased the building for £40,000. The architect *Francis Johnston* was retained to convert it for use as a bank, and in the renovations the House of Commons chamber was altered beyond recognition. The House of Lords chamber, however, was left intact in its original splendour. This section is open to the public during banking hours. Visitors can take a free tour every Tuesday, which is informative and entertaining.

The General Post Office

The story of the General Post Office (GPO) begins unremarkably enough. Built between 1814 and 1818 to the designs of *Francis Johnston*, it was altered and enlarged over a twelve-year period beginning in 1904.

Reopened in March 1916, the newly renovated building was quickly catapulted into the annals of Irish history. Just one month later it was seized by the revolutionaries who made it their headquarters for a violent attempt to establish independence from Britain. The rising began on Easter Monday, which had symbolic value and also meant that the majority of the English garrison would be out of the city at the Irish Grand National. The insurgents were quickly put down. Their leaders were shot, and much of central Dublin was destroyed in the fighting. The GPO was particularly badly damaged, and it would be eight years before it reopened to the public. The importance of the event would never be lost on the building. Even today the six pillars at the front of the GPO bear the marks of bullets fired during the conflict. In 1935 a statue of Cú Chulainn, the legendary figure whose bravery and blood sacrifice inspired the executed rebel leader *Patrick Pearse*, was unveiled in the foyer of the building. A plinth bears the names of the seven leaders of the rising and the opening words of the proclamation of the Provisional Government.

The Four Courts

The Four Courts, home to Ireland's highest courts, has shared a place at the table of history. The building was designed by *James Gandon*, the architect of the Custom House. Work began in 1786, but it was not until 1802, a year after the Act of Union was implemented, that it was finished. The construction period was extended by Gandon's absence, as he feared political and civil unrest toward the end of the 18th century.

Comprising a large pedimented central Corinthian block, capped with a colonnaded rotunda and dome, the building is joined on both sides by a courtyard with open arcades facing the quayside. The five figures on the central pediment represent Moses, Justice, Mercy, Wisdom, and Authority.

The Civil War began at the Four Courts when, following the signing of the Anglo-Irish Treaty in 1921, rebels occupied the building in protest. After a number of weeks, action was taken by the newly formed Irish government to remove them, and the building was shelled by artillery lent to the Irish army by the British government. In the bombardment the Four Courts were badly damaged, and it was not until 1932 that the building was restored to the original design by Gandon.

Dublin Castle

For longevity there are few buildings in Dublin to rival Dublin Castle. Built between 1204 and 1224, it represented the seat of English power in Ireland until 1922, when the Irish Free State was established. The handing over of the Castle was a tense historical moment. *Michael Collins*, a towering figure in the fight for independence, led the Irish army on 16 January 1922 in taking over from the British garrison. When the commanding officer told him, 'You are seven minutes late, Mr Collins,' he retorted: 'We've been waiting over seven hundred years: you can have the extra seven minutes.'

The Castle lies at the heart of Dublin's identity. The name is derived from the former Irish name *Dubhlinn* ('black pool'). This dark lake was created by the confluence of the River Poddle and the Liffey and lay just behind the present site of Dublin Castle, around which the Vikings first settled. They adopted this name, rendering it *Dyfflin*.

Over its lifetime as a British stronghold, various unsuccessful attempts were made to take the Castle by such figures as *Edward Bruce, Silken Thomas Fitzgerald, Robert Emmet,* and the Irish Volunteers in the 1916

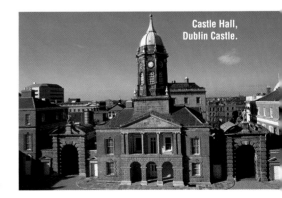

Castle Hall, Dublin Castle.

Custom House and
International Financial Services Centre.

Rising. Much of the original structure has been lost, but at the time of building it ranked in form and construction with the great castles of Europe. It was a roughly rectangular enclosure with four substantial cylindrical towers at the corners, a twin-towered gateway in the centre of a long wall, and a small turret near the centre of the opposite long wall. Today Dublin Castle is very different but equally attractive. It is used for state functions, such as the inauguration of the President of Ireland, and is open to the public.

The Custom House

Popularly regarded as the best example of an 18th-century public building, the Custom House was built between 1781 and 1791. It is the work of Dublin's best-known and most highly acclaimed architect, *James Gandon*. The 375-foot-long building, with a central Corinthian column, arcades on each side linking the end pavilions, and a copper dome topped by the figure of Hope, must surely have been an impressive sight for 19th-century seafarers. The other four statues on the central column represent Neptune, Mercury, Plenty, and Industry.

The entire building was destroyed by fire in 1921 during the War of Independence, and many historic documents were lost as a result. The Custom House was later faithfully restored to Gandon's original specifications; it is now the home of the Department of the Environment and Local Government as well as a visitors' centre.

Kildare Street

Kildare Street and the parallel Merrion Street offer quite a bit in the way of public buildings. Kildare Street contains the **National Library**, **Leinster House** (which houses **Dáil Éireann** and **Seanad Éireann**), and the **National Museum**, all of which adjoin each other. You will need a visitor's card to get inside the main section of the National Library. The Dáil accommodates visiting groups, but they must be invited by a TD (Dáil deputy) or senator. Alternatively, you can write in advance to the Captain of the Guard at the Dáil to arrange an excursion. (The museum is discussed in detail on page 22 of this guide.)

Merrion Street

Merrion Street can be found within a two-minute walk of Kildare Street, running on the same north-south axis. **Government Buildings**, in Upper Merrion Street, are flanked to the left by the Department of Finance and to the right by the back of Leinster House and Leinster Lawn. In the centre of the lawn, which faces onto Merrion Square, an obelisk stands in quiet commemoration of the founding members of the modern Irish state. Beside this you will find the **National Gallery of Ireland**. Visits to Government Buildings are possible only on Saturday mornings and can be arranged through tourist offices or the nearby National Gallery. The gallery boasts an impressive collection of paintings from all the major European schools as well as a strong Irish collection. Admission is free, and the collection is certainly worth viewing. A statue of *George Bernard Shaw* in the Dargan Wing on the ground floor reminds us that he left a third of his estate to the institution, in recognition of the role it played in his education. The nearby **Natural History Museum** sports a large collection of stuffed animals from around the world, with a comprehensive collection of Irish mammals.

Grafton Street

This pedestrianised thoroughfare has all the atmosphere of exclusive retailers and the allure of talented street musicians and buskers. A bronze statue of Molly Malone, heroine of a 19th-century music-hall ballad, invites those approaching the city-centre end of Grafton Street to buy cockles and mussels from her cart. As if in a time warp, the traveller arrives at the opposite end of the street to the spectacle of St Stephen's Green Shopping Centre. **Bewley's Oriental Café**, the world-famous coffee-house situated half way along the street, provides a coffee-scented haven in this busy area.

Georgian squares

There are five Georgian squares in Dublin: two on the north side, Parnell Square and Mountjoy Square, with the remaining three—Merrion Square, St Stephen's Green, and Fitzwilliam Square—in close proximity to each other on the south side.

St Stephen's Green

In its first incarnation, St Stephen's Green was an enclosed park when the west side, close to a leper colony, was used for hangings. It became fashionable with the aristocracy in the second half of the 18th century and was formally opened as a public amenity in 1800 by *Arthur Edward Guinness*, owner of the Guinness brewery. The park offers city workers, families and visitors a relaxing and pleasant open space in the heart of a busy, vibrant city.

Merrion Square

This square is considered to epitomise Georgian Dublin. With their uniform height, impressive doorways complete with brass door-knockers and letterboxes and wrought-iron balconies, the surrounding houses are surviving examples of how 18th-century town-houses looked at the time. The square once had the distinction of forming part of the longest line of uninterrupted Georgian houses in Europe, until 1961, when a development on the east side of Fitzwilliam Street interrupted the legacy.

In the past, Merrion Square has had many famous residents, including *Oscar Wilde*, whose life-size statue now faces his house (number 1); *Daniel O'Connell*, the first Catholic MP to sit in the House of Commons; and the poet *William Butler Yeats*, who lived in numbers 52 and 82.

Parnell Square

Parnell Square, originally called Rutland Square, was completed in 1755. Seven years later *Lord Charlemont* bought the land to build his mansion, Charlemont House, which now houses the **Hugh Lane Municipal Gallery of Modern Art**. The **Rotunda Hospital** on the south side of the square was originally Dr Mosse's Lying-In Hospital. It is thought to be the oldest

A horse carriage tour of Dublin.

maternity hospital in the world. Part of the square is today taken up by the **Garden of Remembrance**, with its impressive sculpture depicting the Children of Lir, a monument to those who lost their lives in Ireland's struggle for freedom.

Mountjoy Square

This square was originally called Gardiner Square, after the 18th-century developer, *Luke Gardiner*; when he later became Viscount Mountjoy, the name was changed accordingly. Construction of the square started in 1792 and finished in 1818. While it was a fashionable area in the early days, it fell victim to inner-city decay, and it is only in recent years that the area has been restored to its former glory. However, much of this development came too late for many of the original buildings on the square's southern and western sides. The playwright *Seán O'Casey* lived at number 35; but, as with many other buildings, it has been razed and the site built upon. *Brian Bórú*, the leader who defeated the Danes at the Battle of Clontarf in 1014, is said to have camped on the high ground on which the square now sits.

Fitzwilliam Square

Fitzwilliam Square, the smallest and the last of the five to be built, was laid out between 1791 and 1825 and brought an end to a tradition of building that had lasted almost a century. The houses, which are smaller than their counterparts in the other four squares, are predominantly used for business purposes, and the park is reserved for the use of residents.

Powerscourt Town-House

A sense of old-world charm comes easily to the visitor at Powerscourt Town-House. Lord Powerscourt of County Wicklow retained the services of *Robert Mack*, the architect of Grattan Bridge, to build him a town-house in Dublin. This was completed by 1774 and sold to a textile firm in 1835. It came to public prominence in the 1980s when it was turned into a bright and tasteful shopping area, complete with restaurants and eclectic craft shops. The centre was revamped in 1998. The glass ceiling gives this large and colourful space a light feeling, set against the extravagant interior design work. The complex acts as a pleasant pedestrian route between Grafton Street and South Great George's Street.

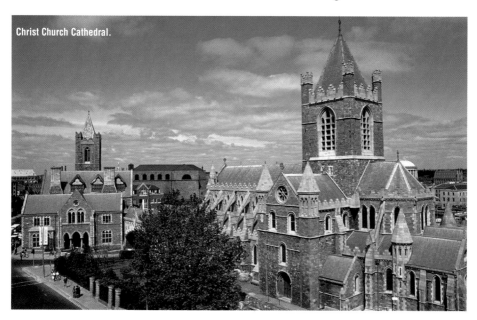

Christ Church Cathedral.

The Mansion House

The Mansion House, situated towards the St Stephen's Green end of Dawson Street, is the official residence of the Lord Mayor of Dublin, and the private quarters are not open to the public. It is mainly used for civic and state receptions; it also features in the film *The Commitments*. The house merits mention, however, for its historical importance. The Queen Anne architecture dates back to 1710, and the **Round Room**, designed by *Francis Johnston*, was installed in 1821 for the visit of King George IV. Almost a hundred years later the Mansion House was used as its chamber by the clandestine first Dáil.

Christ Church Cathedral

Christ Church has always been an ecclesiastical site. *Sigtrygg Silkenbeard*, the Hiberno-Norse king of Dublin, built a small wooden church here for the first bishop of Dublin in 1038. The church was later developed into a stone structure by the Norman *Richard de Clare*, Earl of Pembroke—more commonly known as Strongbow—for the archbishop of Dublin, *Lorcán Ó Tuathail*, who was later canonised and created patron saint of Dublin. Both men died before the church was completed. A memorial to Strongbow can be seen in the cathedral's nave, while the heart of St Lorcán lies in a 13th-century reliquary in the chapel of St Laud, a small interior chapel. The cathedral's crypt is the oldest intact building in Dublin, dating back to the original construction in 1172.

The cathedral faced many difficulties over the centuries. During the late 16th century its vaults were used as taverns and the nave as a market-place. When the nave vaulting collapsed in 1562 it brought with it the south wall. The replacement work was far from satisfactory, and by the middle of the 19th century the survival of the building was in doubt. Salvation came from a strange source. *Henry Roe*, a Dublin distiller, provided £250,000 for its restoration. He volunteered the money in a competitive rather than a pious spirit: another drinks magnate, *Sir Benjamin Lee Guinness*, had paid for the restoration of nearby St Patrick's Cathedral in 1864. The charitable investment in Christ Church Cathedral gave Roe an opportunity to 'go one better' than the Guinness family, who had a tradition of providing large sums of money for public projects in Dublin.

St Patrick's Cathedral

Several hundred yards south of the hill on which Christ Church stands is St Patrick's Cathedral, bearing the name of the patron saint of Ireland, the only Irish cathedral to maintain its complete mediaeval cathedral close, church buildings, deanery close, and library.

St Patrick's is best known for its connection with the writer *Jonathan Swift*, who was dean of the cathedral from 1713 until his death in 1745. The author of many books, most notably *Gulliver's Travels*, is buried near the entrance of the cathedral, as is his lifelong love, *Esther Johnson* (whom Swift called 'Stella'). It is appropriate for this man of letters that he should be buried close to **Marsh's Library**, to our left as we leave the cathedral. This is the oldest public library in Ireland and was founded in 1701 by *Archbishop Narcissus Marsh*. The architect was *Sir William Robinson*, designer of the Royal Hospital, Kilmainham. The library contains about 25,000 books, some surviving from the 16th century. A rare feature is the three caged alcoves where especially rare books are chained to the walls to prevent readers from 'borrowing' them.

The Liberties

The Liberties is the oldest surviving community of Dublin. Originally it was an extensive area to the south and west of the walled city, and today it can be found shoulder-to-shoulder with Christ Church Cathedral and St Patrick's. It gets its name from laws that put it outside the jurisdiction of the mayor and council of the mediaeval city. There is a high concentration of churches here, such as **St Werburgh's** and the **Augustinian Church** in Thomas Street, as well as a number of shrines to the Virgin Mary.

Ancient Ireland

Leachanabuaile Stone Fort, Co. Kerry.

At first, Ireland was not an island at all. It became separated from Britain around the end of the Ice Age. To this day you can see the Mull of Kintyre in the south-west of Scotland quite clearly from the Antrim coast road—and little wonder, for the sea is a mere 12 miles across here at the narrowest point. There was seaborne traffic in people and animals from the very earliest days, especially in the north-east corner.

The oldest Irish Stone Age settlement, at Mount Sandel in County Derry, near the mouth of the River Bann, dates from almost 6000 BC. So Ireland is an ancient land in every sense. It has been continuously inhabited since the end of the Ice Age; yet a casual glance at an atlas might make you wonder why. Ireland lies between 52 and 55° north of the Equator, the same latitude as the wastes of Labrador and much of Siberia. Unlike those places, however,

it has an exceptionally temperate climate. For this we can thank the Gulf Stream, a great looping warm sea current that flows north-east from the Caribbean, right past the west coast of Ireland. Its effect is dramatic: it saves all north-western Europe from the sort of harsh, inhospitable weather one might otherwise expect. Instead the Irish climate is damp but mild, ideal for pasture, cattle-rearing, and cultivation. It is little wonder that this small island has provided a home for different peoples since the dawn of history.

Early settlers such as those at Mount Sandel lived a nomadic life, hunting, trapping, and fishing. About 3500 BC, however, these nomadic people were superseded by pastoralists. Agriculture—the ability to grow crops and to domesticate animals—offered the chance of permanent rather than nomadic settlement. In Ireland, as elsewhere, the coming of agriculture is regarded as the start of civilisation.

These early pastoralists are generally referred to as Neolithic (New Stone Age) people. They have left us the first permanent, surviving monuments that still grace the land of Ireland. None are more impressive than the portal tombs, huge pairs of standing stones supported by a capstone. The engineering skills required to raise these extraordinary structures, especially the capstones, were formidable, all the more so in a thinly populated island where vast armies of labourers could not be called upon. Among the most famous portal tombs are those at Poulnabrone, County Clare, and Proleek, County Louth.

Indeed we have much evidence that Ireland's Neolithic people were far more than simple farmers. Since they understood basic engineering, they must also have been competent in the elements of mathematics. Moreover, we know that they studied the heavens and made astronomical observations—impossible to do without a knowledge of mathematics and the means to measure the passage of time.

The best evidence for this is at Newgrange, the most spectacular pre-Celtic site in Ireland. Situated in a bend in the River Boyne in County Meath, it is a burial site dating from about 2500 BC. It was completely excavated in the 1960s and is one of those places that no visitor to Ireland should miss. It is the most celebrated of the Irish passage tombs: it is over 300 feet in diameter and almost 50 feet high; the passage leading to the burial site in the centre of the mound is almost 150 feet long; many of the stones are decorated in elaborate and beautiful spiral patterns; and there is a series of stone gutters on the outside of the mound to carry rainwater away from the centre and to deposit it harmlessly. But most spectacular of all is the fact that the entire structure is so aligned that, uniquely on the day of the winter solstice, the rising sun penetrates the full length of the passage and strikes the back wall of the burial chamber itself. The astronomical and geometrical skills required to achieve this astonishing feat need no elaboration.

The Stone Age yielded to the Bronze Age around 2000 BC. For almost two millennia bronze was the dominant metal in Ireland. Of course any form of metal is vastly superior to stone, whether for decorative purposes or for warfare; but bronze is a relatively soft metal, and some time after 500 BC it was replaced by a harder, more durable one: iron.

With iron came the Celts. It is as well to remember that pre-Celtic Ireland had been continuously inhabited for over six thousand years. The Celts were simply the latest in a long wave of settlers to occupy the island. But, armed with their iron weapons, they superseded the existing people, of whom we know little with any certainty and who have left us no records of their language or lore.

With the coming of the Celts, Irish history begins in earnest. There were probably successive waves of them; but the last group, who may have arrived about 250 BC, established themselves as a unitary culture throughout the island. Prehistoric Ireland was not a unitary state, however. There were over 150 *tuatha* or minor kingdoms, each of them subordinate to regional kings, who were in turn the clients of provincial kings. The common currency was cattle, and the incessant cattle raids from one *tuath* to another were designed to bring booty and prestige. This gave rise to the greatest of all Irish mythological sagas, the *Táin Bó Chuaille* or Cattle Raid of Cooley. In this, the armies of *Méabh,* queen of Connacht, invade Ulster in order to capture the Brown Bull of Cooley. They are repulsed by the Ulster hero *Cú Chulainn,* who slays his blood-brother *Fearghas* in single combat. This tragic tale of heroism and ambition is Homeric in scale and has influenced the Irish imagination ever since. The insurrectionaries of 1916 looked to Cú Chulainn as a symbol of Irish heroic virtue, and he is a potent symbolic figure in the later poetry of *Yeats.* Cú Chulainn epitomises the mixture of myth and memory in Ireland.

Museums and Galleries

Irish Museum of Modern Art, Royal Hospital, Kilmainham.

Dublin has a long, complex and interesting history and has experienced much over its thousand-year life. Wave after wave of invasion, tragedy and triumph, poverty and prosperity, are just some of the ingredients that have formed it into the city it is today. It is an epic tale best witnessed in the halls of the different museums and galleries spread throughout the city.

Old Jameson Distillery, Bow Street

Dublin is popularly renowned for the production of stout, yet the city has a tradition of distilling that is just as venerable. Jameson whiskey has been distilled here since 1780, just twenty-one years after Guinness opened its gates. The Jameson family quickly established the company as one of the largest in Ireland, and in 1966 a merger between John Jameson and Son, John Power and Son and the Cork Distillery Company forged a new whiskey conglomerate, Irish Distillers. The group was joined by Bushmills Distillery of County Antrim in 1972. The visitor centre, a detailed reconstruction of a working distillery, opened to the public in 1997.

The guided tour of the distillery begins with an eight-minute multilingual audiovisual presentation on Jameson whiskey. The next leg of the tour follows all the stages of distilling, from the malting, milling and mashing of barley to the bottling of whiskey. The tour finishes in the Jameson Bar with a complimentary glass of Jameson. Visitors can offer to act as tasters in a test that shows the difference in flavour between a number of different Irish and Scotch whiskeys; participants receive a certificate to show that they are 'a qualified Irish whiskey taster'. This is an entertaining and informative way to spend an hour or so.

There is an admission charge. For further information telephone (01) 8072355.

Guinness Hop Store, Crane Street

While you cannot get access to the 60-acre complex that is the Guinness production plant, the Hop Store offers a great insight into the brewery's operations and history. The store can be found in Crane Street in a converted 19th-century warehouse.

As a drink, Guinness has become synonymous with Ireland but more particularly with Dublin. In 1800 some fifty-five breweries were operating in the capital, but even at this early point in the company's history Guinness was being sold in a third of

Dublin's pubs. The authorities regarded Guinness as a social evil, yet the wickedly good taste of this stout was very popular among the drinking public.

An audiovisual presentation on the history of Guinness is followed by a visit to the Hop Store's own bar. Over ten million pints of the 'black stuff' are exported around the world from the Guinness brewery every day; yet it is in the Hop Store that you will taste the drink at its best, just a few hundred yards from where it is made.

There is an admission charge. For further information telephone (01) 4538364.

Genealogical Office and Heraldic Museum, Kildare Street

The search by the present-day descendants of Irish emigrants for their roots has grown into a major tourist industry, and the serious investigator should certainly visit the Heraldic Museum. The museum and the Genealogical Office are situated on the corner of Kildare Street and Nassau Street in a fine Venetian-style red-brick building that was built in 1860–1. Designed by *Thomas Deane and Benjamin Woodward,* it was once the home of the conservative Kildare Street Club. In 1971 the building became the property of the Phoenix Assurance Company, and its interior was completely changed in a renovation programme. The Genealogical Office is administered by the National Library and is a good place to make initial enquiries about your Irish roots. The building is also home to the French cultural centre, Alliance Française.

Royal Hospital, Kilmainham, and Irish Museum of Modern Art

Based on the design of Les Invalides in Paris, the Royal Hospital was built towards the end of the 17th century as a home for retired soldiers. It was used for this purpose for almost 250 years yet progressively fell into disrepair and eventual ruin. In 1986 the Government invested £21 million in a restoration programme for the building, and five years later it was reopened as the **Irish Museum of Modern Art**. Its restored formal façade, spacious courtyard and fine interior remind us of its status as the first classical public building in Dublin. The museum houses a permanent collection of Irish and international art of the 20th century, as well as visiting exhibitions throughout the year. In addition, the annual programme features live music and theatrical performances. It is well worth a visit.

Admission is free. For further information telephone (01) 6129900.

Kilmainham Gaol

Kilmainham Gaol was decommissioned in 1924, but even today it is possible to experience some small sense of the original atmosphere of desperation that once dominated it. Throughout the course of Irish history it has incarcerated many prominent political and military leaders. Protagonists of the 1798, 1803, 1848 and 1867 risings were remanded here. In its final days the prison served the first Irish government as a detention centre for prisoners of the Civil War. The brutality of this war seeped into Kilmainham, and a number of 'irregular' (anti-Free State) prisoners were shot in retaliation for the murder of senior politicians at the time.

Éamon de Valera, leader of the irregular forces and later Taoiseach and, in 1959, President of Ireland, was one of those held here during the Civil War. It must have been with mixed emotions that he opened the jail as a museum in 1966.

Kilmainham was also used by the British to intern many participants in the failed Easter Rising of 1916. In particular, fourteen of the leaders, including *Patrick Pearse* and his younger brother, Willie, were shot in the prison yard. *James Connolly,* who was badly injured in the fighting, was carried into the yard in a chair and bravely ordered the firing-squad to take aim properly like true soldiers. In the 1880s *Charles Stewart Parnell,* the 'Uncrowned King of Ireland', was imprisoned at Kilmainham but was allowed to reside in a more comfortable room; he even had a housemaid.

There is a guided tour, an audiovisual presentation, and an exhibition of materials from the jail's archives. There is an admission charge. For further information telephone (01) 4535984.

The East

Chester Beatty Library and Gallery of Oriental Art, Dublin Castle

This prestigious collection of oriental, Islamic and Christian manuscripts and eclectic works of art is perhaps the most unusual on display in Dublin, if not in Ireland. It was brought together by *Sir Alfred Chester Beatty* (1875–1968), a mining engineer who spent his life and personal fortune buying valuable artefacts from throughout the Middle and Far East. The collection, once housed close to the RDS grounds in Ballsbridge, can now be found in the more central location of the Clock Tower in Dublin Castle and will be reopend in February 2000.

Admission is free. For further information telephone (01) 2692386.

Dublinia, High Street

Across the street from Christ Church is **St Michael's Church**. The Synod Hall contains the Dublinia experience, a high-tech exhibition covering the period of Dublin's history from the arrival of the Anglo-Normans in 1170 to the closure of its monasteries in 1540. There are life-size reproductions of the most memorable episodes from that era, a scale model of the mediaeval city, and a reconstruction of the 13th-century dockside at Wood Quay and a 15th-century merchant's household. An audiovisual presentation in the Great Hall is supported by a collection of artefacts from the National Museum of Ireland.

There is an admission charge. For further information telephone (01) 6794611.

Dublin Civic Museum, South William Street

Next door to the entrance to Powerscourt Town-House shopping centre you will find Dublin Civic Museum. Dedicated to the history of the capital city, the museum houses an unusual exhibition of artefacts that recount the history of Dublin. It provides the visitor with a good opportunity to get into the psyche of the city, its people and major events.

The damaged stone head of Admiral Nelson, for example, is all that remains of the Nelson Pillar, a popular monument that once stood in O'Connell Street close to the GPO. However, the towering image of an English admiral was less popular with some people, who, on the fiftieth anniversary of the 1916 Rising, blew it up. They failed to completely demolish it, however, and the complete removal of the remains was left to the army.

Admission is free. For further information telephone (01) 6794260.

Ceol—the Irish Traditional Music Museum, Smithfield

The centre is housed in **Chief O'Neill's Hotel**, named after an emigrant, *Daniel Francis O'Neill*, who rose through the ranks of the police in Chicago in the last century to become chief of police. He was also the author of *1,001 Dance Tunes of Ireland*, which quickly became the bible of Irish musicians in America and at home in Ireland.

'Ceol' is a high-tech £35 million interpretative centre with interactive displays, offering the visitor a detailed view of the evolution of the music. Media consoles allow the user to take a trip through the labyrinth of traditional music's long history, while an auditorium with a 180° screen provides for entertainment all round. The film, produced using a five-camera rig, presents panoramic images of Ireland's best musicians in full swing.

There is an admission charge. For further information telephone (01) 8173838.

National Museum, Kildare Street and Benburb Street

The National Museum of Ireland was established by the Dublin Science and Art Museum Act (1877), and the Kildare Street premises was built in 1890 to the design of *Thomas Newenham Deane*. The museum houses many breathtaking exhibits, including the Irish Gold Collection, the finest display of prehistoric gold artefacts in Europe, and the Treasury Exhibition, which features such remarkable works of Early Christian art as the Ardagh Chalice and the Tara Brooch. Archaeological evidence from the Viking age is on view, as are many other interesting exhibits.

The National Museum now includes the

National Gallery of Ireland, Merrion Square.

former Collins Barracks, Benburb Street. The barracks is one of the oldest in Europe and the oldest continuously occupied barracks in the world. It was reopened in 1997 as Ireland's new museum of the decorative arts and of the economic, social, political and military history of the country and will be further extended over the next decade.

Admission is free. For further information telephone (01) 6777444.

Natural History Museum, Merrion Square

Immediately south of Leinster Lawn is the Natural History Museum, which houses a large collection of stuffed animals from all over the world, with a comprehensive collection of Irish mammals.

Admission is free. For further information telephone (01) 6777444.

Hugh Lane Municipal Gallery of Modern Art, Parnell Square

Charlemont House (1762–5) was designed by the architect *William Chambers* for the *Earl of Charlemont*. In 1927 the government presented the house to the city, and Dublin City Council renovated the building for use as an art gallery. In 1933 the Hugh Lane Municipal Gallery of Modern Art was opened. It takes its name from a famous Dublin patron of the arts who perished in the sinking of the *Lusitania* in 1915. Admission is free. Telephone (01) 8741903/4.

National Gallery of Ireland, Merrion Square

The National Gallery has been open to the public since 1864. The original collection was formed a year before the gallery opened, when a massive industrial exhibition on the adjoining Leinster Lawn was staged by the railway magnate *William Dargan*. For his own part, Dargan was commemorated by a statue that stands outside the front of the gallery today. The stature of the collection has grown, and today it boasts an impressive range of paintings from all the major European schools. The Milltown Wing on the ground floor is devoted to the work of Irish painters; *Jack Yeats,* brother of *W. B. Yeats,* features prominently.

Admission is free. Telephone (01) 6615133.

National Library of Ireland, Kildare Street

The National Library was designed and built at the same time as the National Museum, and by the same architect, *Thomas Newenham Deane.* A rich source of archive material, with newspapers and books of historic and social interest available for reference, the library is open only to those with a reader's ticket. However, you may enter the foyer and get some sense of this splendid building's interior.

Free admission but limited access. Telephone (01) 6618811.

Treasures of Ireland

Burial Chamber,
Newgrange, Co. Meath.

The breadth of achievement of Irish craftsmen, especially between the 7th and 9th centuries, is astonishing. Whether working in stone, vellum, or metal, Irish monks have left masterpieces behind them that confirm the incredibly high technical standards they achieved and the great range of applied skills and inventiveness brought to bear in each chosen medium. Apart from the Book of Kells and the Ardagh Chalice, items like the 8th-century **Tara Brooch** and **St Patrick's Bell Shrine** certainly deserve mention, as does the early 12th-century **Cross of Cong**.

But long before the monks, Continental Celtic craftsmen were masters of goldwork and design; and the early Irish benefited from their example in producing splendid gold ornaments such as the Bronze Age **Gleninsheen Gold Collar** and the 1st-century **Broighter Collar**.

Perhaps the most undervalued of Irish treasures, the free-standing **high crosses,** also show signs of earlier Celtic decorative influence. Erected in large numbers between the 9th and 12th centuries, these expertly carved monuments are a product of the monasteries, and many feature interlace and spiral design. The most outstanding of them are at Monasterboice, Clonmacnoise, Kells, and Ahenny. Their neatly sectioned panels are covered with superbly sculpted scenes from the Scriptures comprising a visual narrative concentrating, more often than not, on the Passion of Christ. In a modern context, each cross can be thought of as an upright sandstone comic-book incised with sacred images, not for entertainment but for meditation and reflection.

But the most richly adorned and embellished treatment of sacred material is surely the **Book of Kells**, an illuminated manuscript dating from the end of the 8th century and recognised as the crowning achievement of Irish Celtic art. A cunning masterpiece of colour and design, it is the magnificent product of ornamental fantasy carried to astonishing extremes of intricacy and abstraction. Improbable beasts entwine themselves around capital letters or crouch enigmatically and decoratively within colourful ink-framed cages. Insects, birds and human figures lie half-concealed in the colourful and scripted camouflage of superbly conceived individual sections. In principle, art is the handmaid of the word; but here, because of its inventive brilliance, it tends to eclipse it.

A complex work, the Book of Kells is also an unfinished one, and certainly not the achievement of a single artist. Possibly begun in Scotland, possibly completed in Ireland, its sophistication can be seen in its incorporation of stylistic elements not just from Continental and Celtic sources but even from Coptic models. Yet, regardless of the debate about its exact provenance, or the extent of its indebtedness to foreign influences, there is agreement that this lavishly illuminated reproduction of the Vulgate Gospels, containing depictions of the Evangelists and their symbols as well as of Christ and the Virgin and Child, constitutes the magnificent final flowering of a highly developed native art of illumination predating the Viking invaders.

The much earlier **Broighter Collar** is considered one of the supreme achievements not just of Irish but of European Early Iron Age art. A golden *torc* or neck ornament, the collar is characterised by an extremely subtle and complex foliage design with delicately incised surface areas possibly inspired by the lotus-bud motif. The clasp mechanism by which the collar is fastened shows great sophistication.

The better-known **Tara Brooch**, made of silver gilt with gold filigree, amber and cast polychrome glass studs, represents a brilliant synthesis of Germanic, late Roman and later La Tène influences. Copper designs set against a silver background form one of its most striking features. A technically dazzling ornament of birds and trumpet scrolls, with abstract animal interlacing and a thistle motif, it represents the summit of Irish metalwork. The only possible item to rival it for finesse of conception and execution is the **Ardagh Chalice**. The plain silver surface of the chalice is rimmed by a band of gold filigree punctuated by red and blue glass studs, the design of each of the studs based on the cross. Below this gold band, the names of the Apostles are engraved in silver, and on each side of the chalice is a central ornamented cross set within a circle and linked symbolically to the band by the adjunction of spiral gold filigree and more glass studs.

All the highlighted treasures listed here are found in the National Museum, except for the Book of Kells which is kept in the Old Library of Trinity College Dublin. The high crosses are, of course, in situ.

Dublin Pubs

Mulligan's pub,
Poolbeg Street.

A Dublin riddle poses the question, 'How do you get from Rathmines to Glasnevin without passing a single pub?' The answer, 'Go into them all,' is hardly realistic, but it reveals how entrenched a feature the pub is in the life of Dublin. With some four hundred pubs in the capital city, it is not uncommon for wayward visitors to be given directions in terms of pubs they will pass before reaching their destination. For natives, 'going for a quick one' is still the most popular social pastime.

Traditional pubs
A good traditional pub should have at least the suggestion of the phantom of some famous Dublin character skulking in a corner, wooden counters and floors, and good drink. Televisions are taboo, as are mobile phones; some pubs even ban their use on the premises. Cigarettes are normally sold behind the bar and not—perish the thought—from a vending machine. These pubs lack any sense of real urgency and prefer to be left to the simple murmur of punters in conversation. They should not be confused with a new breed of pub, the pseudo-traditional pub.

Bars such as O'Dwyer's in Mount Street, McCormack's in Monkstown and the Queen's in Dalkey are examples of this phenomenon. Pubs of this type are carefully constructed replicas of the original Irish pub; and while they are popular and comfortable spots, they are still imitations of the real thing.

Mulligan's
In Poolbeg Street, tucked behind Burgh Quay, the distinctive façade of Mulligan's will first attract your eyes and then invite you in. Established in 1782, it has become one of Dublin's most famous pubs, for reasons that are not hard to explain. It is divided into four small sections, offering the drinker varying degrees of solitude and privacy, though when the pub is busy these qualities can be hard to find. A 'pint of plain' from the taps of Mulligan's is regarded as one of the best in Dublin. Such is the strength of character of the pub that it has survived the impact of local tragedies. The nearby Theatre Royal was demolished in 1962, and with it went a large clientele of artists and thirsty audiences. In 1995 the neighbouring Press Group newspaper offices were closed, wiping out

another reliable and colourful group of locals. However, Mulligan's never lost its allure and is now visited by tourists and city slickers alike. Its reputation as a pub of note is assured, thanks to *James Joyce's* reference to the bar in his short story 'Counterparts'. *Brendan Behan* blessed the head of many a pint of Guinness here; but perhaps the most famous visitor was the late American president *John F. Kennedy*, who spent some time here while working with Hearst Newspapers.

Three for one

Three of Dublin's best-known 'traditional' pubs can be found close together near Merrion Square. **O'Donoghue's** in Merrion Row is one of the best-known pubs in the city. It was here that the Dubliners, the famous ballad group, began their formidable musical career over thirty years ago, playing to a packed house. If the dark wooden interior is too cramped for your comfort, it has an enclosed beer garden to the side and a less smoke-filled environment. Traditional music is still very much part of O'Donoghue's, with regular impromptu sessions a common feature of the pub.

Doheny and Nesbitt's in Baggot Street is a popular haunt of lawyers, journalists, and politicians. It is therefore a place of business where rumours are traded and allegations denied or confirmed and the source of more than a few media leaks. For all this the atmosphere is light and enjoyable. The bar has a magnificent antique front, a heavy mahogany bar counter sub-divided by fine wooden partitions, and soft lighting throughout. Floor space in Doheny's has been extended with the addition of a lounge upstairs and the opening of an old back room. Thankfully, these improvements have not been made at the expense of the original 19th-century bar.

Across the street from Nesbitt's on a corner site you will find **Toner's**, another 19th-century pub, complete with snug. The interior looks old, perhaps even a little tired, yet the original Toner's was gutted in the 1970s. Some features were retained, but it is mostly pastiche. At one point it was not uncommon for pubs to double as shops of one kind or another, giving thirsty drinkers a legitimate excuse for dropping in on some pretext. In Toner's the old drawers were once used for storing groceries and tea, while the pump handles once served beer. Toner's has the distinction of being the pub in which *W. B. Yeats* had his one and only drink in the capital.

Around Grafton Street

The side streets off Grafton Street lead to some of the city's other best-loved pubs. The Chatham Lounge, better known as **Neary's**, is to be found in Chatham Street and is immediately recognisable by its cast-iron decorations. It is a natural meeting-point for actors from the nearby **Gaiety Theatre**. Inside the pub the well-worn marble-topped bar, mahogany surrounds and brass fixtures remind the visitor of its reputation as a place with a plush atmosphere. The bar area is quite tight, but more space can be found upstairs. The author of *The Third Policeman*, Flann O'Brien, was a patron of Neary's.

Down the narrow street directly opposite Neary's, Harry Street, parallel with Chatham Street, you will discover **McDaid's** on your right. Known now for its free, often outrageous blues sessions every Wednesday and Sunday night, it was the 'local' for three major Irish writers: *Brendan Behan, Brian O'Nolan* (Flann O'Brien), and the poet *Patrick Kavanagh*. Renovated in the early 1990s, the pub's interior is now very different from its 1950s appearance. However, it does feel like an old pub, and the creative spirit and wit of these writers finds some echoes in the music of the resident blues band.

Directly opposite McDaid's is **Bruxelles**, a Gothic-revival building designed by *J. J. O'Callaghan* in 1890 and regarded as his most successful pub. Bruxelles has two levels. At ground level it is a small, wooden and often busy pub. Downstairs a larger bar caters for the needs of an eclectic clientele, including rockers, students, and cure heads.

Leaving McDaid's and Bruxelles, walk the few remaining yards of Harry Street and turn left down Grafton Street and then right into Duke Street. Here on the right is **Davy Byrne's**. It has had its fair share of notable customers. The revolutionary *Michael Collins*,

The Castle Inn.

the Sinn Féin leader *Arthur Griffith, Brendan Behan* (again), the writer *Liam O'Flaherty* and the painter *William Orpen* all drank here. *James Joyce* refers to it in *Ulysses* when Leopold Bloom, the novel's protagonist, drops in to the 'moral pub' at lunchtime for a Gorgonzola cheese sandwich and a glass of burgundy. There is nothing left of the original, but it is a friendly and entertaining pub.

Kehoe's of South Anne Street is another pub considered to be the 'real thing'. Its genuine exterior, wooden floors and furniture, finely carved partitions sub-dividing the long bar, cosy snug at one end and small, intimate lounge at the other were recently supplemented by the opening of the upper stages of the house. This move may have doubled the floor space of the pub, but such is its popularity that many patrons must take their drink to the front and sides of the premises.

There is absolutely nothing pretentious or fancy about **Grogan's**, officially called the Castle Inn, in South William Street, but it is one of the best pubs in Dublin. Its simple, old-fashioned décor hasn't been changed in years, and that's the way the locals like it. The clientele is formed of a mix of old Dublin characters and a younger generation of freethinking individuals. The pub is thinly divided by a partition, but in both sections of this small pub the conversation, like the Guinness, is always solid, strong, and good.

It would be wrong to give the impression that the best 'traditional' pubs are to be found south of the River Liffey. O'Connell Street may not have any 'decent' pubs, but you don't

have to go far to find one. Take the **Flowing Tide**, for example. Found diagonally opposite the Abbey Theatre, it is normally frequented by actors and artists, who feel comfortable in the wood-panelled interior, every inch of which is covered in old and new theatrical posters. At the other end of O'Connell Street, across from the Gate Theatre, is **Conway's**, another no-frills authentic pub. **Slattery's** and **Keating's**, found in Capel Street and Jervis Street, respectively, offer quality traditional music sessions every night. Further out in the suburb of Glasnevin, the **Gravediggers** merits the effort it takes to get here. Formerly trading under the name John Kavanagh, the macabre modern name for this six-generation family-run old-style pub comes from its location at the gates of Glasnevin Cemetery. Another 'classic' is **Ryan's** in Parkgate Street.

Modern life-style bars

In contrast to the traditional Dublin pub, a new generation of drinking-houses has emerged that bear little resemblance to their predecessors. In essence they offer a trendy, younger and more affluent market a fresh choice of social outlet. These bars (the word 'pub' doesn't seem to fit easily when describing them) are brash and modern and designed in a format that arguably puts style before content. They are frequently large, multi-tiered premises with an international rather than domestic outlook. Evidence of this is found in their names. At the north end of the Ha'penny Bridge, for example, you will find **Pravda**. Built on the site of an old woollen goods shop, its exterior gives the passer-by little indication of the sheer size, its empty, sparse use of space and the communist iconography inside.

Around the corner from Pravda and along the Liffey lies **Zanzibar**. As soon as you enter the doors it is as if you have been transported to a remote, exotic village in some strange land. The combination of palm trees with architecture reminiscent of Marrakesh and the bustling clientele really do give the premises a sense of a decadent, busy market town.

The European equivalent of Zanzibar can be found in **Café en Seine** in Dawson Street.

The extravagantly long bar and unusually high rounded ceiling are more suggestive of a boulevard in Vienna or Paris.

Not all new life-style bars are so elaborate—for example **Life** in Lower Abbey Street or the **Odeon** at the top of Harcourt Street—but they are all modern establishments, regarded as the meeting places of Ireland's up-and-coming élite. If you want to find this kind of bar, look for a queue outside the door. The very idea of queuing to get into a bar is a new concept and simply unimaginable for those who drink in traditional pubs. You've been warned! It is often said that these bars represent a new-found confidence. However, it is perhaps ironic that at a time when the traditional Irish pub is enjoying commercial success around the world (at one point a new 'Irish pub' was being opened every day somewhere in the world) they should prove unpopular at home.

Theme bars

These mix the distinction between bar and restaurant. Good for group occasions, they usually have to be booked in advance. **Captain America's**, at the top of Grafton Street, is the city's original theme bar. In more recent years, perhaps as a result of the economic boom, larger and more adventurous theme bars have mushroomed. Just past the nearby St Stephen's Green Shopping Centre is the **Chicago Pizza Pie Factory**, and beside this again is **Planet Hollywood**, complete with film memorabilia. In Fleet Street the **All Sports Café** and **Thunder Road Café** add to the range of theme bars. What they lack in culture and character they compensate for with loud, wild entertainment and fun, food, and drink.

And the rest

There are bars that exist on the boundaries of these broad and rough definitions that have a distinct character of their own. The **Dawson Lounge** in Dawson Street is the smallest pub in Dublin, so don't bring a crowd. The **Brazen Head**, which stands on the site of a much older inn (dating from 1198), is reputedly the oldest pub in Dublin, while the **Stag's Head** in Dame Lane derives its name from the stuffed and mounted stags' heads on its wall. Dublin pubs once brewed their own beer, but until the opening of the **Porter House** in East Essex Street it was a lost tradition. This section should serve only as a sample of the variety of Dublin's pub culture. A little exploration will unearth many more interesting pubs.

Enjoying a drink.

Literary Dublin

Dublin Writers' Museum,
Parnell Square.

If, as Shakespeare wrote, 'All the world's a stage,' then Dublin is surely the Black Hole of the literary universe. In the same way that nothing can escape the gravity of an imploded star, the constellation of Irish writers who owe their existence to Dublin spent their lives struggling with the immense pull and influence of this city. As the home to no less than three Nobel Literature Prize winners—*George Bernard Shaw* (1856–1950), *Samuel Beckett* (1906–89), and *William Butler Yeats* (1865–1939)—it is a place of intense literary creation.

A love-hate relationship

Dublin has always provoked strong emotions from its literary protégés and those who decided that they must leave it in order to thrive artistically.

Patrick Kavanagh (1904–67), a poet from rural County Monaghan, felt that to rise to literary heights he would have to abandon the stony grey soil of his native county to scale greater heights. It was with this in mind that he travelled to Dublin for 'a peep into the Temple of the Muses.' What he discovered was quite different from his expectations, yet it had the effect he desired. Instead of finding some sort of divine haven he heard the 'demon's terrifying yell.' But he wrote to his brother, 'I am writing away. I have got a good deal out of Dublin which I have established as Hell.'

'Hell' to Kavanagh, Dublin represented moral and historical paralysis to *James Joyce* (1882–1941), who felt stifled by the city. After he graduated from university the young Joyce left for Paris, only to be driven back to Ireland by destitution and news of his mother's impending death. While he returned only a few times to Ireland, his nomadic life in Europe, embracing Trieste, Zürich, Rome and Paris, was always dominated by his native city. He once wrote to a friend that 'I always write about Dublin, because if I can go to the heart of Dublin I can get to the heart of all the cities of the world.' Joyce went so far as to suggest that if Dublin was to be demolished, it could be rebuilt from the detailed pages of *Ulysses*.

Writers were either married to the concept of Dublin or chose the painful path of emotional and intellectual separation of self-exile. The most popular alternatives to Dublin were London in the case of *Oscar Wilde* (1854–1900) and *George Bernard Shaw*, and Paris for Joyce and Beckett. Curiously, these latter two would sit together in a small Parisian studio, staring at each other in utter silence for hours in a strange confrontation of contemplative wit. Shaw wrote that Dublin would never figure in his writings, yet he never forgot the educational value of the time he spent in the National Gallery as a young man, and he left the gallery a third of his estate. A statue of Shaw stands in the Dargan Wing on the ground floor of the gallery in honour of his contribution.

Men of letters, men of the world

The Dublin literary tradition and its men of letters came from very different social backgrounds, yet all shared a profound understanding of their native city. *Jonathan Swift* (1667–1745) and *Oliver Goldsmith* (1728–1774) were both educated at Trinity College, and both rose to prominence for their sardonic prose. *Seán O'Casey*, a self-educated man, was a labourer for thirty-five years before he became a full-time playwright. *Brendan Behan*, asked once why he took to writing drama, responded, 'Because it's easier than decorating,' the trade he practised for a number of years. Both *Bram Stoker* and *Flann O'Brien* (1912–66) were civil servants, while Shaw was the only son of an unsuccessful wholesale merchant. Yeats, Synge, Wilde and Beckett were all born into wealthy families, which meant they had the benefit of a good education.

A sense of belonging

Establishing a sense of place in Dublin for these writers was never an easy task. *Brendan Behan* (1923–64) and his family, brought up in a Georgian tenement, were moved in the 1930s to the newly created suburbs of Kimmage and Crumlin. In his play *Moving Out* his main character refers to the newly fabricated Dublin environs as 'Siberia', such was the trauma of the move for the character and for Behan himself. Joyce was born into a privileged middle-class background, but with the declining fortune of his family they were forced to move from one abode to another, each more modest than the previous one. Joyce had his alter ego, Stephen Dedalus, refer to St Stephen's Green as 'My Green'. Joyce wanted to depict the city's streets with such accuracy that he used maps and a stop-watch to time the routes of his characters.

If Dublin writers found it hard to gain recognition in their own time and city, things have certainly changed. In 1988 the city authorities established the 'Literary Parade'. It commemorates eleven writers: *Jonathan Swift, James Clarence Mangan* (1803–49), *Oscar Wilde, George Bernard Shaw, W. B. Yeats, John Millington Synge, Seán O'Casey, James Joyce, Brendan Behan, Austin Clarke* (1896–1974), and *Samuel Beckett*. The novelist *Éilis Dillon* has been added to this canon since then.

St Patrick's Cathedral is perhaps the grandest memorial any writer could hope for. For Jonathan Swift it shaped his life. He was its dean, and is now entombed there.

All the former residences of the recognised writers, at least the ones that have escaped the wrecking-ball of the developers, carry plaques with details of their lives. A number of statues and busts around the city's streets and parks add to the sense of hero worship.

Joyce is the most visually prominent writer with regard to landmarks in the city. The **James Joyce Cultural Centre**, 35 North Great George's Street, was made possible only through the dedication of the Joycean scholar, conservationist and Seanad member *David Norris*. Among its most prized displays is the door of 7 Eccles Street, the house of Leopold and Molly Bloom in *Ulysses*. It is all that remains of the property and was saved from destruction when the house was razed. The **James Joyce Museum** in the Martello Tower of Sandycove is closely linked to the writer. Though he resided in the tower only for a short time, he immortalised it in his writing. The opening scene of *Ulysses* is set here, and so it marks the first stage of the annual literary pilgrimage that is Bloomsday. On the 16th of June each year, academics, writers and visitors participate in this lively re-enactment of that one day on which the novel is based. The museum itself houses a collection of letters, documents, photographs and first editions, as well as two death masks of the author.

George Bernard Shaw was a contemporary of Joyce, and in 1925 he won the Nobel Prize for Literature. This prolific and outspoken writer was born at 33 Synge Street, which is now a museum in his honour.

In a poem, *Patrick Kavanagh* asked to be commemorated where there is water, 'canal water preferably.' His wish was granted after his death when a seat and statue of him in contemplative pose were erected beside Baggot Street Bridge, close to where he had lived in 62 Pembroke Road.

Abraham (Bram) Stoker (1847–1912), the author of *Dracula*, was born at Marino Crescent in north Dublin. This novel, his major achievement, inspired a genre of horror films and thrilled audiences throughout the world. Appropriately enough, Stoker worked in a castle—Dublin Castle—where acts of torture were once carried out against Irish people. Stoker is thought to have taken elements of stories about the Great Famine and incorporated them in his masterpiece. A plaque at 30 Kildare Street, close to the National Museum, announces that he lived here for a period. The crypt of **St Michan's Church**, where mummified bodies have been preserved to this day, is said to have been another inspiration for his writings.

Oscar Wilde truly emerged as a literary force in London, but it was in Dublin that he spent his formative years. Today a life-size statue sits in the corner of Merrion Square, across the street from the house where he was born.

Seán O'Casey was born at 85 Upper Dorset Street, and a plaque marks the house. He also lived at 35 Mountjoy Square.

James Joyce statue in North Earl Street.

John Millington Synge is famous for his depiction of rural Ireland and was a major force in the Abbey Theatre. He was born at 2 Newtown Villas, Rathfarnham.

The spirit and story of the Dublin writers is contained in the **Dublin Writers' Museum**. Situated at the top of Parnell Square, this museum is a dedicated and comprehensive resource about the Dublin writers. Set in a beautifully restored 18th-century building, the museum houses collections of rare editions, manuscripts and relevant artefacts used by the artists. You might look out for a typewriter that belonged to Brendan Behan; he is thought to have thrown it through a pub window in a fit of rage. By the way, Behan is buried in Glasnevin Cemetery. There are two exhibition rooms, charting the course of Dublin's literary legacy, with a library of rare books, a gallery of portraits and busts, and a bookshop.

Born into the affluent suburb of Foxrock, *Samuel Beckett* spent most of his life in France. He was educated at Trinity College, and the university's theatre is appropriately named after him.

Oliver Goldsmith (1728–74), author of *The Deserted Village* and *She Stoops to Conquer,* was another graduate of Trinity, and he is commemorated by a statue at the front of the college.

Writers and pubs

The 1950s were the heyday of the Dublin literary pubs. Brendan Behan, who was introduced to alcohol at the age of eight when his grandmother gave him whiskey to 'cure the worms,' explained drinking thus: 'When I was growing up, drunkenness was not regarded as a social disgrace. To get enough to eat was regarded as an achievement, to get drunk was a victory.' But despite their reputation as heavy drinkers, the pub also served as a place of business. Kavanagh, Behan and Brian O'Nolan (Flann O'Brien) used to meet at the **Bailey**. Its owner, *John Ryan*, was an editor, publisher and champion and advocate of many writers during the fifties and sixties. Meanwhile at the **Palace Bar** in Fleet Street the poets *Austin Clarke, John Betjeman, F. R. Higgins*

and *Patrick Kavanagh* used to socialise in the company of the editor of the *Irish Times, R. M. Smyllie.*

Dramatic Dublin

The Irish literary renaissance originated in Dublin and is best represented by the opening of the Abbey Theatre in 1904. The Abbey provided a new generation of Irish artists with a venue for cultural expression. On two separate occasions, in 1907 and 1926, the raw, savagely honest drama of *John Millington Synge* (1871–1909) and *Seán O'Casey* (1880–1964), respectively, caused audiences to riot. On both occasions Yeats took to the stage in defence of the writers with a few remarkable words. 'You have disgraced yourselves again. Is this to be an ever-recurring celebration of the arrival of Irish genius? Synge first and then O'Casey.'

In 1951 the original Abbey was destroyed by fire, and it was not until 1966 that the present theatre was opened. Not before time, there are plans to give this somewhat bland building a deserved revamp.

A new constellation is born

The art of writing is cherished in contemporary Dublin. It is appropriate that the city should be home to the IMPAC literary award, the largest of its kind in the world, valued at £100,000. Irish talent continues to make inroads on the world stage. The Dubliner *Roddy Doyle* came to prominence as the author of the novel on which the successful film *The Commitments* was based. Literary prestige followed in 1993 when he won the Booker Prize with *Paddy Clarke Ha Ha Ha.* The novel also reached the number 1 position in the American best-seller list in early 1994.

John Banville, a novelist from County Wexford, is regarded as one of Ireland's finest living writers and now lives in Dublin. The Nobel laureate *Séamus Heaney,* a northern poet, lives beside the sea in south Dublin. *Neil Jordan,* the novelist and internationally renowned film director, *Brendan Kennelly,* Kerry-born poet and professor of English in Trinity College, and the disabled writer *Christopher Nolan* all live in Dublin.

Dublin by Night

There is plenty of choice for entertainment and 'going out' in Dublin. As a rule of thumb, plays, concerts and films finish by 11 p.m., but if you want to carry on into the night there are more options. The free *Event Guide* can be found readily in most pubs, cafés and restaurants and provides a good source of up-to-date information on all aspects of Dublin's night life. Admission charges to clubs can vary from nil to £8 or £9, and they are all generally busy, especially at the weekends. The price of drink also varies. What doesn't change, however, is the 'party animal' mentality, which is alive and well in this young, modern capital that sees visitors and natives shoulder-to-shoulder in the city's pubs, bars, and night clubs. Perhaps the biggest problem about night-time Dublin is the availability of taxis. Public transport shuts down at 11:30 p.m., though the 'Nitelink' network of buses is reliable, cheap, and fairly comprehensive with regard to the areas it serves. Buses leave every hour on the hour until 3 a.m., and you can catch them around College Green and D'Olier Street.

The National Concert Hall
The National Concert Hall in Earlsfort Terrace is the original home to University College, Dublin, where *James Joyce* was a student. Before that, Earlsfort Terrace was the site of the Royal University of Ireland, established in 1879. In the 1960s the university was moved wholesale and controversially to its present site, Belfield. The concert hall is a sumptuous setting for any musical event and boasts a busy schedule throughout the year.

Concert venues
Dublin is now considered to be an important 'leg' of any international tour by most rock bands and pop acts, and when it comes to venues for pop concerts, Dublin is not lacking. Your choices range from improvised venues such as the **National Stadium**—a boxing venue—and the **RDS** to the established **Point Depot** and the new **Vicar Street** and **Hot Press** music centres.

Cinema
Early in the century Dublin was densely populated with small cinemas. Such was the interest in films at the time that *James Joyce* opened the city's first, the Volta, backed by Italian businessmen. However, the Volta was not a commercial success, a story of failure common to many Dublin cinemas. Directly across O'Connell Street from the **Savoy**, the **Carlton** was shut down a number of years ago. Middle Abbey Street used to be the home of the **Lighthouse**, a small art house that was knocked down and replaced with a multi-storey car park. The role of the Lighthouse has been taken up by the **Irish Film Centre** (IFC) in Eustace Street and to a lesser extent by the **Screen** in College Green. During the summer the IFC screens classic films *al fresco* in Meeting-House Square at the rear of the centre.

Despite the decline in the number of operating cinemas, Ireland has the largest cinema-going audience per capita in Europe. A number of UCI Omniplex centres have mushroomed around the city's suburbs, and Virgin has a multi-screen cinema in Parnell Street. The nearby Imax centre offers a different type of cinema experience but has a limited range of shows on offer.

For an up-to-date listing of films, the *Irish Times* and *Evening Herald* are the best sources of information.

Night clubs
There is one night club in Dublin where you can watch a classic film if you get tired of dancing, when the **Gaiety Theatre** opens its doors after hours as a night club. The auditorium is used to screen old popular films, while the rest of the premises—three floors and five bars in total—caters for a large number of revellers. The Friday night club **Salsa Palace** is usually Latino-based, while Saturday night's **Soul Stage** has a blues-jazz sound, with live performances

both nights.

The **POD**, the **Kitchen** and **Lillie's Bordello** are three of the clubs where visiting musicians, film stars and celebrities are most likely to socialise. These clubs are open to the public but they tend to have a strict door policy for members and a rigid dress code. Look sharp and act confident.

Directly across the road from the Gaiety is **Major Tom's**, a discothèque that plays a strong mix of music from the last three decades. Tom's is owned by the same company that runs the nearby **Break for the Border**, a large country-and-western club with a repertoire of modern music.

Evening in Temple Bar.

Harcourt Street, just off St Stephen's Green, is populated by a number of clubs aimed at different age groups. **Copper-Face Jack's** and the **Vatican** are aimed at a younger clientele, while the **Court** welcomes slightly more mature patrons.

The city centre is well served for night clubs, with the greatest density to be found in Temple Bar. This quarter may have been envisaged as a cultural centre, but it is more like a social and entertainment park. The many late-licence pubs and night clubs in this district ensure that you are never far from 'somewhere to go.'

The last resort of those seeking to extend the night is Leeson Street. A busy office environment by day, many of the basements of these fine Georgian houses are opened at night as 'wine bars'. Where once they stayed open until 6 or 7 p.m., they now tend to close closer to 3 a.m. The beverages are anything but cheap, but if you are thirsty enough you will be served the latest 'last orders' in Dublin.

Cabaret

There is the Irish cabaret format and the European style. For the latter there is not much choice in the capital city, but the funky **Da Club** regularly stages conventional cabaret shows. An evening's entertainment at an Irish cabaret usually involves a mixture of song, dance, and slapstick humour. Some of the shows include dinner, while others offer it as an option. **Jury's Irish Cabaret** has been packing them in for more than thirty years, six evenings a week from May to October.

Cabaret is primarily aimed at the tourist market, yet many Irish people are surprised at how much they enjoy these shows when they bring visiting friends. Other Irish show venues include the **Abbey Tavern** in Howth, **Clontarf Castle**, and **Doyle's Irish Cabaret**.

Gay, lesbian and bisexual bars

In recent years Dublin has become quite tolerant of the gay scene, and this is reflected in the number of bars that have opened catering to the needs of a sizeable homosexual market and the growing value of the 'pink pound'. Bars such as the **George** in South Great George's Street and the **Front Lounge** are 'gay-friendly'. **Flirt**, in the **Tivoli Theatre** every Saturday night, is a new night club for gay and non-gay alike. **Out on the Liffey**, close to the Four Courts, caters for a north-side audience of lesbian, gay, bisexual, cross-dressers, and the simply curious. These bars encourage a mix of clientele, straight and gay, and are frequently among the liveliest in the city.

A Musical Nation

Impromptu session.

Music and poetry had a privileged position in ancient Gaelic society. This tradition has survived. Ireland never developed a school of court or classical music but a vibrant folk tradition has always flourished. In the last twenty years, it has witnessed a fantastic revival.

Until the 1970s, however, that was about all there was in the world of distinctively Irish music. The earliest suggestion of the power of Irish rock music emerged in the early seventies in the form of two guitarists, *Phil Lynott* and *Rory Gallagher.* Gallagher (1948–95), is regarded as one of the finest blues guitarists of all time, if not the best ever. His prowess on the fretboard earned him an invitation from the *Rolling Stones* to join them as their guitarist, an offer he turned down because he said the international group were not close enough to their roots.

Phil Lynott (1949–86), lead singer with *Thin Lizzy,* gave the world its most famous rendition of the ballad 'Whiskey in the Jar', a new interpretation that would change for ever the way musicians looked at their musical heritage and their place in the world. In the late seventies the ground-breaking punk group *Stiff Little Fingers*

enthralled England and the Continent with their energetic, hard-hitting lyrics, a forerunner if you like of the music of *Shane McGowan* and the *Pogues. Van Morrison* of Belfast is one of the truly great surviving and influential figures. His career as the white master of soul has spanned more than three decades, and his solo debut album in the late sixties, *Astral Weeks,* is still regarded as one of the finest records of all time. He has taken another native of his home city, *Brian Kennedy,* under his wing in the hope that this new talent might aspire to similar heights.

The 1980s saw significant developments as Irish rock musicians distinguished themselves by taking a stand on social and global issues, setting them apart as the new messengers in a world of rapid change searching for meaning. Horrified by the scale of famine in Africa, *Bob Geldof,* the former front man of a rock group called the *Boomtown Rats,* organised a massive charity concert in 1985. 'Live Aid' was a remarkable success for the cause it set out to champion. And it was notable for another reason: it was the first major appearance for a Dublin group called *U2.* In this case the apprentice had learnt much from this event, and in 1999 'Net Aid', a global campaign by international musicians to wipe out Third World debt, is now being spearheaded by U2's front man, *Bono*. *Sinéad O'Connor*, once derided for ripping up a picture of the Pope in a protest against the Catholic Church, became a Tridentine priest in 1999. A bizarre move, perhaps, but as her career developed, O'Connor's music reflected growing social and human rights concerns, which prompted her decision.

The mask of Irish music in the 1990s has been worn and adopted by the 'boy band' *Boyzone*. Where U2 were once the most recognisable label of Ireland for young people abroad, that tag has passed to *Ronan Keating* and company. It seems that Boyzone will eventually disband, but their legacy will be carried on by yet another Irish group, be it the *Cranberries*, the *Corrs,* or a group of their calibre.

Ireland's ancient history and its position as the last frontier of western Europe has always inspired a sense of mystery, which has appealed to the creative nature of musicians. *Mike Scott*, lead singer of the Waterboys, *Marianne Faithful*, *Donavan Leech*, the voice behind that hit synonymous with the sixties, 'Mellow Yellow', *Ronnie Woods,* Rolling Stone's guitarist, *Elvis Costello* and *Joe Elliot* of Def Leppard fame are just a few of those rock stars who have specifically moved to Ireland.

Ireland has triumphed in the Eurovision Song Contest no less than five times since the contest began. This is probably not the greatest benchmark by which to measure Irish music, or indeed any music, but the sheer weight of Irish success, including three consecutive wins (1992, 1993, and 1994) hints at the pool of song-writing talent. The 1994 Eurovision Song Contest was also the accidental spawning ground for the greatest Irish music and dance event ever, 'Riverdance.'

The Commitments, though a film about a fictitious Dublin band based on the novel of the same name by *Roddy Doyle*, gripped the imagination of cinemagoers everywhere. *Andrew Strong*, the lead singer in that group, went on to a solo musical career—a case of life imitating art? Not necessarily: his father, Rob, is a well-known singer, and the bass player from the Commitments, *Outspan,* alias *Glen Hansard*, has kept the idea of the 'hardest-working band in rock and roll' alive in the form of his band, the *Frames*.

Emigration has had many profound effects on the Irish psyche and on its eventual ramifications and contribution to the world at large, not to mention the world of music. Descendants of these emigrants have produced some of the greatest names in rock music. Both *Paul McCartney* and the murdered singer *John Lennon* of the Beatles have Irish roots, as have their self-proclaimed nineties counterparts, *Oasis*. The Gallagher brothers, *Liam* and *Noel*, are second-generation Irish people who grew up in England. The same is true of the *Smiths'* front man, *Morrisey,* and the band member *Johnny Marr*, whose 'music of despair' captured the mood of a lost generation during the 1980s, rewarding them with cult status.

The future of Irish rock and pop music is now more assured than ever. There is no sign of seminal figures such as Van Morrison or U2 flagging in their mass appeal or creativity, and a new generation of Irish musicians are in their own distinctive ways carving out a new concept of Irish music. From the *Corrs* of Dundalk to *Boyzone*, *B*witched*, *Westlife*, *Divine Comedy*, *Gavin Friday* and the *Cranberries* of Limerick, a constant flow of talent (no one-hit wonders here) promises new life into the future.

Behind these success stories, countless bands in draughty garages dedicate themselves to a single dream, of musical world domination. This, after all, was how *U2* began their illustrious career, as schoolboys practising in a shed, while the *Hothouse Flowers* got their break in Grafton Street, Dublin, where they used to busk as the *Bendini Brothers*. It is not remarkable that any country should produce a number of great artists, but for a country with such a small population to move from *terra incognita* just thirty years ago to the centre of a global musical empire is.

The story of mainstream Irish music can be captured at the Hot Press Irish Music Hall of Fame in Middle Abbey Street, Dublin, an interactive and modern exhibition of Irish rock and popular music.

Dublin City Centre Map

Fishing Boat, Howth Harbour, Co. Dublin.

Ireland's East Coast

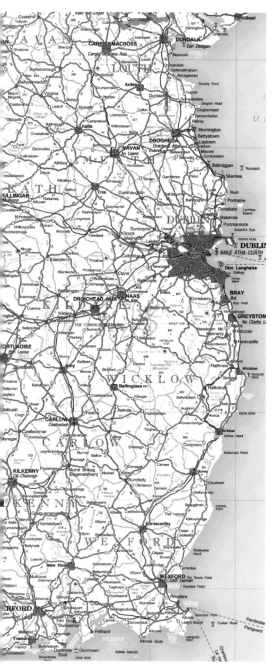

The eastern region of Ireland, consisting of Counties **Louth** and **Meath** in the north, **Dublin**, **Wicklow** and **Kildare**, **Wexford**, **Carlow** and **Waterford** to the south, presents the visitor with a sumptuous and diverse spread of geographical and historical insights pertinent not only to their own past but to that of the country as well.

For a relatively small country, Ireland's landscape contains a multitude of identities, and the differences can be quite stark from east to west or north to south. There is little doubt that the image of small stone-walled fields with wild seas and mountain ranges in the background synonymous with the west of Ireland is most common in the public imagination, but this one-sided perception belies the scenic value of the eastern region. From the flat, almost limitless open spaces of the **Curragh** in County Kildare to the mountainous areas of County Wicklow or the coastal belts of Counties Wexford and Waterford, there are many spectacular natural views to rival anything in the rest of the country.

The evidence of a long, often troubled but periodically peaceful history is clearly mapped out on the natural landscape in this part of the country. Those early settlements begun by the Celtic peoples would develop as trading centres under the Vikings, be overtaken by the Normans, and finally moulded by the English monarchy. Under mediaeval English rule, the stretch of land from County Louth to Wicklow was known as the Pale, a realm where the crown exercised most control. It was also one of the most fertile tracts of land in the country. Many centuries later within this relative safety, the Anglo-Irish aristocracy would commission the building of wonderfully exuberant country residences that formed the nucleus of many of the formal gardens scattered around these counties. In the fight for independence in the early 1920s many of these 'big houses' would fall victim to destruction, but thankfully a large number of them have been saved from disrepair.

Muiredach's Cross and Round Tower at Monasterboice, Co. Louth.

jealously to those events that occurred in its own locality as a source of local pride.

Every county in the eastern region was to suffer at the hands of *Oliver Cromwell* and his brutal armies; and later, when the call to arms was raised in the 1798 rising, they all responded to the cause of national independence. A copious number of cathedrals, churches and monastic sites with their distinctive round towers populate these counties. Set up as spiritual centres, they were attacked by Viking and Irish chieftains alike for their wealth (namely gold), and often became centres of commerce and trade, as was the case in County Kildare and in **Glendalough** in County Wicklow.

Yet for all their underlying similarities, each county is set apart from the others by a number of factors. There is nothing in the eastern region, or the rest of Ireland, for example, to compete with the magnificence of the sites of the **Boyne Valley**. As the capital city, **Dublin** has a character unlike that of any other part of the country. Famous for its writers (past and present), its Guinness and pub culture, witty characters and Georgian architecture, the city is unrivalled for such traits in quantity or quality. Likewise, County Kildare's predominance in the horse-racing industry, County Wicklow's magical combination of wild and domesticated landscapes, Wexford's Opera Festival and Waterford's inextricable link with the sea define the essence of each of these counties.

This varied past is now an integral part of the Irish people, and this sense of history is preserved and displayed with pride in restored jails, cottages, castles, and exhibition centres. Each community clings

41

Counties Louth and Meath

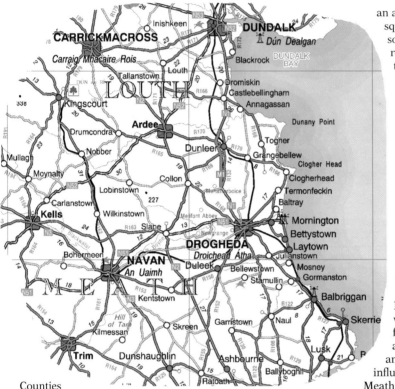

an area of just 317 square miles. It is sometimes referred to as the 'wee county', though it includes the urban centres of Drogheda and Dundalk. For a brief 5 miles or so Meath reaches out to the coast, taking in **Gormanston**, **Laytown** (where the Tara Brooch was found on the beach in 1850), and **Bettystown**, while Louth is firmly fixed against the sea and irrevocably influenced by it. Meath and Louth store a mighty treasure trove of ancient and modern heritage sites that are among the most important in the country, if not in western Europe. People have lived in this area for at least eight thousand years, and it had particular significance as a centre of symbolic and real power for the early Celtic people, the Vikings, Normans, and English, and the Catholic Church. From the earliest epoch to more modern times, the role of this district in the determination of Irish history cannot be overstated. The legendary *Cú Chulainn* was born and died in this area; the **Hill of Tara** represented a thousand-year reign by the Celtic kings; the body of *Brian Bórú* was supposedly laid out in the village of **Duleek** after his death at the Battle of Clontarf; and it was here that

Counties Louth and Meath distinguish themselves from the rest of the east coast in many ways. The land is flat and incredibly fertile, unlike the terrain found in County Wicklow, and the majority of farms are large holdings. It is only to the north of County Louth, across the border, that the landscape becomes mountainous again. The proximity of these two counties to the North has forged their political outlook to no small extent. In **Dundalk** in County Louth and in the fringe areas of County Meath that touch on Westmeath and Cavan there is a marked change in feelings about the North compared with Dublin.

Meath is a large county, sparsely populated. County Louth, on the other hand, is the smallest county in Ireland, covering

Detail of a carving, Newgrange, Co. Meath.

legend claims *St Patrick* made some of his earliest victories for the Christian faith. There is still a lot that is not understood about the earliest times here, and archaeologists continue to discover old and strange clues that slowly but progressively add to our comprehension. For now this area offers an intriguing blend of fact and mystery.

On 11 July 1690, near the village of **Oldbridge** (the birthplace of *St Oliver Plunkett*, 1628–91), one of the most significant battles in Irish history was fought between *King James II* of England and *William of Orange.* In the Battle of the Boyne the Irish and French forces supporting King James were routed by William, and the cause of Catholic Ireland was lost. Protestants in the North commemorate this victory each year by marching on the 12th of July (a miscalculation following the adoption of the Gregorian calendar is responsible for the discrepancy in dates). There is little evidence of the conflict now, but a large orange and green display stand marks the site of the battlefield.

County Meath's association with the high kings of Ireland has given it the name of the Royal County. Louth has no snappy or suggestive title of this kind, though it could viably trade under the heading of the Chapel or Church County. Almost without exception, every town and village in the county claims its origins from, or some long-standing connection with, St Patrick, with one of his disciples or some Christian order. Louth also figures prominently in many ancient sagas, particularly the famous Táin Bó Chuaille (Cattle Raid of Cooley). County Meath has the only Irish-speaking district on the east coast, at **Ráth Cairn**. In County Louth a similar district existed in **Omeath** until the beginning of this century.

Christianity

Aerial view of Clonmacnoise, Co. Offaly.

According to the ballad, *St Patrick* was a gentleman and came of decent people. And so he did. He was the son of a deacon in western Britain, which at the time of Patrick's birth was still part of the Roman empire. When the boy was sixteen he was captured by Irish raiders and spent six years in slavery as a herdsman, probably in what is now County Mayo. Like many another person far from hope and home, he found comfort in the solace of his religion. And that meant Christianity, the official religion of the empire.

He eventually escaped and made his way back to Britain. Safely home again, he began to be troubled by dreams. In these he was addressed by voices from Ireland crying, 'We beg you, holy youth, to come and walk again among us.' Though not sufficiently well educated for the priesthood, Patrick nonetheless answered this call, returned to Ireland about the year 461, and began his mission to convert all the Irish to Christianity.

Patrick is the first individual person in Irish history of whose identity we can be certain. He was almost certainly not the first Christian missionary, nor did he evangelise the whole of Ireland, confining himself largely to the northern half. Other missionary bishops, such as *Palladius*, were probably responsible for the slow conversion of the other half. And it was a gradual process, by no means complete when Patrick himself died about the year 493.

Ireland was at the very furthest margin of the European world. Its peculiar social and political arrangements were reflected in the form of Christianity that established itself here. There were no towns to serve as diocesan centres, so the Irish church was based on a network of monasteries. Moreover, a lot of traditional religious practices were absorbed into the new faith and took new form in Christian ritual. The Irish church combined its Celtic and Roman elements in a mixture that was unique in the Christian world.

But if Irish Christianity was unique, it was also potent. The monasteries developed into powerhouses of scholarship and piety, almost like early mediaeval universities. The greatest of them, Clonmacnoise in County Offaly, on the east bank of the River Shannon, was founded by St Ciarán in 548. Despite successive raids, plunderings and attacks, it survived until 1552—just over a thousand years. The glory years of Clonmacnoise and other monasteries were from the 6th to the 9th century, the so-called Dark Ages. After the collapse of the Roman empire, Christian Ireland was a beacon of light and learning. And it was from Ireland that generations of missionaries later went forth to re-evangelise the Continent. Irish missionaries ranged from Iona off the west coast of Scotland to Kiev.

There are many Continental associations with these heroic early missionaries. St Gallen in Switzerland is named for the Irish missionary who was its first bishop; St Colmán founded the great monastery of Bobbio in northern Italy and many others besides; St Fearghal was bishop of Salzburg, and St Cillian of Würzburg in Bavaria. There were many more; and while one must not exaggerate, it may fairly be said that Irish missionaries made a contribution to the recovery of Europe after the Dark Ages out of all proportion to their numbers.

In Ireland a rigorous ascetic tradition developed beyond the ordinary monasteries. As in the Eastern and Coptic churches, hermits sought out remote and inhospitable places in order to find their own salvation and to pray for that of the secular world. No such site is more remarkable or dramatic than that of the Great Skellig Island, a ferocious triangle of rock off the Kerry coast. Even today a journey out to the monastery of Sceilg Mhichíl is an adventure; one can only imagine what it was like in early Christian times. And when the monks reached the island, home was a beehive hut sitting on a saddle of rock over 500 feet above the sea, with a sheer drop at its feet.

A gentler tradition was the passion for scholarship in the monasteries. Writers such as the English ecclesiastical historian Bede (c. 673–735) remarked upon it. The Irish monasteries were early centres of classical learning. But they also produced work such as lives of the saints in Irish, unusual at a time when the vernacular was not encouraged in the Roman church. Stonework, in particular elaborately carved high crosses, attained a very high standard. Most of all, the monasteries were justly famed for their fabulous illuminated manuscripts. Of these the most celebrated is the great Book of Kells, a transcription of the Gospels in Latin made at the monastery of Kells, County Meath, in the early 9th century and now in the Library of Trinity College, Dublin.

Early Christian Ireland was impressive. Remote and insular, it was distinguished internationally for its scholarship, its artistic accomplishments, its exceptional missionary vigour, and its genuine piety. Though its wealth and achievements made it a tempting prize for outsiders, the sea was its great protection. But all that changed in the late 8th century. Out of Scandinavia came an intrepid and ruthless group of people, known to history as the Vikings, who mastered the sea and built the finest ships of the age. They made the sea their highway, sailing in search of plunder and trade. They went as far as Russia in the east, France in the south, and America in the west. They settled most of northern Scotland and eastern England. In 795 they first appeared in Irish waters.

County Meath

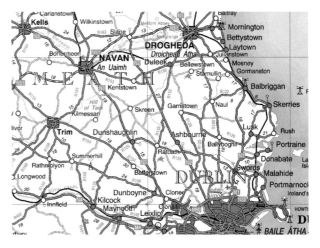

Not far from Drogheda, the most important historical sites in County Meath can be found within a relatively close distance to each other in the basin of the Boyne Valley.

The mound of **Newgrange** was built about the year 3200 BC as a burial site for local chiefs. This circular tumulus had a standing stone on top of it up to the 17th century and just twelve standing stones of a circle that used to surround the mound. The most intriguing surviving elements of Newgrange are the carved kerbstones to the front, with their mysterious carved symbols, and the roof-box. This feature allows the rising sun of the winter solstice (21 or 22 December) to flood through the 'window', flooding the main passage with light for almost twenty minutes. It is a rare sight that only happens once a year, and booking a place many years in advance is the only way to see the real thing. However, there is an alternative. Fearing damage to the site by millions of people over time, the authorities have built a replica of Newgrange at the **Brú na Bóinne Visitor Centre**, complete with a simulated solstice experience.

Newgrange sits beside **Donore**, from where you can enter the other sites of **Knowth** and **Dowth**, the other two major tumuli in the necropolis. These burial mounds are not as developed as their famous sister, but each one has a distinct history and personality. Dowth was ransacked by 19th-century treasure hunters and also quarried for road building material. It boasts a number of beehive structures, as does Knowth, which was once a Celtic stronghold and

was later developed with a motte and bailey by the Normans.

Ashbourne is a thriving market town fast becoming a satellite community of Dublin. It played a major role, directly and indirectly, in the 1916 Rising; to the north of Ashbourne a monument to an insurgent recalls the only significant incident in the rising to take place outside the capital city. **Fairyhouse Racecourse**, to the south-west of Ashbourne, stages Easter meets; and it was partly because the English garrison in Dublin was out of town at this race in 1916 that the rising was scheduled at that time.

To the north on the N2 road is **Slane**. A serene stone-cottaged village, Slane grew up around the castle, built in 1785, which, with its grounds, presents an imposing backdrop and amphitheatre for rock concerts. In the 1980s *Bruce Springsteen* and the *Rolling Stones* played here, but local reaction went against the influx into this tiny community of legions of revellers, and a number of drownings followed as ticketless fans tried to swim across the River Boyne, which cuts through the demesne. In 1991 a large section of the castle was destroyed by fire,

Entrance to Newgrange passage tomb.

Knowth,
Co. Meath.

and its owner allowed further concerts to take place on the grounds as a form of fund-raising. Security was tightened, especially around the river, and acts such as *REM* and *Robbie Williams* have been attracted to play here.

Just half a mile north of the village is the **Hill of Slane**, where legend once claimed that *St Patrick* lit an Easter fire to show the light of Christianity in Ireland. The High King of the time, *Laoire*, forbade any such act, but in a meeting the hostile king supposedly capitulated to the saint and allowed him to evangelise.

Sitting on the River Boyne in the western half of the county, the handsome town of **Trim** encapsulates a number of important heritage sites. One of the oldest ecclesiastical centres in Ireland, its architecture of military occupation dominates, even assimilates, other aspects of the town. Impossible to miss, **King John's Castle**, the largest Norman castle in Ireland, was visited by no less than three English kings: *Richard II, Henry V,*

and *Richard of York*. The castle would fall to *Oliver Cromwell* in 1649 and eventually fall into disrepair, at least until modern times.

Talbot Castle, also called **St Mary's Abbey**, is a 12th-century Augustinian abbey. It was damaged by fire in 1368, and in 1415 part of the abbey was turned into a manor house for the then Viceroy of Ireland, *Sir John Talbot*. The castle was later purchased by *Jonathan Swift's* companion *Esther Johnson*. Swift lived here for a year after buying it from her. The castle would also serve the Protestant community as a school; and the Duke of Wellington was a pupil here as a boy. *Queen Elizabeth I* even considered establishing Trinity College in Trim instead of in Dublin.

The 13-foot **Yellow Steeple**, north of the abbey, was originally the belfry of the abbey. Other curiosities in Trim include the **Echo Gate** on the Dublin road, which resonates a perfect echo across the river; the **Cathedral of St Peter and St Paul**;

the 18th-century **Newtown Abbey**; **St Patrick's Cathedral**; and the **Crutched Friary**, a hospital set up by friars who used to wear red crosses on their habits.

Navan, once a walled town, is surrounded by a number of interesting areas but is not itself a particularly colourful town. It did produce *Sir Francis Beaufort*, an admiral in the British navy who, in 1805, calculated the Beaufort Scale of wind strengths, which is still used by meteorologists today. The banks of the old canal through the town provide a good walking route.

Monks fleeing the island of **Iona** because of vicious Viking attacks went to the monastery in **Kells**, also founded by *St Colm Cille*. With them they took many valuable items. One of their works, a finely decorated version of the Gospels, would be stolen from here, taken for its gold casing, and later discovered in the area, hence the name Book of Kells. Kells offers some other distinctive insights into Early Christian Ireland. Some round towers, **St Colm Cille's House** and scriptural crosses are still evident a thousand years later. Nearby the 18th-century **Tower of Lloyd** and a structure resembling a lighthouse (dedicated to the *Earl of Bective*) stand out on the skyline.

The village of **Moynalty** is one of the best-looking in County Meath and a winner of the Tidy Towns Competition. However, its real attraction is its **Steam Threshing Festival**, which takes place each year during August. The entire local community, and thousands of people from outside, mix in this unique display of farming as it was once practised in Ireland. The festival sports Irish dancing sessions and a temporary museum of antiquated farm implements and antiques.

DON'T MISS

- Newgrange—A passage grave built over five thousand years ago, Newgrange is older than the Egyptian pyramids and Stonehenge.
- Hill of Tara—The Hill of Tara was the seat of the High Kings of Ireland, and the largest section on the Hill is part of the 'Royal Enclosure' where the **Stone of Destiny** can be found.
- **Butterstream Gardens** – one of Irelands finest gardens. A gothic bridge makes a theatrical entrance to the gardens while a tower affords a view over sections of the garden.
- Loughcrew—Outside the village of **Oldcastle** in County Meath are the **Loughcrew Cairns**, an extremely important heritage site but one that receives considerably less attention from visitors, who can more easily reach the more developed Boyne Valley tumuli. However, Loughcrew is just as old, and **Cairn T** has one of the most impressive collections of prehistoric art and the famous 'Hag's Chair'.

ALL-WEATHER OPTIONS

- The **Brú na Bóinne Visitor Centre** (Donore), an interpretative centre for the whole Boyne Valley.
- The **Ledwidge Museum**. About half a mile from Drogheda, this farm cottage was the birthplace of the poet *Francis Ledwidge*, who was killed in 1917 during the First World War. There is also a folk and transport museum.
- The **Hill of Tara Visitor Centre**. Established in a renovated Protestant church, this centre offers a detailed history of Tara and surrounding features, which are generally hard to appreciate at ground level.

County Louth

Lavabo at Mellifont Abbey, Co. Louth.

Dissected by the River Boyne, **Drogheda** (*Droichead Átha*, bridge of the ford) is now some 4 miles inland from the coast, but the Boyne Estuary allowed it to first develop and trade as a busy Viking port town. It owes much to its Norman settlers. The narrow streets and preserved barbican defensive structure of **St Laurence's Gate** stem directly from the Norman era. In the 17th century Drogheda experienced two sieges. In 1641 *Sir Phelim O'Neill* tried to overrun the centre. In 1679 *Oliver Cromwell* and his army carried out their most brutal

massacre here, when three thousand men, women and children were killed; many of the survivors were transported to the Barbados. In the middle of the 19th century engineers would build the railway viaduct that reaches across the Boyne, providing the town with a remarkable landmark.

The head of *Oliver Plunkett*, the Catholic Archbishop of Armagh, is on view in **St Peter's Church** in West Street. He was arrested for treason in 1679 and tried in London, where elements in the English government were determined to find this innocent man guilty. They succeeded, and he was summarily executed in 1691. In 1975 he was canonised and earned the title of Saint.

Just north along the coast road, the villages of **Termonfeckin** and **Clogher Head** feature 15th and 16th-century tower-houses, respectively, built by two different and powerful local families. Termonfeckin was also the seat of the Protestant Primates of Armagh from the Middle Ages until the middle of the 17th century, and it houses a high cross that goes back to the 10th century on the site of a lost monastery from the 6th century.

Between Clogher Head and **Castlebellingham** the village of **Annagassan** is thought to be the first Viking settlement in the country.

North again to Castlebellingham, a village that sprang up around an 18th-century mansion that is now a hotel and restaurant. It is built on the site of an earlier castle, which had connections with William of Orange. Another two miles north lies **Dromiskin**, which became an important ecclesiastical site from Early Christian times. There are a number of religious ruins here, including a round tower, in which the monks used to seek shelter from raiding Vikings, a Celtic ringed cross, and a 10th-century carved spiral pillar.

At the head of the bay, **Dundalk** is now a vibrant manufacturing town and the home of the famous group the *Corrs*, who used to play traditional music in their family's pub. Dundalk is said to have been the home of the legendary *Cú Chulainn*. The sister of the Scottish poet *Robert Burns* is buried in the grounds of **St Nicholas's Church**. She was married to the local rector. The ornate **St Patrick's Cathedral** was designed on the model of

King's College Chapel in Cambridge.

Dundalk stood at the northernmost edge of the English stronghold area known as the Pale; beyond this point the 'wyld Irysh' chieftains ruled, at least until the Plantation of Ulster. Dundalk lies quite close to the border, just 8 miles (13 kilometres) away. Even closer to the North are the towns of **Carlingford** and **Omeath**. Carlingford was once an industrous port in the 15th and 16th centuries, but the opening of the Newry Ship Canal gave Newry the advantage by the beginning of the 18th century. Set against the scenic backdrop of the mountains on this peninsula, the mediaeval traits of Carlingford—small houses with whitewashed fronts studded in narrow streets—has seen it become a heritage town and a winner of the prestigious Tidy Towns Competition.

Next door to County Down, **Omeath** is set in equal natural splendour. Across **Carlingford Lough** the **Mourne**

The East

Mountains combine with the 1,935-foot volcanic ring of **Sliabh Foy** for remarkable vistas, unrivalled on the east coast. The **Long Woman's Grave** in the Windy Gap of the Cooley Peninsula is said to be the burial site of a Spanish princess who emigrated here to marry her lover, an Irish chieftain, but died when she saw the barren, cold landscape of his kingdom.

Despite the fact that the county takes it name from the village of **Louth**, there is a relatively poor selection of historical sites here. There are some points of interest, however. St Patrick is reported to have built the first church in Louth, appointing *St Mochta* as the first Bishop of Louth. A house in his name built in the 12th century stands beside the village. The ruins of **Louth Abbey** can also be seen nearby.

Five miles inland from Drogheda is the village of **Collon**. Laid out in the English style of the late 18th century, the village is made up of two rows of two-storey houses with a market green at one end. The nearby **Mellifont Abbey** is the most significant site here. In its time the abbey was the first and most significant house of the Cistercian order in the country. Established in 1142 by *St Malachy* and several monks from Clairvaux on lands donated by the king of Oriel, *Donncha Ó Cearúill*, it rapidly became the focal point for no less than forty smaller monasteries. Mellifont produced not only a hybrid of Irish and Continental religious thinking but a new, progressive style of architecture that was not practised elsewhere in the country. The partially restored cloister dates back to about the year 1200, and the most interesting piece of surviving architecture is the *lavabo*, a 30-foot diameter octagonal washing-house where the monks would wash their hands before prayers. *Hugh O'Neill*, the vanquished leader of the Irish forces during the Battle of Kinsale, surrendered to *Lord Mountjoy* here before fleeing to the Continent in the Flight of the Earls, a moment in history that marked the decline of the old Irish society.

A meandering country road connects **Mellifont Abbey** with another important monastic site, **Monasterboice**. One of the oldest monasteries in Ireland, it was founded by *St Buithe* possibly as early as the 4th century. Vikings attempted to take the site in the year 968, only to be repelled by the king of Tara. The ruins of the abbey contain two 13th-century churches, a fine round tower, and three sculptured high crosses in varying degrees of repair. The cross closest to the entrance of the abbey is **Muiredach's Cross**, an outstanding 10th-century cross dedicated to the memory of the Abbot of Monasterboice, who died in the year 923. The **West Cross**, one of the tallest examples of its kind, dates from roughly the same era but is not as well preserved, while the **North Cross** is much simpler in design, and its head is now supported by a modern stem. Historians and archaeologists suggest that these crosses, with their engraved passages from the Bible, were originally painted in strong colours, but of course any hint of pigmentation has been eroded by hundreds of years of exposure to the elements.

North of Monasterboice on the N1 road, **Dunleer** is the first town in the barony of Ferrad. It is the site of the early Christian monastery of **Lann Léire**, 'Church of Léire', a settlement with Welsh connections.

West of Dunleer, on the N2 road, the market community of **Ardee** is distinct from its neighbouring towns in that its history is dominated by military rather than religious considerations. **Ardee Castle** to the south and **Hatch's Castle** to the north automatically set the mood for its background. It was here, along the River Dee, that the legendary *Cú Chulainn* single-handedly fought the armies of the south to defend Ulster in the epic 'Cattle Raid of Cooley', in an era when livestock was valued as much as gold. For two months before the ill-fated Battle of the Boyne, *King James II* made this town his military headquarters.

Carlingford Lough,
Co. Louth.

DON'T MISS
- **Mellifont Abbey**—12th-century Cistercian monastery, the lavabo of which is particularly worth seeing.
- **Monasterboice**—Early Christian monastery renowned for its three high crosses, the tallest of which, **Muiredach's Cross**, is one of the finest examples in the whole country.

ALL-WEATHER OPTIONS
- The **Millmount Museum** in Drogheda is a converted army barracks that recounts the history of the town and its environs. On display is a letter from *William of Orange* to the Corporation of Drogheda 12 days after the Battle of the Boyne.

Boyne Valley Drive

Leave Dublin by the N2 road through the rich, fertile lands of County Meath and head towards the village of **Slane**, built on a hill overlooking the River Boyne, a little inland from **Drogheda**. Just north of the village is the **Hill of Slane**, where *St Patrick* was once believed to have lit a fire at Easter to begin his evangelisation of Ireland. There is a fine view of the Boyne valley from the summit. The village is dominated by **Slane Castle**, the residence of *Lord Mountcharles,* in whose grounds rock concerts have been held. A fire swept through Slane Castle some years ago, partially destroying some of its magnificent rooms.

A few miles to the east, on the northern bank of the Boyne, lies the prehistoric funeral chamber of **Newgrange**, dating to about 3000 BC and the best-preserved monument in the region. This important circular tumulus is an artificial 200,000-ton pile of black and white stones, largely covered with earth and grass, some 250 feet in diameter and 40 feet high. The entrance, dominating a stretch of the river, leads by a narrow passage 65 feet long to an interior chamber decorated with geometrical and spiral drawings.

The tumulus is part of the three principal centres of **Brú na Bóinne** ('Palace of the Boyne'), which includes **Dowth** and **Knowth**, along with many other lesser tumuli in the area.

Close by an obelisk marks the site of the Battle of the Boyne, fought in 1690 between the forces of *King James II* and *William of Orange.* Three centuries later, Ulster Protestants still commemorate this victory in marches throughout the province on the 12th of July.

Follow the T26 road through rolling countryside to **Navan**, the principal town of County Meath, situated on the meeting of

the Rivers Boyne and Blackwater. On the left, the ruined square form of **Dunmoe Castle** dates from the late 15th century. Nearby a Romanesque doorway and crucifix have been added to the **Donaghmore Round Tower**.

Continue towards **Trim** on the T26. On the left, **Bective Abbey**, a Cistercian establishment on the banks of the Boyne, was founded by the king of Meath in 1130 as the first daughter-house of Mellifont. Trim, a quiet country town, is dominated by **King John's Castle**, an imposing fortress built by *Hugh de Lacy* in 1173, then enlarged and fortified in the 13th century to become the largest Anglo-Norman citadel in Ireland, when it was seized by *King John.* The other castle in Trim, **Talbot Castle**, now completely modernised, was built in 1415 by *Sir John Talbot,* Lord Lieutenant of Ireland.

From Trim take the L25 road through **Laracor**, where *Jonathan Swift* was curate, and on past **Dangan Castle**, where the *Duke of Wellington,* conqueror of Napoléon Bonaparte at Waterloo, was born.

Turn left on the R156 road and continue towards Drogheda by way of **Dunsany**. On the left is the **Hill of Tara**, ancient capital of the kings of Ireland, a royal acropolis where every three years the kings of Ireland held political and religious meetings presided over by the High King. Continue via **Duleek**, site of a 7th-century monastic foundation, with interesting 10th-century Celtic crosses, to Drogheda.

Situated almost on the mouth of the Boyne, **Drogheda**, like many other coastal towns, owes its origins to the Danes, who established a settlement in 911 on the river ford. A strategic site in the Pale, the Normans made it the most heavily fortified town in Ireland. In 1641 *Cromwell* laid siege to the town, and all those who resisted were either massacred or transported to the Barbados. Part of the old town ramparts survive, notably at **St Lawrence's Gate**; while the **Tholsel** (on the corner of West Street and Shop Street) is the former 17th-century town hall, now occupied by a bank. **St Peter's (Catholic) Church**, built between 1628 and 1691, contains the relics of *St Oliver Plunkett*, former Bishop of Armagh, martyred in London in 1681 and canonised in 1975. The **Millmount**, an ancient tumulus surmounted by an 18th-century barracks, is now a museum.

Leave Drogheda by the T1 road and head north-west for **Mellifont**, site of the ruins of the first Cistercian monastery in Ireland, founded in 1142. Situated on the Mattock River, Mellifont was established by *St Malachy* and several monks from Clairvaux on lands granted by *Donncha Ó Cearúill*, King of Oriel. The partially restored cloister dates from about the year 1200, while the monumental octagonal lavabo, some 30 feet in diameter, where the monks washed their hands before entering the refectory, is the most interesting of the existing buildings.

Leaving Mellifont, rejoin the T2 road for **Collon**, where we turn right and then left for **Monasterboice**, one of the oldest monasteries in Ireland, founded by *St Buithe*. The site was occupied by the Vikings, who were driven out by the king of Tara in 968. The ruins of the abbey comprise two 13th-century churches and a round tower. The site is also the setting for three sculptured high crosses, including **Muiríoch's Cross** (closest to the entrance), an outstanding 10th-century example, dedicated to the Abbot of Monasterboice, who died in 923. The **West Cross** dates from the same era but is less well preserved, while the **North Cross** is much simpler, with the original head now supported by a modern stem.

Rejoin the N2 road and continue to **Ardee**, a small town at the edge of the Pale, which boasts two castles: the 13th-century **Ardee Castle**, now a courthouse, and **Hatch's Castle**, a late 13th-century fortified residence, offered to the Hatch family by *Cromwell*. Leave Ardee on the T2 and continue to **Dundalk**.

Newgrange,
Co. Meath.

Counties Kildare and Wicklow

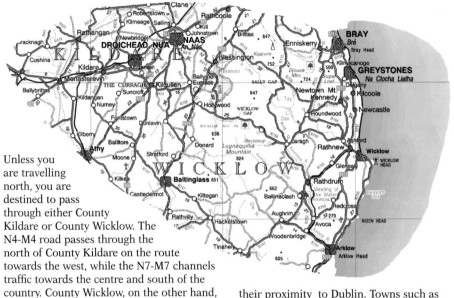

Unless you are travelling north, you are destined to pass through either County Kildare or County Wicklow. The N4-M4 road passes through the north of County Kildare on the route towards the west, while the N7-M7 channels traffic towards the centre and south of the country. County Wicklow, on the other hand, lies directly on the busy N11 route, an important connection between Dublin and the port of Rosslare and indeed the southern counties of Munster. This route, squeezed between the coastline and the highlands of County Wicklow, is undoubtedly a more scenic route than the one through County Kildare, a county that is often 'passed through' rather than visited.

The mountain ranges of County Wicklow are certainly at odds with the glaciated and gentle rolling plains of County Kildare; but these two counties are intimately connected along their boundaries. This contrast results in some of the most interesting landscapes in either county. The R410 road from **Naas** to **Blessington** and its deep lakes leads to the **Sally Gap**, while further south the Quaker village of **Ballitore** rests on the **River Greese**, touching on the fringes of the verdant **Glen of Imaal** in County Wicklow.

County Kildare has no direct connection with the sea, while the major towns in County Wicklow were born on it and profoundly influenced by it. However, the two counties have been equally affected by

their proximity to Dublin. Towns such as **Celbridge**, **Kilcock**, **Clane**, **Maynooth** and **Leixlip** in north County Kildare and **Bray**, **Enniskerry** and **Newtown Mount Kennedy** in the corresponding part of County Wicklow have been demographically transformed. Between 1971 and 1981, for example, the population of County Kildare grew by 50 per cent. Since then, that rate has been surpassed twice over. This trend has brought with it a certain amount of prosperity, but villages that were once tranquil places in the country are no longer recognisable in this form.

The southern reaches of these two counties have not grown at the same rate, and this has helped accentuate economic, geographical and social differences that have always existed. Yet as the race for space and the need to accommodate the exploding population of Dublin increases (some estimates see the population of the greater Dublin area doubling to 2 million by 2011), the encroaching suburbs could extend deep into these two agricultural communities.

From another perspective, Dublin has

Glendalough, Co. Wicklow.

men joined their counterparts in Kildare to fight against the English. Some 350 of them fought and died together on the plain of the **Curragh** at a place called **Gibbet Rath**. A monument in the market square of Kildare stands to their combined bravery and sacrifice.

County Kildare has its fair share of formal gardens and big houses; but County Wicklow truly deserves its reputation as the 'Garden County'. However, towards the end of 1999 moves towards labelling County Kildare the 'Horse County' were being been made. It would be a suitable sobriquet for a county that is famous the world over for its equine industry.

There is no doubt that the county benefits from its level topography; but equestrian pursuits are also popular in County Wicklow. And despite the contrast in landscape, both counties boast major turf-producing areas. Large tracts of land in the western and central flanks of County Kildare consist of ancient boglands. The **Bog of Allen** and **Hill of Allen** are the best-known areas. The Hill of Allen, just five miles north-west of **Droichead Nua** (also called **Newbridge**), is thought to have been an Iron Age fortification used by ancient warriors. The Bog of Allen, the largest bog in Ireland, is home to **Lullymore**. Once a turf-powered electricity station, it has found a new purpose as the 'Island of Discovery'. This small mineral island rises out of the bog on which stands the Lullymore Heritage and Discovery Park, a complex of woodland and bogland walkways, reproduced ancient dwellings, and even a golf course.

Dissimilar in many ways, there are more common threads connecting these two counties than at first appear.

benefited from these neighbouring counties. The **River Liffey**, the life force of the city, springs from the Wicklow Mountains, then turns off for a gentle, sluggish meander through County Kildare before reaching Dublin and its eventual departure into the Irish Sea. Both the Royal Canal and Grand Canal pass through County Kildare, providing a once-valuable trade and transport connection between Dublin and the rest of the country. The capital city has always exploited the Blessington lakes in west County Wicklow as a reservoir for its water needs, and still does; without this natural resource Dublin would be left 'high and dry'.

Both regions rested well within the 'Pale' but played major roles in various revolutions. In the national uprising of 1798, for example, a large number of Wicklow

County Kildare

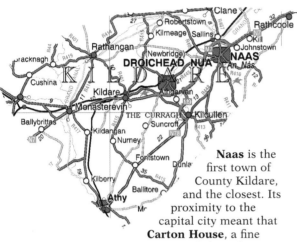

Naas is the first town of County Kildare, and the closest. Its proximity to the capital city meant that **Carton House**, a fine 18th-century Georgian mansion with formal gardens, was designed by the architect behind Leinster House in Dublin and Russborough House near Blessington, *Richard Cassel*. This classical designer was laid to rest in the grounds of St Mary's Church, adjacent to Maynooth College.

St Patrick's College, the first clerical training centre in Ireland, was founded in 1795. Before that, priests would have to travel to France and Spain to train for the priesthood. The English government felt it could exercise greater control over the clergy if it sanctioned the college. St Patrick's still functions as a seminary, but the number of vocations has declined dramatically, and the majority of students study secular subjects.

Maynooth also has a 13th-century castle, situated close to the college entrance. A revolt by an important local figure, *Silken Thomas Fitzgerald*, was quashed at this castle when English forces reneged on a promise of leniency and slaughtered Fitzgerald and his men. The castle itself suffered greatly at the hands of Cromwell's forces and was abandoned in the 17th century.

A few miles south of Maynooth, in Celbridge, **Castletown House** merits some attention. Built between 1722 and 1732 for *William Conolly*, the Speaker of the Irish House of Commons, it is Ireland's largest and best example of a Palladian country house. It owes much of its character to *Edward Lovett Pearce*, the architect who also designed the Bank of Ireland in College Green,

Japanese Gardens,
Kildare.

Dublin. Because Kildare was a wealthy county firmly within the English stronghold, local aristocrats felt secure in building large country houses throughout the area.

Bodenstown

Bodenstown, County Kildare, will forever harbour the spirit of the 1798 rising. *Theobald Wolfe Tone* (1763–98), one of the main leaders of that event, who solicited French assistance in overthrowing English rule in Ireland, was captured and imprisoned in Dublin, where he slit his throat. His body is buried here, and each year many political groups convene at his graveside to honour Ireland's national struggle and aspirations for the future.

The little village of **Robertstown**, accessible via the R409 road from **Naas**, was once an important leg on the Grand Canal but now is a quiet, relaxing place to visit. During the summer a barge tour offers visitors a nostalgic and gently paced alternative way of passing an hour or so. Robertstown's only landmark, the Grand Canal Hotel, complete with its distinctive Crosthwaite Clock, recently repaired, stands at the head of the village.

Droichead Nua (also called **Newbridge**), once an important garrison town for the English army, is now another thriving business and retail town, and the home town of the folk singer *Christy Moore*. Newbridge Cutlery, with an exhibition centre, is its most famous industry.

The town of **Kildare** is centred around an old-fashioned market square that is now used for this purpose only on Thursdays. Its origins are as a cathedral town, and **St Brigid's Cathedral** and round tower can be readily visited, as they stand imposingly close to the square. According to legend, when Ireland's female patron saint asked the ruling chieftain for land on which to found a convent in the 6th century, he said he would grant her as much land as her cloak would cover. When she placed her cloak on the ground it spread out and grew until it covered many acres. The round tower was added in the 9th century, and in the 13th century the cathedral was built on the site of the convent. The cathedral exists in a triangle of the Black, Grey and White Abbeys. Kildare may have more to offer in heritage than its neighbouring towns, but it has little else to detain the visitor.

The village of **Kilcullen** on the westbound R413 road from Kildare boasts a macabre relic. Ireland's finest 19th-century bare-knuckle fighter, *Dan Donnelly* (1788–1820), fought his greatest fight against the English boxer George Cooper in the nearby **Donnelly's Hollow**. Famous for his long arms (he could tie his knee-breeches without bending), Donnelly reputedly carried the defeated Cooper up the slope of the hollow. His giant footsteps, the 'Steps of Strength and Fame', were carved out by fans and can still be seen today. A monument in the hollow recalls his achievements. Donnelly's funeral procession was one of the biggest in Irish history, but his corpse was stolen by body-snatchers. Today one of his arms is mummified in a glass case in the 'Hideout' in Kilcullen, a welcoming old-world type pub.

Horse-racing

The plains of the **Curragh**, stretching between and around Kildare and Newbridge, form the centre of the horse-breeding industry in the county. This land, many thousands of acres in all, forms a limestone plain from which the rich grass provides natural pastures for developing good bones. This terrain makes for prime training and racing conditions, and an abundance of small independent studs in this area make use of this open land for running horses. Just outside Newbridge the **Curragh Racecourse** looms large to the right. It is home to the largest race meeting in the country, the Budweiser Irish Derby and the Irish 2000 Guineas, Irish Oaks, and St Leger.

The Curragh has a long association with the military. Once the warring grounds of *Fionn mac Cumhaill* and other legendary factions, it is now the site of the largest military installation in the country, built by the British army as a training camp for soldiers before they fought in the Boer War. During the Second World War both German and Allied prisoners who were shipwrecked or crashed in neutral Ireland were interned here.

There is a horse museum and rare breeds farm in Bridestream near **Kilcock**; but the most important bloodstock exhibit in the county is without doubt the **National Stud**, one mile outside Kildare on the main road. Established in 1900 as a centre for excellent breeding standards, it has lived up to that role, earning the town a twinning with Lexington-Fayette in **Kentucky**. For a small admission fee it is possible to potter around this well-maintained equestrian compound, visit a small museum, and learn about horse husbandry. The admission fee also admits visitors to the **Japanese Gardens**, which sit in one corner of the complex. They were built between 1906 and 1910 by the founder of the National Stud, *Colonel William Hall-Walker,* who travelled to Japan to recruit two gardeners for his project. The gardens represent a person's journey through life, from birth to death, but you will need a guide to appreciate their full symbolism.

Athy is a pretty though perhaps slightly run-down town towards the Carlow end of the county. Earlier this century it was a popular circuit for *Gordon Bennett* car-racing; today it boasts the sound of modern cars, slugging through viscous traffic. The **Motte of Ardscull** lies outside the town. Folklore has it that this mound is the home of the fairy people. Historically it was developed by the Normans for the superior position it commands of the surrounding low-lying lands. The motte, a large oval mound up to 35 feet high, is surrounded by a ditch and rampart; its plantation of trees was laid down during the 19th century.

Between **Ardscull** and **Crookstown** there is another impressive earthworks complex at the **Rath of Mullaghmast**, where a number of earthworks, ring-forts and a standing stone are in evidence. This was the scene of a massacre in the late 16th century by one family over its enemies; and in 1843 the Liberator, *Daniel O'Connell,* staged one of his last mass meetings here for the repeal of the Act of Union.

Perched on a hill beside the N9 road, **Moone High Cross** juts into the skyline. Originally erected in the 8th century, this 15-foot granite ringed cross fell down and became buried in Moone Abbey churchyard, but it was restored in 1835. False-relief engravings record scenes from the Bible. The ruins of another cross can be seen spread around the graveyard.

DON'T MISS
- The Japanese Gardens and the new Garden of St Fiacre one of the finest in western Europe, combined with the grounds of the National Stud.
- The Curragh, Naas or Punchestown racecourses if there is a meet. Horse-racing is still a major social event and an opportunity to see priests, politicians and the general populace mixing in a spirit of enjoyment and passion.

ALL-WEATHER OPTIONS
- St Brigid's Cathedral and Round Tower, just off the market square in Kildare.
- The Crookstown Heritage Centre, featuring a working watermill and Quaker Museum. This museum is a former school where the philosopher Edmund Burke was a pupil.
- The Steam Museum, Straffan, County Kildare. The exhibit includes several full-size stationary engines and twenty 19th-century models.

Wicklow: The Garden County

Just 12 miles south of Dublin, County Wicklow offers a rich and diverse alternative to the urban atmosphere of Dublin. The Dublin-Wicklow boundary begins unnoticed on the N11 road between **Shankill** and **Bray**. County Wicklow's proximity to Dublin is something of a boon to visitors, who can get here quickly and easily; yet for the north of the county this proximity has had other, more damaging effects. An expanding population in the capital city has put massive pressure on the housing infrastructure and forced many people to look towards the neighbouring counties for a domicile. Wicklow, like Kildare and Meath, has felt the full impact of this population spread. In the last decade Bray and its environs have increased beyond recognition, with countless housing developments mushrooming around its nucleus.

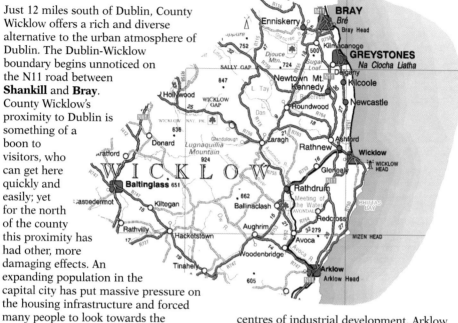

This trend has robbed the town of its identity, and to most Dubliners Bray is now simply an extension of the capital city and not the main town of County Wicklow. The municipal authority and business community have fought back by marketing it as the 'Gateway to the South-East' in an attempt to establish its strategic position in relation to this part of the country.

The accelerated growth of Bray has also emphasised natural differences that exist between it and the more southern towns. To a lesser extent, Wicklow town has grown in response to the same inward pressure, but this has not been the case in Arklow. While Bray and Wicklow are centres of industrial development, Arklow is seen as an economic black-spot, an image it is fighting hard to shrug off.

The coastal strip of County Wicklow is served by the rail network from Rosslare Harbour to Dublin; but in the interior of the county, movement by public transport becomes very complicated and inefficient. There are tours of the various heritage sites, but these can be expensive and restricted to limited areas. If you have the time to spend and want to see a good deal of what County Wicklow has to offer, the most viable option might be to rent a car.

County Wicklow's reputation as the 'Garden of Ireland' is well deserved. It is certainly a county of gardens; and there are many different garden centres in this botanical haven. Wicklow has the only national park in the eastern region; the other four are outside Leinster. The park covers much of upland County Wicklow, approximately 50,000 acres. The uplands were formed more than 400 million years

St Kevin's Kitchen, Glendalough, Co. Wicklow.

ago, when molten igneous rock swelled and cooled. Exposure to the elements and the Ice Age has worn them down into the features we see today. The national park is a sanctuary of landscape and wildlife, including rare orchids and the peregrine falcon. There is an information point and education centre for the park in the valley of Glendalough.

County Wicklow's 'outback' also offers a host of possibilities for adventure holidays, including everything from angling to horse-riding, hill walking and quad trekking. The proliferation of services and facilities to accommodate these activities has been quite pronounced in recent years. The mountains and villages also provide film-makers with a rich and interesting backdrop; *Excalibur, Braveheart, Far and Away* and *My Left Foot* are just some of the films shot in part or entirely here. Ardmore Studios in Bray provides the technical services necessary for a thriving film industry.

Ireland is renowned as a golfing venue, and the country is now a patchwork of hundreds of golf courses. This is especially true in County Wicklow, which has over twenty courses. The terrain offers scenic and challenging variety, from seaside and traditional links courses to inland parks and amazing hillside courses. Courses in the east of the county offer sand links, and some have stunning sea views and incorporate the coast in their make-up. The courses in the north of the county generally have flat fairways, while in the south they are at one with the mountainous layout of the landscape. The biggest golf event in Ireland, the Irish Open, was staged in the **Druids Glen** for some years. Many of these courses are under-used during the week and are inexpensive in comparison with overseas green fees. Contact the secretary or club manager beforehand to book a tee time.

Bray is the largest town in County Wicklow, once a fine 19th-century resort—the Irish Brighton of its era—with a mile-long esplanade ending at the foot of **Bray Head**. Thousands flocked here during the summers of that era for a 'day by the sea'; with the demise of summer it would return to its life as a sleepy town. The buildings on the sea front now look tired and show their age; but those days are not so much over as replaced. Because of the DART suburban railway, Bray is readily accessible from Dublin, and tens of thousands still invade the town during the summer. It is a town geared towards the needs of this new generation of pleasure-seeker. Bray Bowl, close to the railway station, provides bowling and amusement arcade facilities, adding to many others in the town. The **National Sea Life Centre**, on the sea front, was opened in the late nineties, replacing an older aquarium that never achieved commercial success. The new centre allows visitors to get amazingly close to the fish through multi-level viewing platforms,

Wicklow winter scene.

and children can handle crabs and starfish in the 'touch-pools'.

The increase in population has seen Bray become a commercial town, with an abundance of shops and pubs, a busy urban centre all year round.

To reach the **National Garden Exhibition Centre** from Bray, turn off the N11 road at Kilpedder. It is well signposted from here. The centre boasts no less than nineteen display gardens, designed by some of Ireland's leading landscape gardeners. A nursery sells plants, and there are tours and special-event weekends. The range of gardens is as global as it is intriguing, from the Harlequin walk and Acid Garden to Pythagoras at play and the Geometric Garden.

The nearest village to Bray, **Kilmacanogue**, sits in the shadow of the Great Sugarloaf Mountain. Lavender grows here, scenting the air of this village. These flowers are used by Fragrances of Ireland, the country's sole perfume manufacturer. There is also a weeping Monterey cypress and a yew tree, thought to be two thousand years old.

Enniskerry is close to Powerscourt and seen as a point to pass through to get there; yet, like so many of its counterparts in the county, it is a small picturesque community in which it is worth spending at least the time it takes to drink a coffee. The **Powerscourt Estate**, with its grounds and spectacular waterfall, is perhaps the best-known and most visited of all the exhibition gardens in the county, advertised as 'a sublime blend of formal gardens, sweeping terraces, statuary and ornamental lakes together with secret hollows, rambling walks, walled gardens and over 200 varieties of trees and shrubs.' This depiction is true to life, and the grounds are very well kept. Kildare boasts its Japanese Gardens, but it faces a rival in the Japanese gardens of Powerscourt.

The main attraction, however, has always been the waterfall. Formed over ten thousand years ago by an ice formation, it is the highest waterfall in Ireland, dropping almost 400 feet into the Dargle Valley. Since the middle of the 18th

century it has enchanted visitors with a magical spell that seems certain never to lose its binding powers. The waterfall takes its water from the surrounding mountains and bogs, hence its distinctive brown colouring. A nature trail around the base of this magnificent feature allows you to explore it and its unique habitat in close detail. The area is something of a natural haven for flora and fauna. The waterfall is open all year round but is perhaps best seen after a heavy shower.

Greystones, 5 miles south of Bray, was once a small fishing village; and while it no longer has a fishing community, the harbour is well kept and set in a broad bay with a long beach that curves towards Bray Head. The village has lost much of its character because of the explosion in housing developments here, and it is now one of the most expensive areas in the country in which to buy a house. Plans are well advanced to extend the DART to Greystones, and this will no doubt affect future growth.

Further south on the N11 road, **Ashford**'s greatest heritage claim is **Mount Usher Gardens**. The grounds are well known for the quality and quantity of their tree population, and this 20-acre site provides one of the best examples of the romantic Robinsonian garden style, with well-laid-out trees and shrubs from around the world.

The village of **Rathnew** was once quite distinct from Wicklow, but it is now little more than the entry point to the larger town. **Wicklow** itself falls almost in the dead centre of the county's coastline. Like Arklow, it has Viking origins and always maintained its maritime heritage. It takes its name from the Norse name *Vikingrló*, 'Vikings' meadow'. The ruins of the **Black Castle** on the southern end of the town's coastline date back to 1178. When it was used as a defensive structure it was linked to the mainland by a drawbridge. The **Wicklow Regatta** is a major maritime event and harks back to a time when the sight of ships in the bay was a common feature.

The seafaring legacy of **Arklow** is not as

great as it once was, but its spirit has never died. *Sir Francis Chichester* sailed the *Gypsy Moth*, built in the shipyards here, around the world. The naval training ship *Asgard* was also built here. A maritime museum outlines the town's relationship with the sea, a history the local people still cherish.

Carnew is the most southerly of all County Wicklow's villages but has little to offer that cannot be found in more accessible regions of the county.

The small village of **Avoca** is better known to the world as 'Ballykissangel'. This popular television series is shot in the postcard-perfect village and its environs and has become something of a goldmine for its British backers. In the past this was a gold and copper-mining community and home to Ireland's oldest woollen mill. RTE's television serial 'Glenroe' is named after a village of that name in County Wicklow but shot in **Kilcoole**, in the north of the county. At the peaceful confluence of the Avonmore and Avonbeg rivers, two miles north of **Avoca**, is the area known as the 'Meeting of the Waters'.

Next stop the village of **Rathdrum**. A long village that extends along a hillside, it culminates in a splendid market square that has not changed much over the years. It is a ready-made film set, and some of the film *Michael Collins* was shot here. The excitement generated by a shoot is now almost second nature to many of the local people, but they were still surprised when the 'Spice Girls' landed on the town one day in 1997 to shoot a video for their song 'Stop'. The Rathdrum Cartoon Festival used to be a welcome annual event in the life of the village but it has been allowed to disappear, which is a shame. The festival attracted cartoonists from around the world, who gave workshops to the public. The Cartoon Inn still goes by that name and has photographs and drawings from the festival. In place of the cartoon festival the local people have taken to painting the sky with colour in the form of a fireworks festival in August.

A couple of miles east of Rathdrum the road leads to **Avondale**, the birthplace of *Charles Stewart Parnell*, the 'Uncrowned King of Ireland', in 1846. The **J. M. Synge Summer School** is held in the grounds of Avondale House.

North of Rathdrum, **Laragh** and **Glendalough**, and further north-west **Hollywood** and **Blessington**, are set in or near the rugged beauty of the **Wicklow Gap** and the **Sally Gap**. Blessington houses the Beit collection of paintings in **Russborough House**, a world-renowned collection of fine art, as well as the **Lacken Reservoir**, which provides Dublin with much of its water and a recreational space for its citizens. Note that water sports are not allowed in the lakes, as they are deceptively dangerous.

Glendalough is more than the remnants of a 6th-century monastery: it also has a petite village nearby, and sometimes it is hard to imagine just how such a small village can cope with the busloads and hordes of visitors that pass through it each year, some half a million in total. To the east of this monastic heritage site, **Roundwood** claims to be the highest village in Ireland but is perhaps more notable as the setting for films such as *Dancing at Lughnasa* by *Brian Friel* and *Pierce Brosnan's* film *The Nephew*. It is a popular stopping-point for walkers, and the excellent pubs in the village are usually busy, especially at the weekends.

Sitting in the bottom inland corner of the county, **Baltinglass** is closer to Counties Kildare and Carlow than to its own neighbours in Wicklow. Situated on the banks of the River Slaney, it is the site of the Abbey of Vallis Salutis, founded in 1148 by *Diarmaid Mac Murchú*, whose invitation led to the Norman invasion and subsequently English intervention in the country. At the top of **Baltinglass Hill** you will discover **Rathcoran**, a large hill-fort and a Bronze Age cairn, complete with passage graves.

Walking in County Wicklow

The **Wicklow Way** was the first long-distance mountain-walking route in the country, but this was opened for public use only in 1981. This 82-mile (132-kilometre) route begins in **Marlay Park** in **Rathfarnham**, a suburb of Dublin, and runs through Knockree, Roundwood, Laragh, Glenmalure, Ballygobban Hill, and the villages of Tinahely, Shillelagh, and finally Clonegal. The Wicklow Way offers many inspiring views of the glens along the way, especially Luggala and Glendalough. The stone-walled remains of Rathgall are thought to have been the residence of the kings of Leinster.

Two major walking festivals are organised each year, in May and October; and County Wicklow Tourism is to produce two guides about walking and archaeology in the county. These festivals offer different challenges to experienced and novice hill-walkers alike and a very strong social aspect, with meals and visits to pubs and traditional music sessions in the evening.

Day-trippers can walk in the **Glen of Imaal** but should heed the marked routes. Not only would it be easy to get lost in this expanse but the army uses parts of the glen as a training site; and while the danger of straying upon a wayward shell is remote, it is possible.

Long before mountain walking was fashionable the playwright *John Millington Synge* spent his time walking the glens, hills and mountains of Wicklow, learning about nature. He enjoyed the solitude, as is obvious from his poem 'Prelude': 'Still south I went and east and south again, through Wicklow from the morning till the night and far from the cities and sites of men, lived with the sunshine and the moon's delight.' Such was the impact of this environment on Synge that it would feature prominently in his writing, sharing his affections with the Aran Islands. It was also along the roads and lanes of the mountains that Synge met many tramps, travellers and peasants in the fields. His Anglo-Irish background and wealthy family would have distinguished him as a 'nobleman' to these people, yet Synge never patronised them: instead he spent hours listening to them, their stories and ways of speaking, which heavily influenced his writing.

DON'T MISS

- **Glendalough** is the ultimate 'must see' site of County Wicklow. This 6th-century monastic settlement, with seven churches and a round tower, is set in a deep glacial valley with comfortable walking routes set against the backdrop of the glen's two lakes, from which the name derives. It was founded by *St Kevin* and quickly became a major settlement in Early Christian Ireland but went into decline following attacks by the Vikings. An interpretative centre outlines the geographical and historical story of the glen.
- South of Blessington on the road between **Hollywood** and **Donard** are the **Athgreany Piper's Stones**. Some fourteen prehistoric stones form a circle, with another stone just outside the formation. Folklore has it that these stones are the bodies of people turned to stone for dancing on or near pagan ground, with the outside rock said to be the piper.

ALL-WEATHER OPTIONS

- **Wicklow's Historic Gaol**, Kilmantin Hill, Wicklow, was used to imprison tens of thousands of people from the 1798 rising before they were transported to Australia or New Zealand. The tour of the prison museum takes over an hour, and the building also houses a genealogy centre, a shop, and a café.
- The **Dwyer McAllister Cottage** is at the end of a grassy lane off the Donard–Rathdangan road in west County Wicklow. It was here that the Wicklow rebel *Michael Dwyer* fought a pursuing British force in 1799 before making good his escape.
- **Powerscourt** – beautiful formal gardens, steep terraces, flamboyant fountains and sanctuary and the dramatic backdrop of the Sugarloaf mountain make this one of the loveliest gardens in Ireland.

TOURING ROUTE
Suggested tour

The Tour de France, the largest cycling race in the world, came to Ireland in July 1998, drawing massive attention to the east coast areas through which it passed.

The starting point of stage 1 of the race was the south Dublin suburb of **Dundrum**, home of an Irish Tour winner, *Stephen Roche*. The entourage quickly entered County Wicklow through **Bray**, from where the cyclists blazed a trail around the outline of the county, as far south as **Arklow** and along the western boundary from **Woodenbridge** to **Blessington** in the north. The Tour route offers motorists a ready-made framework through many of the best sites in County Wicklow. There is the added advantage that these roads were resurfaced for the race and are now among the best in the country. (At the time, one pundit commented that it was a pity the Tour didn't cross the entire country.)

Bray, just 12 miles south of Dublin on the N11 road, most remarkable for its sea front, quickly leads on to the village of **Kilmacanogue**. From here we get a good view of the **Great Sugarloaf Mountain** and come across Avoca Handweavers, the world-renowned textile shop. Twenty minutes away is the village of **Ashford**, set beside the woods of the **Devil's Glen** and Tiglin outdoor activity centre. A completely thatched village up to the turn of the century, **Rathnew** is steeped in musical and sporting history. It was also the home village of *Captain Robert Halpin,* the man who laid the first transatlantic cable.

The half-way point of our coastal trip, **Wicklow** is a suitable diversion for an hour or so in which to look around, have a meal, or shop. The tourist office is in the market square at the end of this elongated town.

The tip of County Wicklow culminates

in the small but growing seaside resort of **Arklow**. The beach area (there is a north and a south beach) provides the most interesting sites here. An impressive pyramid can be seen on the Beach Road, beside a graveyard; some relatives of the Home Rule leader *Charles Stewart Parnell* are buried underneath this strange tomb.

Leaving Arklow and the N11 road, we head inland towards **Woodenbridge**, a small village that richly deserves its name. The Woodenbridge Hotel is also Ireland's oldest coaching inn. By now you will notice a difference in the road, as it bends to cope with the meandering mountainous terrain and links a chain of villages. Pushing north, the valley of **Avoca** opens up before us. Ruined red-brick buildings, half hidden in the verdant hills, are all that is left of a once thriving copper and mining tradition. It is also the home of Ireland's oldest woollen mill and the inspiration for Avoca Handweavers.

Rathdrum is a splendid village with tons of charm. A textile town in the 18th and 19th centuries, its northern end swoops down a hill to a fine aqueduct. **Avondale** is a close neighbour to this south Wicklow village and worth a visit. The house of *Charles Stewart Parnell,* built about the year 1780, is a museum, while the grounds offer 200 acres of forested land, ideal for picnics or outdoor activities. The poet *Thomas Moore* (1779–1852) immortalised Avondale in his poem 'The Meeting of the Waters'. Continuing directly north through the vale of **Laragh** and the village of the same name, the road leads to **Glendalough**. The Tour route takes us next through the **Wicklow Gap**, heading into the west of the county. The Gap provides a number of open scenic views and the artificial lake of **Turlough Hill**, the country's sole pumped-storage power station.

We are now approaching the northern boundary of County Wicklow; but first we pass through the village of **Hollywood** (no film stars here, however), and then **Blessington**, a former stage-coach stop on the Dublin to midlands run. From here the terrain slips gently towards County Dublin.

Wicklow mountains.

O'SHEA'S HOTEL
9 Talbot Street
Dublin 1
Tel: 836 5670
Fax: 836 5214

O'SHEA'S MERCHANT
12 Lower Bridge Street
Merchants Quay
Tel: 679 3797
Fax 670 7938

Offers accommodation as well as traditional ballads, music and dancing

Take off your caipín (cap) and come a prancing

Dine in one of our restaurants, late bars as well

If you are interested give us a bell ...

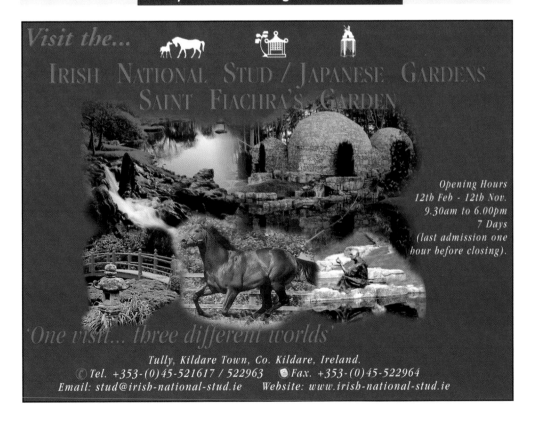

Visit the...

IRISH NATIONAL STUD / JAPANESE GARDENS
SAINT FIACHRA'S GARDEN

*Opening Hours
12th Feb - 12th Nov.
9.30am to 6.00pm
7 Days
(last admission one
hour before closing).*

'One visit... three different worlds'

Tully, Kildare Town, Co. Kildare, Ireland.
Tel. +353-(0)45-521617 / 522963   Fax. +353-(0)45-522964
Email: stud@irish-national-stud.ie   Website: www.irish-national-stud.ie

Counties Wexford, Carlow & Waterford

The further south from Dublin you travel—starting with County Wicklow, passing through County Wexford and ending in County Waterford—the more the landscape changes. The gently rolling hills and valleys of Wexford and Waterford are the archetypal green fields of Ireland, a patchwork of open, fertile and healthy spaces that make for enjoyable driving through a colourful region punctuated by numerous human-made features dating from prehistoric times to the present.

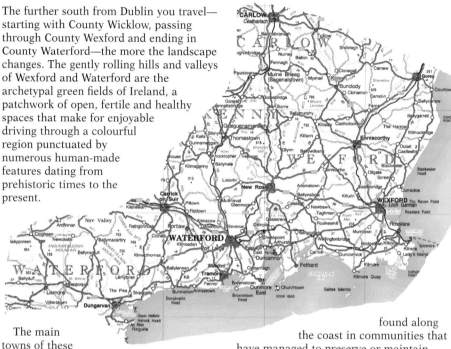

The main towns of these counties all originate from a common point in history, the invasion of the Vikings. Subsequent invasions, such as that of the Normans in the 12th century, who landed in County Wexford, and the English, have sent these towns in different directions. What has not changed for these counties is their close relationship with the sea. **Rosslare Harbour** in County Wexford is a gateway to Britain and the rest of Europe, with hundreds of thousands of people entering and leaving Ireland on the ferry service that operates here. Cargo transport is the business of Waterford harbour, the most modern port in the country. Regattas, sailing competitions, visiting tall ships and naval vessels keep this tradition alive, both on a professional and an emotional level. Some of the most interesting and appealing villages to visit in these counties are to be found along the coast in communities that have managed to preserve or maintain their connection with the sea.

Waterford and Wexford were prominent centres of resistance in the rising of 1798 by the United Irishmen against British rule. Some of the fiercest fighting in the country took place in County Wexford, as thousands of peasants, armed only with pitchforks and other farm implements, held out against superior forces for six weeks, before they were crushed at **Vinegar Hill** just outside Enniscorthy. A statue of the *Lone Pikeman* in the centre of the Bullring in Wexford commemorates their sacrifice and bravery. The song 'The Croppy Boy' emanates from an incident of betrayal that took place in Waterford and has become something of an unofficial anthem for the rebellion.

Wexford and Waterford are known collectively as the 'Sunny South-East', a reputation they deserve as the region with the lowest rainfall and greatest number of days with sunshine. It is fortunate then that they should have some of the finest beaches in the country, along the route of the warm Gulf Stream, which brushes past the coast of these two counties on its journey north.

Both counties offer much in the line of unspoilt scenery to rival anything found in the west of Ireland. The 'Slobs', a wildlife reserve just north of Wexford, offer protection to many forms of flora and fauna not found anywhere else in the country. A diverse range of animals and plants flourish along the shoreline of County Waterford and inland in the county's mountainous sections. For the hill walker, bird-watching community, angler or outdoor enthusiast the choice could not be better.

An almost bewildering array of 'big houses', complete with excellent grounds and gardens, adds to the scenic value of the countryside. As a general rule, from somewhere in the middle of County Wicklow the towns and villages have kept much of their original identity, and around them can be found many ancient tombs, stone markings and remnants of Celtic and prehistoric civilisation. The visitor in search of adventure and activity can choose such sports as golf, angling and sea fishing, horse-riding, hill walking, and sailing. At night there is little shortage of social entertainment in the huge number of bars and pubs scattered throughout the region; and because the sea is such an intrinsic element of life here, seafood is often a speciality in hotels and restaurants.

Harbour, Passage East, Co. Waterford.

County Wexford

Flanked as it is by the mountains of south Wicklow, Carlow and Kilkenny and cut off at the outer extremities by the Irish Sea, Wexford has the appearance of a small county, yet it is the largest one in Leinster, with an area of 981 square miles. It was dominated by the Vikings, but there is little evidence of their reign; by contrast, the landscape holds many clues to the Norman and subsequent English invasions.

Curracloe, **Courtown** and **Rosslare** along the eastern coast are three of the four Blue Flag beaches in County Wexford. **Ferns** (*Fearna,* 'elder trees') may now be a quiet village with most of its activity coming from the busy N11 road, but it was once a place of some substance. It was founded in the year 598 by *St Maodhóg,* and during the Early Christian period no less than thirty churches and several monastic foundations were established here. Today the town's skyline is dominated by two church spires. In the 13th century it lost its status as a major diocese and administrative centre in the province of Leinster. The kings of Leinster made it their base, and it was from here that *Diarmaid Mac Murchú* set out to seek the help of the English crown in his claim to the high-kingship. The ruins of the castle, built in the early decades of the 13th century, stand on the original site of the first Mac Murchú fortification.

In the 1950s and early 1960s the traditional industries of **Enniscorthy**, including bacon-curing, cutlery, and flour-milling, went into decline. The buildings and factories of those industries are still part of the town's landscape, but light and heavy engineering companies and food processing are now the main employers. In more recent times attempts have been made to renew the urban centre; but the 16th-century castle and county museum that sits on top of the first Norman earthwork mound will always dictate the centre and look of this town. Riverboats dock along the quays and offer the chance to move down the estuary.

New Ross, to the west of Enniscorthy on the N30 road, saw heavy fighting in the 1798 rising, but its principal heritage site is **St Mary's Church**, a roofless 13th-century building. South of New Ross, the village of **Dunganstown** has links with one of the most famous American presidents, **John F. Kennedy**. This small town was the birthplace of Patrick Kennedy, JFK's grandfather, who in 1858, like many other Irish people, was forced to emigrate to the United States. During his visit to Ireland in 1963, Kennedy made an emotional return to the town and his Irish roots. The Kennedy house no longer exists, but a plaque marks the spot, and a

Sailing off Hook Head,
Co. Wexford.

family of direct descendants owns a
cottage here. The **John F. Kennedy
Arboretum** testifies to this local heritage.
Open all year round, this 600-acre site
boasts 200 forest plots, some 4,500
different trees and shrubs, and signposted
walks. A road leads to the panoramic
vantage point of Slieve Coillte.

Over the last few years the Kennedy
Trust, a charitable organisation, has
raised £3 million for the construction of
the *Dunbrody*, a full-scale replica of the
ship of that name that carried many
emigrants to the New World between
1845 and 1870, built in Québec for the
Graves family of New Ross. The replica of
this 176-foot long ship was built in a local
boatyard and has attracted many visitors
during the construction period. Now that
it is complete the ship will allow them to

see at first hand what the *Dunbrody*
would have looked like at the time. A
gangplank allows you to board the main
deck, from where you enter the captain's
quarters and the state room, reserved for
wealthy and important passengers. Next
the visitor is brought into the main
passenger section, a world apart from the
space and luxury of the upper quarters.
The tour culminates in an audiovisual
show about the emigrants, their
contribution to American society, and of
course the Kennedy clan.

The **Wexford Opera Festival** is a big
noise in this small town. Founded in 1951
by the Wexford Opera Study Group, it
quickly established itself as the principal
operatic event in Ireland, and it wasn't
long before the festival achieved
international prestige. Indeed many

The East

Italian opera stars owe no small debt to their participation in the Wexford festival. The town comes alive for this 17-day event each October, but accommodation, parking and tickets all become quite difficult commodities to find. By booking well in advance—up to three months—you can avoid most of these difficulties and take in the best of what the season has to offer; otherwise you might fare better staying in one of the surrounding towns or villages, such as Gorey, Ferns, or Clonroche.

The **Irish National Heritage Park** at **Ferrycarrig**, off the N11 road, offers a different kind of culture. This 35-acre amenity offers a fair sample of Irish heritage, stretching back nine thousand years. It is an open-air museum with a high educational value and offers the perfect experience for family outings. As soon as you enter the park, replicated homesteads, graves and ring-forts come into view. A *crannóg* (a small wooden dwelling built in the centre of a lake) and Celtic farmstead as well as a Viking house are among the most interesting sights, while children may enjoy the chance to grind grain in the horizontal water mill. The park opens from March to October, and last admissions are at 5 p.m., but for a thorough look you will require at least a couple of hours.

Just two miles north of Wexford the **Slobs**, a region of land reclaimed from the sea, is the natural setting for the **Wexford Wildlife Reserve**. In winter about half the world's population of white-fronted geese, approximately 10,000 in all, fly here from Greenland. They are

Johnstown Castle, Co. Wexford.

joined every year by flocks of Brent geese from the arctic region of Canada. The reserve protects these and many other breeds of bird that seek sanctuary here throughout the year.

Horse-racing, show-jumping, hunting, breeding and training are commonplace in and around Wexford. During the racing season there is top-class racing at the **Bettyville** track in the town. Slightly further afield in **Enniscorthy**, **New Ross** and **Bannow-Rathangan** there are annual show-jumping events as well. Both *Aidan O'Brien,* winning trainer of the Irish Classic and the English Derby, and the flat trainer *Jim Bolger* hail from Wexford. A number of equestrian centres offer the visitor the opportunity to ride horseback indoors or outdoors and even to go beach trekking. Polo-cross, a popular form of polo, is the latest equestrian sport to come to Wexford.

Bannow Bay in the south of County Wexford was the point at which the Normans entered Ireland, and the village of **Bridgetown** was the first part of Ireland to be colonised by them. The cultural interchanges that took place over the centuries in the isolated region of the south-east led to the formation of a hybrid dialect called Yola, an old version of English with an admixture of Irish, Welsh, Flemish, and Old French.

The coastal route from the port of **Rosslare** to **Kilmore Quay** combines the beauty of the land and the sea with a number of secluded coves and inlets. The peninsula of **Hook Head** is home to the oldest lighthouse in Europe. Folklore claims that the monks had a warning beacon here from as early as the 5th century, and the Vikings were so grateful for their safe passage that they left them alone. The Normans built a lighthouse on this site, and a planned visitors' centre will recount its long history. **Slade Castle** is nearby, and **Tintern Abbey** is also on the peninsula.

Duncannon in the south-west is the other Blue Flag beach in the county. There is a wonderful view of this beach from the adjacent **Duncannon Fort**, which was built in 1586 to secure Wexford Harbour against the threat of the Spanish Armada. Such was the strategic importance of this star-shaped fort that Napoléon Bonaparte himself intimately knew its layout. Duncannon has a clear view over Waterford Harbour and a network of small winding streets.

North of Duncannon on the 'Ring of Hook Head' drive the fishing village of **Ballyhack** features the renovated tower-house that was built by the Knights Templar about the year 1450. The castle displays artefacts from the Templars, who fought in the Crusades, mediaeval monks, and Norman nobility. It is open daily during July and August and from Wednesday to Sunday during April, June, and September.

DON'T MISS
- **Kilmore Quay**. This extraordinary fishing village is the closest land point with a boat service to the Saltee Islands. Ireland's last lightship, the *Guillemot,* is also here.
- The **Irish National Heritage Park**, outside Wexford, for a comprehensive account of how Irish people lived over the millennia.
- Europe's oldest lighthouse at the head of the Hook Peninsula, and Slade Castle.
- Ireland's only surviving windmill at Tacumshane, near Tagoat, Lady's Island on Carnsore Point.

ALL-WEATHER OPTIONS
- The **Wexford County Museum** in **Enniscorthy Castle**, with its displays of Norman artefacts and other pieces from the 1798 and 1916 risings.
- The **John F. Kennedy Arboretum** provides outdoor and indoor activity.
- In New Ross the replica ship *Dunbrody* provides an informative and interesting way to spend an hour on a wet evening.

Waterford: The Crystal County

From **New Ross** to **Dungarvan** and beyond, the land boundaries of County Waterford are marked by the mountain ranges of south Carlow and Kilkenny and

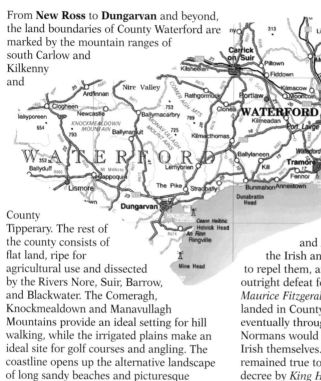

County Tipperary. The rest of the county consists of flat land, ripe for agricultural use and dissected by the Rivers Nore, Suir, Barrow, and Blackwater. The Comeragh, Knockmealdown and Manavullagh Mountains provide an ideal setting for hill walking, while the irrigated plains make an ideal site for golf courses and angling. The coastline opens up the alternative landscape of long sandy beaches and picturesque fishing villages.

Waterford city and county are also quite distinct, blending the urban and the rural in one convenient geographical parcel. County Waterford is not wanting in ancient and modern attractions, from prehistoric stone sites to the green appeal of multiple golf fairways.

Waterford

The city of **Waterford** is sometimes referred to as Ireland's unconquered city, for reasons that need to be explained. It was of course overrun in the first place by Norsemen, who took control of the settlement from the indigenous people, the Déise. Between them they battled for control; but the Vikings held the town for several hundred years. With the imminent arrival of the Normans, led by

Strongbow and *Raymond le Gros*, in 1170, the Irish and Vikings banded together to repel them, an attempt that ended in outright defeat for the newly formed allies. *Maurice Fitzgerald*, Strongbow's cousin, landed in County Waterford in that year; and eventually through intermarriage the Normans would become 'more Irish than the Irish themselves.' But in Waterford they remained true to the English throne. A decree by *King Henry II* to the effect that Waterford was a royal city ensured this allegiance for almost five hundred years. When this strategically important town successfully resisted the sieges of two ambitious mavericks in the 15th century, *Lambert Simnel* and ten years later *Perkin Warbeck*, it adopted the motto *Urbs intacta Waterfordia manet*, 'Waterford remains the inviolate city.' The city remained Catholic in religion, and when *Oliver Cromwell* tried to storm it in the middle of the 17th century he found that its reputation for tenacity was well deserved and just as strong as ever. Cromwell's first sally against Waterford lasted just eight days in 1649, and when his forces returned in 1650, laying siege to it for another four months, they could not break the spirit or resolve of the townspeople, and a negotiated deal ensured its continued

Admiring Waterford Crystal.

position as a port and Catholic centre.

Waterford's most distinctive building must be **Reginald's Tower**, on the corner of the Mall and the Quay. It was originally the site of a wooden Viking fortification begun by *Reginald the Dane* in 1003, on which the Normans constructed a circular tower in the 13th century, with a second phase in the 15th century, bringing it to today's height of 80 feet, with walls up to 13 feet thick. The tower was the main fortification in the town's defences. At various stages it has been used as mint, military store, and prison, but today it has been restored as **Waterford Civic Museum**, with an impressive range of artefacts related to the tower and its history. Behind the tower are Reginald's bar and restaurant, constructed out of the same stone. Remnants of the original Viking walls, built in the year 1000 and developed two hundred years later by *King John* of England, can also be seen towards the back of the tower. Some of the smaller Norman towers are still in prime condition along the wall.

The city maintains much of its original character, with winding streets and buildings of different periods the norm in the old part

of the town. In the years after King John granted Waterford a charter (1215) it prospered as Ireland's premier port for European trade. This status as a mercantile centre has not changed, as ships from all over the world continue to collect and deposit cargoes here.

The Mall, a broad 18th-century street that runs from the quays into the old town, is built on a stretch of land that was reclaimed in that era. It houses the **City Hall**, built in 1788, and inside this building with a rather bland façade hangs the sword of *Thomas Francis Meagher*, who fought as a general in the battle of Fredericksburg during the American Civil War. Having survived this brutal conflict, he was to die by accident when he fell overboard from a paddle steamer on the Missouri River. The **Municipal Library** and the **Courthouse** are two other buildings worthy of merit in this district.

The **French Church** (called **Friars** locally) in Grey Friars' Street was built in 1240 by *Hugh Purcell* as a monastery for the Franciscan order. If the church received the patronage of *King Henry III*, it was later closed by *Henry VIII*, who granted *Henry Walsh* a charter to turn the Friary into a hospital in 1545, a function it served for hundreds of years. The church fell into ruin during the 18th century, and of the original building only the nave, chancel (with a triple-light east window) and north isle remain standing. Many local noble families were also buried here. It is known as the French Church because it was last used as a place of worship by immigrant Huguenots in the 17th and 18th centuries.

Christ Church Cathedral in Dublin was built up by the Normans, chiefly *Strongbow*, on the site of an older ecclesiastical site. This was also the case with the cathedral of the same name in Waterford. Strongbow cemented his power in Ireland by marrying the daughter of the Irish chieftain *Diarmaid Mac Murchú* in the town's cathedral. Waterford had held out against Cromwell, but the town suffered a lot of structural damage, and the cathedral was seriously damaged in the siege and eventually knocked down and replaced with the building you see today. It was designed by the local architect *John Roberts*, who also created the nearby Catholic cathedral.

The success of the Wexford Opera Festival prompted Waterford to replicate this model, and today the Waterford Festival of Light Opera takes place in the city each year in September and October. It hasn't gripped the world's imagination to the same extent, but it does add a new dimension to Waterford life, and it is easier to get into the concerts and events.

Without doubt, Waterford is best known for its crystal. Situated just outside the city centre on the N25 road, the factory receives close to a million visitors a year to its display centre and guided tour. The first glass factory was set up in Waterford in 1783 by the businessmen *George and William Penrose*, who set out to make glass and crystal on a par with anything else in Europe. Their combined resources and knowledge of glassmaking gave the crystal a unique quality, and Waterford crystal won acclaim and several gold medals at the Great Exhibition of London in 1851. But it was at this point that harsh excise duties forced the closure of the factory. It took another hundred

years for it to reopen, with a resurgence of interest in the Irish arts and another combination of enterprising businessmen to revive the legacy. It took five years of training for the craftsmen to learn this skilled trade, and in 1951 Waterford Crystal made a comeback on the world market. Success followed once more, and by the 1980s the Waterford company was the world's largest producer of handcrafted crystal.

Sailing at Dunmore East, Co. Waterford.

Passage East

Today the village of **Passage East**, 7 miles downriver of Waterford, is a pleasant short-cut between Counties Wexford and Waterford, across the Barrow estuary. The car ferry takes about 40 miles off the journey and is a popular option for touring visitors. Throughout its history, Passage has seen a lot of traffic, starting with the Vikings, who founded the village in the 10th century. The low-lying banks made it easy for them to land their ships, and a settlement quickly grew up here. The Normans in turn valued the usefulness of the village; and later it would serve as a convenient point of entry for invading English forces. Passage was more than a strategic point to the people who lived here: for them it was a vibrant fishing village. Salmon was the most common fish at one time, but when hard times visited this community everyone was affected. In times of desperation when fishing was poor, fishermen would be forced to gather seagull eggs. There are still a number of preserved cottages in the village that serve as a reminder of those simpler, if harder, days.

South of Passage, **Dunmore East** has managed to keep its history as a fishing village alive, and, like Passage East, it has a number of well-maintained thatched cottages. The harbour is usually busy with small vessels, especially during the summer, and the nearby beaches are equally popular destinations. The Doric lighthouse (1823) combines with the natural splendour of the area to provide great vistas across the water to **Hook Head**.

Tramore

West of this point, **Tramore** is known to many Irish people as a popular seaside resort. It is only in recent years that it has begun to modernise its image. The resort had become somewhat tacky, but there are signs of improvement. Lazerworld, Splashworld and Tramore Plaza, a multi-purpose venue and a 50-acre amusement park, are bright attractions compared with the small, dark video shops that were once the norm. The town, which is terraced above the beach, is also working hard to enhance its appeal in the hope that tourists will visit it as well as the famously long sandy strand that is 3 miles long and whose waves make perfect surf for surfing. At the top of **Great Newtown Head**, the **Iron Man**, a massive iron replica of an 18th-century sailor, stands with his arm jutting out towards the sea as a warning to passing ships. Numerous ships and hundreds of people were lost around this area, prompting Lloyd's of London to erect this and other towering landmarks in 1816.

There are a number of other small and less tourist-oriented villages that deserve a look. **Annestown**, on Annestown Stream, is part of an ecological conservation initiative. **Dunhill Castle** overlooks this picturesque community, and a cliff walk takes you to **Dunbrattin Promontory Fort**, an Iron Age site. **Bunmahon** follows, and then the award-winning tidy town of **Stradbally**, complete with a number of tidy cottages, the largest mediaeval church in rural Ireland,

and the **Drumlohan Ogham Stone**. **Clonea** boasts a Blue Flag beach and Turkish baths. This stretch of coast, from Tramore to Clonea, offers great waves for surfing.

Dungarvan

The market town of **Dungarvan** (*Dún Garbhán*, 'Garbhán's fort'), 30 miles from Waterford, has deep roots, dating back to the Stone Age. In the late 19th century archaeologists discovered a collection of bones that belonged to mammoth elephants in a local cave, the only discovery of its kind in the country. The bones were dated to 40,000 years ago. In the 3rd century the Déise settled around this area, which is still referred to as the 'Decies' by local people. The town developed around a monastery founded in the 7th century by *St Garbhán*. In 1185 *Prince John of England* visited the town, ordering the construction of fortifications to protect it. **Dungarvan Castle** was built at this time but has been changed much over the years; today it is the administrative centre of Waterford County Council. It has a choice scenic location in **Dungarvan Harbour**, where the River Colligan spreads out before it reaches the sea. **Abbeyside**, the eastern suburb of the town, was the birthplace of *Ernest Walton*, who won the Nobel Prize for physics in 1951 for his pioneering work on nuclear fission. It also features the well-preserved ruins of a 13th-century Augustinian priory, with a 60-foot square tower that was renovated as a belfry for the adjoining Catholic church.

More of a curiosity than a landmark worth visiting is the limestone monument to Master McGrath 3 miles outside the town. It stands in memory of a greyhound that won the Waterloo Cup no less than three times—in 1868, 1869, and 1871—and was beaten only once in its career over thirty-seven races.

Taking the R674 road to **Rinn** and **Baile na nGall**, you enter an Irish-speaking district and a different world.

Ardmore

Christianity came to Ireland before *St Patrick*, and some say it came first to **Ardmore** in the form of a Welshman, *St Declan*. He supposedly arrived in this southerly point about thirty years before Ireland's national saint, and legend has it that his bell and vestments were carried across the water by a glacial boulder that now lies tossed on a rock formation on the beach. The boulder is meant to have healing powers for anyone who climbs underneath it, but you are more likely to come away with scuffed shoes and ripped skin than a miracle cure. As well as the ecclesiastical ruins of **St Declan's Oratory and Cathedral** (10th to 14th century), Ardmore shelters **Temple Disert**, an early hermitage church and one of the best-preserved round towers in the country. Some 154 members of the Confederate army in 1642 sought refuge here from pursuing English forces, and when they surrendered, 117 of them were hanged on the spot.

Reginald's Tower, Waterford.

DON'T MISS

- Just over 2 miles outside Waterford, in the abandoned burial ground of **Kilburrin**, there is a massive portal tomb that reaches a height of 12 feet. The site is a national monument, but it is badly maintained and overrun with weeds. All the same it is an impressive structure.
- Five miles north of Tramore, off the L26 road, the portal tombs of **Knockeen** and **Gaulstown** merit attention for their antiquity.
- From **Kilmacthomas**, visit the prehistoric standing stones of the **Comeragh Mountains** and **Nire Valley Drive**, as well as the *fulachta fia* (ancient cooking-pits), **Knockboy ogham stones**, and assorted cairns.
- Around Dungarvan there are a number of ancient sites, castles and round towers within easy reach of other.

ALL-WEATHER OPTIONS

- **Waterford Crystal.** See this famous hand-blown glass transformed into magical crystal by master craftsmen, and the range of Waterford Crystal products in the company's display centre. The art of glass-blowing looks deceptively easy, but it takes at least five years to perfect this skill.
- Behind the tourist office in Waterford, in the **Granary**, a well-restored stone building, a new multimedia exhibition recounts the history of the city and county from earliest days to the present. If you can only afford to make a whistle-stop tour of the county, then this exhibition is a prerequisite. The tour lasts about an hour, but you can spend much more time browsing among the artefacts if you want. It might also be a good option on a wet day for passing the time.

County Carlow

County Carlow, the second-smallest county in Ireland, is bordered by Counties Wicklow, Wexford, and Kilkenny. It is dominated by flat agricultural land and by two of Ireland's main rivers: the Barrow, which forms the boundary with County Kilkenny, and the Slaney, which flows along the foot of the Wicklow Mountains. This fertile land close to the rivers attracted a host of settlers over the centuries, many of whom left their permanent mark in the form of castles, tower-houses, and monastic remains. Being an inland county, Carlow does not attract nearly as many visitors as neighbouring Wicklow and Wexford and is in fact frequently overlooked by those on their way from Dublin to the south-west. However, for those who want to take the time to discover the rural heart of Ireland, this is an ideal place, with its unspoilt villages and towns, endless miles of hedgerows, slow, meandering rivers, and relaxing, unstrenuous walks.

The town of **Carlow** is situated at the main crossing of the River Barrow and once marked the most southerly outpost of the English crown in Ireland, right at the border of the Pale. The 13th-century Norman castle with its two drum towers still stands but has suffered much through the centuries, not least during the 19th century, when it served as a mental hospital. Other prominent buildings in the town are the 19th-century Gothic Revival **Catholic church** off College Street and the **Courthouse** at the junction of Dublin Street and Dublin Road. The **Carlow Museum** is housed in the Town Hall, in Centaur Street, and has an exhibition dealing with the county's history, archaeology, and folk life. Today most people in and around Carlow work in agriculture or at the nearby sugar factory, while an increasing number commute into Dublin, as house prices there have risen astronomically in the past few years.

Only 2 miles east of Carlow is the **Browneshill** portal tomb, which boasts Ireland's largest capstone, at well over 100 tons. At **Killeshin** a ruined 12th-century church merits a visit for its exceptionally beautiful Romanesque doorway. In the town of **Leighlinbridge** a 12th-century Norman castle still stands, and a lovely stone bridge over the Barrow. Not far from here, but well away from the main road, lies **Old Leighlin**. The first monastery here was founded in the 7th century and once housed up to 1,500 monks. In the year 630 a synod took place here that decided on the date on which Easter should be celebrated throughout the world. The remains of the 12th-century cathedral of *St Laisreán* still tell of the town's former importance as a bishopric between the 12th and 16th centuries. After its joining with the diocese of Ferns in 1600 the town went into decline; but Carey's pub seems to have survived the centuries with fewer problems, having been in the same family since 1542!

Another example of the changing fortunes of whole communities is **Muine Bheag** (also called Bagenalstown), which, according to the plans of the local landowner *Walter Bagenal,* was destined to become Ireland's answer to Versailles, but it never made it, because of lack of funds. Nearby **Ballymoon Castle** was one of the earliest Anglo-Norman strongholds in Ireland and remains quite impressive to this day, with its granite walls over 8 feet thick.

Borris, another charming town, was the seat of the McMorrough Kavanagh family, once the rulers of Leinster, who were at odds with the English crown for generations. One of the best-remembered and best-liked family members was *Arthur McMorrough Kavanagh,* a reforming landlord of the 19th century who was born without limbs but managed to become an excellent sportsman and painter (holding the brush in his mouth), and an **MP**. Visits to the house are by appointment only.

One of the most idyllic ancient ecclesiastical sites is at the village of **Saint Mullin's**. At the ancient burial ground of the kings of Leinster, beside a 7th-century monastery founded by *St Moling,* a small stone cell, the stump of a round tower, a holy well and the remains of an old church stand today overlooking the River Barrow.

Hidden away in the village of **Clonegall** is **Huntington Castle**, dating from the 16th century, with a beautiful yew tree avenue; both castle and gardens are now undergoing restoration and can be visited only by appointment.

Tullow, the largest town in the county, is surrounded by raths, the most prominent of which, **Castlemore**, lies about a mile to the west of the town. Not much further away on the eastern side of Tullow the ancient stone fort at **Rathgall** is also of note. Heading towards Bunclody, follow the signpost for **Altamont Gardens**: the formal garden, herbaceous borders and water garden always guarantee a stunning display but are especially renowned for the carpets of cyclamen that bloom in autumn. **Rathvilly**, which has won the Tidy Towns Award more than once, affords pleasant views of the Blackstairs Mountains and the Slieve Bloom Mountains, both excellent terrain for those who prefer a brisk but relaxing walk to driving.

Browneshill portal tomb, Co. Carlow.

The Midlands

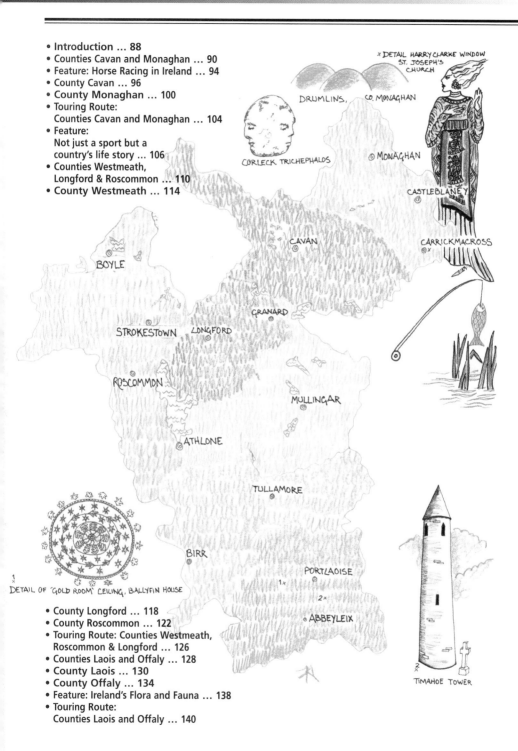

x DETAIL HARRY CLARKE WINDOW
ST. JOSEPH'S
CHURCH

DRUMLINS, CO. MONAGHAN

CORLECK TRICHEPHALDS

MONAGHAN

CASTLEBLANEY

CARRICKMACROSS

BOYLE

CAVAN

GRANARD

STROKESTOWN LONGFORD

ROSCOMMON

MULLINGAR

ATHLONE

TULLAMORE

DETAIL OF 'GOLD ROOM' CEILING, BALLYFIN HOUSE

BIRR

PORTLAOISE

ABBEYLEIX

TIMAHOE TOWER

86

Timahoe Round Tower,
Co. Laois.

Midlands

For the purposes of this guide, the counties reckoned as coming within the purview of the midlands are **Laois**, **Offaly**, **Westmeath**, **Longford**, **Roscommon**, **Cavan**, and **Monaghan**—inland counties lying to the east of the River Shannon. This means an area of lakes, rivers, canals, pasturelands, and bogs—enough to give you a watery, sinking feeling, even without the bogs! At least that is a common first reaction from those who haven't been here. However, on closer inspection the impression is misleading, and if you persevere it's not sinking you'll be but just plain buoyed up by the exceptional quality of what's on offer, not only on the calming watery stretches of these counties but on the dry bits as well!

Lack of knowledge about the midlands, and an unfair bias against flatness, are two factors that have traditionally predisposed visitors to either skirt the region or pass through it at high speed on the way to somewhere else. On learning that Ireland is a saucer, flat in the middle and with stunningly beautiful mountains on its outer rim, many tourists simply head for what they have been told are the most scenic parts of the country. This is unfortunate, because even physically and geologically the central limestone plain is of immense interest; and paradoxically, the midlands merit more attention than many of the more popular areas, on at least three counts: the inherent value of the boglands themselves; the leisurely holiday navigation possibilities afforded by the extensive river and canal network; and the cultural and historical significance of early monastic sites, representing the flowering of Irish spirituality and scholarship, together with the castles and fortified dwellings that convey so vividly the determination of the Anglo-Normans and the native Irish to defend themselves and to survive.

Covered with a mantle of boulder clay deposited during the Ice Age, and overlaid in the centre by raised bogs, the midlands constitute a unique water-centred natural environment, with its own fauna and flora. (Who could guess that eleven species of outwardly innocuous carnivorous plants, ready to trap and digest insects, flourish in this unassuming locale?) At first the post-glacial thaw left central Ireland covered with shallow lakes, and the alliance over time between this abundance of water and the accumulating, decomposing compressed vegetation led to the gradual appearance of bogs. Today these boglands are themselves in the process of disappearing in what is seen as an ecological disaster, especially for rare plants and birds, for whom the dark-brown moorlands form an ideal natural habitat.

Although one of the characteristic geological features of the region is the presence of *eskers* (long ridges of post-glacial gravel)—most notably in Counties Offaly, Westmeath, and Roscommon—the most dominant characteristic of the midlands in the mind of travellers is the abundance of bogland and water. The sphagnum moss found everywhere on these bogs holds water like a sponge and then releases it slowly, just as the bogs themselves absorb and retain human bodies and artefacts and surrender them up after a gap of hundreds or thousands of years. In this sense a bog is both a depository and a medium of preservation of inestimable worth to the archaeologist and the historian.

The bogs of the midlands constitute a beautiful natural museum, filled with every kind of secret exhibit, ranging from the human remains, clothes and food of earlier 'bog people' to reliquaries, gold chains, bridle-bits, and the ornate crosiers of missing bishops. They form a wonderfully varied excavation site and archive, offering instant access to the past, both geologically and archaeologically. To illustrate: the earliest example of La Tène Celtic art found in Ireland—a gold collar with fused buffer-terminals—was discovered in a bog at Knock, Ardnaglug, County Roscommon. Apart from more ornate pieces like this, midland bogs have also yielded up tools, weapons, and household utensils—exhibits in sufficient number to document the history of Bronze Age people in Ireland. And, as if to show how closely intertwined bog memory and monastic Ireland are, the scholastic site of **Clonmacnoise** stands not far from the turf-fired power station at Shannonbridge and within the 350 square miles of the **Bog of Allen**, stretching between the Rivers Liffey and Shannon.

Both the Grand Canal and the Royal Canal cut their way through the raised and damp peatlands of the Bog of Allen, formed over five thousand years ago. It is even possible to leave from the Shannon waterway and follow the Grand Canal system to Dublin, and *en route* to see the mechanised harvesting of turf and the lines of dried sods awaiting transfer to Ferbane power station in County Offaly. Fortunately for canal-travellers, river communication is simplified, as the Grand Canal links with the Shannon at Shannon Harbour, and the Royal Canal joins the river west of Longford.

Though it may seem astonishing today, up to the mid-1800s the Grand Canal carried 100,000 passengers a year in 'flyboats' pulled by teams of galloping horses at anything up to the dizzying speed of 8 miles an hour; and it continued to be used by freight barges up to the 1960s. Further north in County Leitrim, the **Shannon-Erne Waterway** was reopened to leisure use in 1994. It crosses a chain of lakes and passes under thirty-four stone bridges. All these canals provide tourist access to midland beauty-spots as well as opening onto the limitless holiday diversions of Ireland's most historic waterway, the River Shannon.

By far the most important monastic site of the midlands is **Clonmacnoise** in County Offaly; but there are many other monastic remains of great interest, as well as a large number of castles and heritage houses throughout the region. **Trinity Abbey** on Lough Key in County Roscommon, the **Cistercian Abbey** at Boyle, also in County Roscommon, **St Comhghán's Monastery**, Killeshin, County Laois, **Multyfarnham Franciscan Friary** near Mullingar, County Westmeath, and **Castletown Franciscan**

Lough Key Forest Park, Co. Roscommon.

Friary in County Kildare give some idea of the richness and widespread distribution of this spiritual heritage.

But the island of saints and scholars is also the island of warriors and invaders, and the fortress mentality is much in evidence throughout the midlands. **Tyrrellspass Castle** in County Westmeath, **Lea Castle** in County Laois, **Birr Castle** in County Offaly, **Cloughoughter Castle** in County Cavan, **Timahoe Round Tower** in County Laois and the general evidence of *motte* building at critical control points to transit routes over the bogs show the architectural diversity typical of the region. This mixture of monastic and fortified attractions makes the midlands an ideal area for the historically minded visitor.

The life-style of the region is calm and settled, regulated by pleasantly small country towns, with leisure activity centred around fishing and cruising. Probably the best way to see the midlands is to cruise through them, to take an old-fashioned narrowboat or a modern cabin-cruiser and to go at your own pace, drifting by canal banks decorated with yellow spots of iris, cheerful white-faced dog daisies, and demure purple and white orchids—or else not to move around at all, simply to take a fishing-rod and stand in one place, taking in the greenness and the millennial vibes while waiting patiently for that one great crucial moment of surprise …

89

Counties Cavan and Monaghan

Counties Cavan and Monaghan are in many senses forgotten or overlooked, for historical and political reasons. Historically part of Ulster, they have suffered from a general confusion that bedevils the public's view of border counties. This is less true of that other border county, Donegal, simply because its isolation and geographical singularity signpost it in a clearer way. But in the case of both Cavan and Monaghan, the full impact of partition in 1921 has not really sunk in on either side of the border. A kind of 'wait and see' attitude still characterises the inhabitants of the two counties. To confuse matters even further, County Cavan began by being part of the western province of Connacht, and it was only in 1584, when the kingdom of *Bréifne* or Breffni was 'shired', that it became part of Ulster. Up to the late 1300s the south of the county around Lough Sheelin was part of Leinster. Touristically, it is often placed in the north-west; for public health matters it is part of the north-east; and journalistically its local newspaper, the *Anglo-Celt*, describes it as being in the north midlands. Given this degree of topographical, historical and political

ambiguity, and the high stakes for a native in identifying himself with anything in a definitive way, is it any wonder that Cavanmen (and Monaghanmen too, for that matter) are regarded as being canny and have a reputation for carrying their cards close to their chests!

Bounded to the north by County Fermanagh, on the west by County Leitrim, on the south by Counties Longford, Westmeath and Meath and on the east and north-east by County Monaghan, Cavan consists of gentle rolling hills or *drumlins* (long oval mounds dating from the Ice Age) and is famous for the multiplicity of its lakes. It lies half way between the Atlantic and the Irish Sea and is no further than 20 miles on either side from the ocean. To the west the soil is poor, but to the east and south-east of the county the land is fertile. Over a quarter of the population live in towns and villages, but the principal occupation of the people is agriculture, and a slow pace of life prevails outside

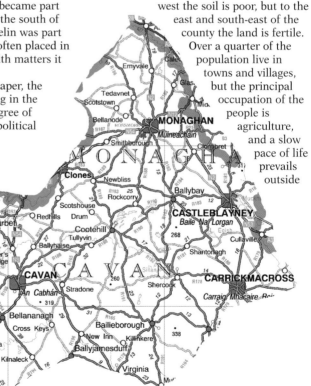

Pony-trekking,
Killykeen Forest Park,
Co. Cavan.

the main centres.

Because of difficult lake and bog terrain, County Cavan proved surprisingly resistant to Anglo-Norman invasion, and the O'Reillys, who ruled west Cavan, managed to resist colonisation by the English up until late in the 16th century. The county was included in the Ulster Plantation from 1608 onwards, when it was settled by Scots and Englishmen. Following *Owen Roe O'Neill's* unsuccessful attempt to make the cause of the ousted native Irish prevail, Cromwellian forces took total control of County Cavan, and the renewed spell of land and property confiscation ensured that the county would remain under English domination. From that time on, the canniness described above may have become a necessary attribute for survival in a dangerous politico-historical situation, pending the emergence of more liberal attitudes.

As a trait of character, canniness seems far removed from the gossipy and scandal-mongering creatures who conspire socially in *A School for Scandal*, written by one of County Cavan's most famous sons, *Richard Brinsley Sheridan* (1751–1816). *William Percy French* (1854–1920), the amusing composer

Castle Leslie,
Glaslough,
Co. Monaghan.

of stage-Irish pastiche and caricature for the gentry ('Are you right there, Michael, are you right?' and 'Slattery's Mounted Foot') was also a Cavanman; and the ancestors of *Henry James* (1843–1916), the great American novelist, were tenant farmers on Bailieborough Estate.

Cavan's neighbour, **County Monaghan**, is also an area of small hills and lakes. Like Cavan, it resisted foreign influence quite successfully for a long time, though in 1589 a large part of it came under the English crown, and in 1591 it was divided into estates between seven MacMahons and a McKenna. Its hills and valleys have been peopled and worked for over five thousand years; and small farmers carrying on cattle-rearing and dairying, with some cultivation, who meet regularly at marts and fairs in the towns form the backbone of County Monaghan economically. Monaghan peasant life in the 19th and even early 20th century was often hard, unrewarding, and frustrating.

But the picture of rural life provided in *The Great Hunger* by *Patrick Kavanagh* (1905–1967), one of Monaghan's, and Ireland's, greatest poets, has changed with the years. Even if individual farms are still restricted in size, poultry-raising co-operatives and mushroom-production enterprises have developed and help account for the improvement in farming incomes. At the same time, traditional ventures such as lace-making continue to thrive in such time-honoured centres as **Carrickmacross** and **Clones**.

In recent times, both Cavan and Monaghan have suffered a good deal from the indifference of holidaymakers who prefer to opt for what they may consider more exciting venues. There are signs, however, of a turnaround. The revival in 1994 of the old **Ballinamore–Ballyconnell Canal**—now linked with the Shannon waterway and covering the Lough Erne lake system—has excited great interest. Now known as the **Shannon-Erne Waterway**, it joins together streams, rivers and lakes and makes possible an additional 40 miles of carefree sailing or cruising. Part of the route, linking Counties Leitrim and Fermanagh, passes through County Cavan and has made tourists more aware of that county and, by association, of Monaghan. Indeed County Cavan is the birth-place of the River Shannon—at 185 miles the longest river in Ireland and one that finds its source in the so-called **Shannon Pot**, on the slopes of the **Cuilcagh Mountains**. The county's other river, the Erne, rises east of Lough Gowna and makes a daisy-chain of three lakes, **Lough Oughter** in County Cavan and **Upper and Lower Lough Erne** in County Fermanagh. In addition to touristic developments at local level, the success of the Belfast Agreement has boosted confidence with respect to all border counties and for Cavan and Monaghan in particular has brought about a new awareness of the superb and unspoilt natural environment they represent.

Because of the ubiquitous availability of lakes, rivers, and streams, Monaghan and Cavan have always enjoyed a reputation as great angling counties. They are also attractive areas in which to practise canoeing, or to walk. County Monaghan has a wealth of prehistoric sites and archaeological remains, and this window on the past is complemented by a variety of fine museums, ranging from the County Museum itself, a vintage steam museum, a heritage centre, and a folk museum, not to forget the **Patrick Kavanagh Centre** in **Iniskeen**. And for a border county like Monaghan, one of the best examples of north-south co-operation is the **Tyrone Guthrie Centre** at **Annaghmakerrig**, which operates with combined grants from the British and Irish Arts Councils. County Cavan also has a good number of stone monuments from the Bronze and Iron Ages, as well as *crannógs* (lake dwellings), and its central place in ancient tradition can be seen by visiting **Maigh Sléachta**, a sacred place of the Celtic gods. Both counties possess their scenic attractions: in County Monaghan the **Bragan Mountain** area, **Glaslough Lake**, and **Lough Emy**, along with **Lough Muckno**; in County Cavan, **Lough Oughter**, **Killykeen Forest Park**, **Bruce Hill**, **Lough Inchin**, and **Dun a Ro Forest Park**.

Horse-racing in Ireland

The parade ring at the Curragh Racecourse.

Horse-racing in Ireland is known as the 'sport of kings'—with good reason. In Celtic times the sport was strictly governed by the ancient 'Brehon' laws and limited to 'princes and the sons of noblemen'. Archaeological excavations of the remains of horses in the Boyne Valley reveal the high esteem in which these animals were held by the Celts, and the prowess of the Irish horse would continue to gain credibility throughout history. *Napoléon Bonaparte,* for example, equipped many of his horsemen with animals purchased from the Ballinasloe horse fair in County Galway, which is still dealing today. Owners, breeders and trainers from around the world turn to Ireland for high-quality bloodstock with a reputation for winning, while Irish jockeys are equally in huge demand in England and further afield.

The reasons for this reputation have always been the same and can be best summed up by the findings of the Commission on Horse Breeding in Ireland, which was established in 1900 by the Department of Agriculture. From the outset the commission stated that 'the excellence of the Irish horse is attributable to the comparative purity of the blood, to the natural advantages in respect of climate and soil which the greater part of the country enjoys, to the habits of the people, their innate love of the horse and the keen interest they take in its welfare.'

Horse-racing has always been a popular sport. Until the 17th century Sunday racing was the norm, at least until it was outlawed by

'And they're off'. Racing at the Curragh.

a puritanical *Oliver Cromwell*. Horse-racing is once again practised on Sundays and most public holiday weekends. Each year hundreds of flat and national hunt fixtures are staged throughout the country; but there are a number of meetings that draw attention from around the world. Classic flat races are typically run at the Curragh, and the **Budweiser Irish Derby**, the most prestigious of them all, is held there every summer. The annual **Dublin Horse Show**, one of the premier events in equestrian circles, has been in existence since 1830; while Leopardstown racecourse, in the southern suburbs of Dublin, is the main race venue for the capital (it also boasts a golf course and the ICON Centre tourist attraction). Like the Curragh racecourse, both Fairyhouse—home of the **Irish Grand National** every Easter Monday—and Punchestown are within an hour's drive of Dublin and are well worth a visit.

The race meeting is a splendid affair of colour, noise, and excitement. Decoratively attired women in festooned hats hoping to win the 'Best-Dressed Lady' competition stand out like pheasants in the shoulder-to-shoulder melee of punters, priests, trainers, and racing enthusiasts. Fortunes are made and lost, and the excitement of the horses darting past the post throws the crowd into convulsions of shouting and screaming, which is followed by passionate debate about the performance of rider and animal. It is a cycle that begins once again with the parading of the entrants for the next race.

These celebrations are part of the cult of the horse, which is so strong in the Irish psyche and landscape. There are, for example, no less than ten places around the country with the name Knocknagappul (*Cnoc na gCapall,* 'hill of the horses').

The racing season extends throughout the year. The **National Stud** at Tully, County Kildare—'the Thoroughbred County'—is the horse-breeding capital of Ireland. The massive tracts of limestone plain produce the ideal environment for building bone and training horses. For anyone seriously interested in the bloodstock industry, a visit to a stud is a must; for everyone else, Irish horse-racing offers a chance to indulge themselves in this noble sport and to enjoy these majestic animals.

County Cavan

A busy market town, commercial centre and county town, **Cavan** was in ancient times the seat of the rulers of east Breffni, the O'Reillys. Of the **Franciscan friary** founded in 1300 by *Giolla Íosa Ó Raghailligh*, only the belfry tower remains. For the rest, the main town buildings date from the last two centuries, with the **Church of Ireland church** and the **Courthouse**, both by *John Bowden*, constructed in the 19th century and the **Catholic cathedral** built in 1942. Two parallel streets—Farham Street, which has some solid Georgian houses, and Main Street, with its shops and bars—comprise the urban centre of what remains in essence a typical Irish county town. On the town's outskirts, visitors can see handcrafted crystal being made at the Cavan Crystal glassworks, or journey to nearby **Lough Oughter**, the largest lake in the county, for a spell of coarse fishing. **Lough Oughter Castle**, a 12th-century Anglo-Norman fortress surrounded by water and standing on a lake island, has

recently been restored by the Office of Public Works. The Ulster Confederate hero Owen Roe O'Neill is reputed to have lived here for a time before being poisoned by his enemies. The garrison of the castle was the last in Ireland to surrender to Cromwellian forces, on 27 April 1653, thereby ending a twelve-year war. **Killykeen Forest Park** on the shores of the lake has fine walks and nature trails and is an excellent spot for fishing.

Cootehill, in east County Cavan, is a small town named after the Cootes, a settler family who founded it in the 17th century. *Sir Charles Coote* is remembered as one of Cromwell's most ruthless deputies; another member of the family, *Richard Coote*, became governor of New York and later of New Hampshire and Massachusetts. *Thomas Coote* arranged for the building of **Bellamont House**, a Palladian mansion designed by the famous architect *Sir Edward Lovett Pearce* in 1730. The town, pleasantly situated between the Analee River and its tributary the Dromore, has a large number of churches. A field-marshal of the Austrian army and privy counsellor of

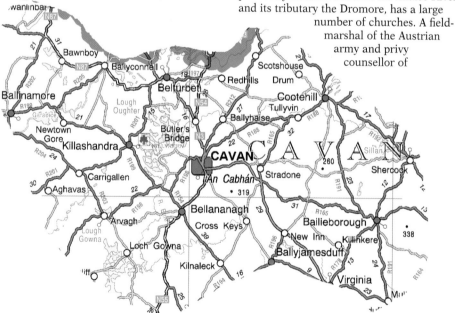

Brackley Lake,
Co. Cavan.

Austria, *Thomas Brady* (1752–1827), was born here, and the Irish-American author *Mrs Sadleir* (1820–1903) was a native of the town. There is good coarse fishing at **Drumlane Lake**.

Built on rising ground beside the River Erne, **Belturbet** was intended as a point of defence against invaders. It is a Plantation or resettlement town, founded by the Butlers, who were granted lands as part of a scheme to plant the area with English and Scottish settlers. An austere 17th-century Protestant church stands on the crest of a hill behind the town, which is dominated by the domed bell-tower of the Italianate Catholic church placed next to it. The town is principally a lively angling and boating resort and has a marina and cruiser station. Nearby **Ballyconnell** was famous for its 7th-century monastery of **Tomregon**, a centre of healing and learning. A famous carving now placed against the side wall of the town's Protestant church shows *St Bricín*, a 7th-century surgeon, performing an operation. But today the town is better known as forming part of the Ballinamore–Ballyconnell canal extension.

The origins of **Bailieborough** resemble those of Belturbet. In the early 17th century the Scottish Bailie family was granted land in the area, and Bailieborough was born. Traditional Plantation focal points—a Protestant church and a market house—are at opposite ends of the town's main street. A traditional focus of the native population, a Catholic cathedral (1942), with stations of the cross by *George Collie*, stands opposite the Protestant church. The grandfather of *Henry James*, the American novelist, and *William James*, the Pragmatist, was a tenant farmer at Bailieborough estate before leaving for the United States. Today the main employers in the area are the Golden Vale Creamery and Bailieborough Foundries.

'Go back to your roots and live longer' is the lesson to be learnt from a visit to **Ballyjamesduff**, the village made famous by a *Percy French* song, 'Come Back, Paddy Reilly, to Ballyjamesduff'. An acquaintance

97

of French's, *Paddy Reilly* spent fifteen years in exile in Scotland before deciding to return to his home town. The virtues of so doing are evident in his living to the ripe old age of eighty-eight. As well as Paddy, Ballyjamesduff now has the new **Cavan County Museum**, with exhibits of prehistoric stone pieces and a dug-out canoe from the 9th century.

Virtues of another kind are apparent in **Virginia,** a town named after *Queen Elizabeth I* of England, the 'Virgin Queen', and settled in the early 17th century. Whether or not this paragon of moral excellence ever gave rise to scandal is immaterial, but *Thomas Sheridan*, who lived in this attractive and well-planned town, had a dramatist grandson, *Richard Brinsley*

Trout-fishing,
Lough Sheelin,
Co. Cavan.

Sheridan, who certainly established a reputation from writing about a school devoted to the subject. Grandfather Sheridan was frequently visited in **Cuilcagh House** by his great friend *Jonathan Swift*, who wrote much of *Gulliver's Travels* during a stay here.

The impetus for the building of the village of **Kingscourt**, situated close to **Dún an Rí Forest Park**, came from a local landowner, *Mervyn Pratt*, in 1760. Today **St Mary's (Catholic) Church** contains some of the best stained-glass windows in Ireland. These are by *Evie Hone* (1894–1955), who worked with famous French abstract artists at the beginning of the century. The windows depict important events in the lives of Christ and the Virgin Mary.

Pleasantly situated on the Analee River, **Ballyhaise** is a quiet, attractive village. Overlooking it is a red-brick and sandstone building with a delightful oval saloon and some fine plasterwork. **Ballyhaise House** owes much to the work of reconstruction carried out on it by the German architect of Leinster House, *Richard Cassel*. It features a curved bay window and, at ground level, innovative steel shutters, with apertures through which the occupiers could direct their muskets against intruders. It is now an

agricultural college, but still worth seeing for its unusual features.

Two relics evocative of County Cavan's past deserve special mention here. The first, the 7th-century **Well of St Cillian** at **Mullagh**, serves as a reminder that even saints can arouse murderous desires. Born at Mullagh, *Cillian* was a missionary whose name is now proudly carried by a ferryboat travelling between Rosslare and the Continent. But the real Cillian was considerably less buoyant following his assassination by the wife of the Duke of Würzburg, who, fearing that her newly converted husband was about to throw her over for the allurements of Hibernian-style religion, directed her anger at the saint, and made him a martyr as well.

The other exemplary tale concerns County Cavan's little tower of Babel, known locally as **Fleming's Folly**. The said Fleming embarked on the construction of a tower, convinced that once it was finished he would be able to see the sea. Needless to say, he didn't; but at least he had learnt something ... To survey this monument to unfulfilled expectation, drive 5 miles out from Cavan along the Granard road and just gawk ... Indescribable ocean view guaranteed!

DON'T MISS
- Don't miss **Killykeen Forest Park**, set around the lake and islands of **Lough Oughter**. There are marked trails flanked by Norwegian and sitka spruce, with ash, birch, oak, beech, sycamore, and alder. A great variety of birds and wildlife is on show, as well as sites of great historical interest, from an Iron Age ring-fort to **Lough Oughter Castle**.
- It's not every day one has a chance to see the exceptional work of *Evie Hone*, but **St Mary's Church** at **Kingscourt** provides not just one window of opportunity to do so but many—all of them stained-glass masterpieces.
- Visit **Ballyhaise House** to see perhaps not America's but Ireland's first oval room, designed by *Richard Cassel*. Lots of other interesting features besides.

ALL-WEATHER OPTIONS
- When the weather's a mess, you need to see junk—three barns of it at **Mrs Faris's Pighouse Collection** near **Killeshandra**. Waistcoats, evening gowns, old lace and domestic items abound.
- If you're cold and damp and low on energy, visit the **Life Force Mall** in Bridge Street, Cavan. You can prepare a loaf of wholemeal brown bread on your arrival, and then, at the end of a 40-minute tour, dried out and resuscitated, you can pick it up piping hot from the oven.

County Monaghan

The county town of **Monaghan** is a thriving agricultural centre that owed much to the

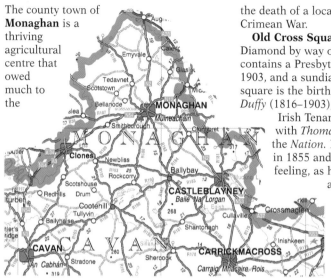

industrious Scottish Presbyterians who built up a prosperous linen business in the town in the 18th century. Earlier the MacMahons, who ruled the county, had forts in the area and made a *crannóg* on the island of the present-day **St Louis' Convent** their headquarters. After the family had joined forces with *Hugh O'Neill* in the war against the English towards the end of the 16th century and been defeated, they were dispossessed of their lands.

Three connected squares compose the town centre. Two of these are bordered with solid 19th-century civic buildings, and the squares are linked by narrow 18th-century lanes. At the centre of the arrangement is the **Diamond**—originally the market-place—which contains the attractive **Rossmore Memorial**, a 19th-century drinking-fountain, and the arched **Market House**, built in 1792. The latter now houses the tourism office. The contiguous Church Square has a fine courthouse with Doric columns built in 1829 and a Regency Gothic church. There is also a massive obelisk commemorating

the death of a local colonel killed in the Crimean War.

Old Cross Square is reached from the Diamond by way of Dublin Street. It contains a Presbyterian church built in 1903, and a sundial. Number 10 in the square is the birthplace of *Charles Gavan Duffy* (1816–1903), who helped found the Irish Tenant League and who, along with *Thomas Davis*, helped set up the *Nation*. He retired from politics in 1855 and left Ireland for Australia, feeling, as he put it, 'like a corpse on a dissecting table.' However, despite this harsh 'posthumous' appraisal of himself, he can be said to have begun a second life down under when he became Prime Minister of Victoria in 1871.

High on a hill outside the town is **St Macartan's Cathedral**, a hard grey limestone church built between 1861 and 1892 to designs by *J. J. McCarthy* in the French Gothic style. Following the Second Vatican Council, three tapestries were placed on the east wall: these evoke different scenes in the life of *St Mac Cáirthinn*. Other notable buildings are **St Louis' Convent**, situated by a lake, and the **Monaghan County Museum** in Hill Street. The convent has its own heritage centre, providing information on the history of the order throughout the world; while the County Museum, which won a Council of Europe Museum prize in 1980, houses the 15th-century Cross of Clogher, along with a permanent collection of archaeological exhibits and mediaeval artefacts, as well as more recent local crafts, paintings and prints from the late 18th century onwards.

About two-and-a-half miles from Monaghan on the road to **Newbliss** is **Rossmore Forest Park,** a low-lying beauty-spot with small lakes and agreeable woodland walks. Newbliss itself is a linen village, created in the 18th century by *Robert Kerr*. Just 3 miles away is **Annaghmakerrig House**, former home of *Tyrone Guthrie* (1900–71) and now a residential centre for artists and writers. Nearby **Rockcorry** is a former flax-growing area where *John Robert Gregg* (1867–1948), inventor of a system of shorthand, was educated.

To the north of Monaghan, near the village of **Glaslough**, is **Castle Leslie**, home of *Sir Shane Leslie*. The house is filled with art treasures and in its present form dates from 1878. Also known as **Glaslough House**, it has been occupied by descendants of the Scottish scholar and bishop *John Leslie* (1571–1671) ever since

he first took over the mansion in 1665. It has seventy rooms, one for each of the seventy years the bishop had when he married an eighteen-year-old bride and fathered no less than ten children. Apart from this spritely contribution to procreation, he managed to find time to build a small church by the lake, which still survives, thereby ensuring both genetic and architectural continuity. A historical tour of the house covers the connections and history of the family and provides access to the many fascinating antiques, including a fireplace by *Francesco della Robbia* and a chest and fireplace from Perugia and, last but not least, a haunted room.

The west County Monaghan town of

Castle Leslie,
Glaslough,
Co. Monaghan.

Monaghan County Museum,
Cross of Clogher.

Clones is a market town and angling centre. The town's beginnings go back to *St Tiarnach* in the 6th century. A roofless 12th-century church still survives off Abbey Street, and curious 18th and 19th-century round stones standing in St Tiarnach's graveyard and filled with thematic carvings such as the skull and crossbones, an hourglass and the bell and coffin remind the visitor of the passage of time's winged chariot. An early **round tower** and a 12th-century stone sarcophagus can also be seen. In the central Diamond, a splendid **high cross** from the 10th century has sculpted scenes from the Old Testament on one side and from the New Testament on the other. The Church of Ireland church, a market house—now housing the County Library—and a courthouse are some of the fine 19th-century buildings illustrating the architectural tone of Clones in its later stages of development.

An exhibition of Clones crochet lace—a heritage craft here—is available at the **Canal Stores**, a newly refurbished visitor centre that opened in 1996, and samples of the lace can be bought at the **Clones Lace Guild**. Among the town's famous sons are *Thomas Bracken* (1843–1898), who emigrated to Australia and settled in Dunedin, New Zealand, where he acquired a newspaper; *Barry McGuigan*, former world featherweight boxing champion; and *Patrick McCabe*, author of *Butcher Boy*, *Breakfast on Pluto*, and *The Dead School*. A further McCabe—*Eugene*—the author of *King of the Castle* and other works, farms in the neighbourhood.

Castleblayney, site of an Early Christian church, takes its name from *Sir Edward Blayney*, to whom *King James I* of England granted land in 1611. A later descendant, the eleventh Lord Blayney, who raised a regiment in the Napoleonic Wars felicitously referred to as 'Blayney's Bloodhounds', contributed greatly to the development of the town. The Blayneys were in occupation from the 17th to the 19th century and were succeeded by the Hopes. **Hope Castle** (named after *Henry Hope*, the owner of the Hope diamond, the largest blue diamond in the world) is a 19th-century house situated next to the largest and most beautiful of County Monaghan's many jewelled lakes. The demesne, with its house, lake, and grounds, makes up **Lough Muckno Leisure Park**, which attracts anglers and nature-lovers in great numbers. *Eoin O'Duffy* (1889–1944), Commissioner of the Garda Síochána (1922–33) and controversial leader of the Blueshirt movement in the 1930s, was a native of **Lough Egish**, near Castleblayney.

Carrickmacross, in the southern part of County Monaghan, is a market town with a reputation for handworked lace featuring a typical swan motif. (Examples of the style can be seen at the Lace Co-operative in Market Place.) At opposite ends of the main street are the 200-year-old **St Finbarr's Church** and the **Courthouse** (1844). Some fine Georgian buildings lie between them. **St Joseph's (Catholic) Church**, a neo-Gothic edifice built between 1861 and 1897, contains no less than ten *Harry Clarke* stained-glass windows.

About 5 miles to the north-east of Carrickmacross is the town of **Iniskeen**, best known as the home of one of Ireland's greatest poets, *Patrick Kavanagh* (1904–1967). The **Patrick Kavanagh Rural and Literary Resource Centre** is situated in the historic **St Mary's Church**, next to the cemetery where Kavanagh is buried.

DON'T MISS

- Don't miss the award-winning **Monaghan County Museum**, featuring archaeology, folk life, crafts, transport, coinage, industry, and an art gallery.
- Make a trip to **Castle Leslie** to look over jewellery that belonged to the wife of *King George IV*, a baby's dress worn by *Winston Churchill*, and a whole range of art treasures and antiques and an eerie haunted room.
- Visit the splendid amenity of **Lough Muckno Leisure Park**, a 900-acre park with woodland walks set around a beautiful lake and offering every conceivable kind of sport, from angling, trekking, canoeing and waterskiing down to an adventure centre and a nine-hole golf course.

ALL-WEATHER OPTIONS

- If the rain is coming down in sheets, try 'lacing' your depression by visiting the **Gallery**, Carrickmacross, where a variety of samples of the local lace-making craft are on display and for sale.
- If you're really depressed by all that rain, just remember that 'we are not alone in our loneliness I Others have been here and known I Griefs we thought our special own.' Visit the **Rural and Literary Resource Centre**, created in Inishkeen to honour the poet *Patrick Kavanagh*, writer of these consoling words.
- Defy the rain by visiting the **St Louis' Convent Heritage Centre** in Monaghan to learn something of that order's remarkable history.

TOURING ROUTE
Counties Cavan and Monaghan

Leave Monaghan (but not before you visit the **County Museum**, with its 14th-century Cross of Clogher), taking the N54 road in the direction of **Clones (St Tiarnach's Church**, high cross, and round tower). Driving parallel to the canal, continue on the A3, and again the N54, to **Butler's Bridge** to see nearby **Ballyhaise House**, designed by *Richard Cassel.* Follow the N3 to **Cavan**, and **Killykeen Forest Park.**

From Cavan take the N55 to **Granard** (venue of the biggest harp festival in Ireland, held each August, and also the site of the largest Norman *motte* in Ireland). At nearby **Abbeylara**, part of the Black Pig's Dyke is to be seen. From Granard take the R194 eastwards to **Ballyjamesduff** (with **Cavan County Museum** and its

Coarse fishing on Lough Allen Canal, Co. Leitrim.

stone idols), passing Lough Sheelin on the right-hand side. From Ballyjamesduff take the R194 to **Virginia** (4 miles to the north-west is **Cuilcagh House**, linked with *Sheridan* and *Swift*), crossing the River Blackwater and driving close to **Lough Ramor**.

From Virginia take the R178 to **Bailieborough** (Catholic church with Stations of the Cross by *George Collie*). From Bailieborough take the R165 to **Kingscourt** (**Dun na Rí Forest Park** and *Evie Hone's* stained-glass windows in **St Mary's Church**). From Kingscourt take the R179 to **Carrickmacross** (hand-made lace, appliqué work on tulle, and Catholic church with ten stained-glass windows by *Harry Clarke*).

From Carrickmacross take the N2 to **Castleblayney** (Georgian courthouse, **Lough Muckno Leisure Park**, and **Hope Castle**). From here continue on the N2 to **Clontibret** and through Monaghan to **Emyvale**, a picturesque town circled by woods, with an abundance of wildfowl and swans, and nearby **Tully Fort** worth a visit. From Emyvale take the road south-east to **Glaslough**; see the demesne of **Glaslough House**, as it's sometimes called, or **Castle Leslie**—a 19th-century Italianate mansion and a favourite haunt of such dissimilar figures as *W. B. Yeats* and *Mick Jagger*. Return from Glaslough by the R185, which joins the N12 before entering Monaghan once more.

Not just a sport but a country's life story

The Gaelic Athletic Association (GAA), the organisation that caters for traditional Irish games, has had a remarkable significance throughout the 19th and 20th centuries. Not only did it develop a thorough involvement in field games but it stimulated the resurgence, parish by parish, of the once humiliated Irish people. Its eminence today, despite the attraction of international sports such as soccer and rugby, is overwhelming evidence of its persistent vibrance.

Irish or 'Gaelic' football, in its simple use of hands and feet, claims to have contained the seminal thrust of rugby, soccer, and Australian football. International games with an agreed convergence of Irish and Australian rules now take place before crowds of over 60,000 in Australia and Ireland. It is unlikely, however, that Gaelic and Australian football, or for that matter hurling, will become world games.

Yes, hurling! Now here is another, quite different phenomenon, rejoiced in with outrageous success by the GAA and by Ireland as a nation. Hurling is reputedly ancient. It is possible to interpret the early Irish sagas—which recount the speed and prowess of the great warrior Cú Chulainn, who could hurl a ball into the air while running forward and be under it where it landed—as a prototype of hurling. Be that as it may, it was certainly played, though in an uncodified fashion, for at least a thousand years prior to the foundation of the GAA in 1884.

Nationalist Ireland veered sharply towards cultural and political independence in the 19th century with the founding of two organisations that could not be classified as subversive. One was the Gaelic League, founded by a group including Dr Douglas Hyde (later the first President of Ireland), which struggled to revive Ireland's embattled language and literature; the other was the Gaelic Athletic Association, founded in Thurles, County Tipperary, in 1884.

The aims of the GAA were to organise the purely Irish games, particularly hurling, Gaelic football, and handball, with regulations governing the rules for the games, the administration, and the co-ordination of every parish and county in a nationwide movement. The GAA, still amateur today, enjoyed extraordinary growth, with each parish in Ireland providing fertile ground for the growth and organisation of the native games.

Hurling is akin to hockey; but so great is the difference that it can be defined only as a third cousin. In hurling the ball can be picked up on the hurley and belted into the air. There are no offside rules. The ball can be carried on the hurley, a beautiful art that can split defences. The ball can of course be played on the ground; it can be raised off the ground with a full arm swing (or otherwise). There is a grace of movement with accuracy that is a delight to watch in proper execution. There are goals, of course, with the usual netting; but the posts are high, as in rugby football. A ball that is hurled from any part of the field over the bar in between the posts is a point; and three points equal a goal. This allows for a plethora of scores—unlike soccer or hockey, where one can groan from deadly boredom in that absurdity that would be anathema to hurling, the scoreless draw.

It is not a dangerous game. Every player knows that his hurley is a weapon that has an 'each way' potential. There is respect for the 'ash' and for craft knowledge. When a high ball lands between a group of contending players, they do not stand back, unleash their ash scimitars, and strike out: they protectively bunch, shoulder to shoulder, and play the ball only.

Hurling.

Crowds in modern times for the great inter-county hurling and football confrontations have seen numbers like 85,000 or more in Croke Park, Dublin, now reduced to a safer 65,000. Provincial finals in Munster, once boasted of as 'the home of hurling', have regular crowds of 40,000 to 60,000.

Every visitor should make a point of going to see a game. You will not see a spectacle like it anywhere else in the world.

Dúchas The Heritage Service

An Roinn Ealaíon, Oidhreachta, Gaeltachta agus Oiléan
Department of Arts, Heritage, Gaeltacht and the Islands

Open your eyes to Ireland's exciting heritage!

Yearly Ticket Available!

We offer a guide-information service & visitor facilities at over 65 sites throughout Ireland

For further information contact

www.heritageireland.ie or email **info@heritageireland.ie** or telephone **+353 1 647 2461**

Please send me details about the Heritage Card and Dúchas sites.

Name _____

Address _____
_____
_____

Send to: 'Heritage Card', Dúchas, Education & Visitor Service,
Department of Arts, Heritage, Gaeltacht and the Islands,
6 Ely Place Upper, Dublin 2, Ireland.

IRLGUIDE

Waveline Cruisers is based in Quigley's Marina at the South end of Lough Ree, right in the centre of Ireland and also right in the middle of the Shannon system. All the permanent staff have plenty of experience in what it is all about to be on the Shannon. We'll be only too happy to share our experience with you.

Killinure Point, Glassan, Athlone, Co. Westmeath.
Tel: (0902) 85711. Fax: (0902) 85716.
Email: waveline@iol.ie
Website: http://www.waveline.ie
Cruising Base: Quigley's Marina.

Counties Westmeath, Longford & Roscommon

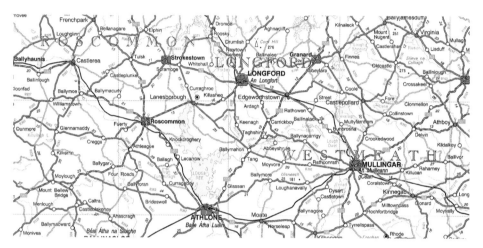

In the old days, the typical Dublin 'hard man's' attitude to this county of cattle farmers was summed up in the pejorative comment about a heavy-legged woman: 'She's beef to the heel, like a Mullingar heifer.' This expression of ignorance both about what makes a woman worthy and what makes County Westmeath interesting is happily a thing of the past. Whatever about a few decades ago, **Mullingar**, the main urban centre, is now a prosperous marketing town, and the women who live in it are as trim and svelte as any of their Dublin sisters.

The county is bounded by County Cavan on the north, County Meath on the east, County Offaly on the south, County Roscommon on the west, and County Longford on the north-west. The lower part of **Lough Ree** and the River Shannon form its western boundary. It has an area of 680 square miles and is a mixture of lakeland, pastureland, and bogland. It has four large lakes: **Lough Owel**, **Lough Ennell**, **Lough Derravaragh** and **Lough Lene** and to the north of the county shares **Lough Sheelin** with County. Cavan. A fertile inland county, it was once integrated with County Meath (*Contae na Mí*, 'the middle county'). Together

the two formed Ireland's fifth province— quite a prosperous one, thanks to its two great rivers, the Boyne and the Blackwater. In the days when Meath and Westmeath were unified, the seat of the High King was at **Uisneach**, a small hill in County Westmeath; nearby stands **Aill na Mireann** ('rock of the divisions'), a boulder traditionally marking the centre of Ireland. On a clear day it is possible to see twenty counties from the summit. Unluckily for the county, the king moved from Uisneach in the year 360 and made his headquarters at Tara. But then Uisneach was chosen as home for the king once more in the 11th century. Earlier *St Patrick* is said to have set up monasteries in the 6th and 7th centuries at **Killare** and **Fore** and on **Hare Island** in Lough Ree. Once the Normans took over the area in the 12th century, mottes and baileys multiplied, and finally stone castles, enabling them to consolidate their hold on the area. Local resistance continued, however, and because of the difficulties posed by the rebellious county, the Plantagenets squeezed Westmeath from Meath in 1542. Later the Irish people had their lands confiscated in the wake of the Cromwellian conquest and the bitter conflicts of the late 17th century.

Largely pastoral, with lakes, County Westmeath contains some great scenery—chiefly towards the centre of the county, where wooded shores and gently rising hills provide many charming views. The Westmeath countryside has a number of great houses and historic castles, many of which are open to visitors. To the north lies countryside made familiar to his readers by the 18th-century poet and writer *Oliver Goldsmith*. On the west the protected shores and water of **Lough Ree** offer great opportunities for fishing and boating. Apart from its fascinating range of Gothic constructions, County Westmeath also has a number of varied regional attractions, such as Mullingar's **Military Museum**, Athlone's **Devenish House**, and the celebrated **Seven Wonders** of Fore.

Many of the local curiosities and landmarks in and around **Mullingar** have storied and anecdotal associations. Worth tracking down are *James Joyce's* associations with County Westmeath. Having come to Mullingar as a teenager in 1900, and again in 1901, to visit his father, who was compiling an electoral register, he stayed at **Levington Park House** near Lough Owel and set parts of *Stephen Hero* in Mullingar. In *Ulysses*, Bloom's daughter, Milly, is put to work as a photographer's helper by Joyce in what is now Fagan's newspaper shop, formerly owned by the photographer *Phil Shaw*. Outside Mullingar, **Belvedere House and Gardens** form the background of a tale that ended up in Joyce's *Ulysses*.

The valley of **Fore**, near the shores of Lough Lene, is another part of the county rich in tradition. An Early Christian settlement here gave rise to a legend according to which the area became associated with 'seven wonders'. Regardless of whether one accepts the legitimacy claimed for these wonders, the Fore valley itself is a wonderful place in which to walk or cycle—an activity that in such beautiful surroundings can quickly become miraculous in its own right.

Westmeath is a county high on local colour, and it has architectural follies to prove it. The most outstanding of these is undoubtedly the **Jealous Wall**, built by a cantankerous earl to prevent him from being exposed to an especially disturbing sight (details on pages 114-16). This vindictive county curiosity, constructed in the 18th century, is situated in the home of Lord Belfield, the first Earl of Belvedere, and is within easy reach of Mullingar.

Bounded by Counties Leitrim and Cavan to the north-west and north-east, by County Roscommon on the west and County Westmeath on the south-east, Longford is a flat, water-filled county, smack in the middle of Ireland and set directly in the Shannon river-basin. Lakes and small streams typify its physical relief, and it has some large areas of bog, though the county is well afforested. The highest point in the county is **Carn Clonhugh** (985 feet), one of a range of low hills extending south-west from **Lough Gowna** on the County Cavan border. Like County Westmeath, it was originally part of the county of Meath. Granted to *Hugh de Lacy* by *King Henry II* of England in the 12th century, it was quickly colonised and, on the separation of Westmeath from Meath in 1543, was included in the former. Today most of its inhabitants live from farming or work in related industries. Agriculturally, most of the land is divided into small farms, and an important activity is the pasturing of cattle for export. Over a third of the population lives in towns, of which the largest is **Longford**.

County Roscommon has an area of 950 square miles and is bordered by County Sligo to the north, County Leitrim to the north-east, Counties Longford and Westmeath to the east, County Offaly to the south-east, County Galway to the south-west, and County Mayo to the west. The greater part of the county lies between two rivers, the Suck and the Shannon, and varies between elevated limestone surfaces and depressions taking the form of bogs or water-meadows. Cattle and sheep are raised here and sold at regular fairs in the town of Roscommon.

The north-west of County Roscommon traditionally belonged to the MacDermotts, and part of the south to the O'Kellys. Under the terms of the Composition of Connacht (1585), many native chieftains acquired tenure under English law in respect of their territories. As a result of this rather exceptional arrangement, the native Irish social character of the county lasted longer than elsewhere and began to disintegrate only with the Penal Laws and land reforms.

Though County Longford has an attractive reputation with coarse fishermen, its literary associations are even more impressive and can be fished out by visitors anxious to see, for example, where *Oliver Goldsmith* was born at **Pallas**; where **Maria Edgeworth**, that exceptionally gifted writer and one of twenty-one children, entertained such eminences as *Walter Scott* and *William Wordsworth* at **Edgeworthstown**, and more recently where the poet and dramatist *Pádraic Colum* was born in the town of **Longford**. Or again one can look to the descendants of the town's famine exiles, many of whom settled in Buenos Aires, and find that one of them, *Edel Miro O'Farrell*, became President of Argentina in 1914.

County Roscommon has rather more outdoor strings to its bow. Enormous flood meadows stretching out from the River Suck provide a magnificent natural habitat for birds and opportunities for bird-watching. And throughout the countryside one finds a superb variety of prehistoric sites and historic monuments, ranging from megalithic tombs and ring-forts to Anglo-Norman castles and early Christian abbeys, with the Cistercian abbey in **Boyle** the most remarkable of these. Its principal natural attraction is **Lough Key**, a lake situated in the spectacular surroundings of an unspoilt forest park.

Though it cannot claim as many literary connections as Longford, County Roscommon was home to the great Gaelic League enthusiast and first President of Ireland, *Douglas Hyde*. And it can also be said that without County Roscommon, *Oscar Wilde* would not exist, as his father, *Sir William Wilde*, was born at **Castlerea**. And though Longford claims *Goldsmith*, the idea for *She Stoops to Conquer* came to him on a visit to Rahalen House near **Elphin**—a town in which he is indisputably buried.

While the rivalry between the counties is healthy, there is little doubt that both have a complete range of attractions to put before even the most critical of tourists, and complement one another admirably.

Lough Owel,
Co. Westmeath.

County Westmeath

Without going overboard with regard to its architectural beauties, one can say that **Mullingar** has an attractive 18th-century **Market House**, now the home of the town museum, and a well-designed **Courthouse** dating from 1825. Its main street is lined with lively pubs and grocery shops that even stock Brie cheese for the German and French tourists who come to enjoy the shooting, fishing and hunting for which the area is famed. The town's **Catholic cathedral**, with its twin towers, was consecrated in 1939 and contains mosaics by the Russian artist *Boris Anrep*. **All Saints' Church** (Anglican) incorporates stonework from the Augustinian priory and was reconstructed in the 17th and 19th centuries.

Mullingar was originally established by the English settlers of County Meath, and during the Williamite wars *Baron Ginckel*, the Dutch general, fortified it, making it the rendezvous for his forces before the Siege of Athlone in 1691. Today the wheel has come full circle and Mullingar is again a garrison town, but this time of the Irish army.

Apart from its role as an agricultural and market centre, Mullingar has extensive communication links with the rest of the country. Linked directly with Dublin by rail and road, it is also a harbour town served by the Royal Canal.

A number of entertaining museums add to the town's appeal. The best of these is the **Military Museum**, with its collection of First World War and Second World War firearms, uniforms, and flags, a special section on the old IRA, and what is claimed to be a pistol used by *Michael Collins* during the War of Independence. An **Ecclesiastical Museum** attached to the Cathedral contains a number of crosses made by Catholics to help preserve their faith in Penal times, as well as the 17th-century vestments of *St Oliver Plunkett*, the martyr. In the main street is the **Market House Museum**, filled with Iron Age implements and weaponry as well as priceless information about *Adolphus Croke*, a local eccentric who identified one of the turkeys in his farmyard as his reincarnated father. Concerned for the future life, he ordered a tomb to be built in the shape of a beehive, because he had the enviable privilege of knowing in advance that he was going to be reincarnated as a bee. A bzzzy man, you might say …

Around Mullingar

Three-and-a-half miles south of Mullingar is picturesque **Lough Ennell**, with its elegantly proportioned 18th-century **Belvedere House**, whose rococo plasterwork ceilings are among the finest in the country. Extensive, well-kept gardens run gently onto terraced slopes on the banks of the lake. Belvedere House was constructed by *Robert Rochfort*, Lord Belfield, much of whose life was wasted in disputes with his younger brothers, George and Arthur. In 1736 Robert married a sixteen-year-old and then, within a few years, after building Belvedere House, accused her of having an affair with Arthur. He virtually imprisoned her for thirty-one years in a nearby house. Arthur meanwhile had run away to England, but when he returned in 1759, the earl, who was a model of consistency, sued him for adultery. Unable

Market House,
Mullingar,
Co. Westmeath.

Locke's Distillery,
Kilbeggan,
Co. Westmeath.

to pay his expenses, the unhappy Arthur went to jail for the rest of his life. That left Robert with one brother less to have a row with; but the earl accepted his loss quite philosophically and proceeded to enter into a fierce argument with his remaining sibling. George didn't know what kind of a construction to put on his brother's strange behaviour. But Robert did: he ran up what has been known ever since as the **Jealous Wall**—an attractive Gothic façade planned by an Italian architect and built to cut off the Earl's home from the view of nearby **Tudenham House**, where George had the misfortune to live. If this folly was indeed the work of a madman, as some suppose, at least he was a madman with taste! And for your greater pleasure, his folly is still on view in

the gardens of Belvedere House, where, no matter how jealous you are, you can still find some 'concrete' reasons for not being overlooked!

For a more expeditious way of dealing with altercations, a visit to **Lough Owel**, about 3 miles north of Mullingar, is recommended. It was in this lake that *Maeleachlainn* drowned the Danish chief *Torgjest* or Turgesius, in the year 843. But that was way back then, and the lake is now the leisurely playground of the perfectly peaceful Mullingar sub-aqua and sailing clubs.

Also north of Mullingar is **Lough Derravaragh**, a lake associated with the legend of the Children of Lir. No beastly brother saga here but a nasty stepmother,

Aoife, who turned her four stepchildren into swans and decreed that they should remain in this state for nine hundred years. Unlike most chastised offspring, this gifted quartet actually sang in such a way as to bring joy and pleasure to all who heard their singing. With the arrival of Christianity the spell was broken, the singing ceased, and the ex-choristers were baptised and welcomed into the ranks of the faithful. A pity about the music ...

East of Lough Derravaragh is **Castlepollard**, a good base for fishing. But most people visiting the area are here to see **Tullynally Castle**, one of the largest and most striking of Ireland's castles and home to ten generations of the Pakenham family, otherwise known as the Earls of Longford. The castle was laid out in 1760 by the first Earl of Longford but later overhauled and expanded by the Gothic designing genius of *Francis Johnston*. Formerly **Pakenham Hall**, it is referred to several times under that name in the memoirs of the 18th-century novelist *Maria Edgeworth*, whose father was a frequent guest here. Set in rolling parkland and featuring four towers and impressive ranged battlements, the castle combines several architectural styles, though the Gothic Revival predominates. Highlights of the guided tour are the 8,000-volume library, a main hall often used for concerts, a huge 19th-century kitchen, a pleasant garden walk, and the largest kitchen garden in the country.

Three miles east of Castlepollard is the village of **Fore** (*Baile Fhobhair*, 'townland of the spring'), with its nearby Christian antiquities. In the graveyard is the partially restored 11th-century **St Feichín's Church**, with its massive 2-ton lintel. Fore is renowned for its 'seven wonders', one of which is the 'monastery in a bog'—the Benedictine Abbey founded in 1200 by the De Laceys and which comprises the largest group of Benedictine remains in Ireland. Some of the further wonders are 'the water that never boils' (a housewife's nightmare?), referring to St Feichín's Well, and the 'hermit in the stone', an allusion to *Patrick Beglin*, the last hermit in Ireland, who lived until 1616 in the Anchorites' Church on the hillside.

To the south from Mullingar, **Kilbeggan** is worth visiting to see **Locke's Distillery Museum**. Built in 1757, the distillery operated up to its abandonment in 1954. The museum has a working mill-wheel, with a back-up steam engine from 1878, and displays every facet of the whiskey-making process to visitors through glass-screened walkways, including the action of *mashtons* or huge vats where the grain mash is stirred by rotating arms and levers.

Moate, on the road from Kilbeggan to Athlone, is a cattle market town founded by Quakers. The district round Moate has many ancient sites, and a Harvard Expedition to the area in 1932 to carry out excavations on *crannóg* sites produced archaeological finds now kept in the National Museum. Half a mile from the town is a cultural heritage centre called **Dún na Sí**, 'the Fort of the Otherworld'. It serves as base for a travelling folklore group and as a school for students of Irish culture as well as displaying a miniature Early Christian village with thatched houses, grouped figures, and agricultural tools.

DON'T MISS
- Don't miss the largest castellated family house in Ireland, **Tullynally Castle**, with its portraits, library, great hall, and landscaped park and kitchen gardens.

ALL-WEATHER OPTIONS
- When the weather's putrid, think pewter! See experts turning Mullingar's silver-grey claim to fame into cups and bowls at the **Mullingar Bronze and Pewter Centre**.
- **Athlone Castle and Visitor Centre** incorporates an audio-visual presentation on the flora and fauna together with the power resources of the Shannon.

County Longford

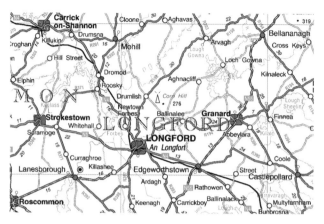

Despite being a small inland county, **Longford** has always maintained strong links with the world at large. Its connections with Argentina, France and Switzerland are both surprising and fascinating and belie its superficial air of innocuous provinciality. In the period 1842–60 alone over 11,000 Irish people left for Argentina, and family names with Longford roots are among the most common among those Argentines laying claim to an Irish background. As already mentioned, the best-known of these is *Edel Miro O'Farrell*, President of Argentina in 1914. The French ties lead the visitor to **Ballinamuck**, one of the most historic towns in north County Longford. It was here in 1798 that a combined Irish and French force under *General Humbert* was defeated by the English under *Lord Cornwallis*. Filming of *Thomas Flanagan's* novel *The Year of the French* refocused attention on the town. But the French connection does not end there. The *Abbé Edgeworth*, a member of the famous Edgeworth family of **Edgeworthstown**, became a historic figure when he attended the condemned French king, *Louis XVI*, on the scaffold during the French Revolution.

With regard to Switzerland, the ties are with **Ardagh**, where both the clock and the planned scheme of houses are unique in Ireland for their Swiss design. Today traffic is as much towards County Longford as out of it, and the visits by sizable groups of Continental and British anglers to Longford's fishing centres, such as **Lanesboro** and **Granard,** proves that its past reputation for establishing foreign connections was no passing phase.

The town of **Longford** (*An Longfort,* 'the fortress') is a progressive, spaciously laid out urban centre with broad streets, solid bourgeois buildings, and plenty of shops. Its main architectural feature is **St Mel's Cathedral,** a 19th-century building with a 160-foot tower. Begun in 1840, its construction was delayed by the Great Famine, and it was not completed until 1893. It has a spacious forecourt, and elegantly arched colonnades support a fine vaulted roof. A stained-glass window by *Harry Clarke,* featuring a composition of red, gold, and blue, merges effectively with the delicately rose-tinted roof and the sober cream of the stone pillars. At the rear of the cathedral is a small **Diocesan Museum** containing *St Mel's* 10th-century crosier and miscellaneous items from the past, including elk antlers, Bronze Age spearheads, and crosses from Penal times, as well as a Ballinderry gaming-board with forty-nine peg hooks in even rows of seven.

The former post office, also in the main street, is now the site of the **County Museum,** which, in addition to exhibiting memorabilia from the independence struggle of the 1920s, also provides a genealogical service.

Readers of *Jane Austen* may enjoy tracking down an intriguing biographical connection in County Longford by visiting

Carrigglas Manor, Ireland's first 19th-century county house, situated just 3 miles north-east of Longford. Originally the Jacobean seat of the Bishop of Ardagh, the building was taken in hand in 1837 by the Huguenot Lefroy family and completely transformed, with the addition of Tudor-Gothic turrets. The superb stables were designed in 1790 by *James Gandon*, architect of the Custom House in Dublin. As a young man, *Thomas Lefroy*, who masterminded the restoration and embellishment of the manor, became romantically involved with *Jane Austen* in England, and the assumption is that he served as a model for the romantic Mr Darcy in *Pride and Prejudice*.

Though he did marry eventually, *Hugh Lefroy*, another member of this interesting family, was an eccentric who normally preferred courting apples and potatoes to the dangerous business of pursuing women. His special passion was cultivating potatoes on rooftops. He also believed it caused less distress to apple trees if he pruned them at night.

In County Longford, moving from *Jane Austen* to *Maria Edgeworth* and *Oliver Goldsmith* is a simple matter. **Edgeworthstown** has a history of association with the Edgeworth family stretching back to 1583, when the first family members settled here. *Richard Lovell Edgeworth*, inventor and surveyor, one of the most eminent members of the family, had twenty-two children, among them *Maria*, the novelist, who wrote *Castle Rackrent*. *Goldsmith* received his early education in the town, and *Oscar Wilde's* sister, *Isola*, is buried in the grounds of **St John's Church**. A new **Visitor Centre** is being developed in the town to inform tourists of its rich literary and historical heritage.

Ballymahon, on the Inny River, is the heart of Goldsmith country, which spans Counties Longford and Westmeath. Though Goldsmith was born at Pallas, County Longford, in 1729, his father was Rector at **Forgney**, near **Ballymahon**, and he drew extensively on his youthful Longford experience in his writings. An incident in which he enquired for an inn and was sent in jest to the squire's residence forms the basis of the plot of *She Stoops to Conquer*. An annual Goldsmith Summer School is held each June in the county. **Ardagh**, not far from Ballymahon, was the scene of Goldsmith's youthful scapegracing, and it was the Fetherson family home that was mistaken by him for an inn. The Fethersons had acquired local estates in the 18th century. When *Lady Fetherson* decided to build houses for her tenants in the 1860s she was inspired by a Swiss town planning model, and this neat, well-organised look, still visible today, may have helped Ardagh to a recent National Tidy Towns Award.

St Patrick himself is said to have brought Christianity to the town in the 5th century and left his nephew, *Mel*, behind as first Bishop of Ardagh. But before this, Ardagh was supposedly the setting for the myth of *Mír and Éadaoin*—a story of timeless love in which a jealous woman, the wicked *Fuamnach*, turns her rival into a butterfly but fails to halt the course of true romance. Despite her best efforts to entrap them, the two lovers escape her net, and in a clear case of 'follow the Leda' they find an escape route to happiness as swans. More details of the story and of other local myths, archaeology and history are available at the newly opened **Heritage Centre.**

Myth also looms large in the shadowy past of **Granard,** a thriving market town that dates back to prehistoric times, when it was associated both with sun worship and *Crom Cruach*. History still marks the town, in the form of Ireland's highest Norman motte and a projection from it that causes the main street to veer sharply to the south (if a twinning of towns is on the cards, it may well be with Pisa). **Granard Motte** was built by *Richard de Tuite* in 1199 as part of an initiative to extend Norman control in the area. Nine counties and five lakes can be seen from the summit. Granard is an excellent centre for angling on the nearby **River Inny** and **Lough Gowna** and **Lough Sheelin**.

Abbeyleix, two-and-a-half miles south-west of Granard, contains a semicircular earthwork once believed to be the site of the

Ardagh Cathedral,
Co. Longford.

original church founded here by *St Patrick*. Parts of the mysterious prehistoric earthwork known as the **Black Pig's Dyke** are also visible in the area. This stretched from Donegal Bay to the Irish Sea, and parts of it still survive in Counties Cavan, Monaghan, Longford, and Meath. Its exact purpose is still unclear, and speculations vary between a military function and the idea that it was designed to act as a deterrent to cattle-raiding.

Another example of the abiding interest of the past is provided by the bog that in 1984 yielded up a fascinating trackway. This is an arrangement of large oak planks discovered in a Bord na Móna bog at **Corlea** near **Kenagh**. A number of other trackways have been discovered since then and form the basis of the purpose-built **Corlea Trackway and Exhibition Centre**, created in 1994. The Iron Age timber trackway dates from about 147 BC and had gradually subsided into the bogland because of the wheeled traffic over it and the unstable nature of the terrain. An audiovisual display explains the background to the primitive thoroughfare and details of its discovery.

Nearby **Newtown Cashel** has a **Folk Museum** set in a whitewashed cottage; its exhibits include a collection of agricultural and domestic artefacts. It contains a number of outdoor sculptures by *Michael Casey*, who works with bog-wood unearthed by Bord na Móna machinery and has his studio close to the town in **Barley Harbour**.

Mosstown Estate, Co. Longford.

DON'T MISS
- Visit **Carrigglas Manor** to see the world through the eyes of *Jane Austen's* suitor. The Lefroy homestead opens the door on a bygone country life of great elegance; and if you'd like to see what they wore in the period, why not visit the **Costume Museum** in the manor stableyard?
- Make sure you step into **St Mel's Cathedral** in Longford to see *Harry Clarke's* magnificent stained-glass window presenting Christ in glory.

ALL-WEATHER OPTIONS
- When it rains, make tracks for **Corlea Trackway Exhibition Centre** to learn how a team of archaeologists excavated a 2,000-year-old bog trackway of oak planks, secured by pegs and designed to carry wheeled vehicles.
- The **Heritage Centre** in the old schoolhouse of **Ardagh** is a good place to take shelter from the showers while learning something of pre-Christian folk tales, the rivalries of the O'Farrell family, and the 1619 Plantation.

County Roscommon

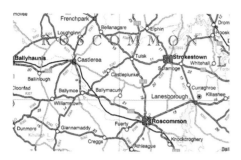

Much of the eastern and south-eastern section of County Roscommon bordering on the River Shannon and its lakes has been covered as part of the Shannon region proper, as with **Athlone**, for example, or **Boyle** and environs, neither of which will be discussed in what follows.

Roscommon (*Ros Comáin*, 'St Comán's wood') is a market town and county town rich in historical associations and a good base from which to tour the region. One of its main landmarks is the ruins of a **Dominican priory** founded in 1253 by *Féilim Ó Conchúir*, King of Connacht. A late 13th-century effigy of the founder has been placed on a later 15th-century tomb decorated with eight mail-clad warriors representing *gallowglasses*—mediaeval Irish professional soldiers.

An even more impressive ruin, standing dramatically on the hillside, is **Roscommon Castle**, a fortification built in 1268 by the Lord Justice of Ireland, *Sir Robert d'Ufford*. Only four years later it was captured by the Irish and razed to the ground. Rebuilt in 1280, and occupied by the O'Conors for more than three hundred years, it surrendered in 1652 to the Cromwellians and was allowed to fall into ruin. It has a solid square layout with rounded bastions at the corners and a double-towered entrance gate.

In Abbey Street the **Church of the Sacred Heart** was completed in 1925, and the west façade and the interior contain some artistic glass mosaics made by the Italian enterprise Salviate and Company. At the top of the main street stands a fine building that began life as the Old Courthouse (1736), served as the Catholic church (1833–1903) and now survives as the Bank of Ireland—an instance of the moneylenders not being driven out of the temple but entering into it!

On the north side of the town square is the **Old Jail**, an institution with a lurid past. Towards the end of the 18th century a well-dressed stranger knocked on the door of a Kerry woman called Betty, who lived in the town. She admitted him, let him stay, and then killed him for his money. On going through his papers, she discovered to her horror that she had murdered her own son, who had become a stranger to her over the

Strokestown Park House,
Co. Roscommon.

years. She confessed her crime, was arrested, and, along with other prisoners, was condemned to death by hanging. Unfortunately for the state, the hangman was ill, and the sheriff refused to do the job. Betty volunteered her services, provided she received a pardon. Her offer was accepted and, in an exemplary demonstration of gratitude, she despatched her shaken companions into eternity. Thereafter she was the jail's hangwoman, with a yearly salary. The same Betty has also gained a place in history for having done charcoal portraits of her victims on her walls, thereby giving a new twist to the familiar twentieth-century concept of taking one's work home …

Adjacent to the jail is **Roscommon**

County Museum, where visitors, fresh from prison, can examine such varied exhibits as a sheela-na-gig from Rahora, a dug-out canoe, and a replica of the Cross of Cong. The building also houses the Roscommon tourist information office.

Five miles to the west of Roscommon is the village of **Fuerty**, where tradition has established a rival in ghoulishness to Lady Betty. The ruins of a **Franciscan church** recall the massacre of at least a hundred priests by a Cromwellian, *Colonel Robert Ormsby*, better known as 'Robert of the jingling harness'—a man long recognised for his 'unbridled' murderousness.

The **Castlestrange** demesne, between Fuerty and **Athleague**, contains an Iron Age boulder known as the **Castlestrange Stone**. This boulder, covered with curvilinear ornament in the ancient Celtic style, has been dated to 250 BC and epitomises the La Tène style. It is one of only four in the country.

Donamon Castle to the west of Roscommon, beyond Fuerty, is one of the oldest inhabited buildings in Ireland, referred to in the Annals of the Four Masters as early as 1632–6. Though the most ancient part of the building dates from the 1400s, it has undergone many reconversions since then and is now in the hands of the Divine Word Missionaries. On the eastern side of Roscommon, on a peninsula stretching into **Lough Ree**, are the 13th-century ruins of **Rindoon Castle**, with a rectangular keep set within curtain walls.

Strokestown Park House, to the north of Roscommon, is a beautifully restored 18th-century mansion designed by *Richard Cassel* that from 1660 to 1979 was the ancestral home of the Mahons. A landlord and black sheep of the family, *Major Denis Mahon,* chartered 'coffin ships' or unseaworthy vessels to transport his evicted tenants to America in Famine times—an activity for which he was widely criticised. In 1847 he was shot dead on the estate. In a reversal of his baleful influence, the Strokestown Park

House Stables have now been turned into a **Famine Museum**, and among the exhibits and images documenting the origins and effect of the Great Famine are letters written by former tenants of the time. The Famine Museum was opened in 1994 by the President of Ireland, Mary Robinson.

Outside the mansion an 18th-century walled pleasure-garden has been restored to its original splendour. It contains the largest herbaceous border in Ireland. Nearby St John's Church in Strokestown is now the **County Heritage Centre** and contains an interpretative display on pre-Christian Ireland, as well as supplying information concerning the monuments of Rathcroghan and the Táin Bó Chuaille.

Rathcroghan, not far from **Castlerea**, is one of the most important archaeological sites of Ireland. In the 1st century the Connacht queen *Méabh* had her headquarters here. An area of 15 acres contains fifty-three ancient sites and embraces the traditional coronation and burial place of the kings of Ireland and Connacht. A 6-foot standing-stone marks the grave of *Dáithí,* the last pre-Christian king of Ireland. But access to the site is difficult, as many of the ring barrows and ring-forts are on private land.

Three miles south-east of Rathcroghan is

La Tène stone,
Castlestrange,
Co. Roscommon.

Carnfree, the inaugural mound of the O'Conors, kings of Connacht. Much legendary speculation surrounds other figures supposed to be associated with it, including *Conn of the Hundred Battles*, and the queen of Tuatha Dé Danann. But whatever the truth of these suppositions, the views from the mound are magnificent.

Castlerea, in the west of County Roscommon, is a market town situated in wooded country on the banks of the River Suck. Three quite disparate celebrities were born in the town. The first was *Féilim Ó Conchúir*, the last king of Ireland, born here in the 12th century; the second, *Oscar Wilde's* father, *Sir William Wilde* (1815–76), and the third, *Douglas Hyde* (1860–1949), first President of Ireland. Just west of the town is **Clonalis House**, the seat of the O'Conors, a family that included eleven High Kings of Ireland and twenty-four Kings of Connacht. The 45-room mansion was constructed in 1878 and contains over ten thousand archival documents and one of *Ó Cearúlláin's* harps. It has Sheraton and Louis XV furniture; and a good range of family costumes, uniforms and laces are on display. At the entrance to the house is the ancient coronation stone of the Connacht kings.

To the south-east below Castlerea is **Ballintubber Castle**, built by the O'Conors in the 13th century. In 1652, Cromwellian forces took it, but it was restored to the O'Conors in 1677. It was taken over a second time after the Battle of the Boyne, in which the O'Conors backed the wrong horse, and paid the price. Though it began to fall into decay at the beginning of the 18th century, the remains of the castle are substantial and are laid out in quadrangular form, with polygonal towers at the angles. It is worth looking at because traditionally the Irish built in timber, and this is believed to be the earliest example of an Irish stone castle.

Like most of the counties of Ireland, Roscommon has produced its fair share of writers, and they are associated with towns within striking distance of **Boyle**. The **Diocesan School** at **Elphin** educated *Oliver Goldsmith* and *William Wilde*, surgeon and father of *Oscar*; **Frenchpark** was the birthplace of *Douglas Hyde*, writer and professor, founder of the Gaelic League, and President of Ireland; and **Cootehall**, where the Annals of Lough Cé were compiled, secured its second literary claim to fame when *John McGahern*, one of Ireland's foremost contemporary novelists, grew up here and masterfully described the minutiae of provincial life, as well as later going on to win the coveted *Irish Times* Literature Award for his novel, *Amongst Women*, in 1990.

DON'T MISS

- Don't miss **Strokestown Park House**, for at least two reasons: because of the neo-Palladian architecture of *Richard Cassel*, and because of the moving and imaginative exploration of the Great Famine of the 1840s.
- Don't miss **Rathcroghan**, burial place of the Irish kings and Connacht kings—an area of the county steeped in prehistoric mystery and an archaeological treasure-trove, with twenty ring-forts, ring-mounds, and megalithic tombs.
- Don't miss **Clonalis House**, home of the O'Conors, to see the harp played by Ireland's greatest harper, the blind Ó Cearúlláin, the stone on which Connacht kings were crowned, and the period furniture and family portraits.

ALL-WEATHER OPTIONS

- Perfect for children on a wet day, the **Animal Farm Visitor Centre**, 3 miles from Boyle, is mainly under cover, has thirty variations of animals, craft shops, pony rides, and demonstrations of modern dairy farm techniques, as well as old-world tea-rooms for recuperating parents.
- Pagan or Christian, you'll still want to avoid the downpour, and you can by dropping in to the **County Museum** in Roscommon to view a range of pre-Christian and Christian exhibits. They run the gamut from the superb sheela-na-gig of Rahara to the history of the Dominican Priory, and terrifying tales of the Old Jail, where you'll 'hang' on every word!

Counties Westmeath, Roscommon & Longford

Leave Athlone on the N61 road, driving parallel to Lough Ree and passing through Knockcroghery on the way to **Roscommon**. An attractive short stop would include a visit to **Roscommon County Museum** (sheela-na-gig, dug-out canoe, and potted histories of the Castle, Dominican Priory, and Old Jail); the **Old Jail** itself, with memories of the hangwoman, Lady Betty; and the **Priory**, to admire the mail-clad gallowglasses. From Roscommon, continue on the N61 past Clogher Lake on the right-hand side to the historic town of **Boyle**. Here you can visit **King House**, the stately 18th-century residence of the King family overlooking the Boyle River, featuring three-dimensional displays and audiovisual special effects; look in on **Frybrook House**, with its fine Georgian

plasterwork and Adams fireplace; and see the magnificent restored ruins of **Boyle Abbey**, with its useful interpretative centre.

From Boyle take the N4 road in the direction of Carrick-on-Shannon. If time permits, make a short trip on your way to **Lough Key Forest Park**, part of the former Rockingham Estate and one of the most beautiful lakeland areas in Ireland, filled with nature trails and mediaeval ruins and situated just 2 miles east of Boyle. At the same time keep an eye out on the left-hand side of the road towards Carrick-on-Shannon for **Woodbrook House** (the setting for David Thomson's *Woodbrook House*), a mansion set in countryside around Lough Drumharlow and Lough Key, just across the river from Cootehall, where *John McGahern* grew up.

Lakelands,
Co. Westmeath.

Once the bustling fisherman's haven of Carrick-on-Shannon is reached, take the R368 road towards **Elphin**, where *Oliver Goldsmith* and *William Wilde* went to school; the sight of a restored and fully functional 18th-century windmill may tempt you to become Quixotic and throw caution to the winds. At the fork outside Elphin, continue on with the R368 towards **Strokestown**. Take a break here to enjoy the neo-Palladian splendour of **Strokestown Park House and Famine Museum**, and visit **St John's Church** to explore the **County Heritage Centre**, which has a fine introduction to pre-Christian Ireland and a genealogical service under the same roof. From Strokestown take the N5 in the direction of **Edgeworthstown**, associated with *Maria Edgeworth* and the resting-place of *Oscar Wilde's* sister, *Isola,* which has a recently created visitor centre.

At Edgeworthstown take the R395 road through the town of Lisryan to Coole, continuing on to **Castlepollard**, an area rich in lakes (Lough Derravaragh, of Children of Lir fame, and Lough Lene are in the vicinity). However, if they have to choose, hard-pressed travellers are more likely to enjoy a visit to **Tullynally Castle**, a house referred to by *Maria Edgeworth* as **Pakenham Hall.** It is a large castellated mansion, and its gardens are open to the public in the summer; the combination of attractions on offer has something to please all ages. While in Castlepollard make a short excursion to **Fore**, just 3 miles to the east, an ancient village with a memorable collection of antiquities, each one more storied than the next (**Benedictine priory, St Feichín's church**, and the **Anchorites' cell**). From Castlepollard take the R392 towards Ballymahon, and then, having rejoined the N55, proceed directly back to **Athlone**, passing through some of the most traditional parts of Goldsmith country, Ballymahon to Glassan, with the 'mix-up' hostelry of the Three Jolly Pigeons from *She Stoops to Conquer* clearly signposted on the way.

Counties Laois and Offaly

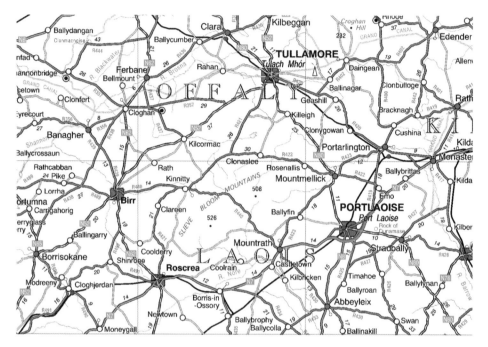

Historical and other precedents exist for coupling Counties Laois and Offaly. A plan for colonising these two counties was formally implemented by the English government under *Queen Mary*, though because of the fierce resistance of the Irish, the full success of the policy was not visible until the reign of *King James I* in 1603. Today the two counties are united under a single county manager, though each is independent in that it possesses its own county council. Both lie at the centre of the plains and bogland forming the midlands and are often spoken of as a single entity.

County Offaly covers 770 square miles and is bounded by Counties Westmeath and Meath to the north, County Kildare to the east, Counties Laois and Tipperary to the south, and Counties Galway and Roscommon and the River Shannon to the west. In the south-east of the county are the heather-filled **Slieve Bloom Mountains**,

with some pleasant valley landscapes. But the rest of the county is mainly a mixture of bogs and cultivable land created by glacial drift. Its best-known tourist attraction is the monastic setlement of **Clonmacnoise** on the banks of the Shannon.

Divided in two by the Grand Canal, Offaly's bogland extends from the **Bog of Allen** in the east to **Boora Bog** in the west. A good deal of the Bog of Allen supplies fuel for power stations, but the smaller Boora Bog is the site of archaeological discoveries that prove that nomads were in the area over nine thousand years ago. Passages through the treacherous bogs, known to local people, were guarded in the past by a chain of mottes, and the county also has an abundance of raths, or prehistoric hill-forts. Today the bog generates employment, and in the area over five thousand people work for Bord na Móna, the national turf board.

Slightly less than half the population of

Slieve Bloom Mountains, Co. Laois.

the county live in towns and villages. **Tullamore** is the county town and has a worsted mill, brewery, distillery, and sausage and bacon factory. There are footwear factories in **Birr** and **Edenderry**, and smaller towns hold monthly livestock fairs. The farmland is mainly pasture, with some tillage and the rest in meadow. Barley and wheat are grown. Southern Offaly tends to be green and agriculturally prosperous, with genteel towns like **Birr**, whereas to the east the Slieve Bloom Mountains represent a more picturesque area for walking tours (the **Slieve Bloom Way**) that take in an ancient high road to Tara and a prehistoric valley. To the west lies the Shannon and the remains of Clonmacnoise, one of the largest and greatest monasteries ever to exist in Ireland.

County Laois is bounded by County Offaly on the north and west, County Kildare to the east, Counties Carlow and Kilkenny to the south, and County Tipperary to the south-west. To the north lie the Slieve Bloom Mountains; to the east are the Grand Canal and the River Barrow and, on the western side, the River Nore. Between the Slieve Bloom Mountains and the Castlecomer Plateau, most of the county is lowland. **Port Laoise** is the seat of the county council. As is true of County Offaly,

mixed farming is the rule, and the county supplies sugar-beet for the Carlow sugar factory. Some sheep farming is carried on, and there are also a number of forestry plantations.

For the visitor, the county contains many heritage and monastic sites, and outdoor activities are well catered for. With the Rivers Barrow, Nore and Erkina and their tributaries, fishing is a natural choice; but for those who simply want to walk, County Laois has plenty to offer. Apart from the 50-mile **Slieve Bloom Way** there are pleasant woods such as those of **Abbeyleix**, **Durrow**, **Cullohill**, **Spink** and **Wolfhill** to be explored.

Neither Laois nor Offaly corresponds to the unjustified charge of tediousness and flat banality often brought against them. On the contrary, they are counties of enormous depth, both historically and physically. The area is one marked by the great colonising and fortifying energy of early English and Anglo-Norman settlers, just as it is marked by the dynamic scholarly, religious and missionary achievement of the native Irish. At once seigneurial and monastic, a riddle of prehistoric ruins, castles and ancient friaries, it has managed to work out its own blend of historical truth in an unmistakable midlands landscape of bog and hedgerow.

County Laois

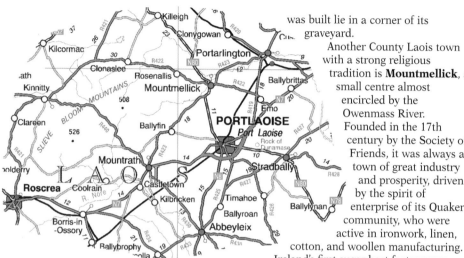

was built lie in a corner of its graveyard.

Another County Laois town with a strong religious tradition is **Mountmellick**, a small centre almost encircled by the Owenmass River. Founded in the 17th century by the Society of Friends, it was always a town of great industry and prosperity, driven by the spirit of enterprise of its Quaker community, who were active in ironwork, linen, cotton, and woollen manufacturing. Ireland's first sugar-beet factory was built here in 1851. Just 4 miles north-west is the oldest Quaker burial ground in Ireland at **Rosenallis**. Many of the 18th-century houses and work buildings of Mountmellick have survived, though the original Quaker meeting-house and school are no longer functioning as Quaker establishments. In the 18th century the town became well known for the making of lace, and it is still being produced by the local Presentation Convent nuns.

To the west of Mountmellick lie the **Slieve Bloom Mountains**, a delightful area for walkers, with endless miles of signposted tracks and paths. At the foot of the mountain range is **Mountrath,** a market town that in the 17th century had a flourishing iron industry. Just outside Mountrath is **Roundwood House,** a striking Palladian manor in its own grounds, built in 1740 for the Quaker *Anthony Sharp* and now run as a heritage guest-house.

Three miles to the north of Mountrath is beautiful **Ballyfin House**, completed in 1826 at the behest of *Sir Charles Coote* and one of the most splendid buildings of its kind in Ireland. Most of the design for the house was carried out by *Richard Morrison*, a pupil of

Port Laoise, a prosperous commercial centre, was laid out in the 18th century, and its main buildings include **St Peter's Church** (partly designed by *Gandon*), the **Courthouse** by *Sir Richard Morrison,* and the late 19th-century Gothic **Methodist Church**. Port Laoise is first referred to in the Annals of the Four Masters in 1548 and originally served as a military outpost for the defence of settlers. On the main railway line between Dublin, Cork and Limerick, it is the county's principal town and administrative centre.

The role played by Huguenots in the life of the county is visible in **Portarlington**, the county's second-largest town, where the **'French Church'** and other reminders of the presence of French Protestants are still to be seen. A number of fine examples of Georgian, Huguenot and 19th-century architecture, and the so-called French style of the old town-houses, constitute a living memorial to a historic past that is also perpetuated by an annual French Festival. **St Paul's Church** was built in 1851 on the site of the 17th-century French church for the Huguenots; now many of those for whom it

Rock of Dunamase,
near Port Laoise,
Co. Laois.

Brittas House,
Co. Laois.

James Gandon. Sir Edward Lutyens landscaped the gardens, and the conservatory is attributed to *Richard Turner,* designer of the Palm House at Kew Gardens, London. Some of the features of the interior of the house are its parquetry floors, vaulted ceilings, marble columns, and sumptuous plasterwork. Today the house is in the hands of the Patrician Brothers.

Another stunning piece of County Laois architecture is **Emo Court and Gardens,** begun in 1790 by *James Gandon* but left incomplete in 1798, after which it was finished in two stages by *Lewis Vulliamy* in 1834–6 and by *William Caldbeck* in 1860. In 1920 the magnificent neo-classical house was sold, along with the vast demesne, to the Land Commission and then bought by the Jesuits in 1930 for use as a novitiate. In 1969 the Jesuits in turn sold Emo Court to *Major Cholmeley-Harrison,* and he embarked on an enlightened restoration programme, which made sure it became the classical county villa. Gandon had intended to construct for his friend, *Lord Portarlington*. In 1994 the house and parklands were presented by Cholmeley-Harrison to *President Robinson*, who accepted it on behalf of the people of Ireland. In addition to trees and shrubs, the gardens contain statuary showing the four seasons and provide a variety of agreeable walking routes. Near Emo Court stands **Coolbanagher Church**, another graceful building designed by Gandon and built in 1786.

The village of **Stradbally**, 6 miles southeast of Port Laoise, was once the seat of the O'Mores. For a long time the family held the Book of Leinster, a priceless mediaeval manuscript compiled between 1151 and 1224 and now in the possession of Trinity College, Dublin. Today the town is famous for the more down-to-earth **Steam Museum**, which has a fine collection of fire engines, steam tractors and steam rollers restored to working order by the Irish Steam Preservation Society. Each August the grounds of **Cosby Hall** are the rallying point for steam-operated machines and vintage cars.

Further to the south of Port Laoise is **Abbeyleix**, a settlement that grew up around a 12th-century Cistercian monastery. In the 18th century *Lord de Vesci* established Abbeyleix as a planned estate town with fine public buildings and town-houses. The three-storey family house where the De Vescis still live was erected in 1773 from a design by *James Wyatt*. It received a new façade in the 19th century and gives onto extensive gardens. Now designated a heritage town, Abbeyleix maintains an excellent **Heritage Centre,** detailing local history and exhibiting the Turkish-style carpets woven in the town from 1904 to 1913.

Five-and-a-half miles to the south of Abbeyleix is **Durrow**, another planned estate town with neat rows of houses set around a green and close to **Castle Durrow**, the first great Palladian house in the area, built in 1716.

Near the border with County Carlow, **Killeshin** was at one time a centre of culture and learning. Its 6th-century monastery, founded by *St Comhghán*, was razed in the 11th century, and the ruins now surviving date from the 12th century. Of the remains, the most notable item is a well-preserved carved doorway, the capitals of which feature human faces, many of which have seen better days ...

DON'T MISS

- Don't miss **Ballyfin House**, a classical masterpiece created by the father-and-son team of Richard and William Vitruvius Morrison: the splendid Gold Room with its intricate rococo plasterwork, the Saloon with marble and gypsum columns and the colonnaded Ballroom or Library are especially noteworthy.
- An absolute must is **Emo Court**, the magnificent neo-classical house designed by Gandon, surrounded by extensive parklands, restored with taste and flair and generously donated to the Irish people in 1994.
- Don't miss the bonus of going from Emo Court to the nearby village of **Coolbanagher** to view the only church known to have been designed by Gandon.

ALL-WEATHER OPTIONS

- Why get hot under the collar about the rain when you can really let off steam in the village of **Stradbally** at the **Steam Traction Museum** by viewing a Merryweather horse-drawn fire-engine from 1880!
- If the downpours and the state of your wallet are getting to you, you should be getting to **Donaghmore Workhouse and Agricultural Museum.** There's nothing like an introduction to the history of real poverty to make the sun come shining through ...
- Too cold, too wet? Take off in a sunny direction by looking at the Turkish-style carpets on view at **Abbeyleix Heritage Centre**.

County Offaly

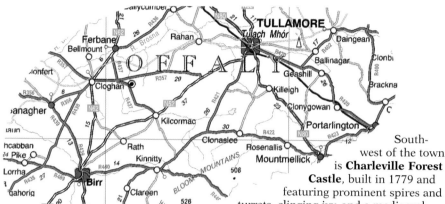

Tullamore, the county town of County Offaly, is a prosperous market and manufacturing centre traversed by the Grand Canal. Its present town centre came about as the result of a freak accident in 1785 when a hot-air balloon flying over the town hit the ground and exploded, destroying a hundred houses and rendering a massive rebuilding programme necessary. In 1798 the arrival of the Grand Canal from Dublin gave the area a commercial boost, and brewing, distilling and flour-milling activities quickly developed.

The town has some fine buildings, in particular **St Catherine's (Protestant) Church**, a Gothic Revival construction of 1815, designed by *Francis Johnston*, the architect responsible for nearby **Charleville Forest Castle**. The local Catholic church was destroyed by fire in 1982 but has been restored, and a number of windows by *Harry Clarke* brought from Rathfarnham Castle have been installed. In spite of the removal of the Irish Mist company to Clonmel, a new **Tullamore Heritage Centre** attached to the tourist office provides information in the right spirit on the history of Irish Mist and Tullamore Dew, as well as local history.

South-west of the town is **Charleville Forest Castle**, built in 1779 and featuring prominent spires and turrets, clinging ivy, and a mediaeval-style grotto, held to be the finest Gothic Revival building in Ireland. The fan-vaulted ceiling of its ballroom is modelled on that of Strawberry Hill, a Gothic extravaganza near Twickenham, Middlesex. There are fifty-five rooms in all, as well as a magnificent gallery running the whole width of the building.

Less visited is **Durrow Abbey**, close to Tullamore, source of the celebrated 7th-century Book of Durrow, now in Trinity College, Dublin. The only authentic surviving elements of the abbey, which was plundered and burnt during the Dark Ages, are the 9th-century **High Cross**, **St Colm Cille's Well**, and a few early tombstones. On the site today are a Georgian mansion and a ruined 19th-century Protestant church.

Edenderry, also situated on the Grand Canal, is a picturesque market town that marks the westward limits of the Pale—the English-controlled territory administered from Dublin. Formerly a trading centre on the canal route linking Dublin to the Shannon, it serves as gateway to the Bog of Allen and is today an important town for the turf-processing industry.

Birr is the most attractive town in County Offaly. Founded in the 6th century at the junction of two rivers, its more

Birr Castle Gardens,
Co. Offaly.

Bog cotton, Co. Offaly.

recent history began when the Parsons family from Norfolk were granted 1,000 acres in the area in 1620 and proceeded to build the town around their castle. *Sir Laurence Parsons*, who built the castle, laid out the streets, and established a glass factory, also had the habit of issuing decrees to the local population. One of them specified that all women caught serving beer would be 'sett in the stocks by the constable for three whole market dayes.' Poor things! How sad that, when it came to dealing with misdemeanours of this type at the time there were no clear precedents, only 'stock' answers ... In later

history the Parsons became Earls of Rosse, and family members still reside on the estate.

Birr Castle withstood many a siege in the wars of the 16th and 17th centuries. Alterations were made to it in the 19th century, and no major changes have been made since. In 1845 the third earl built what was at the time the largest telescope in the world; it remained so for over seventy years. It was used by the fourth earl to establish the first accurate measurement of the temperature of the moon and to catalogue the spiral nebulae, and is still in working order today. A

Historic Science Centre, opened in the stable block of the demesne, records the scientific achievements of the Parsons family and of other Irish scientists in the fields of astronomy, photography, engineering, botany, and horticulture. The town of **Birr** has now set up its own **Heritage Centre**, built in the style of a miniature Greek temple and furnishing a detailed account of the town's history.

The gardens of the castle are worth seeing in their own right. Laid out in the 1830s and 1840s, they contain over a thousand species of shrubs and trees from all over the world and are noted for their spring flowering and autumnal colouring. The centrepiece of the demesne is 120 acres of magnificent landscaped gardens arranged round a large artificial lake. The tallest box hedges in the world, planted over two hundred years ago in 1780 and still on show, now stand over 40 feet high.

An O'Carroll family residence, **Leap Castle**, south-east of Birr between **Kinnitty** and **Roscrea**, used to guard the valley separating Munster and Leinster. It was burnt down in 1922 and is now in ruins. Today it is renowned for the smelliness of one of the ghosts that frequents it, and its reputation with local people is that it is the most haunted castle in Europe.

Seven miles north-west of Birr is **Banagher**, a quiet riverside village, one of the few Shannon crossing-points in the area. It inspired *Anthony Trollope* to write *The MacDermots of Ballycloran* (1843-7) and *The Kellys and the O'Kellys* (1848). *Charlotte Brontë's* husband, *A. B. Nicholls*, rector of Birr (died 1906), is buried in the local graveyard. The local Catholic church contains a statue of the Madonna by *Imogen Stuart.*

Not far from Banagher to the south is the 12th-century **Cloghan Castle**, the oldest inhabited castle in Ireland. A 19th-century house adjoins the well-preserved keep. A 45-minute tour permits visitors to examine heavy Cromwellian armaments. To the north-east of Banagher is the village of **Croghan**, and 5 miles from Croghan is the impressive **Clonony Castle**, a four-storey square tower now enclosed by an overgrown castellated wall.

Eight miles north-west of Cloghan is the village of **Shannonbridge**, with its fine bridge of sixteen arches. Huge artillery fortifications dating from Napoleonic times create a strange contrast with the tower of the nearby turf-burning power station that dominates the town. The road running north leads to the most important site in the north-west of the county, that of **Clonmacnoise** (covered in the Shannon region). To the south of Shannonbridge, a 45-minute train tour takes the visitor through a section of the **Bog of Allen** on the railway line used to transport the turf, with commentary covering the characteristics of the bog landscape and its distinctive flora.

DON'T MISS
- Don't miss **Birr Castle**, home to the remarkable Parsons family since the 17th century; wander through magnificent gardens and admire the historic telescope, for seventy years the largest in the world.
- Because you may have missed it in the Shannon coverage, don't miss **Clonmacnoise** now, burial place of kings and one of the finest monastic sites in Ireland. See the fascinating ruins, the famous thousand-year-old cross, and the most important collection of graveyard tombstones in the country.

ALL-WEATHER OPTIONS
- Spend a rainy day rambling though the fifty-five rooms of **Charleville Forest Castle**, or settle down to read a Gothic novel in a Gothic setting, that of the finest Gothic Revival building in Europe.
- See what it felt like to be a Cromwellian soldier by examining Cromwellian armaments after visiting **Cloghan Castle**, the oldest continuously inhabited castle in the county.

Ireland's Flora and Fauna

Foxgloves.

The Irish climate provides ideal conditions for the growth of grass; this explains the verdant appearance of the countryside throughout the year. About a thousand species of flowering plants and ferns are native to Ireland. Many questions remain unanswered about how the main body of flora arrived on Irish soil. For instance, how many made the journey across the land bridges between Ireland and Britain between the end of the last Ice Age and the submersion of the exposed land 1,500 years later, and how many managed to survive through the Ice Age? After the Ice Age, plant migration and colonisation took place rapidly, and it wasn't long before the entire country was covered by oak, elm, alder, hazel, birch, willow, pine, ash, whitebeam, cherry, poplar, apple, holly, juniper, arbutus, yew and a diverse range of grasses, sedges, and flowering plants.

As soon as the first farmers arrived, almost six thousand years ago, they set about with their stone axes felling trees to make clearings for farming and for their dwellings. This felling was continued at a more rapid pace by, in succession, the Celts, the Vikings, and the Normans, until finally, during the 17th century, the last of the native woodlands disappeared.

Today a mere 8 per cent of the land is under tree cover, the lowest tree density in Europe.

Arguably the most interesting flora in Ireland are the Arctic, Alpine and Mediterranean plants to be found in the crevices of the moonlike limestone pavements of the Burren district in County Clare. Also rich in plant life are the raised bogs of the midlands and the blanket bogs of the west and mountain lowlands. Both types of bog are complex eco-systems and give life and shelter to a wide variety of plants, among them ling heather, cross-leaved heath, deer sedge, bog-moss, and bog-cotton.

Many thousands of years ago the countryside was inhabited by Arctic lemming, wolves, giant Irish deer, brown bears, wild boar, and woolly mammoth. All are either long since extinct or have moved north to colder climes. Today the landscape is populated by a wide variety of animals and birds; and some of the most common and a few of the lesser known are described here.

Three types of deer are to be found. The imported fallow deer are widespread, except in the extreme north-west, south-east, and south-west; red deer are found mainly in Glenveagh, Killarney National Park (which holds the only native red deer), and Wicklow National Park; while sika deer, introduced to Ireland in the 19th century, are mainly found in County Wicklow, Killarney and the south-west, and parts of Counties Tyrone and Fermanagh.

The fox is common throughout the country, as are badgers, rabbits, hedgehogs, and pygmy shrews. Stoats are often found by hedgerows or dry-stone walls, whereas otters are widespread and can be expected to inhabit any lakeland or river area where fish thrive. The red squirrel is plentiful, living mainly in coniferous woodland, but is difficult to glimpse, whereas its cousin the grey squirrel is less shy and more easily observed. It can frequently be seen in parks and gardens. The Irish hare has survived, with its distinctive white tail and red-brown coat.

There are seven species of bat, compared with fifteen in Britain. The most common here is the pipistrelle.

The pine marten is Ireland's rarest mammal. It is roughly the size of a domestic cat, is shaped like a weasel, and has a bushy tail. It finds shelter among the Slieve Bloom Mountains in Counties Laois and Offaly and near the coastline between Counties Sligo and Clare.

Ireland has only two-thirds the number of bird species that Britain has. This is because of the latter's larger area, its more varied climate and higher altitudes in places, and a resulting greater number of natural habitats.

In winter in Ireland, lakes, estuaries and wetlands provide a haven for hundreds of thousands of waterfowl from the Arctic and northern Europe. Whooper swans and flocks of brent, barnacle and white-fronted geese sweep in from Greenland, Iceland, and Canada, together with waders such as golden plover, black-tailed godwit, and knot. From the Baltic region and from Scandinavia, ducks and waders such as teal and lapwing fly in on the prevailing wind, together with great flocks of thrushes and finches. During spring and autumn the islands and headlands of west Cork, Kerry and Clare provide spectacular views of migrating shearwaters, petrels, and auks. In summer the cliffs of the western seaboard and islands are busy with breeding seabirds, including some of the largest colonies of gannets in the world on the small island of Little Skellig off the Kerry coast.

One of Ireland's most threatened bird species is the corncrake, also rare throughout Europe. With its distinctive jarring call, this shy and rarely seen bird migrates from Africa and nests in hay meadows, mainly in the west. Efforts to protect it have involved a number of willing and conservation-minded farmers delaying their hay-making until the nesting season is over.

What does the future hold for Ireland's flora and fauna? The demands of a rapidly changing life-style fuelled by a vibrant economy and exacerbated by sometimes poor decisions at either Government or EU level have combined to pose real dangers. Massive drainage, mainly driven by agriculture, has already resulted in the destruction of many wetlands that were important wildfowl and botanical habitats. A rapid and unsustainable three-fold increase in the number of sheep—to almost 9 million at the beginning of the 1990s—has meant severe over-grazing of many peatlands and sand dunes, especially in the west. Throughout the countryside, many ancient grasslands and meadowlands have been destroyed by a combination of drainage, ploughing, re-seeding and over-use of fertilisers and herbicides. Water pollution, principally from intensive farming, is a continuing problem, while an extensive short-term forestry policy is seeing the proliferation of sitka spruce and lodgepole pine across large areas of lowland heath and bogland, destroying the native flora and making large areas inhospitable for much of the indigenous wildlife.

Despite these dangers, we must gain strength from the knowledge that nature is resilient and will in time, if allowed, recover its former glory. And this will be a treat for all, for its present glory is often a wonder to behold.

TOURING ROUTE
Counties Laois and Offaly

Leave Tullamore by the N80 road (but not without seeing the nearby **Charleville Forest Castle**, a neo-Gothic house fit for a mystery film), heading in the direction of Clara and crossing the River Brosna before arriving at **Farnagh**. Here take the R444 to **Clonmacnoise**, the foremost mediaeval site on the River Shannon and the most renowned early Irish scholastic site, with cathedral, church, and round tower. Continue on the R444 to **Shannonbridge**, where the 19th-century fort with its heavy artillery was designed to prevent an invasion by Napoléon Bonaparte.

At Shannonbridge take the R357, passing over the confluence of the Rivers Blackwater and Gowlan, as well as a tributary of the Shannon, to reach **Cloghan**. Here take the N62 (which becomes the N52 just before entering **Birr**). There is plenty to enjoy here, between the castle, demesne and gardens, a huge 19th-century telescope, and a neatly laid-out heritage town. From Birr take the N62 to **Roscrea**; of special interest are the 18th-century **Damer House**, 13th-century castle and Ireland's only silk farm at **Mount St Joseph**, just 2 miles to the west of the town.

From Roscrea take the N7 through Borris-in-Ossory, Castletown and Mountrath (just 3 miles from **Roundwood House**, a Palladian mansion with fine stairs, renovated by the Irish Georgian

Society and associated with *Henrietta Moraes*, model of *Francis Bacon* and *Lucien Freud*, who spent a number of years here). Continue on to **Port Laoise**; from here take the M7 motorway to **New Inn**. (Those with a little time on their hands could take the N80 from Port Laoise to see the **Rock of Dunamase**, one of the most impressive sites in Ireland, possibly including in the visit a trip to **Stradbally** to see its **Steam Museum**, and returning by the N80 to rejoin the N7 to New Inn.)

From New Inn take the R422 towards **Mountmellick** (with its Quaker Visitor Centre) to see **Emo Court**, a superb Georgian residence designed by *Gandon* in 1790, with ornamental lake and pathways with Greek statues; make sure also to drop in on nearby **Coolbanagher Church** (also by Gandon), with its finely carved 14th or 15th-century font. To return to base, leave Mountmellick by taking the N80 to **Tullamore**, passing by the River Barrow en route.

Sunset on Lough Owel, Co. Westmeath.

The Shannon Region

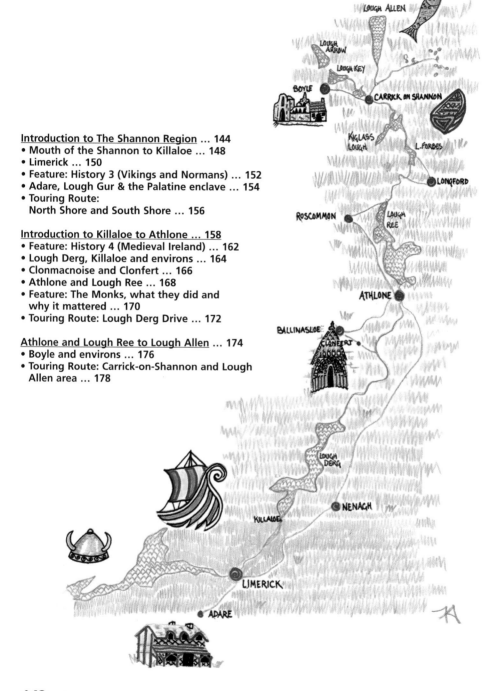

Cruising on the Shannon.

Introduction

Boating on the Shannon.

Rivers are no respecters of boundaries, and this is so with the River Shannon. It flows through many counties, from its source in County Cavan to the estuary formed by Counties Limerick, Clare and Kerry before disappearing into the vast expanse of the Atlantic Ocean. Its very autonomy and scale—it drains over a fifth of the entire Irish landmass—means that, for touring, it needs to be considered as a separate regional area, and a superb natural resource meriting treatment in its own right. Over 200 miles in length, the Shannon is the largest and most attractive river-playground in Ireland. For all its length, however, it possesses a mere six locks, so that it offers an unimpeded and tranquil transit route for every variety of commercial and pleasure craft. Navigation either on the lakes or on the slow-moving river is a real source of pleasure, and more than 150 miles of the inland waterway are available for exploration by cabin-cruiser.

Part of the undeniable appeal of this historic artery can be put down to aquatic diversity. There's nothing boring about the Shannon. By turn lake, river, and sea, it moves easily and gracefully through its sparkling transformations, presenting travellers with a rich and varied landscape, featuring wild life in settings of great natural beauty and affording the versatile angler the full range of fresh-water and salt-water fishing. Bird-watchers are especially well catered for: there are grey herons, swans, cormorants, tern, coot, herring-gulls, great-crested grebes, meadow pipits, and kingfishers, as well as winter sojourners such as Greenland geese, golden plover, and widgeon. In a word, the Shannon possesses unique appeal as a natural amenity for holiday-makers and naturalists alike.

For those contemplating water sports it's a safe and friendly river. From **Battlebridge** in the north down to **Killaloe** in the south, there is little to trouble voyagers or swimmers. Once it leaves County Cavan, the Shannon branches out to form broad welcoming lakes, of which the two largest—**Lough Ree** and **Lough Derg**—are 18 and 24 miles long, respectively. For most of its course the river meanders along, idling quietly over the central limestone plain. It is only when it passes Killaloe that it changes character, producing a surprise package of rapids and torrents before sweeping majestically past **Limerick** and out to sea. Otherwise—apart from the danger of being caught out on the lakes in bad weather—it presents a calm, easily navigable surface. And in the unlikely event that the delights of the river pall, a range of on-shore activities and entertainment is always at hand in the shape of cycling trips, walking tours and pony-trekking, as well as unexpectedly good local inns and restaurants in friendly, unpretentious riverside towns and villages.

But even for the casual holiday-maker, a river like the Shannon has the added appeal of being something more than a mere resort facility: it's also an intriguing natural connection with the past, reminding the traveller at each turn of the bend of former times, of historic adventurers like *Patrick Sarsfield* and infamous brigands like *Murcha 'the Burner' O'Brien*, of the generations of men and women who settled on its banks and built dwellings there, of a thousand and one events, both good and bad, ranging from lost battles and traitors to the founding legend of the king's daughter, *Sionainn*—punitively transformed into the river itself after she stole hazel nuts from beside a sacred well in a vain effort to become as wise as the greybeards at her father's court.

In both an ancient and a modern sense, the Shannon is Ireland's Nile: it offers us the enticing possibility of accessing history while happily sailing or cruising along its

Coarse fishing on the Shannon.

The Shannon Region

Shannon wildlife – swans.

calm waters. As with the Egyptian river, prehistoric remains and holy places dot its banks. From the 6th-century monastic remains at **Clonmacnoise**—a site endowed by Irish kings through subsequent centuries—to **Killaloe**, seat of the Dalcassians, the river is alive with regal and religious memories.

In this respect its cultural richness has been undervalued. And if one considers the Shannon region as a whole, many exceptional geological, archeological, architectural, botanical and historical attractions are a mere stone's throw away. The limestone rock formations of the **Burren** area, for example, with its underground caves and intriguing mix of Mediterranean, Arctic and Alpine flora, the amazing standing stones of **Lough Gur** (considered one of the most complete Stone Age and Bronze Age sites in north-western Europe), **Strokestown Park House**, the superb 18th-century creation of a German architect, *Richard Cassel*—the list is long and varied. Even a quick review of the region's literary associations—*Anthony Trollope, Charlotte Brontë, Oliver Goldsmith, John Milton, Maria Edgeworth, James Joyce,* and *Dion Boucicault*—is more than enough to stir the imagination.

From a purely historical standpoint, Limerick and Athlone are the most important towns. Both evoke one of the few European battles ever fought on Irish soil: the Battle of the Boyne in 1690. At **Athlone** the soldiers of *King James II* offered a vain resistance to the forces of *William of Orange,* eventually surrendering after a week-long bombardment of the castle, in which they had taken refuge. And in **Limerick,** a site settled by the Vikings as early as the 9th century, the Treaty Stone, on which the surrender of the city to William was supposedly signed, still stands for all to see. Because the terms of the surrender (respect for the rights of Catholics) were immediately breached, Limerick is known to this day as the 'City of the Broken Treaty'.

Beyond Limerick lies the estuary. Even here the Shannon manages to stake its claim to historical grandeur through **Carrigaholt** (*Carraig an Chabhaltaigh,* 'rock of the fleet') and **Foynes**. In 1588 the Spanish galleon *La Annunciada* sheltered here, along with six other ships from the ill-fated Armada expedition. In the end the *Annunciada* had to be scuttled on the spot; but despite this setback its crew managed to make the long journey back to Spain.

Over three hundred years later the town of **Foynes** was destined to become the centre of international attention as the landing-place for the first commercial transatlantic crossings using flying-boats. The outbreak of the Second World War put an end to commercial flights, but military operations, still involving flying-boats (and carried out in a surreptitious manner so as not to imperil Ireland's neutrality) replaced them.

Those Spanish and American visitors of bygone days may have been among the first, and bravest, of their kind, but as long as the Shannon continues to beckon in all its contemporary glory, they will certainly not be the last.

Aerial view of the Shannon.

Mouth of the Shannon to Killaloe

One of the lower Shannon's more compelling claims on the attention of the traveller is that nothing is as visually and emotionally exhilarating as contemplating the spectacle of a vast, river-fed body of water running seawards between two headlands. Beautiful in their own right, **Loop Head** and

fresh as ever, the spectacle as gripping.

For essentials, nearby Shannon Airport remains the natural touch-down and take-off point for millions of

air travellers, and **Limerick** the crossroads and supply centre for all those heading off to other parts of the country. The area out to the west where the estuary runs on to form the rugged headlands and coastline of Counties Clare and Limerick possesses its own unique charm. To the east lie the rich pasturelands of Counties Limerick and Tipperary, enclosing the fertile **'Golden Vale'** and nestling at the base of the **Galty Mountains**—a part of the region with its own brand of quieter, more settled appeal.

Kerry Head are also ideal locations for viewing the no-holds-barred spray and mist, wave and cloud extravaganza of the Shannon's entry into the open sea. Never mind that the event has been repeating itself for millennia: the actors are as

King John's Castle, Limerick.

Carron Church, Co. Clare.

But for those willing to rough it a little, forget the rat race and simply enjoy the exciting sea and bird-life vistas of the **Cliffs of Moher**—one of the wonders of the area—a journey to the western limits may provide an even more memorable experience. Here, 700 feet of sheer cliff-face made up of black shale and sandstone plunge into the raging Atlantic below. But for all the noisy pounding of the sea against its base, the sound that prevails is the incessant cacophony of those other, more seasoned air travellers, the puffins, seagulls, choughs, and razorbills, as they wheel and dive recklessly from their cliff-side fastnesses, or hang impressively in the gale-force winds of Atlantic storms. Tired of birds? Climb into nearby **O'Brien's Tower** and take in a panoramic view that sweeps from the outer extremity of **Loop Head** and the Kerry mountains in the south, all the way round to the **Aran Islands** and the purple-tinted mountains of **Connemara** in the north.

Only a few miles further inland from the cliffs, and constituting in fact their north-easterly point of departure, is the other great natural wonder of the region, the no less impressive limestone plateaus of the **Burren**.

At first view a barren area of rocky land, it is, despite the bleak surface conditions, the natural habitat for an incredible variety of animals and plants. For those feeling fit enough, its slabbed natural relief also affords a fascinating terrain for walking trips and geological and botanical exploration.

In its lower reaches, the River Shannon touches on four counties: Limerick, Tipperary, Clare, and Kerry; but from the beginning of the estuary to the sea only Limerick, Clare and Kerry are concerned. A more convenient, 'cartographic' way of viewing it is to note that the river divides into two shorelines, running outwards from Limerick towards Loop Head and Kerry Head, respectively. This creates a north bank and a south bank, each with its own points of interest. But the divide is not as definitive as it might appear, and motorists who tire of one bank or the other may bridge their difficulty by taking the car ferry at either **Tarbert** in County Kerry or **Killimer** in County Clare, thereby saving themselves the rigours of a 100-mile detour via Limerick and, even more importantly, getting to see the other side …

Limerick

King John's Castle, Limerick.

In 922 the Vikings sailed up the Shannon estuary and established a colony where the city of Limerick now stands. Just over two hundred years later, in 1194, the fortress-building Normans appropriated the city; the castle of King John and the cathedral of St Mary date from this period. The Munster Fitzgeralds, or Geraldines, as they were known, who were the major landowners in the area, had gradually become Gaelicised and in 1571 revolted against Tudor rule, only to lose their estates in the process of a savage war. Further wars of resistance followed in the years 1594 to 1602, and in October 1651 Limerick capitulated to Cromwellian troops, following a year-long siege. The city was the target of two further sieges during the war between William and James II (1689–91), and the associated series of battles were brought to a close with the Treaty of Limerick (1691).

In the 18th century—a time of agrarian revolt and religious persecution—the city walls were dismantled, and wide streets and fine Georgian houses were built in the Newtown Pery area. This progress was halted in the 1840s with the outbreak of the Great Famine, which also saw the decline of Irish here. The unsuccessful uprising of 1848 followed, but then the highly effective Land League campaign against landlordism in the 1880s, along with the development of the co-operative creamery system on the part of dynamic new landowners, created a climate of rural prosperity from which Limerick, as the main city of the region, benefited extensively. In more recent times this prosperity has been enhanced through the establishment of Shannon Airport.

In many tourist guides to Ireland, Limerick has often been represented as large, dull, and stubbornly conservative—a place to pause briefly in, and move quickly out of, in order to reach the more attractive scenic beauties of the rural hinterland. This image is quite unfair, and hopelessly out of date. The sodality-dominated Limerick of the 1950s, with its depressing statistics of continuous emigration, on which negative profiles are based, and the upbeat, high-tech city of today, with its thriving art galleries, performance centres and magnificent new **University of Limerick Concert Hall**, are like chalk and cheese. Apart from a new dynamism in the city itself, the wise use of EU funds a massive input of foreign investment in computer enterprises, medical and pharmaceutical manufacturing and the development of telecentres have all played their part in transforming the city beyond recognition.

Limerick is an important port and industrial centre, with an international airport only 15 miles distant. Long famous for its cured hams and bacon and its lace-making, the city has moved into the modern era in style, adding to its traditional arts and crafts new technological training facilities and expertise and a reinvigorated cultural life. At the same time its perennial tourist attractions, such as **King John's Castle**, with its five drum towers, solid curtain walls, battlement walkways, and interpretative centre, and **St Mary's Cathedral**, with its pre-Reformation stone altar and *son et lumière* spectacle, remain important drawing-cards for the city.

Close to King John's Castle, visitors can also enjoy **Castle Lane**, an authentic streetscape of bygone years, illustrating Limerick's urban architectural heritage. The complex houses **Limerick Civic Museum** and **Castle Lane Tavern**, a venue for regular performances of Irish music and dancing.

In the arts and culture, Limerick has benefited from enlightened decentralising policies at national level as well as the entrepreneurial talents and energies of its own citizens. The **Irish World Music Centre**, with its fine new concert hall, is based in the University of Limerick; and Limerick was also chosen as the location for the classical music radio station, Lyric FM, recently set up by the national broadcaster, RTE. The **Belltable Arts Centre** in O'Connell Street operates a lively theatre programme and maintains a gallery for local, national and international exhibitions of all forms of art, as well as films, video, installation and performance work.

Over in John's Square the **Limerick Museum**, divided between two elegant houses, has a permanent display covering the long and varied history of the city and surrounding areas, from the Stone Age up to today. In 1992 it obtained the first Gulbenkian Foundation Irish Museums Award. **Limerick City Gallery of Art** in Pery Square, set up with help from Andrew Carnegie, has a permanent collection of 18th, 19th and 20th-century art and plays host to travelling exhibitions of contemporary work. It also holds readings and concerts of traditional and classical music.

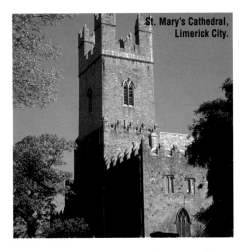

St. Mary's Cathedral, Limerick City.

Just 3 miles away at **Castletroy**, in the University of Limerick, is the **National Self-Portrait Collection**, an innovative selection of paintings, watercolours, prints and collage—mainly, but not exclusively, representative of 20th-century artists. Also deserving of special mention is the **Hunt Museum**, a major private collection of art and antiques brought together by the archaeologist *John Hunt* and his wife *Gertrude* and now open to the public in Rutland Street. Here the range of material is quite staggering, from Egyptian, Greek and Roman exhibits, through mediaeval items, right up to 18th-century metalwork and ceramics. Highlights include works by *Picasso*, a bronze horse by *Leonardo da Vinci*, and the cross worn by *Mary Queen of Scots* on the day of her execution. All this in much-maligned Limerick? Guidebook scoffers of the last generation, beg absolution here!

DON'T MISS
- Englishtown (**St Mary's Cathedral, City Hall, City Museum, St John's Castle**)
- Irishtown (**Custom House and Hunt Museum, St John's Cathedral**)
- Newtown Pery (the heart of modern Limerick)

ALL-WEATHER OPTIONS
- Enjoy a mediaeval banquet at **Bunratty Castle**
- Visit the pubs of nearby **Castleconnell** for Irish music
- Compose a limerick!
- Visit any of the Traditional Irish Music pubs (Brochure available from Tourist Office)

Call the USA direct   Just call 1-800-COLLECT

Vikings and Normans

The Vikings burst out of Scandinavia at the end of the Dark Ages. They were one of the most potent and energetic people in the early rebuilding of Europe. Their own homeland, with limited space and much poor land, could not contain their surplus population. They took to the sea.

The Vikings had a genius for shipbuilding. They built narrow, shallow-draught longships, the finest ocean-going craft of their day. Not only that but they could manoeuvre these craft inland on navigable rivers, something that was to be particularly significant in Ireland. Altogether, their achievements were astonishing. They created a huge ocean-bound kingdom centred in Norway but also embracing the Scottish highlands and islands; they created a kingdom in eastern England; they colonised Normandy (the Normans were their descendants); and they settled much of the southern Baltic coast and penetrated as far into the Russian interior as Novgorod, which they founded and which was the first town of any size in the vast Russian interior. And they discovered America.

These energetic, aggressive and ferocious people first appeared off the Irish coast in the year 795. Ireland, with its wealthy monasteries, offered easy pickings. The Vikings were much more advanced militarily than the Irish, and they met little effective resistance. Most of what we know about them in Ireland comes from annals recorded in the monasteries they attacked, so they were naturally represented as rapacious barbarians plundering and raping a superior civilisation. There was more to the Vikings than this, however. They were also traders. They founded the first Irish towns at the mouths of the principal rivers and used them as settlements that traded with other Viking centres, such as York and the Isle of Man. Traders need stability as well as warriors. Dublin, Wexford, Waterford and Limerick all owe their origin to the Vikings.

In time, many Irish lords and chieftains made alliances with the Vikings. There was intermarriage between the two groups. In addition, the Irish kingdoms learnt much from the military prowess of the newcomers, and the consequent advance in military skill made wars between the kingdoms more violent. Out of this growing instability a new force emerged. The tiny kingdom of Dál gCais in what is now east Clare found a particularly gifted warlord in *Brian Bórú*. He first overran Munster and eventually, in 1005, achieved what no-one had ever done before him: he effectively established his rule over the entire country.

The many kingdoms that he reduced to client status resented this. The eastern province of Leinster, in particular, was restless. In 1014 a Leinster rebellion supported by some Vikings was defeated by Brian at the Battle of Clontarf, near Dublin. But Brian himself died, and with him died the chance of a lasting united Irish kingdom. Despite later myths, Clontarf was not a battle between Irish and Vikings fought to expel the invader: it was a battle between different groups of Irish, in which Viking elements fought on both sides.

For 150 years after Clontarf there was a nervous stability punctuated by inter-communal conflict. Wars between the Irish kingdoms persisted, and it was one of these that led to the Norman landings of 1169. *Diarmaid Mac Murchú* became king of Leinster about the year 1126. In the 1150s he abducted the wife of *Tiarnán Ó Ruairc,* king of Bréifne (modern County Cavan). Ó Ruairc defeated Mac Murchú in battle and forced him to flee; he made his way to the court of *King Henry II* of England.

Henry was a descendant of *William the*

Viking boat, Wexford Heritage Park.

Conqueror, the Norman who had taken England from the Anglo-Saxons a century earlier. He was far too busy to get involved with the squabbles of Irish kings, but he gave Mac Murchú permission to seek the support of Norman lords in Wales. The result was the fateful landing of the first Norman soldiers in Baginbun Bay, County Wexford, in 1169. The Normans, under the leadership of the forceful *Richard de Clare*—better known as Strongbow—soon captured Waterford, Wexford, and Dublin. Their military skills were far in advance of anything yet seen in Ireland.

Suddenly alarmed at his vassals' sweeping success on the smaller island, Henry came across in 1171 and received the submission not only of the new Norman colonists but also of many Irish kings as well. Ireland was now officially attached to the English crown, though the connection was fairly loose. Nonetheless the English monarch has had a presence in Ireland ever since; only since 1922 has that presence been removed from most of the country.

The Normans quickly used their superior military and engineering skills to establish themselves throughout much of the country. They conquered land and built enormous castles and fortresses to control it. Places like **Trim Castle** in County Meath and **Carrickfergus Castle** in County Antrim were vastly bigger than any structures built in Ireland up to that time. They were impregnable; whoever held them controlled the countryside for miles around. The Normans were in Ireland to stay.

153

Adare, Lough Gur & the Palatine enclave

Franciscan Abbey, Adare, Co. Limerick.

The first impression given by **Adare**, situated south of Limerick on the Maigue River, is of a sleepy but elegant rusticity. A Fitzgerald fief, the town is made up of solid stone houses with well-maintained thatched roofs, colour-coded shop fronts, and moss and ivy-covered churches from the Middle Ages.

Adare first came into prominence when it was occupied by the Anglo-Normans in the reign of Henry II. Later the town became the property of the Fitzgeralds, Earls of

Kildare, following which it underwent incorporation in the 14th century, and a grant was made for the erection of walls. But the dominant dressed-cottage style that is its contemporary feature is the work of the third *Earl of Dunraven* (1812–71), master of the manor and a landlord who, unusually for the time, enjoyed a reputation as someone who looked after his tenants' interests.

The mediaeval history of the town has left its traces. In its main street stands the **White or Trinitarian Priory**. This was founded by *Geoffrey de Marisco* in 1230. Destroyed during Henry VIII's suppression of the monasteries and restored in the 19th century by the Earl of Dunraven, it remains in use as a Catholic church. Behind it is a renovated stone columbarium or dovecote dating back to the Middle Ages.

On the outskirts of Adare an Augustinian abbey, founded in 1315 by the Earl of Kildare, serves as a Church of Ireland place of worship. Though less imposing than the

Trinitarian priory, its restored 15th-century cloister and Dunraven mausoleum make the **Church of St Nicholas**, as it is now known, well worth seeing.

A third mediaeval building, and one of the most delightful golfing hazards found anywhere, is a 15th-century **Franciscan friary** consisting of a nave and transept with side chapels and a miraculously well-preserved central tower, standing smack in the middle of the Adare golf course. To visit it, check first at the clubhouse for directions.

Also in the vicinity of the golf course is the **Church of St Nicholas of Myra**, which was built and rebuilt between the 13th and 17th centuries.

Close to the main road-bridge over the River Maigue is the **Desmond Castle**, a strongly fortified keep built in the early 13th century on the site of an ancient ring-fort. The extensive ruins are of an inner ward surrounded by a moat and enclosed by a large courtyard. The castle, which was in decay by 1329, was besieged by the English in 1580 and occupied by the Earls of Desmond during the 17th century. At some point in Cromwellian times it faded from consideration, militarily and socially, and was allowed to go to ruin.

Adare Manor, a limestone mansion built in Gothic style by the second Earl of Dunraven in the 19th century and featuring carved oak staircases and a carved greystone fireplace by *Pugin,* has now become a luxury hotel. Its large formal gardens contain a superb 300-year-old cedar

Lough Gur, Co. Clare.

of Lebanon.

For those keen to learn more about the growth of Adare from the 13th century on, the **Adare Heritage Centre**, situated in the main street, contains a useful permanent exhibition, as well as maintaining an audiovisual display dealing with contemporary developments.

Situated only 5 miles from Adare, the **Celtic Park and Gardens** must be counted among the area's attractions. On the site of an original Celtic settlement in what was one of the most important Cromwellian estates in Ireland, it combines many authentic and re-created features from Ireland's past, including an ancient portal tomb and an authentic ring-fort. Its classical-style gardens with their hundreds of roses and flowering shrubs, colonnades and gravel paths open out onto unspoilt countryside.

DON'T MISS
- Don't miss the graceful, stylised ruins of the 15th-century **Franciscan Friary**.
- See the carvings of animals and human heads in the 14th-century **Augustinian priory**.
- Admire the feudal grandeur of the 13th-century **Desmond Castle** with its keep, curtain walls, and great hall.

ALL-WEATHER OPTIONS
- Visit the **Palatine Museum** in nearby Rathkeale and learn how German Lutherans came to settle in Ireland.
- Visit **Castle Matrix** and examine the collection of Wild Geese documents covering the history of the Irish serving in Continental armies.

Don't forget to pick up your Global Refund Tax Free Shopping Cheques as you shop.' www.globalrefund.ie

GLOBAL REFUND

North Shore & South Shore

The outermost point of the Shannon estuary on its northern shore is **Loop Head**. To reach it, whether one comes via the N68 road from Ennis further north or by the N18 and N473 from Limerick through Shannon, it is necessary to pass through Kilkee and proceed southwards on the R487. At the end of this drive stands the village of **Kilbaha**, which is separated from Loop Head by a mere 3 miles.

Standing in the Atlantic off Loop Head is an isolated section of cliff known as **Diarmaid and Gráinne's Rock**. Between it and the mainland is a channel called the Lovers' Leap. This comes with a tourist health warning: visitors are actively dissuaded from attempting to emulate the feat of *Cú Chulainn,* the mythical hero who leaped from solid ground across the divide and onto the rock to escape the unwelcome attentions of a woman. The assumption is that no local rock should prove fatal to visiting men, and no female visitors feel so aggrieved as not to want to pass this way again.

Leaving Loop Head and moving along the shore road we reach Kilbaha once more. In the 1850s this village was the scene of the 'Little Ark' episode. A local priest, Father Meehan, was forbidden by bigoted landlords to celebrate Mass, but he decided that if he did so between high water and low water on the beach he was outside the jurisdiction of those persecuting him. In 1852 he got a carpenter to make a hut on wheels, inside which he placed an altar. This little ark was them regularly trundled down to the beach,

and local people were able to be present at the outlawed ceremony. The ark in question is preserved in the parish church of **Monleen**, just beside Kilbaha.

After Kilbaha we come to **Carrigaholt**, an Irish-speaking village with a sandy beach, the well-preserved **Castle Macmahon**, and historical memories of the Spanish Armada. From the top of the castle there is a good view out over the estuary. From Carrigaholt the R487 road winds up to **Kilkee**, a family holiday resort built around a crescent-shaped sandy beach. Kilkee is a noted snorkelling and scuba-diving venue, and the river outlets close to it offer good brown-trout fishing.

From Kilkee the N67 road runs downwards to **Kilrush**, a bustling market and seaside town with extensive marina development. It then extends a further few miles out to **Killimer**, the point of departure for car ferries to the north shore at **Tarbert**. Killimer churchyard is celebrated as the burial place of *Ellen Hanley,* the inspiration for the tragic heroine of *Gerald Griffin's* novel *The Collegians.*

The road back via Kilrush offers a choice of driving directly to **Ennis**, through **Lissycasey** and **Darragh** (on the N68 road) or taking the R473 road through **Labasheeda**, **Kildysart** and **Ballincally** to link up with the Ennis–Limerick road at **Clarecastle**. This is a more scenic route, hugging the estuary coastline for most of its length and, in its final section, offering tourists the possibility of stopping to explore the wonders of **Bunratty**

The Shannon Estuary,
North and South.

Folk Park, with its re-creation of typical 19th-century urban and rural life, or enjoying a mediaeval banquet at **Bunratty Castle** or, alternatively, before heading back to Limerick, the range of ancient and modern craft products at nearby **Ballycasey Craft and Design Centre**.

SOUTH SHORE

Moving along the coast (R551 road) from **Kerry Head**, which stands opposite its northern counterpart, Loop Head, at the mouth of the River Shannon, we reach the lively resort town of **Ballybunnion**, with its attractive beach and justly celebrated links golf course. A short distance outside the town a memorial stone marks the spot where a Marconi wireless station established the first east-west wireless telephone communication, to Cape Breton, Nova Scotia, in March 1919.

From Ballybunnion the road proceeds to **Ballylongford**, to the north of which are the striking Gothic ruins of **Lislaughton Friary**, constructed by *John O'Connor Kerry* in 1478. On towards the coast the road meets **Tarbert**, the terminal for ferries to County Clare, then links up with the N69 road to Limerick. Just past Tarbert the road rises to **Glin**, a dairy centre, and on the outskirts of the village stands **Glin Castle**, a magnificent 18th-century structure, seat of the Fitzgerald family, who have been in residence here for over seven hundred years. The castle has a unique collection of historical furniture as well as a kitchen garden. The beautiful demesne of the castle is open to visitors.

A focal point of interest beyond Glin is **Foynes**, with its flying-boat museum. Among the features of the museum are a 1940s-style cinema, the original terminal building, and the radio and weather room, with the original transmitters, receivers, and Morse code equipment. Close to Foynes at **Shanagolden** is **Manisternagalliaghduff Convent**, one of the few known mediaeval nunneries. It consists of a church and cloister. A room to the south of the church is called the 'Black Hag's Cell' through mistranslation of the Irish term for a nun.

For those interested in flowers and rockeries a visit to the **Boyce Gardens**, a private 1-acre garden at **Mount Trenchard** in Foynes provides an agreeable horticultural diversion before leaving the area.

The road from Foynes cuts past **Askeaton**, a Desmond stronghold, with its castle and 15th-century Franciscan friary. The castle, founded on an island in the River Deel about the year 1199, contains a great banqueting-hall that, with its finely carved windows and blind arcade, constitutes one of the finest mediaeval secular buildings in Ireland.

From Askeaton the road then reaches **Curraghchase Forest Park**. An exceptional 600-acre park with abundant wildlife in its woodlands and lake, it features walk-ways, a lake, and a nature trail. Hidden within the forest are the ruins of **Curraghchase House**, the 18th-century home of the poet *Aubrey de Vere*. The Curraghchase garden, well worth seeing, is open to the public from Easter to September. Not far away, perched on volcanic rock, stands the ruined **Carrigogunnell Castle**, a 15th-century edifice affording fine views of the Shannon. Beyond the castle at **Mungret**, two churches survive from a monastery founded here by *St Neasán*, who died in the year 551. East of the village one finds the striking ruins of Mungret Abbey; from here the road leads to Limerick, past the Shannon hydro-electric scheme at **Ardna-crusha** (R464 and R463), and on to peaceful Killaloe.

Killaloe to Athlone

Killaloe, a natural cross-over point on the Shannon's southerly course, and Athlone, its mid-point, are joined by the great expanse of a single lake, **Lough Derg**. In the days of flourishing canal and river traffic this, the largest lake on the Shannon, played a central part in the commercial exchanges linking Dublin and Limerick. Today things are different: it fulfils instead a function as the primary holiday venue for all those enjoying fishing, water sports and other outdoor activities. But the old and the new cohabit easily. Not far from where barges formerly plied their leisurely way and white-faced pilgrims voyaged to **Holy Island** in the lake's centre in quest of absolution and salvation, bronzed young holiday-makers now water-ski in search of more tangible earthly joys.

The approximately 100-mile road ringing Lough Derg offers some splendid scenery. The lake's west bank marks the eastern boundary of County Clare and runs back to the Slieve Bernagh and Slieve Aughty mountains. It includes **Killaloe**, for many the most attractive town in the entire county, a site associated with *Brian Bórú*, the chieftain who taught the Vikings a thing or two at the Battle of Clontarf in 1014. A narrow bridge with thirteen arches connects it with **Ballina** in County Tipperary.

Further on lies **Mountshannon**, a favourite with anglers and pony trekkers and a good spot from which to sail, cruise, or set out to Holy Island. **Portumna**, where the Shannon was first bridged in 1796, stands at the lake's northern end. The town contains a fine castle, now in the process of restoration, and is close to a magnificent forest park. For the rest, the perimeter road goes on its picturesque way, passing by villages with craft-work centres and pubs featuring traditional music.

On its descent from Athlone to Portumna the Shannon collects two tributaries, one from the east, the Little Brosna, from the prosperous market town of **Birr**, County Offaly, the other, the Suck, from the west, from **Ballinasloe**, home of the celebrated Horse Fair, in eastern Galway.

The north-south axis of the Shannon was imaginatively complemented in the 18th century by the building of the east-west Grand and Royal Canals. Though neither of these marvellous artificial waterways is much used for their original commercial purpose, they still make it possible for the stout-hearted traveller to hire a cruiser at Tullamore, County Offaly, and either head off to the west or push down the River Barrow to Waterford. But for those impatient souls who prefer faster access to the middle Shannon region, the main N6 Dublin–Galway road through Athlone remains the quicker and softer option.

Apart from Holy Island in the centre of Lough Derg, the region is of exceptional historical and cultural interest. **Clonfert**

St Flannan's Cathedral,
Killaloe, Co. Clare.

and **Clonmacnoise**, Early Christian centres with fascinating architectural remains, lie on opposite sides of the river close to Shannonbridge. **Aughrim**, site of an epic confrontation between the armies of James II and William of Orange, is only a short distance to the west, near **Ballinasloe**, and possesses its own interpretative centre. And at **Birr**, a short drive westwards from Portumna, the castle and demesne of the Earls of Ross offer the possibility of a visit that's likely to enchant both astronomer and botany enthusiast.

Athlone, standing at the entrance to **Lough Ree**, marks the boundary between the provinces of Leinster and Connacht. An ancient ford on the River Shannon, it's now a busy road and rail junction and a much sought-after harbour for all manner of boats on Ireland's network of inland

waters. Of great historical interest in its own right, it also represents an ideal point of departure for exploring the shores and islands of the quiet lake beyond it.

Between Portumna and Athlone the land tends to flatten out as we move in closer to the boglands of County Offaly. But this kind of landscape, though different in kind from the more spectacular environs of Lough Derg, can also prove fascinating. Probably the best way to experience the difference is to go to Shannonbridge and take a 45-minute tour of 6 miles of low-lying countryside on the **Clonmacnoise and West Offaly Railway**. The ensuing revelations concerning the secret life of turf may make you convert in an instant from being an unqualified lover of mountains to what every Irishman knows he is from birth—a natural bogman!

159

Wild Swans on the River Shannon.

It's delightfully different

✓ The widest choice of holidays to Ireland by Air or Sea

✓ Fly and Drive tours with Aer Lingus

✓ Go As You Please motoring holidays

✓ Coach tours and Country Breaks

✓ Huge choice of accommodation from Guesthouses and Farmhouses to Hotels and Castles

✓ Dublin, Cork and Galway City Breaks

✓ Golfing Holidays

✓ Group Bookings

Mediaeval Ireland

Irish warriors and peasants.

The arrival of the Normans in the late 12th century created a link between Ireland and the English crown. The Normans' strength lay in their military and engineering skills; their weakness was lack of numbers. They were able to conquer and hold most of the good land, but they could not settle the whole country. Side by side with the Norman lordships, the old Irish kingdoms survived. In theory all were subject to the king of England, but London was a long way distant over the sea. Government, in the modern sense, hardly existed. There was no national army or system of uniform taxation; communications were poor; and most people never travelled outside their immediate locality.

Gradually, Normans and Irish learnt to live together in an uneasy alliance. At the same time they paid scant attention to events in London or even in Dublin Castle, the nominal centre of English royal power in Ireland.

In the 14th century the native Irish world experienced a revival. It pressed hard on

Norman lordships, especially in the west. By the middle of the century all of Connacht was once again in Irish hands, except for the walled city of Galway. Similarly in Ulster, only Carrickfergus remained Norman. It was different in the east and south: there the great Norman families of Fitzgerald and Butler more than held their own. Even here, however, there was a problem. Many Normans were becoming Hibernicised, assuming Irish ways, speaking Irish, and adopting Irish customs and usages. The situation became so dire that in 1367 the 'Irish Parliament'—a wholly Norman body—passed a series of laws, known as the Statutes of Kilkenny, forbidding their kinsfolk to wear Irish dress, speak Irish, and so on. These laws were ignored; but the mere fact that they were enacted in the first place underlines the strength of the Irish resurgence.

In the late 14th century the situation was judged to be so serious that the king himself, *Richard II,* came over twice to Ireland to lead military campaigns against Irish raiders on the borders of the Pale, the small area around Dublin that was under the control of Dublin Castle.

Neither expedition was a success, and the king's failure merely underlined the weakness of English power in Ireland. The Norman magnates drew their own conclusions. If the king could not protect them, they would shift for themselves. So it was. In the course of the 15th century the big Norman lordships became more like semi-independent kingdoms. The three most important were those of the Fitzgeralds of Kildare, centred just south of Dublin; the Butlers of Ormond, centred in Kilkenny and controlling the south-east and midlands; and the Fitzgeralds of Desmond, cousins of the Fitzgeralds of Kildare, who held most of the province of Munster and were also the most Hibernicised of the great Norman families.

Of the three, the Fitzgeralds of Kildare gradually assumed the greatest importance. By the 1470s this family was the most powerful in Ireland, connected by an array of marriage alliances to families both Norman and Irish all over the country. The Great Earl of Kildare, *Garret Mór Fitzgerald,* was chief governor of Ireland, in effect the king's representative.

Late mediaeval Ireland was part of the English king's domains but one that operated a highly devolved system of home rule. The Earl of Kildare was for most practical purposes the ruler of Ireland. He levied taxes, raised armies, and controlled the government of most of the country. But he was a ruler in the mediaeval, not the modern, sense. Distance was a problem for him as well. He could not be everywhere, could not move soldiers or tax-collectors around a country with poor internal communications. Instead he controlled things through alliances with local lords and chieftains, whom he made beholden to him.

Even at that there were parts of Ireland that were beyond his reach, or that of anyone else. In central and western Ulster, ancient Irish kingdoms—almost wholly untouched by Norman influence—went on very much as they had done since time immemorial.

By the early 16th century, all this was about to change. The endless problems of the previous century that had kept the English crown weak—the Hundred Years' War in France and the series of civil wars known as the Wars of the Roses—were over. There was a new king on the English throne. *Henry VIII* was a child of the Renaissance, with its emphasis on the rights of princes and kings. The general European tendency was towards the development of strong states and empires with efficient centralised bureaucracies and uniform laws. Henry shared this ambition. He gradually stamped out regional and local particularisms in England and Wales, and in the process finally ended Welsh independence. He tried the same in Scotland, but Scotland was an independent kingdom and resisted him fiercely. Ireland, however, was not independent in the Scottish sense. It was part of Henry's inheritance, and he meant to live up to it. By the 1530s, Ireland was on the brink of a revolution.

Lough Derg, Killaloe & environs

Lough Derg, 25 miles long and 2 to 3 miles wide, is the largest and most southerly of the Shannon lakes. It marks the boundary between Counties Tipperary and Clare and, apart from being a mecca for water sports, also features fine walking trails and cycle routes, as well as a scenic perimeter road that passes through some of the prettiest landscape in Ireland.

Killaloe, a major fishing and boating centre, boasts the country's largest inland marina, thanks in part to its fine situation on the river's west bank. The town, which is connected with the village of **Ballina** (County Tipperary) by a bridge of thirteen arches, is set against an attractive natural backdrop composed of the Slieve Bernagh mountains to the west, the Arra Mountains to the east, and of course the lake itself.

The antiquity of Killaloe can be gauged by its rich mix of historical and mythological associations—stretching back to prehistory from the great Dalcassian princes—and the presence of several ancient sites in the vicinity of the town. The seat of Ireland's high king and most famous Dalcassian prince, *Brian Bórú* (c. 926–1014) stood at **Kincora**, and, though nothing remains of it today, its established romantic place in poetic tradition is analogous to that occupied by King Priam's fortress at Troy in Greek myth and epic. Brian was killed in 1014, fighting the Danes at Clontarf. Kincora lasted a hundred years more, before being finally destroyed by raiding Connacht warriors.

Half a mile to the north of the town, another site, 'Bórú's Fort', evokes further Dalcassian memories and also provides a magnificent view of the lake. Further down the scale of heroic grandeur, **Greenaunlaghna**, on the slopes of Craglea, marks the spot where local chiefs had their stronghold.

With the passing of Dalcassian influence, the prestige of Killaloe waned, but despite its gradual loss of political and economic importance it remained a significant ecclesiastical centre and continued to enjoy a measure of prosperity, thanks to its strategic position on the lake.

Within Killaloe the most impressive site is in fact ecclesiastical: **St Flannan's Cathedral**, dating from the late 12th century. It consists of nave, choir and transepts, with a heavy square central tower. Though not especially striking at first glance, its main claim to fame is a richly carved Romanesque doorway of exceptional artistry. Nearby is the so-called **Thorgrim's Stone**—the shaft of a bilingual stone cross, unique in its juxtaposition of runic and ogham characters. Also in the vicinity, in the churchyard of the modern **St Flannan's Church**, is the 9th-century *St Molua's Oratory*, removed from Friars' Island to save it from being submerged during the inauguration of the Shannon hydro-electric scheme. For those seeking further information about the town's past, present and future, this is to hand in the **Killaloe Heritage Centre**, which shares a building with the town's tourist authority.

Going northwards towards Mountshannon, the area to the west of **Scariff** offers some attractive scenery, particularly **Lough Graney**, where the poet *Brian Merriman* wrote *Cúirt an Mheán Oíche* ('The Midnight Court'), Irish-Ireland's most celebrated poem and a byword since then for women's emancipation!

Mountshannon, an 18th-century village of stone houses and lively pubs on the south-west shore of the lake, is an ideal point from which to set out for **Inis Cealtra** or **Holy Island**, one of the earliest Christian settlements in east Clare. Situated only a mile from Mountshannon and half a mile from the mainland, the island's fascinating Christian remains constitute another reminder of the extensive network of Golden Age monasteries along the River Shannon. Founded in the 7th century by *St Caimín*, the settlement survives in the form of a 30-foot round tower, four ancient chapels, a hermit's cell, and gravestones covering the period from the 7th to the 11th centuries. Though the monastery suffered greatly at the hands of the Danes in the 9th and 10th centuries, it was restored to something of its former splendour by *Brian Bórú* and is now undergoing further preservation work.

A peculiar building on the island, dubbed variously the 'Anchorites' Cell' and the 'Confessional', provides a good index to the hold that ecclesiastical ruins have on the minds of imaginative visitors. Those adhering to the hermit's cell school of thought saw it as a place of self-mortification used by the early monks, while those favouring the 'confessional' point of view saw it as an absolution-seeker's 'sin box'. Unhappily for both, recent excavations now suggest that it was first put up about the year 1700, functioned as a shrine, and was rebuilt again and again in the style of the original wooden construction.

St Caimín's Church is believed to have been commissioned by *Brian Bóru* himself, and the pre-1000 style of the nave lends some support to this belief. At some point in the 12th century the Romanesque arch, chancel and west door were added. These underwent a botched restoration in 1879, but now the church is being upgraded once more, this time using more appropriate stones. It contains a number of grave-slabs from the 8th to the 11th centuries and the remains of several high crosses.

St Brigid's Church, a Romanesque edifice, has a 13th-century gateway providing access to an enclosure. Bronze and iron workings found here, along with evidence of comb-making and other material pursuits revealed by recent excavations, suggest that when it was replaced by the nearby **St Mary's Church** in the 13th century it was transformed into a centralised work area.

Part of the Holy Island site contains an area of earth and stone called the 'Saints' Graveyard', comprising a number of grave slabs, some of which date back to the 11th and 12th centuries. The nearby small graveyard building known as the 'Church of the Wounded Men' is believed to be the mortuary chapel of the O'Gradys, whose family motto, *Vulneratus sed non victus* ('Wounded but not vanquished'), might well have been the perfect catch-phrase for Ireland's epic hero, *Cú Chulainn*.

Further inland on the island lies an enclosure known as **St Michael's Garden**. Local tradition associates it with miraculous cures; but again the truth is otherwise. Far from justifying its popular reputation, excavations carried out in recent years show that it was in fact a final resting-place for unbaptised infants.

The 'Lady's Well' near the shore constituted a focal point for pilgrims, many of whom would toss coins into it as a sign of repentance. In the 1830s unseemly behaviour made it seem less holy well than Trevi Fountain, and permission for the annual Whit Sunday pilgrimage to the island was withdrawn.

Further to the north is **Portumna**, a port of call for river traffic, with fully developed cruiser and fishing facilities as well as a magnificent wild-life sanctuary, **Portumna Forest Park**, less than a mile from the town. On the south-eastern side of the lake, just 5 miles inland, stands **Nenagh**, the main town in North Tipperary and an important stopping point on the main Dublin–Limerick road.

DON'T MISS

- Don't miss a visit to **Inis Cealtra or Holy Island**, monastic ruins and over a thousand years of spiritual tradition.
- Go fishing at scenic **Scariff** near **Cragliath**, a fort where Aoibheall, the fairy queen, had her dwelling-place.
- Visit colourful **Lough Graney** (4 miles north of Feakle), where Brian Merriman wrote 'The Midnight Court'.
- In **Killaloe** examine the exceptionally fine Romanesque doorway in **St Flannan's Oratory** and sneak a look at **Thorgrim's Stone**, a bilingual ogham and runic monument.

IF IT RAINS

- Visit **St Flannan's Cathedral** and **St Flannan's Oratory**, Killaloe.
- Drive to **Bunratty Folk Park**, where many of the most fascinating exhibits are under cover.

Clonmacnoise and Clonfert

When *St Ciarán* and eight other monks founded a monastic settlement close to Shannonbridge in the year 548, they can hardly have imagined that it would become the most celebrated of all Ireland's holy places. For over a thousand years, **Clonmacnoise** was a dynamic religious centre famed for its literary and artistic activity. It also served as a royal necropolis and enjoyed the patronage of successive high kings. In addition it maintained continuous scholarly and missionary contact with the rest of Europe, even during the Dark Ages, and by keeping alive both the teaching of classical languages and the light of religious faith it played a leading part in gaining for Ireland its reputation as the 'island of saints and scholars'.

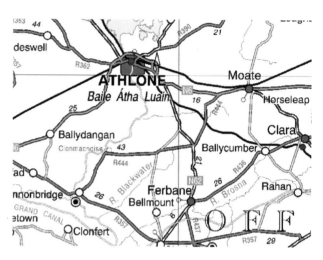

The very accessibility of Clonmacnoise, both by land and water, proved its downfall. In the period 830–1165 the Danes and the Anglo-Normans carried out successive plundering raids on what proved an unprotected and vulnerable enclave. The native Irish did likewise. A major act of desecration took place in 1552 when the English garrison of Athlone completely despoiled the holy city and carried off all sacramental items of value they could lay their hands on, down to the last scrap of glass from the windows. As late as 1647 a last-ditch effort to restore the cathedral was made but equally quickly undone when Cromwell's soldiers overran the site, with devastating results.

Clonmacnoise today

A cathedral, eight churches, two round towers, three high crosses, two hundred grave-slabs (the largest and most significant selection in Ireland) and a 13th-century ring-fort remain. The 10-foot **South Cross**, with its Passion carvings, and the 9th-century **North Cross**, set off with floral and animal motifs, still testify to a high level of artistic excellence. The cathedral, however, has been greatly altered by time, and only the *antae* at the east and west ends belong to the original structure. The grave of *Ruairí Ó Conchúir*, last high king of Ireland, buried here in 1198, is in the north-east corner of the chancel. Some distance eastwards of the 20-acre cemetery, the **Nuns' Church** is one of the finest specimens of the Irish Romanesque style, even though it is little more than 50 feet long and consists only of nave and chancel. Of historical as well as artistic interest, it was built by *Dearbhorgaill*, the wife of a Bréifne chief taken captive by *Diarmaid Mac Murchú*, king of Leinster. It was this abduction that ultimately precipitated the Anglo-Norman invasion of Ireland.

Clonfert

Any excursion to Clonmacnoise should take in nearby Clonfert in County Galway, where a Benedictine monastery was founded by *Brendan the Navigator* in the year 563. Brendan's voyages—almost more legendary than his holiness—are recorded in a mediaeval manuscript. They supposedly took him to Wales, the Orkneys, Iceland and possibly North America and even led one modern adventurer to construct a boat to similar specifications in a courageous attempt to prove that the saint had been the first to cross the Atlantic.

Like Clonmacnoise, Clonfert was a famous centre of learning and underwent fire and destruction between the time of its foundation and the 12th century. The bulk of the building dates from 1200. At the moment the abbey serves as a Protestant church—a change of faith that, ironically, may have played a role in ensuring its survival.

The abbey offers a very pleasing façade. Above a series of recessive circular arches over the west doorway is a triangular pediment playfully decorated with iconic heads, ornament, and animal figures. The capitals, which lean slightly inwards, are carved with grotesque faces. Apart from

Clonfert Cathedral, Co. Galway.

this superb sculpted sandstone doorway, the interior of the abbey contains a delightful chancel arch adorned with haphazardly positioned images of beatifically solicitous angels, sundry rosettes, and an incongruous pin-up mermaid holding a mirror.

DON'T MISS

- Don't miss the thousand-year-old magnificently carved **Cross of the Scriptures** inside the Clonmacnoise visitors' centre.
- Also see the **Nuns' Church**, endowed by Dearbhorgaill, wife of the king of Bréifne, following an extramarital fling with the king of Leinster. (She even stayed here, after her cuckolded husband had passed on in 1172.)

IF IT RAINS

- Visit **Banagher**, where Anthony Trollope spent time as a post office surveyor and Charlotte Brontë endured a tough honeymoon in 1854.

Athlone and Lough Ree

Athlone Castle and St Peter and Paul's Church.

A strategically important east-west and north-south divide fought over for centuries, with most of its ancient buildings destroyed or in ruin, **Athlone** is today a busy road, rail and river junction. Perhaps the last, sad chapter in an unhappy historical record—and the one most illustrative of the effect of constant warring on the town—occurred when the Jacobite army withdrew to the west following the defeat in 1690 at the Battle of the Boyne and made the Shannon its last line of defence. A year later, when the Williamite general *Ginkel* laid siege to Athlone, the harassed Irish retreated to the west side of the river, 'burning

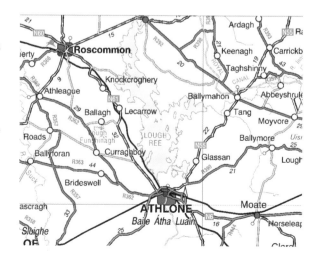

Shannon view, Lough Ree.

their bridges' behind them. It was the last, tragic compliance with the oft-repeated Cromwellian edict to the Irish: 'To Hell or to Connacht!'

Athlone Castle was built in 1210 as a Norman bridgehead for access to Connacht. Thick walls and a drum tower are all that survive, but the remains of the keep now house an interpretative centre covering such varied aspects as the area's history, the famous siege, the life and times of *John McCormack*, Ireland's greatest tenor, the flora and fauna of the Shannon region, and a military museum.

Opposite the castle the Roman Renaissance dome and two spires of the **Church of St Peter and Paul** dominate the town. Inside the church the resolutely 20th-century *Harry Clarke* stained-glass windows form a vivid counterpoint to the austere ecclesiastical surroundings, creating a reposeful ensemble of colour and stone.

Apart from serving as an east-west gateway, Athlone is enjoying steady growth as an industrial and commercial focal point and a high-tech training and recruitment centre, with a number of multinational companies investing heavily in the area. At the same time its traditional role as a base from which to visit the monastic site of Clonmacnoise and the attractive Goldsmith country to the north-east in County Longford, or for exploring the shores and islands of picturesque Lough Ree, has taken on fresh importance as a result of the exceptional development of tourist business in the Shannon region. With a population of 20,000, it is now the largest town in County Westmeath and can boast a wide range of shops and services, made even more accessible to people from out of town by a relief road and bridge completed in 1991.

DON'T MISS

- Don't miss (and you won't, because it catches the eye at every corner) the towering Roman Renaissance **Church of St Peter and St Paul**.
- See **King John's Castle** and its museum (archaeology and folklore).
- Take a cruise on Lough Ree and visit the islands of **Inchclearaun** and **Inchbofin**, with their Early Christian churches and gravestones.
- Don't forget to visit delightful **Glassan** (6 miles from Athlone on the N55 road), a village of roses that claims to be the original of *Goldsmith's* 'Auburn'.

ALL-WEATHER OPTIONS

- Visit the museum of **King John's Castle** and listen to recordings of John McCormack.
- Visit the **Church of St Peter and St Paul** and admire its stained-glass windows.

The monks: what they did, and why it mattered

What the ancient Celts lacked throughout their long history was a written tradition. Some would say it was by Druidic choice. For whatever the reason, they left few records, other than artefacts, and their culture remains for that reason mysterious and enigmatic. Irish became a written language only following the arrival of Christian missionaries bearing the precious gift of Latin and an alphabet. But after the time of *St Patrick*, anything worth preserving was written down and safeguarded in manuscript form in great houses or monastic libraries. For this reason, one of the major features of Irish history in the 6th century is the accelerated development of monastic sites and the associated development of Latin and literary culture. Indeed before the end of the century Ireland had become the chief seat of Latin learning; and by the 7th century, Irish monks had helped to bring about the beginnings of a written literature in the vernacular—the first such undertaking in northern Europe and one that predated by over six hundred years Dante's single-handed efforts to perform a similar service for Italian.

Of the Irish schools, the most famous were Armagh, Clonard, and Kildare, followed by Clonmacnoise, Bangor, Monasterboice, and Lismore. Organised like small towns in groups of monastic cells, there were nearly two hundred of them scattered throughout the country. Each had a head monk, with a hierarchy of scholars under him. In every school there was a scriptorium, where books were copied, and a library. The druidic lore· of the *filí* was orally taught, side by side with the classical language, and by the middle of the 7th century an adventurous monastic soul broke the Druidic taboo against the written form by committing to manuscript everything he had learnt in Irish as well as in Latin. This breakthrough marked the beginning of a rich and surprising fusion of native and Latin learning, releasing Irish literature into textual form and, by a process of imitation in Britain and Germany, helping to generate the development of vernacular written expression in western Europe.

Monks lived in hermits' cells, made from wood or dry stone and grouped around a small stone-roofed chapel, usually flanked by a slab or a cross marking the tomb of the founder. Little by little pilgrims and disciples made their way in increasing numbers into these hidden retreats and changed the character of monasteries from centres of meditation to university prototypes. In the 7th and 8th centuries students from England and the Continent poured into Irish schools, and the basic instruction provided in reading and writing (in Latin) made the monks forerunners of the revival of Latin culture throughout Britain, France, and a large part of Germany.

The familiar image of the mediaeval copyist monk bent over a lectern, made familiar to millions through *The Name of the Rose,* is but one side of the picture. As a 7th-century document, the Life of Colm Cille, shows, apart from their strictly religious duties monks had to perform down-to-earth agricultural tasks, such as looking after animals, expediting dairy chores, and supervising crops and gardens. They combined these practical demands with the copying of sacred texts and commentaries and the decoration of religious objects.

The material dimension of what might seem at first glance a purely spiritual or artistic activity such as manuscript illumination should not be lost sight of today. Each parchment used necessitated the rearing and slaughter of 150 calves. Appropriate sources for the beautiful coloured inks employed in the work of embellishment had to be found and exploited. The colour red, for example, was derived from red lead and cermes (a shield-louse extract); violet, purple and brown came from a Mediterranean plant; orpiment provided yellow, and verdigris the light-green tones; while areas in blue were coloured with a lapis luzuli pigment. Someone may have supplied all these items, but that supply had to be organised, and here again some monk or monks must have done all the

Cross of Clogher, Monaghan Museum.

development, the combined influence of the scribal and metal design traditions was to leave its mark on the carvings of the high crosses at Clonmacnoise. Here, ornament finally became subordinate to the human form and prepared the way for the arrival of Romanesque sculpture in continental Europe.

The obvious motivating force for the monks was art in the service of God. As the illuminated manuscripts show, they more than fulfilled their mandate in this respect. Slowly, however, more contemporary elements found their way onto the margins of the religious texts being copied. These could comprise poetic exercises of a spiritual kind but also included delightful poems celebrating nature, seasonal changes, and verse of a social and satirical nature, the writing of which probably helped relieve the tedium of many a dull winter's day for the monks concerned.

The output of artist-monks in metal, enamel and stone was no less remarkable than that of those who copied and illuminated manuscripts, as can be seen from the surviving bells, chalices, crosiers, crosses, reliquaries and brooches held in various museums. A cross-over point between the art of illumination and metal decoration is provided by the *cumhdachs* or book shrines made from the 9th to the 17th centuries. One of the most celebrated of these is the Cumhdach of St Molaise's Gospels (1001–1025), characterised by Byzantine figures of the Evangelists and filigree interlacing.

With the coming of the 9th century, the greatest creative period of Irish art was nearing its end. The illuminating monks (in both senses of the word) were emigrating to the Continent and preparing to make their contribution to the Carolingian Renaissance. In Ireland the successful creation of a completely original artistic mode of expression in the monasteries was about to give way in the 11th and 12th centuries to Hiberno-Romanesque decoration and a hybrid of Scandinavian and Irish influences in the field of metal design work. But the astonishing contribution of Irish monks, not only to Irish but to European culture, remains a subject of perennial fascination, even more so if one bears in mind that the movement that began as a project to set up places of isolation and retreat away from the world ended up changing those same places into spiritual and cultural centres for transforming it.

necessary donkey-work. Without reliable access to basic materials, no writing was possible.

A typical monastic institution, such as Clonmacnoise, was also a theological and secular entity, drawing large numbers of foreign students and functioning in many respects like a modern university system. Remarkably, students enjoyed free room and board—a situation likely to excite the envy of many a contemporary undergraduate. The monastic scriptorium preserved a great deal of vernacular literature, in addition to ensuring the copying of sacred texts. The monks working there performed an invaluable archival service for historians and literary scholars by faithfully recording genealogies and keeping annals. In the 11th-century Book of the Dun Cow—the earliest and most celebrated manuscript in Irish—they also incorporated early versions of the Voyage of Maoldún and the epic Táin Bó Chuaille, and even included in the collection a number of romantic tales in prose.

The illuminated manuscripts penned by the early Irish monks were in themselves artistic masterpieces, closely related to work in metal and sculpture. The Book of Kells in Trinity College, Dublin, reveals the same creative approach as the crosier of Clonmacnoise, its gold handle inlaid with silver patterns and animal motifs, on show in the National Museum. This inter-relationship of the decorative arts at the time makes it easier to understand why a good many of the motifs in illuminated manuscripts derive from the brilliant designs of earlier workers in metal. At a still later stage of

One of the most enjoyable drives in Ireland is that around the greatest of the Shannon's lakes, **Lough Derg**.

Setting out from **Limerick** by the Nenagh road (N7), the drive takes us left by **Parteen**, where, at **Ardnacrusha**, a huge hydro-electric dam was built between 1925 and 1929, turning the lake into a vast reservoir, the waters of which generate 350 kWh yearly. After Parteen, take a right onto the R465 to O'Brien's Bridge where the road reaches **Killaloe**, founded in the 6th century by *St Lua*. Near the town are the remains of the large ring-fort of **Béal Bórú**, from which *Brian Bórú* (926–1014) received his name . The restored cathedral, said to have been built in 1182 by *Dónall Mór Ó Briain*, features a doorway that led to the tomb of *Muircheartach Ó Briain*, king of Munster (*d.* 1120). On from Killaloe, by the lakeshore, the road passes through **Ogonnoloe** to **Tuamgraney**, with its romantic ruins of a 10th-century pre-Romanesque church and the 17th-century tower of **O'Grady's Castle**. The nearby **Raheen Estate** shelters an ancient oak wilderness and includes the epic Brian Bórú Oak, estimated to be a thousand years old and over 32 feet in circumference. **Scariff**, set back delightfully from the shore, is an important brown-trout fishing centre. **Mountshannon**, another favourite haunt of anglers, holds the national record (30.5 lb) for brown trout.

TOURING ROUTE
Lough Derg Drive

Game fisherman,
Lough Derg,
Co. Clare.

From here the T41 road passes through **Connagh** and **Power's Cross** to **Portumna**, a small agricultural and fishing centre beautifully situated between the Slieve Aughty and Slieve Bernagh mountains and including within its Forest Park **Portumna Castle**, an imposing Italianate residence of the Lords Clanrickard, and a restored 15th-century **Dominican friary**. At this stage one can either continue on through **Loughrea** to **Galway**, with the striking **Derryhiveny Castle** on the left, or drive through **Portland** and **Carrigahorig** to **Terryglass** on the R493. Here on the left lies the village of **Lorrha**, the site of a 6th-century foundation of *St Ruán*, destroyed by the Vikings under *Torgjest* or Turgesius in 844; and **Lorrha Castle**, a restored MacEgan tower-house. Terryglass, overlooking the eastern shores of the lake, is dominated by the ruins of a 17th-century Butler tower.

The lake shore route continues on via **Puckane** to **Dromineer Bay**, a fine boating centre, through **Portroe**, with its pleasant vistas and high-quality slate quarry in the Arra Mountains, to **Ballina** on the R494 road. The R483 return section then passes via Parteen once more, and back to Limerick.

Athlone and Lough Ree to Lough Allen

The pleasantly wooded **Lough Ree**, second-largest of the Shannon lakes, is bordered in the west by County Roscommon and in the east by Counties Longford and Westmeath. At the southern exit from the lake stands Athlone and facing it, at the northern extremity, the town of **Lanesboro**.

Between the Shannon and the River Suck to the west one comes upon green pastureland, rolling countryside, and lakes dotted with small islands. Livestock farming and fishing are the main activities. County Roscommon has a good touring centre in **Boyle**, close to **Lough Key Forest Park**, and boasts a restored Palladian mansion, **Strokestown Park House**, with its fascinating Famine museum. Physically its highest point, 1,385 feet (422 metres), lies in the north, on the County Leitrim border, with other pleasing elevations to the north-east (Curlew Mountains, 867 feet) and east (Slievebawn Hills, 864 feet).

Moving northwards by road from Athlone on the western side of the lake, the traveller encounters **Knockcrockery** (*Cnoc an Chrochaire*, 'hangman's hill')—a name that seems undeserved for such a quaint villa—famous for the manufacture of clay pipes. Facing it out on Lough Ree is **Inishcleraun**, where the Connacht queen *Méabh* is said to have been killed while she was bathing—a murderous act more than compensated for over the years by the founding of a monastery there by *St Diarmaid* in the year 540 and the erection of six churches.

An excursion to the west of Knockcrockery, just two miles from Athleague at **Castlestrange**, brings us to one of the best examples of Celtic La Tène spiral-decorated stones in Europe, and not far from this again to **Donamon Castle**, one of the oldest inhabited buildings in Ireland. The road back towards Lough Ree traverses the town of **Roscommon** and

Parke's Castle,
on Lough Gill,
Co. Leitrim.

carries on to **Lanesboro**, a thriving country town with many facilities for casual visitors and tourists alike.

This is County Longford, one of the prettiest of the midland counties. An area of farmlands and brown bog with occasional low hills and pleasant views of hill and river, it boasts a surprising number of literary celebrities for its size. These range from *Pádraic Colum*, the poet, to *Maria Edgeworth*, author of *Castle Rackrent*, who entertained *Walter Scott* and *William Wordsworth* here. In its downward course the Shannon passes close to **Longford**, the county town—spaciously laid out with wide, pleasant streets.

Continuing the journey up-river brings us past **Lough Key Forest Park** with its 3-mile-wide lake. Only a few miles distant is **Carrick-on-Shannon**, the county town of County Leitrim, a river-cruising town and one of Ireland's top coarse-angling centres, with bream, rudd, roach, tench and pike on offer. In its time it was also a busy terminal for deliveries of timber, cement, hardware, and stout, coming by waterway from Athlone, Limerick, and Dublin.

County Leitrim can be thought of as divided into two parts, almost wholly separated from one another by **Lough Allen**, a lake formed by the broadening of the Shannon as it moves towards Drumshanbo. Its striking scenic beauty tends to be underrated. South of Lough Allen lies an area of *drumlins* or small hills, interspersed with fresh-water pools; on the eastern side stands the impressive **Slieve Anierin**, with mountainous landscape stretching to the north as well. The drive round Lough Allen is highly recommended, and **Glencar Lake and Waterfall** and the **Creevelea Friary** should not be missed. **Drumshanbo**, on the southern shore of Lough Allen, is another fishing and boating centre, with an impressive set of amenities for families on holiday.

Until recently the Shannon was navigable to a short distance above the town of Carrick, but the reopening in 1994 of the restored **Ballyconnell–Ballinamore Canal** has extended the navigable area from the village of Leitrim across the border and into Lough Erne in County Fermanagh. Purists, however, who insist on pursuing a river to its natural source and reject the idea of human extensions have the choice of continuing on north of Lough Allen into County Cavan, where they will come upon the mythical **Shannon Pot** on the southern slopes of the Cuilcagh Mountain.

Boyle and environs

Lough Key and **Lough Gara** are natural extensions of the Shannon waterway, linked to one another by the Boyle River. On the northern bank of the river lies **Boyle**, a fine 19th-century garrison town, pleasantly situated at the base of the Curlew Mountains.

In the eyes of many, Lough Key is the most beautiful of the lakes comprising the Shannon system—especially where fishermen are concerned. It hosts many international fishing contests, and its reputation in this respect was certainly enhanced by the landing on its shores of a 39 lb pike in 1992.

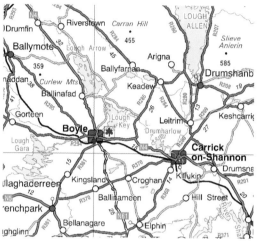

On **Trinity Island** in the lake are the ruins of the **Abbey of the Trinity**, founded by the White Canons, an order set up by *St Norbert* of France in the 12th century. But the island (in earlier times controlled by the King family) also indirectly evokes *John Milton*. Following the death by drowning of one of the sons of the King family with whom he was studying at Cambridge, Milton wrote 'Lycidas' and ensured both his and King's immortality. An even earlier literary association of the island is that concerning the compilation here of the Annals of Boyle, a record of battles fought in the area to ward off attackers and invaders.

On nearby **Castle Island** the famous Annals of Lough Key (beginning with the year 1041) were compiled. These are now preserved in Trinity College, Dublin. The island contains a gable and church door from a 9th-century monastery and a 19th-century castle built on the site of an earlier fortified construction belonging to the MacDermots. Castle Island is also the place where Úna MacDermot was imprisoned by her family to prevent her marrying Thomas Láidir McCostello, a young man from a rival family. After she had died from unhappiness and other, more mortal afflictions, her lover swam each evening to the island until, like Joyce's Michael Furey, he succeeded in falling ill with pneumonia. His death-bed wish was to be buried alongside his beloved. This was granted, and in a poignant memento of sentimental gardening, two rose-trees grew over their common grave, becoming gradually entwined in a lover's knot. Many years later *William Butler Yeats*, himself a lover of transcendental roses, hatched plans to found a secret order on the island, but, unlike the rose-trees of Úna and Thomas, his never flowered.

Close to the southern shore of the lake stand the remains and outbuildings of **Rockingham House**, originally designed by *John Nash* of London and now part of an updated tourist restaurant and parking complex serving as a focal point for visiting and viewing the magnificent 800-acre **Forest Park**. A good platform from which to survey the surrounding countryside is the top deck of the more recently built **Moylurg Tower**. An additional attraction of the park is its richness in archaeological remains, ranging from **Carrowkeel Court Cairn** to various ring-forts and subterranean chambers.

Boyle Abbey,
Co. Roscommon.

Half way between Boyle and Ballaghaderreen, Lough Key's sister lake, **Lough Gara**, is both a good spot for catching trout and an archaeological treasure-trove. Finds include 338 crannógs, 31 dug-out boats, and many implements and ornaments. On the right of the road, westward from Boyle, is one of the largest portal tombs in Ireland. The tablestone—nearly 16 by 13 feet—was formerly supported on five upright pillars.

Boyle is justly celebrated as the site of Ireland's most impressive 12th-century Cistercian abbey. It was founded by *Abbot Maurice O'Duffy* in 1161 and is closely associated with the great abbey of Mellifont, County Louth (set up in 1142 by fellow-monks of *St Bernard of Clairvaux*). The abbey is well preserved and provides a pleasing mix of Gothic asceticism on one side of the nave relieved by flanking Romanesque arches on the other. Also worth examining in detail are the decorative carvings of men and animals on the capitals.

The recent restoration of **King House**, the former residence of *Sir Henry King MP*, in the centre of Boyle has added considerably to the tourist appeal of the town. A splendid 18th-century house, its importance was underlined for the townspeople by its ensuring that Boyle's Main Street led directly to its doors. At present the house maintains a visual exhibition offering fascinating insights into the history of a family that was by turn oppressive and supportive of the native Irish, from the iniquitous point of departure when *Sir John King* was rewarded with land for 'reducing the natives to obedience' up to more recent times.

DON'T MISS

- Don't miss the ruins of **Boyle Abbey**, a Cistercian house of the 12th century.
- See the 18th-century **King House**, the restored mansion of Henry King and now an interpretative centre.
- Don't miss **Lough Key Forest Park** (2 miles east of Boyle), a great place for picnics, walking, and exploring Ireland's prehistoric past.

ALL-WEATHER OPTIONS

- Visit **Frenchpark**, where Douglas Hyde, first President of Ireland, was born and is buried, with its museum and interpretative centre.

TAX FREE SHOPPING *'Don't forget to pick up your Global Refund Tax Free Shopping Cheques as you shop.'* www.globalrefund.ie

GLOBAL REFUND

The N4 road from Carrick-on-Shannon to Drumod crosses the river at **Jamestown**. This town, incorporated by *King James I,* was the scene of a synod in 1650 and also of a successful raid by *Patrick Sarsfield* during the Jacobite wars. The Shannon here forms a loop and is crossed again at **Drumsna**, a village set in the midst of delightful scenery. Further on the river expands on the right into **Lough Boderg** and **Lough Bofin**. On the shores of Lough Bofin is **Drumod**, formerly noted for its ironworks. About 2 miles further south is **Rooskey**, at the point where the river emerges from Lough Bofin. The main road continues on to **Longford**, where the N5 road can be taken to begin the loop back to Carrick, via Scramoge and Strokestown.

Strokestown, a 19th-century market town famous for its **Park House, Famine Museum**, and coarse fishing, is an enticing place for a stop. The area has several crannógs of great antiquity, and the town's handcraft market and craft centre constitute additional incentives for

TOURING ROUTE
Carrick-on-Shannon and Lough Allen area

taking a break here.

From Strokestown the R368 proceeds northwards to **Elphin**, which has been the seat of a bishopric for more than 1,500 years. According to legend, *St Patrick* founded a religious establishment in the area. About a mile north-west is **Smith Hill**, the birthplace, according to some, of *Oliver Goldsmith*. The road runs on from Elphin through **Killukin** and back to Carrick.

Lough Allen drive
The circuit of Lough Allen may be made from Drumshanbo by following the R207 road, which skirts the eastern shore of the lake to **Dowra**, a little town on the boundary of Counties Cavan and Leitrim. This road hugs the lakeshore, crossing a number of streams that rush down from the overhanging mountains. At Dowra it crosses the River Shannon (only a few miles from its source). On the island of

Inismagrath, near the northern end of the lake, are the ruins of a church said to have been founded by *St Beoaodh*. At **Tarmon**, near the west shore, are the ruins of a church believed to have been founded by one of the O'Rourkes.

At **Drumkeeran** the R200 bends southwards and becomes the R280; it soon enters **Roscommon**, with the **Arigna Mountains** prominent on the right. The district around Lough Allen is noted for its veins of coal and iron, and Arigna is one of the few places in Ireland where coal was mined. The route continues on through the small town of **Mountallen**, curving gently round the lake to rejoin Drumshanbo.

River Inny at Abbeyshrule,
Co. Longford.

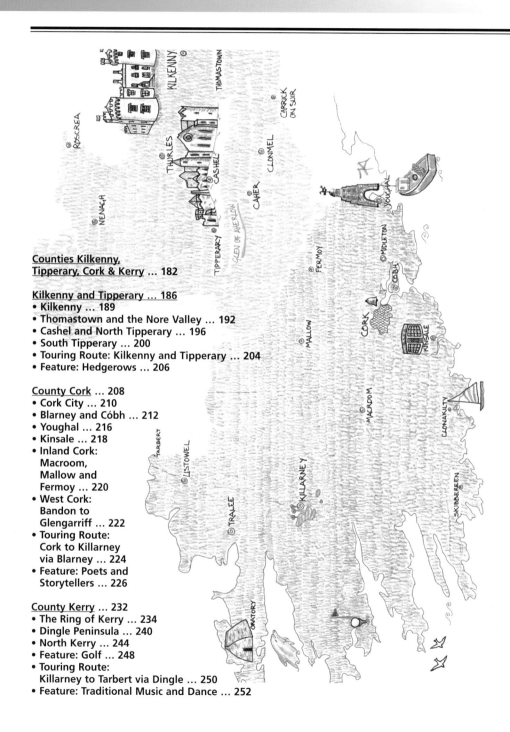

Parknasilla,
Co. Kerry.

Counties Kilkenny, Tipperary, Cork & Kerry

In this attractive southern region, Counties Kilkenny and Tipperary stand out distinctly from Counties Cork and Kerry. The differences are in part the effect of landscape and situation and in part the effect of history.

Rich farmland with a limestone base irrigated by the Rivers Suir, Nore and Barrow, and the calm inland setting of Kilkenny and Tipperary, make for rustic peace and tranquillity. County Tipperary consists of a central flatland flanked on its western side by a continuous hilly relief and ending towards the south-east with the Comeragh Mountains. Binding it all together is the River Suir, running southwards like a silver thread from Thurles in the north, then banking eastwards past Cahir, Clonmel and Carrick-on-Suir to exit in Waterford city harbour. County Kilkenny is also characterised by fertile low-lying farmland, with pleasant river-valley views in the south. It too is a river-dominated county, marked by the River Nore, which moves through Kilkenny, then slants south-eastwards past Thomastown to join forces with the Barrow at New Ross in County Wexford before discharging itself alongside the Suir in Waterford estuary.

In physical geography, the contrast between these two counties and Cork and Kerry is one between counties of exclusively inland pasture and seascape counties with extensive farming areas. County Cork, the largest county in Ireland, is characterised in the east and north by limestone land, traversed by extended east-west sandstone ridges. The region's hallmark is the succession of pleasant river valleys created by the River Blackwater and its tributaries. Southwards, romantic fishing-ports like Youghal and Kinsale illustrate the continuous appeal of the coastline, which, as it moves towards County Kerry, gives rise to rugged peninsulas, impressive deep-set bays

dotted with islands, and luxuriant sub-tropical vegetation in its sheltered reaches.

Apart from a small area of low-lying ground spreading out towards the Shannon estuary at its northern end, County Kerry combines stunning lake and mountain scenery with attractive stretches of sand set between bluff cliffs and jutting headlands. Its three promontories, Beara, Iveragh, and Dingle, stretch into the Atlantic like three hill-backed terrestrial fingers. The rain-swept intensity of Atlantic storms, the temperate warmth of Gulf Stream waters, a profusion of sub-tropical trees and plants, an abundance of golden beaches, endless gradations of light and colour induced by subtle changes in sea and sky—Kerry has it all. From the yellow of furze and stubble, not forgetting the festive red-and-purple fuchsia and the gorgeous pink clumps of heather on the side of mountain roads, to the rich greens of pasture and headland and the calming purple, blue and grey of ocean skies, the colour range of the county is exceptional. Given that it is also home to red deer and wild salmon, and blessed with all that one could ask in lake, sea and mountain scenery, it is one of the most attractive holiday areas in the country: a fishing, climbing, swimming paradise.

Historically and culturally, both Kilkenny and Tipperary are marked by the 12th-century seizing of lands in those counties by the Anglo-Norman Butler family, Earls of Ormonde. The Butlers actively promoted the Norman cause before switching allegiance to the English crown, though even this allegiance in many ways diminished with time as a result of intermarriage with the native Irish.

As the most beautiful inland and mediaeval town in Ireland, Kilkenny still stands today as a fully realised implementation of Norman ideals and values. This heritage dates back to the

Sybil Point,
Dingle Peninsula,
Co. Kerry.

building programme undertaken in the period 1200–45 and was consolidated by the order, rigour and stability of successive administrations from that time on. It is something that Kilkenny people have safeguarded with pride.

The playful imputation to the local people of spitefulness ('Kilkenny cats') is best seen in relation to the dominant literary qualities of the well-known writers educated at Kilkenny College, itself an Ormonde foundation. No strangers to controversy themselves, Congreve, Berkeley and Swift all had sharp intellects characterised by comic wit, metaphysical clarity and satirical inventiveness, respectively. Their focused, incisive mental attitudes would seem to have rubbed off on local people (or vice versa).

In contrast, County Tipperary never had a centre that housed an Irish parliament, as Kilkenny did in the 14th century, when only Dublin outranked it in national importance. Turbulent Tipp, as it is sometimes called— because of its former reputation for market-day fights—has less civic *gravitas* than Kilkenny but is characterised by an equal passion for the soil, marts, and stud farms. This passion tended to erupt at times of landlord-tenant confrontation when the Whiteboy movement became especially active and groups of white-smocked tenant-farmers settled scores with their landlords. Badly hit by the Great Famine, County Tipperary's population declined dramatically

The South

Parknasilla, Co. Kerry.

than Tipperary and Kilkenny to preserve the Irish language and culture. The persistence of the Catholic 'big house' in Counties Kerry and Cork into the 18th century created favourable conditions for the continued speaking of Irish and meant that the traditions of Irish poetry and literature prevailed, in spite of the legal and institutional interdictions ranged against them. The well-known term 'Hidden Ireland' hints at the subtle cultural aspects of national identity that make both counties historically unique. Often referred to as the Kingdom, Kerry is in some ways the Texas of Ireland. Its people are immensely proud of the attention it receives for its natural beauty, rejoice in their own reputation as independent, fair-minded people, and seek daily to perpetuate their standing as practitioners of millennial courtesies and guardians of a tart and puckish sense of humour.

County Cork has a more troubled and revolutionary tradition than Kerry. As the maritime history of the area shows, a number of revolutionary expeditions attempted to land on the south coast, but without success, as the disastrous expeditions to Bantry Bay and Kinsale demonstrate. In more recent times Michael Collins, a great national hero, was born in the vicinity of Clonakilty, County Cork. Ironically enough, his fate was to be killed in a Civil War ambush in his own county. This is not to say that County Kerry did not produce its own share of political and military activists: it did. And where political power is concerned, Tipperary's own ancient site of consecration at Thurles speaks for itself. In County Kilkenny, on the other hand, the mood was more parliamentary, and after the Normans and the Gaels banded together, the spirit of compromise was always sought, if not always obtained, in dealings with the ruling English. But in the Cork character to this day lies a deep-seated distrust of officialdom and power, regardless of the guise in which it presents itself. For Corkmen traditionally there was only one solution to colonial occupation: to oppose it in arms. Hence its deserved reputation as the rebel county.

from 435,000 to 239,000 in the space of twenty years, but today its fortunes have changed radically, and from the 1960s onwards it has enjoyed an enduring prosperity from dairy-farming.

Being further removed from the centres of authority and power, and larger in scope, Counties Cork and Kerry were less amenable to colonial pressures and found it easier

Sunrise at the Old Head of Kinsale,
Co. Cork.

Counties Kilkenny and Tipperary

native Irish. Many remains of Anglo-Norman castles are still visible in the Nore and Barrow valleys, and in the town of Kilkenny the 12th-century castle of the Ormondes is one of their finest achievements. An outstanding heritage county, more marked by successful preservation of its mediaeval past than anything else, the ancient and the modern do nonetheless co-exist here quite happily, as the placing of the Kilkenny Design Workshop in the former stables of Kilkenny Castle amply testifies.

Today, County Kilkenny has succeeded in striking a fine balance by turning its glorious past into a permanent tourist asset, while continuing to pursue its prosperous agricultural destiny. Ancient round towers, monasteries and storied castles are only part of its ancient splendour: it also possesses fine prehistoric sites, incised crosses, megalithic tombs, underground chambers and, at Haroldstown in the south, one of the largest portal tombs in Ireland. On the contemporary side, the county has established a reputation for pottery and design, apparent not only in the county town but also in the spongeware produced at Bennettsbridge. It has also been building a reputation for cultural dynamism, particularly visible, for example, in the innovative and diverse arts festival held

Kilkenny is a well-wooded and well-cultivated county, irrigated by three rivers: the Barrow, the Suir, and the Nore. An undulating limestone plain occupies the central section of the county. To the north are the attractive uplands of the Castlecomer district, while on the Tipperary border to the west, Kilkenny is framed by the Slieveardagh Hills and the Booley Hills. The Nore and Barrow valleys constitute very agreeable landscapes, and for those travelling on foot or by bike, the South Leinster Way passes through many of the most beautiful of them.

The county name, *Cill Chainnigh*, means Church of St Canice; and just as Tipperary has its Cashel and its Holycross, Kilkenny has its outstanding monuments in the castle, cathedral, and Jerpoint Abbey. However, though both Tipperary and Kilkenny were under Butler control for much of their history, in Kilkenny the Anglo-Normans left more enduring and tangible evidence than elsewhere of their presence and their interaction with the

186

each August in the town of Kilkenny. With some of the richest lime-based pastures in the country, especially in the Golden Vale to the south, County Tipperary is synonymous with successful livestock-rearing, dairy farming, and horse-breeding. Set between the Rivers Shannon and Suir and with the eastern shore of Lough Derg creating the impression of an ocean view, it is bounded by Counties Offaly and Laois to the north, Kilkenny to the east, Waterford and Cork to the south, and Limerick, Clare and Galway to the west. This proximity to other counties suggests that it's not such a long way to Tipperary. On the contrary, the largest of Ireland's inland counties benefits greatly from its central position and offers easy access from any point in the country.

St Canice's Cathedral, Kilkenny.

Physically, County Tipperary is a microcosm of what the relief map shows for Ireland: mainly flat in the centre, and surrounded by mountains on its perimeter. The most decorative of these are the Knockmealdown and sandstone Galty Mountains extending across the border between the south-western part of the county and County Limerick. The broad central plain is traversed north to south by the River Suir, with nearly every town of consequence in the county being situated on it, or on one of its tributaries.

Dominated politically throughout most of its history by the Earls of Ormonde, County Tipperary is today divided into a North and South Riding, with Nenagh and Clonmel as the administrative centres for the north and south of the county, respectively. But well in advance of British occupation of the area, the county's prestige was demonstrated by the fact that Cashel was chosen as the seat of the kings of Munster. This was long before St Patrick turned it into a bishopric and laid the groundwork for later exclusive church possession of the site.

The massive 15th-century fortress of Cahir Castle placed on a rocky island beside a bridge over the River Suir underlines the importance of the county historically. And the magnetic drawing power of Holycross Abbey, Tipperary's third great national monument, is a matter of historical record. Thousands upon thousands of pilgrims made their way here in bygone centuries to pay their respects to the presumed relics of the cross of Christ; and now that the abbey has been restored, this power is evident once more—not with pilgrims this time but with tourists.

Kilkenny Castle,
night view.

Kilkenny

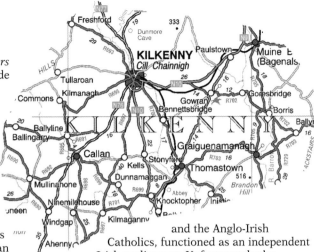

The limestone effigies of *Piers and Margaret Butler* lying side by side in **St Canice's Cathedral** have the perennial appeal of Egyptian mummies. At the same time, their serene sculpted forms epitomise Kilkenny's tasteful preservation of important elements from the Anglo-Norman Middle Ages. If Kilkenny is rightly known as the Marble City, then one can speak here of marbled presences, because when limestone is highly polished it acquires the black, shiny allure characteristic of this strikingly statuesque couple.

In Norman times Kilkenny had two townships, Irishtown, which had its charter from the Bishops of Ossory, and Englishtown, set up by the Earl of Pembroke, William Marshal. The two were joined together in 1843.

Two historically memorable epochs stand out in the town's history. The first was the period of Norman construction and expansion from the 12th to the 14th century, during which it was ravaged by the Black Death (1348–9) and served as the venue for many parliaments, the most notable of which was that of 1366, which passed the infamous Statutes of Kilkenny. These made it high treason for an Anglo-Norman to marry an Irishwoman, prevented Irishmen from living in a walled town, and penalised any Anglo-Norman who adopted the language, customs or dress of the Irish. They were rigorously enforced but failed to prevent the Normans from eventually becoming 'more Irish than the Irish themselves.'

The second notable era was from 1642 to 1648, when the Confederation of Kilkenny, representing both the old Irish and the Anglo-Irish Catholics, functioned as an independent Irish parliament. Unfortunately the confederation soon split into two camps. The Anglo-Irish made a treaty with the English Viceroy, and following the death of Owen Roe O'Neill, leader of the old Irish, defeat was inevitable. In 1650 Cromwell attacked the town, and it surrendered.

Kilkenny Castle, the fortress of the Butlers, stands on a fine natural site overlooking the two fords of the River Nore at the southern extremity of the town. It was put up in the 13th century in place of an earlier motte fortress erected by Strongbow. Though the object of many reconstructions since, it has seen seven hundred years of continuous occupation and still retains the lines of a mediaeval fortress. In 1936 the Butlers vacated the castle, and in 1967 the family presented it to the citizens of Kilkenny, and it has been in state care ever since. The present structure forms three sides of a quadrangle, and three of the four original round corner towers remain. The Long Gallery, with its mixed Celtic and pre-Raphaelite motifs, paintings by *Lely* and *van Dyck* and Butler family portraits, is especially striking. Another outstanding feature is a hammerbeam roof of Norwegian timber, as well as four Gobelin tapestries designed by *Rubens*. The imposing castle has a subterranean side as well as a tunnel under the road leading to the stables. What for, one may ask? A quick getaway? Not at all. It was to permit the 19th-century staff of ninety-three servants to appear and disappear with diffident if mysterious regularity, but never to be conspicuously present.

The **Butler Gallery**, housed within the castle, holds exhibitions of modern art; and the 18th-century stables now contain the **Design Centre**, a top-quality work and display venue for Irish arts and crafts.

St Canice's (Anglican) Cathedral overlooks the northern end of the town. The present building replaced a small Hiberno-Romanesque church, and before

that an early monastic settlement existed on the site. Only the 100-foot round tower (admire the view from the top) survives from the monastery period (AD 700–1000), when it served a double function as belfry and place of refuge in times of danger. Begun between 1202 and 1218 along Early Gothic lines, the cathedral was completed in the period 1260–86. The earliest part is the chancel, possibly completed before 1220. Ireland's second-largest cathedral, it has the finest surviving early Gothic doorway in Ireland. Highly polished grave-slabs are a feature of the walls and floor. One of these, inscribed in Norman French, refers to *Jose Kyteler*, who is presumed to

Rothe House, Kilkenny.

be the father of *Alice Kyteler*, who had the doubtful pleasure of being tried for witchcraft in 1323. She escaped with her life, but her servant, *Petronilla*, paid the supreme price for the suspicions surrounding her mistress and in 1324 was burnt at the stake for her loyalty.

The **Black Abbey**, or Convent of the One and Undivided Trinity, forms part of a Franciscan friary founded in 1225. It was dissolved in 1543 and converted for use as a courthouse, but by the end of the 18th century it had ceased to be used for that purpose and became a roofless ruin. It was partially restored and roofed in 1778. Then in the 19th century it was fully opened for public worship. The south transept has some delicate 14th-century window-tracery decoration, especially the five-light Rosary window. Outside in the graveyard are ten stone coffins from the 13th and 14th centuries.

The grounds of **St Francis Abbey Brewery**, a Smithwick's brewery now taken over by Guinness, contain the ruined tower and chancel of **St Francis Abbey**, a foundation dating from 1234. The decorative window contains seven graduated lights.

One of Kilkenny's oldest mansions, **Rothe House**, was built by a leading merchant, *John Rothe*, in 1594. It played a central role as a meeting-place for religious and political leaders at the time of the Confederation and is made up of three restored buildings opening onto courtyards. Today it functions as a museum, with hand-carved oak furniture and a collection of costumes, but also doubles as a depository for the collections of the **Kilkenny Archaeological Society**.

Among Kilkenny's other well-known landmarks is **St Mary's (Catholic) Cathedral**, built in 1849, with a high tower and statues of the Virgin by *Giovanni Benzoni*.

The **Shee Almshouse**, founded in 1582 by *Sir Richard Shee*, survived as a charitable institution for three centuries. It is one of the few remaining 16th-century almshouses in Ireland and now houses the tourist office and a 20-minute **Cityscope** exhibition, providing an insight into mid-17th-century Kilkenny.

Other historical buildings include the **Tholsel** or toll house. Erected in 1761, it has a strange clock-tower and a front arcade over the pavement. **St John's Priory** was founded in 1200 but devastated by Cromwell; all that remains is a roofless chancel, a fine seven-light window, and a mediaeval tomb. Nearby **Kilkenny College**, dating from 1666, educated *Jonathan Swift* and the philosopher *George Berkeley* but is now in use as Kilkenny's County Hall.

DON'T MISS
- Don't miss **St Canice's Cathedral** with its fine timberwork and stone carvings, round tower, and splendid sepulchral monuments.
- Storm **Kilkenny Castle**, the mediaeval bastion of the Dukes of Ormonde. A dramatic mix of Gothic, Classical and Tudor, set on high ground above the river, it sums up centuries of history and sets the tone for the contemporary town.

ALL-WEATHER OPTIONS
- When bewitching weather is unavailable in Kilkenny, bewitch yourself by following the trail of Alice Kyteler, the town's reputed witch, to her old home at **Kyteler's Inn**. Inside, effigies of witches and other memorabilia ensure that her broomstick reputation is maintained.
- Relive the drama of political intrigue in Confederate times at **Rothe House**, and enjoy local museum exhibits and a small costume collection.
- When there's no scope for hope with the weather, there's always **Cityscope**, a display re-creating 17th-century Kilkenny in the Shee Almshouse.

The South

Thomastown and the Nore Valley

On the west bank of the River Nore, a mile to the south-west of Thomastown, is one of the most impressive monastic ruins in Ireland, **Jerpoint Abbey**. In the 16th century it suffered the fate of many monastic institutions of the period by being suppressed and abandoned, but between the time of its foundation (1160) and its untimely suppression it flourished as a self-sufficient Cistercian daughter-house, with its own infirmary, granary, stables, water mill, outhouses, and gardens. Conceived in line with the typical Cistercian architectural plan of a central cloistered garden and a cruciform layout with aisled nave and two chapels in each transept, Jerpoint Abbey's classical proportions and warm oat-coloured stone compose a perfect meditative setting. Originally set up by *Dónall Mac Giolla Phádraig*, king of Ossory, and colonised from Baltinglass in 1180, it was affiliated with a Yorkshire abbey in line with the Anglicising policy of the Anglo-Normans. However, after more than a century this strict policy began to fall apart, and the abbot of Jerpoint was fined for accepting Irish monks, in contravention of the Statutes of Kilkenny.

The oldest sections of the building are the Hiberno-Romanesque transepts and chancel, where the effigy of *Bishop Felix O'Dullany* (died 1202) represents him holding a crosier that is being gnawed by a serpent. A fine central tower was added in the 15th century, but the east window, with its delicate tracery, is a 14th-century insertion. The restored cloister pillars are decorated with fine sculpted figures of knights and ladies, bishops, dragons, and an unhappy-looking dyspeptic monk clutching his stomach. From the south transept, wooden steps, used by the monks to descend for night office, lead back to the roof of the east range of the monastic buildings, from which there is a clear view of the Dublin–Waterford railway.

Thomastown was the seat of the kings of Ossory. It is named after *Thomas FitzAnthony*, Seneschal of Leinster, who circled it with a wall in the early 13th century and erected a castle as well. He then built a further castle, **Grenan**, along the River Nore. Some fragments of the mediaeval walls survive, as does the partly ruined **Church of St Mary** (13th century) and **Mullins Castle** by the town bridge. The high altar from Jerpoint Abbey is preserved in the local Catholic church. While the main street is an attractive mix of shops and pubs, the town suffers from being situated on the noisy Dublin–Waterford road. As a relief from traffic it offers the **Water Garden**, a walk flanked by herbaceous borders and interspersed with pleasant fountains. A section of the nearby **Mount Juliet Estate** has been turned into a championship golf course by *Jack Nicklaus*. At the centre of the estate is an 18th-century manor-house, now a hotel, whose residents can also avail of the riverside park and lovely walled gardens.

South-east of Thomastown is the picturesque and photogenic village of **Inistioge**. It has a charming 18th-century bridge of ten arches spanning the River Nore, and the ruins of an Augustinian priory founded in 1210. Apart from these it has two important poles of attraction: a tree-lined square surrounded by gaily painted cottages, and the river frontage with lawns running down to the river's edge. Inistioge possesses lots of appeal for film directors in search of a quiet, timeless locale with atmosphere. Mia Farrow's *Widow's Peak* was made here in 1993, and a year later it was the turn of Maeve Binchy's *Circle of Friends* and following that *Where the Sun is King* in 1996.

The climb upwards to **Woodstock Park**, the Tighe family estate, whose superb 18th-century house was destroyed during the Civil War in 1922, is well worth while. The park has the longest monkey-puzzle avenue in Europe.

To the south of Thomastown lies **Dysart Castle**, the birthplace of the famous 18th-

St. Canice's Cathedral
Kilkenny.

architectural style has been dubbed Early English, and it is the largest of the Irish Cistercian buildings. It has a long stone nave, with high clerestory windows. The effigy of a 13th-century knight, resurrected from the ruins, has been placed near the entrance door.

At **Ullard,** 3 miles north of Graiguenamanagh, the ruins of a 12th-century Romanesque church are to be seen, along with granite carvings on the doorway. A 9th-century granite high cross bearing biblical scenes is set beside the church.

Gowran, the seat of the kings of Ossory, is now a village with a racecourse—a natural transition, one might argue, given that horse-racing is the 'sport of kings'. As early as the 13th century the lands were acquired by the Anglo-Norman *Theobald Fitzwalter,* ancestor of the Butlers. **Gowran Castle** was besieged by Cromwellian forces in 1650. Following capitulation, the castle was burnt and its entire garrison, with the exception of one officer, shot. The old Gowran collegiate church dating from 1260 has been incorporated in the 19th-century **St Mary's (Protestant) Church.**

The village of **Kells**, just 8 miles south of Kilkenny and beside the King's River (a branch of the Nore), is the site of one of the most impressive monastic remains in Ireland. Some of the priory ruins date from 1193, but most are from the 15th century. Apart from the fortified gatehouse, seven square towers connected one to another by the protective walls form the framework for the **Augustinian abbey** and the old chapel and house foundations that lie within them. Despite the strong defensive arrangements, little remains of the original monastic buildings created by *Geoffrey de Marisco* and four Augustinian canons from Bodmin in Cornwall, but what has survived is enough to give a strong sense of how difficult it must have been to ensure autonomy and survival for a mediaeval walled settlement. With this Kells there is no book, only the language of broken stones: the other Kells, synonymous with vellum and illumination, is in County Meath.

Work of the Kilkenny potter Nicholas Mosse.

century philosopher *George Berkeley,* who gave his name to a Californian university and his ideas to God.

North-eastwards, **Graiguenamanagh** (*Gráig na Manach*, the monks' village), with the Blackstairs Mountains as backdrop, is situated on a bend of the River Barrow beside the border with County Carlow. At one time it was an important ecclesiastical site; today it is a thriving market-town. Founded by the *Earl of Pembroke,* the 13th-century Cistercian Abbey of **Duiske** (now a Catholic church) occupies a good deal of the present town area. In 1774 the tower collapsed, but since then the abbey has been restored to its original splendour. Its

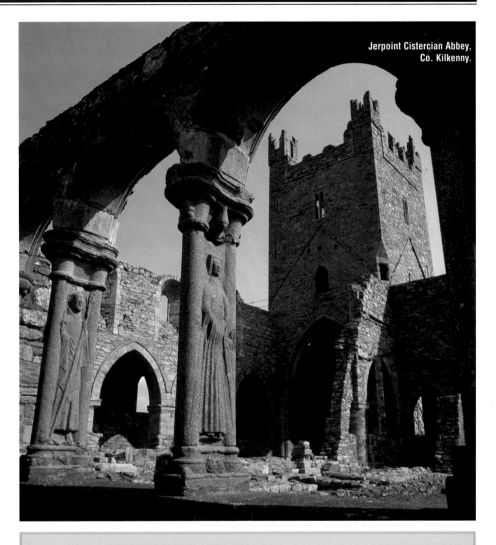

Jerpoint Cistercian Abbey, Co. Kilkenny.

DON'T MISS

- A visit to **Jerpoint Abbey** on the River Nore is a must—the most interesting and best-preserved Cistercian ruins in the country, with sculpted lords and ladies in the cloisters.
- Make a trip to **Kells** to compare Jerpoint Abbey with the Augustinian abbey here—another impressive monastic site with striking architectural remains.

ALL-WEATHER OPTIONS

- Cross the charm of an 18th-century village with cinematographic celebrity and you have **Inistioge**, still an unspoilt setting, with interesting churches and tree-lined walks between the showers.
- See Graiguenamanagh's **Duiske Abbey**, where the 13th-century interior of the building has been well restored and a splendid Romanesque doorway is well worth the visit.
- At **Jerpoint Glass Studio** watch beautifully shaped glassware being made by hand.

Cashel and North Tipperary

By far the most inspirational national monument in County Tipperary, the **Rock of Cashel** has something of the perennial quality of all rocks, including that of St Peter. Like the original, the Rock of Cashel gave rise to a church, and the finest 12th-century Romanesque chapel in the country is still standing on it. But before that, from 370 to 1101, it represented the seat of Munster kings and rivalled Tara in grandeur. It was here in 978 that *Brian Bórú* was made high king—an occasion on

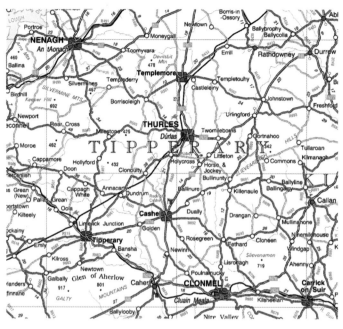

which he also declared it his capital. Thanks, however, to *St Patrick's* baptising of the king *Aonghas*, the ground was already laid for the later predominance of church over state—a constant of Irish political life up to recent times. In 1101 *Muircheartach Ó Briain* officially presented the Rock to the church in order to curry favour with the bishops and in the belief that none of the MacCarthys, with whom they disputed its suzerainty, would ever have the gall to ask the clerical authorities for its return. Taking their defeat gracefully, the MacCarthys moved to Cork and as a gesture of good will constructed the magnificent **Cormac's Chapel** on the site before leaving.

Though the Rock suffered through the centuries from many acts of desecration, the worst of these occurred in 1647 when *Lord Inchiquin*, seeking the presidency of Munster under Cromwellian auspices, attacked Cashel. Many terrified townspeople fled for refuge to the Rock but were pursued.

In a calculated act of terror, Lord Inchiquin had sods of turf piled against the cathedral walls, and in the ensuing fire hundreds of innocent people were roasted to death.

For a twenty-year period in the 18th century the Rock was taken over by the Protestant Church, but in 1749 the Anglican Bishop of Cashel decided to remove the cathedral to the town. Damage from the elements and a history of neglect led to a gradual degradation of the site, before it was finally declared a national monument in 1874 and carefully restored.

The most attractive item in the arresting *corps de bâtiment* perched on top of the Rock is Cormac's Chapel. The chapel, begun by *Cormac Mac Carthaigh*, King and Bishop of Cashel in 1127, was consecrated in 1134. It presents a cruciform appearance, because of the square towers set at the junction of nave and chancel. The exterior walls are faced with blank arcading, capitals and corbels, with a high gable over the doorway to the

Rock of Cashel,
Co. Tipperary.

north. Though described as Hiberno-Romanesque, the chapel seems to have been influenced by Continental ornamental tradition and construction methods. Inside is an 11th-century stone sarcophagus, decorated with an unusual design of ribbons and interlacing serpents. A gilt crosier head (the Cormac crosier) found within the sarcophagus, and now held by the National Museum in Dublin, has been identified as late 13th-century French. It contains animals and fish worked in enamel, turquoise, and sapphire.

The 13th-century **Cathedral of St Patrick** is an aisle-less cruciform building with a central tower, an extremely long choir, an exceedingly short nave, and two east chapels in each transept. The wrought work of the chancel windows is in yellow sandstone, in contrast to the grey limestone of the rest of the building. **Cormac's Chapel** abuts on the south transept, from which winding steps rise to the summit roof-walk of the cathedral's central tower. On the south wall of the choir is the wall-tomb of *Archbishop*

Miler MacGrath, who changed his religious beliefs several times during his hundred years; but, as the wall-tomb unequivocally shows, when it came to the long haul, he ended up on the side of the angels!

The building known as the **Hall of the Vicars-Choral** (15th century) was the residence of the laymen or minor canons who assisted in the cathedral services. It now houses a museum, with St Patrick's Cross and Coronation Stone as its principal exhibits. Over 6 feet high, the cross dates from the 12th century and the pedestal supporting it from the 4th century.

The 100-foot-high sandstone **round tower** was built in the 10th century at a time when the Rock was still in the possession of the kings. It has a simple inset doorway placed 12 feet above ground level.

Close to the base of the Rock is the ruined **Dominican friary** founded in 1243, rebuilt in 1480 following a fire. It has well-preserved chancel walls and a tower. A special feature is its attractive 13th-century east window. Within a mile of the friary are the ruins of

The South

Hore Abbey, a Cistercian daughter-house of Mellifont in County Louth and the last Cistercian house to be founded in mediaeval Ireland. Another monastic ruin of note in the vicinity is the 12th-century Augustinian **Athassel Priory**, just five miles to the south-west of Cashel. In its time the most extensive mediaeval priory in Ireland, today it provides only glimpses of its former grandeur in the shape of cloisters and some of the monastic buildings. The 100-foot-long abbey has carved figures.

Sentimental Guinness-drinkers may be forgiven a spot of nostalgia in the midst of **Cashel Palace Garden**, which leads to the Rock. The gardens contain a mulberry tree from 1702 and, more significantly, hop plants descended from those used in the first brewing of Guinness in 1759, invented by Richard Guinness, agent to the Archbishop of Cashel. In later years Richard's son, Arthur, went on to found the world-famous brewery in Dublin. Irrespective of this fact, Guinness-drinkers in search of martyrdom who dare to assert that the dark brew they love was founded, like the one true church, on the Rock, run the risk of being stoned 'now or later.'

In the town of Cashel the sober-looking Anglican cathedral is an 18th-century building. Its grounds contain the **GPA Bolton Library** with its 120,000 books, including a monk's encyclopedia from 1168 and pages of Chaucer's *Book of Fame* printed by the great William Caxton himself.

The **Cashel Heritage Centre** provides information on the background history of the town with commentary.

Thurles and Holycross

Thurles, on the River Suir between Templemore and Cashel, was created by the Butlers and since Penal times has been the cathedral town of the archdiocese of Cashel and Emly. It is also in the history books as the founding-place of the Gaelic Athletic Association (GAA) in 1884. For sports followers and the curious, **Lár na Páirce**, a 19th-century building in the centre of Thurles, houses an extensive display centre for the history of all sports coming under the GAA umbrella.

The **Catholic cathedral,** built in 1875, is a fine Romanesque-style building with a campanile over 100 feet high and is visible for many miles in every direction. Its Protestant counterpart, **St Mary's**, now houses a museum dealing with the Famine period. One of its most poignant exhibits is a man-trap, used by landowners to prevent the starving Irish from stealing food from orchards and fields. In the church's graveyard is a carved stone tomb from the Middle Ages. Apart from the permanent Famine Display, the church curators are also developing a military museum.

Four miles south of Thurles stands the fully restored **Holycross Abbey**. It was founded in 1168 for the Benedictines by the king of Munster, *Dónall Ó Briain*, and in 1182 was transferred to the Cistercians. Suppressed in 1536, the abbey was made over in 1563 to the Earl of Ormonde, and thanks to the protection of the Butlers, the monks remained at Holycross down to the 17th century. Two relics said to be from the cross on which Christ was crucified are housed in the abbey and account both for its name and for the veneration in which it was held by the many pilgrims who flocked here in times past.

The church is composed of a nave with aisles, transepts with side chapels, and a chancel with a square tower. Inside, the superbly carved black marble *sedilia* on the Epistle side of the altar and the fleur-de-lis carved on the stone pillars illustrate the high level of craftsmanship achieved by the stonemasons. Also worth admiring is the attractive window tracery, especially in the east and west windows.

Nenagh

The chief town of North Tipperary, Nenagh is situated close to Lough Derg but on the main Dublin–Limerick road. **Nenagh Keep**, the town's chief monument, formed part of a larger castle built in 1200 by *Theobald Fitzwalter*. It is 100 feet high and almost 35 feet across and was originally one of three towers in the curtain wall of a fortified Norman castle. In Abbey Street are the remains of a **Franciscan friary** founded in 1250. Apart from the friary and the castle, most of Nenagh's buildings were built from the mid-1700s on, with the town undergoing sustained development once it became the administrative capital of the North Riding.

Nenagh's **District Heritage Centre** in the former county jail has models of the jail complex, Lough Derg, and the lakeside villages of Dromineer and Garrykennedy. In the cells for the condemned, taped commentary and biographical notes are provided on the seventeen men who were hanged here.

The village of **Lorrha**, close to Nenagh, is the site of a monastery founded in 540 by *St Ruán*. The ruin now standing on the site is that of a 13th-century church of the **Dominican priory** founded in 1269 by *Walter de Burgh*. The high crosses in front of the church, dating back to 750, are among the oldest in Ireland. The celebrated **Lorrha Missal**, generally known as the Stowe Missal, possibly the oldest in Europe, is thought to have been written in Lorrha in the late 8th century.

Four miles away, **Redwood Castle** has been restored by a member of the Egan family, to whom the castle belonged. The famous Leabhar Breac and parts of the Annals of the Four Masters were written here in the late Middle Ages.

Roscrea

This prosperous manufacturing and market town owes its origin to the monastery founded here in the 7th century by *St Crónán*. Since then a 12th-century **Augustinian priory** was built on the original site, of which only the west gable and belfry survive. The remains of a 15th-century **Franciscan friary** have been partly incorporated in the Catholic **Church of St Crónán**. The high square belfry of the original building is still standing, and its supporting arches provide an impressive entrance to the modern church.

Roscrea Castle, erected in the middle of the 13th century, now stands in the grounds of **Damer House**, a successful local heritage centre in a fine early 18th-century building, superbly restored by the Irish Georgian Society. There is a splendid staircase and a fine planned garden.

Mona Incha Abbey, 2 miles to the east of Roscrea, is situated on what used to be an island in a bog. The ruins include a church with Romanesque features and later Gothic additions. The nave and chancel have a finely decorated 12th-century west doorway and chancel arch constructed in sandstone.

DON'T MISS

- Don't miss the majestic outcrop of limestone that is **Cashel Rock**, Ireland's Acropolis—crowned with stunningly constructed architectural masterpieces set high above the outspread plain below. In particular, spend time in the ancient **Cormac's Chapel**, the most impressive and complete Romanesque church in the country.
- See what drew thousands of pilgrims to the Cistercian **Holycross Abbey** in the Middle Ages. Fully restored, the abbey is just 4 miles south of Thurles and has superb *sedilia,* exquisite stained glass, and an early 15th-century wall-painting of two hunters and a stag.
- Despite its ruined state, don't miss **Athassel Priory**, the most extensive of its kind in mediaeval Ireland: evocative pinnacles and cloisters in a superb rural setting.

ALL-WEATHER OPTIONS

- Delve into the history of hurling and camogie in **Lár na Páirce**, the GAA display centre, Thurles.
- Visit Roscrea's elegant **Damer House**, an early 18th-century building with heritage centre covering local historical material and providing a genealogical research service as well.
- Be bookish while it rains: visit the **GPA Bolton Library** in Cashel and see the smallest book in the world and some silver altarpieces from the original Rock cathedral.

South Tipperary

Clonmel

Clonmel (*Cluain Meala*, 'meadow of honey') is not, as its name implies, a rustic retreat but the largest town in the county, and the most sophisticated. It is also prosperous on at least two counts: agriculture and industry (cider and medical devices), and functions as a first-rate shopping centre for South Tipperary. Situated on the northern bank of the River Suir, it enjoys one of the most agreeable settings of any town in the county, with the charming **Comeragh Mountains** serving as a backdrop for the town's many historical buildings.

Clonmel was settled even before the arrival of the Danes. It acquired a charter from King Edward I of England and was walled and fortified in the 14th century. Thereafter it became a stronghold of the Butler family and was besieged and then taken by the *Earl of Kildare* in 1513. In 1650 its garrison put up fierce resistance to Cromwell but eventually capitulated.

From a cultural viewpoint, Clonmel is extremely rich. At least four major figures in English literature are closely connected with the town: *George Borrow*, author of *Lavengro*, who went to school here; *Anthony Trollope*, who worked for the Post Office and wrote his first two novels in the town; *Marguerite Power*, Countess of Blessington, who was born near Clonmel and died in Paris in 1849; and *Laurence Sterne*, author of *Tristram Shandy*, who was born in Mary Street in 1713 and who, with Swift, represents the cream of the Anglo-Irish literary tradition.

But a great deal of local colour, if not culture, was also provided by an Italian immigrant, *Charles Bianconi*, who, having proved something of an embarrassment to his father because of a romantic penchant for unsuitable partners, was sent into exile and in 1802 arrived in Dublin at the tender age of sixteen. Thrown back on his own rather limited resources, he began by hawking religious pictures and eventually succeeded in setting up a coach service between Clonmel and Cahir. His company rapidly developed into a national passenger and mail service. By 1843 a hundred coaches were in regular use, and at **Hearn's Hotel**, the starting-point of his system, visitors can see the original clock that timed the arrival and departure of the famous Bianconi cars. In recognition of his contribution to the town's growth in importance, the young Italian was twice elected lord mayor.

Clonmel's most significant ancient building is the old **St Mary's Church**, originally constructed about 1204 but rebuilt in its present form in the 19th century, when the tower was added. The church incorporates parts of 14th-century buildings, and its grounds contain sections of the old town walls. The **Franciscan friary**, dating from 1269 and rebuilt on several occasions since, contains the tomb of the Lords of Cahir. A shrine of St Anthony was added in 1959 and new stained-glass windows in 1960. At the west end of O'Connell Street the town's original 14th-century gate was rebuilt in 1831 along mock-Tudor lines and has had a limestone plaque affixed to it recently to commemorate Sterne's association with Clonmel.

Tipperary (South Riding) Museum, which now occupies a fine 19th-century house in Parnell Street, has an extremely large collection of items of local and archaeological interest, as well as a fine collection of paintings and prints, including work by *John Butler Yeats* and *William Leech*.

Carrick-on-Suir

A settlement defined by Ormonde Castle to the east and a fine 15th-century stone bridge to the west was the point of departure for the growth of Carrick-on-

**Glen of Aherlow,
Co. Tipperary.**

Suir at the tide-head of the river. The first records of the town date back to 1242, and Ormonde Castle (now in ruins) was built in 1309. The strategically important seven-arched bridge linking south Leinster and east Munster was built in 1447, before Columbus voyaged to the New World, as was its original four-towered castle.

Two of the castle towers can now be seen, incorporated in a unique architectural treasure, the **Elizabethan Manor-House**, built by *Black Tom Butler*, 10th Earl of Ormonde, about 1560. Originally constructed in the hope that Queen Elizabeth might visit the town, the Tudor manor incorporates all the queen's favourite symbols and brickwork.

201

The South

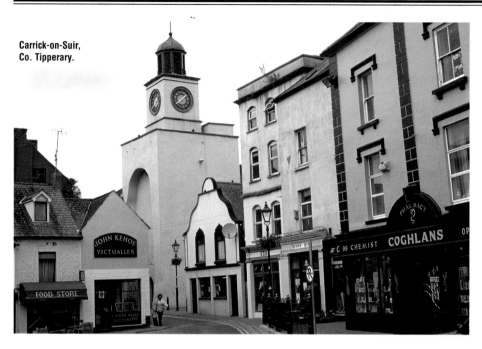

Carrick-on-Suir,
Co. Tipperary.

On either side of the inner courtyard are two frescoes, showing Black Tom and the queen with their initials and the date, 1565. The motifs of an eagle, a griffon and the Carrick knot are repeated throughout the manor. The plasterwork in the Long Gallery on the first floor has been completely renewed, and the room has two fine chimney-pieces. The ceiling is stuccoed, with sections showing the queen's arms and various Tudor heraldic symbols, such as the Tudor Rose.

Seán Kelly was born in the area of Carrick-on-Suir. Kelly, the man who won the Paris–Nice cycling race more times than anyone else and who in recent years, along with Ireland's other outstanding cycling star, *Stephen Roche*, succeeded in bringing some stages of the Tour de France to these shores. In tribute to Kelly's exceptional exploits, the main town square is now renamed after him.

Cahir

The magnificent restored **Cahir Castle** guards a strategic site on the river. Begun in the 13th century and extended in the

15th by the Butlers, it remained in Butler control until it came under state ownership in 1961. It endured its most difficult days when the Butlers sided with the Irish in the Elizabethan Wars and the Earl of Essex took the castle after a short siege in 1599, when the walls were breached by English artillery. In subsequent conflicts it was surrendered first to Lord Inchiquin, the Parliamentary commander, then to Cromwell himself in 1650, but on the second occasion without damage, as no shot was fired.

The castle has a massive keep and three towers with high walls enclosing an outer, middle and inner ward. A working portcullis is stationed in the middle gate. Both the keep, which was originally a gate tower, and the north-west tower date from the 13th century. The roof and two walls of the great hall are 19th-century additions.

Cahir is an agreeably laid-out town with cheerfully painted houses, a fine main square, and plenty of space to move around in. It makes a good centre for hill walking and for climbing the nearby **Galty Mountains**, while good fishing for trout and salmon is available on the Suir.

Swiss Cottage, just less than a mile outside Cahir, was originally designed as a fishing and hunting lodge for Lord Cahir by *John Nash*, the famous Regency architect. A thatched cottage on two levels, it has verandahs, dormer windows, and low sloping roofs. The dining-room walls are exquisitely decorated with hand-painted French wallpaper from 1816 showing leisurely Turks smoking on the banks of the Bosporus.

From Cahir it is a short drive to the **Glen of Aherlow**, sometimes called Ireland's greenest valley; it is certainly one of the most scenic. The glen embraces over 15 miles of unspoilt countryside set against forested foothills and the spectacular Galty Mountains. The idyllic nature of the place is well conveyed by the names 'Hill of Music' and 'Paradise Hill' reserved for favourite areas. For those willing to walk, trail maps and information are available at the Glen of Aherlow Fáilte Centre in Newtown.

At the northern end of the Glen of Aherlow is the town of **Tipperary**, a dairy farming centre that began as an Anglo-Norman settlement at the end of the 12th century. *John O'Leary*, the Fenian leader, was born here, as was *Charles Kickham*, the novelist, another Fenian who has had a statue erected to him in the town. Towards the end of the 19th century Tipperary took an active part in the Land League movement. In 1889, following an increase in rents by a local landlord, his tenants rebelled and, assisted by other tenants from all over Ireland who gave their services free for a week, **New Tipperary** was constructed, but the scheme was later abandoned. Muintir na Tíre, an organised movement to promote all aspects of rural life, was founded here in 1931. It has had a major impact on farming communities throughout Ireland.

The War of Independence is remembered in the **Canon Hayes Sports Complex** at the east end of Main Street. It houses a large display commemorating in particular the exploits of the 3rd Tipperary Brigade of the old IRA, complemented by exhibits of various kinds, including letters, photographs and personal items relating to the period.

DON'T MISS

- Don't miss **Cahir Castle**, a massive mediaeval construction towering out of a great rock in the middle of the River Suir. This masterwork of Norman fortification is magnificently restored and contains a fine interpretative centre.
- At Carrick-on-Suir you must see Black Tom Butler's **Elizabethan Tudor House**, built for a queen. She didn't come, but why not take her place by admiring the Long Gallery on the first floor and the fine stuccoed ceiling and brickwork.
- Don't miss the scenic **Glen of Aherlow**, set between the Galty Mountains and the Slievenamuck Range: corrie lakes, cascading mountain streams and wandering deer await you.

ALL-WEATHER OPTIONS

- Lodge your protest against the weather by visiting **Swiss Cottage**, the fantasy-full hunting and fishing lodge near Cahir, where a 40-minute guided tour will marry romantic extravaganza and rustic domesticity under one (non-porous) thatched roof.
- In spite of the rain you'll be humming 'I can see clearly now' after your visit to the **Tipperary Crystal factory**, where you can watch craftsmen blow and hand-cut the transparently beautiful material with consummate skill.

TOURING ROUTE

Counties Kilkenny and Tipperary

This itinerary makes Counties Kilkenny and Tipperary the main touring area, though it crosses to the Waterford side of the River Suir for the drive from Carrick-on-Suir to Clonmel.

Leave Kilkenny by the R700 road, crossing the River Nore at Bennettsbridge, with its studios and craft shops, 'sponge' and software potteries. From Bennettsbridge continue on the R700 towards Thomastown, with its fine 18th-century bridge, pretty shop-filled main street, and Ladywell Water Garden. At Thomastown take the N9 road south for a short while, until signs appear for Jerpoint Abbey, a wonderfully preserved 12th-century Cistercian abbey, one of the most impressive religious edifices in Ireland, with a variety of splendid carved figures on the colonnade pillars. Continue on the N9 until a sign for Knocktopher appears, and take the R699. At a fork this splits between the R699 and the

R701; take the R701 in the direction of Newmarket and Kilmaganny. At Kilmaganny, going southwards, the route becomes the R697. Continue on this road until until Ahenny (visit **Ahenny High Crosses**), passing through the tree-filled upper reaches of the Lingaun Valley.

Keep an eye peeled for a signposted left turn for 'Kilkeeran Crosses', and follow the small link road to the Kilkeeran High Crosses. These mark the site of a 9th-century monastery. The so-called West Cross has eight horsemen sculpted on its base and is decorated with interlacing and bosses.

Continue on the R697, turning left to Carrick-on-Suir, with the 16th-century Ormonde Castle and 15th-century arched bridge. In Carrick-on-Suir cross the Dillon bridge and make two right turns in succession, the first just beyond the bridge, the second at the next major junction, which has a signpost indicating Rathgormuck. Take the main R680 road. This route, on the edge of County Waterford, follows the bends of the River Suir and passes through the most fetching areas of natural beauty—low stone walls and sylvan repose, ruined castles, and undulating green pastures.

Keep to the R680, crossing a small bridge opposite Tikincor Castle, before entering the outlying areas of Clonmel and turning right at the main crossroads for a brief visit to the town to see St Mary's Church, the County Museum, and Riverside. There are splendid views of the Comeragh Mountains to the south.

From Clonmel take the N24 road to Cahir to see the 13th-century Cahir Castle, a restored Anglo-Norman fortification with keep, north-west tower, working portcullis, and audiovisual presentation. Now take the R670 about a mile south of Cahir in the direction of Ardfinnan to see Swiss Cottage, Lord Cahir's fishing and hunting lodge. From Ardfinnan take the R665 road to Ballyporeen, a town associated with Ronald Reagan, former President of the United States, whose grandfather was born here in 1829. (A Ronald Reagan Centre provides background information.) Continue on the R665 to Mitchelstown, then take the R513, proceeding to Galbally, where the R663 passes by the Glen of Aherlow and the Galty Mountains. At Bansha the N24 leads back to the N8, hugging the River Ara. On the N8 turn north towards Cashel, the ancient ecclesiastical capital of Munster, to see the Rock of Cashel, Cormac's Chapel, and Hall of the Vicars-Choral.

At Cashel take the R660 road to Holycross, with its Benedictine Holycross Abbey, recently fully restored, with cloisters, wall painting, and stained glass. Then continue on to Thurles, with its Romanesque Catholic cathedral. From Thurles take the N75 through Twomileborris to rejoin the N8; head north to Urlingford and turn right to join the R693; head towards Freshford, and then turn southwards to return to Kilkenny.

Rock of Cashel, Co. Tipperary.

Hedgerows

Wild flowers on the roadside.

Ireland's extensive network of hedgerows, as we see them today, began to develop towards the end of the 18th century. Originally planted as fences and to delineate property and townland boundaries, their survival is largely due to the fact that Ireland's agricultural land is primarily pastureland. Extensive tillage typically reduces hedgerows, so Ireland can consider itself extremely fortunate—unlike other European countries, whose hedgerows have been almost annihilated over the past fifty years.

In England and Wales about 4,500 miles of hedgerow were removed each year from 1946 to 1974, approximately a quarter of the total. Since then, many more thousands of miles

have disappeared. In Ireland, by contrast, about 14 per cent of the country's hedgerows were removed in the period 1937–82, an enormously destructive event by any standards, though only half the loss suffered in England and Wales.

Over time, the benefits of hedgerows extended far beyond their original purpose. A typical hedgerow will provide shelter for farm animals and protect vulnerable crops from wind damage. It will help to curb soil erosion and prevent flooding in areas that are prone to heavy, sustained rain. More recently, evidence has shown that hedgerows can act as barriers to the spread of diseases, such as bovine TB. And, as the dawn of understanding breaks on a growing number of enlightened farmers, the

Feature

role of hedgerows in providing a balance in nature has become clear. These farmers have begun to appreciate the crucial role a rich diversity of pests and predators living within the hedgerow habitat play in the control of agricultural pests. In a rapidly expanding organic farming industry, the protection and nurturing of such a diversity becomes of paramount importance.

This latter-day conversion by farmers to the benefits of hedgerows has been a long time coming, for it is to changes in farming practice that we owe the loss of so many hedgerows. Among these changes were the dramatic decline in small farm holdings since the 1950s and the merging of many small fields into ever-larger pastures, most notably in the east and south-east; the advent of large farm machinery, as a result of which farmers experiencing difficulty in manoeuvring around small fields removed those hedgerows that were 'in the way'; the introduction of wire and electric fencing, replacing the traditional hedgerow method of restricting the movement of animals; the adverse effect on crop growth as a result of the loss of sunlight on shady areas of hedged fields and the continuing cost of maintaining hedgerows on a farm, usually requiring the regular hiring of a contractor, a cost that many smaller farmers simply could not afford.

Hedgerows account for 5 per cent of the total stock of broad-leaved trees in Ireland. In a survey in one part of County Mayo some years ago, hawthorn was the most common hedgerow species, with a 97 per cent presence in the hedgerows surveyed. Others were bramble (84 per cent), blackthorn (48 per cent), gorse (48 per cent), ash (32 per cent), elder (10 per cent), ivy (10 per cent), sycamore (10 per cent), beech (3 per cent), and rose (3 per cent). This relates to a specific area; however, in all at least sixty trees, shrubs and woody climbers have been found in our hedgerows.

The older hedgerow trees of elm, oak, beech, lime and chestnut are slowly being replaced by ash and sycamore, as these recover quickly from severe cutting. Ash is today the most common hedgerow tree. The most common shrub is hawthorn, because of its ability to quickly form a dense, animal-proof hedge. Also common are brambles, dog-rose, woody climbers like ivy and woodbine, hazel, holly, ash, and spindle. Many roadside hedges have a stream or drain running alongside, thus providing conditions moist enough for willows and alder to survive.

Hedgerows provide undisturbed shelter for a wide variety of shrubs and flowering plants. Blackthorn, wild cherry and gorse are the first to flower, from March to late April. In early May the lovely white blossom of hawthorn emerges, followed by elder and crab apple from late May to early June. On the outer fringes of many hedgerows are found species such as hogweed, cow-parsley, goosegrass, garlic mustard, lady's smock, primrose, dog violet, robin-run-the-hedge, and hedge woundwort. On more acid soils, wood sorrel and foxglove are common; and where damp soils predominate, meadowsweet and great hairy willowherb thrive.

Hedgerows are reservoirs for a vast array of insects, which themselves are a rich source of food for birds such as wrens, song-thrushes, blackbirds, hedge-sparrows, yellowhammers, chaffinches, bullfinches, whitethroats, and redwings. Hedgerows also provide food and shelter to a wide variety of mammals. Most of these are nocturnal: badgers, rabbits, foxes, field mice, hedgehogs, pygmy shrews, and barn owls.

Even if there were no obvious practical advantages—which is not the case—there are more abstract yet intrinsically important values in an Irish hedgerow. These are values relating to beauty, wilderness, spirituality, and mythology. An Irish landscape devoid of hedgerows would be a barren landscape indeed. In an age in which economic growth and a desire for more and more material possessions dominate, it is reassuring to know that throughout the landscape runs a network of ancient hedgerows, reminding us that past values can and do survive. Let us hope we never lose them.

County Cork

With an area of 2,880 square miles (7,460 square kilometres), County Cork is the largest county in Ireland and contains the third-largest city. Bounded by Counties Waterford and Tipperary to the east, Limerick to the north, Kerry to the west, and the Atlantic Ocean to the south, its characteristic east-west ridges traverse peaceful uplands and hills. Pastureland and farmland, irrigated by a complex of eastward-flowing rivers, occupy the inland valleys. In the east of the county the valleys tend to be broadest, growing narrower as one heads westwards, brewing, distilling, tweed-making and lacework, the county has latterly gone high-tech, both in computers and pharmaceuticals, and the recent success of Viagra, produced near Cork, has led to much local teasing.

Although over a third of the county's population works in the city, the main cash resource of the county tends to be livestock, and many of the farms in the east and centre grow cereals and root crops. Dairy-farming represents a proud tradition; so when visiting the county make sure to taste some milleens, a spicy cheese from west Cork, and a slice of gubbeen from Schull, as well as crubeens (pigs' feet) and drisheens (a blood sausage). Only this mix can give you the right local flavour!

culminating in coastal lowlands towered over by high mountains. This western section, bordering on County Kerry, is regarded as the most scenically attractive area. Its centrepiece, Glengarriff and Garinish, benefits from the temperate influence of the Gulf Stream and features year-round sub-tropical vegetation. But for some the less spectacular and more settled attractions of the Lee and Blackwater valleys to the east offer an agreeable alternative to the rugged appeal of the Beara Peninsula, with its mountain peaks and brilliant gardens.

At the centre of County Cork lies the city of **Cork**, a flourishing metropolis on the River Lee with one of the best natural harbours in Europe, a logical focal point for the manufacturing and agricultural life of the region. Famous over the years for its

Corkonians are full of cockiness, charm, and buoyancy. They had to be. In the Famine years (1846–51) the county lost 200,000 people—a quarter of its entire population—of whom 150,000 died and 50,000 emigrated. Many of those who emigrated passed through the port of **Cóbh**, their last contact with land before America. Today the town is on the circuit for touring luxury liners, a stopping-off point where disembarking visitors can confirm for

Mardyke, River Lee, Cork.

themselves that Cork good humour still keeps the natives afloat!

As one would expect of the largest county in the land, diversity is the keynote of Cork's appeal. The eastern strip, in which Cóbh lies, continues on to take in small fishing villages like **Ballycotton** and delightful historic towns like **Youghal**, tranquilly situated where the River Blackwater meets the sea. West Cork, on the other hand, presents a much more convoluted road and harbour structure, and the traveller can count on a gripping roller-coaster experience through a scenic wonderland where the landscape doesn't allow for such a thing as a straight line.

East or west, north or south, the county offers the traveller a splendid portfolio of tourist choices. Physical exercise is catered for by riding, fishing and boating throughout the area, and especially attractive walking-routes along the **Beara Peninsula**. On the other hand there's the sightseeing and gourmet self-indulgence of **Kinsale** (to be completed, if time and digestion permit, by a trip to **Ballymaloe House** at Shanagarry to enjoy the sophisticated cuisine on offer there). Visually there is gorgeous landscape almost everywhere, and if it rains, visits to the highly developed arts and crafts studio-shops in the area are in order. For the ear, the musical offerings are myriad, for a particularly vigorous tradition of Irish music has survived here. Finally, for the soul, there are the breathtaking colours of the sea in places like **Bantry**, **Dunmanway**, **Courtmacsherry** and **Clonakilty**, and the ultimate pneumatic bliss of Atlantic ozone. All that remains for the stressed-out visitor to do is to unpack, unwind, and enjoy!

Cork City

The point of departure for what subsequently grew into Ireland's third-largest city was a 7th or 8th-century settlement around an Early Christian monastery on the south bank of the River Lee. Then, before the end of the 9th-century, Viking invaders began putting down roots in their newly conquered lands. Anglo-Norman warlords were later granted the town by King Henry II of England, taking it over in 1177, at which time it became a royal borough, receiving a set of charters from 1189 onwards. A thriving trade in wool and cow-hides helped promote its development at this juncture, but it went through a lean period in the 14th and 15th centuries. In 1491–2 the city imprudently supported the claims of *Perkin Warbeck*, the English pretender, and lost its city charter as a result. As part of the plantation of Munster in 1586, large estates were assigned to English planters such as *Sir Walter Raleigh*, but the entire scheme came unstuck in 1598 because of violent armed opposition. Following this breakdown, Spanish forces

St. Patrick's Bridge, Cork City.

attempting to help *Hugh O'Neill* of Ulster were defeated in 1601 in a decisive battle at Kinsale. The city then made common cause with *Cromwell* in 1649, and in 1690 *John Churchill, Earl of Marlborough,* took control of it for *William of Orange,* after it had again backed a loser by throwing in its lot with *King James II.*

Despite these setbacks, Cork grew rapidly in size and importance in the 17th and 18th centuries, building up its commerce on the basis of a successful butter trade. However, it also became increasingly radical politically, and remained an important base for Fenian activism throughout the 19th century. Up to and during the War of Independence (1919–21), Cork's reputation as the rebel county increased, and it found itself once more on the receiving end of authoritarian repression because of the ambushing of military convoys and general resistance to British rule in Ireland. The pattern of stubborn resistance followed by violent repression continued apace. *Terence MacSwiney,* the heroic figure who replaced the murdered Lord Mayor, *Tomás MacCurtain,* was himself jailed, and died in Brixton Prison after a 74-day hunger strike. But even the signing of the Anglo-Irish Treaty of 1921 failed to put an end to the fighting, with anti-Treaty elements taking control of the city for a time. These were overcome eventually, but the leader of the pro-Treaty forces, *Michael Collins* (recently dramatically evoked in Neil Jordan's film of the same name), was killed in an ambush not far from his own home town of Clonakilty.

Market in Cork City.

Shandon,
night view,
Cork City.

Blarney and Cóbh

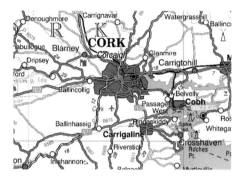

The only time the Irish are lost for words is when they have to say goodbye. Two celebrated tourist spots around Cork symbolically recall both the gift of eloquence and the silent pain of parting. These are Blarney and Cóbh.

Tradition dictates that those in search of the gift of the gab had to kiss a certain stone. They still do: a block of rough limestone set high in the battlements of **Blarney Castle**. Similarly, history shows that those in search of a fresh start had to leave the country, and this is what millions did over the centuries through **Cóbh**, Ireland's most famous point of departure for the New World, taking leave of their nearest and dearest in recurrent separation scenes of great poignancy, then waving a last farewell from the decks of ships as they sailed, grim-faced and heartbroken, into exile.

Both tourist locations are almost obligatory stopping-places on any visit to County Cork and bring the full range of human emotions into play. Where Blarney Castle is filled with comic resonance, Cóbh has the aura of tragic destiny. Together they sum up the Irish reality, a value system based on the power of language and the spoken word, and a famine and emigration experience that has marked the Irish people for ever.

Blarney Castle was built in 1446 by *Cormac Mac Carthaigh* and successfully resisted siege after siege through the 16th and 17th centuries, only to be finally captured in 1690

by the army of King William III, and in large part destroyed. Today only the massive square keep (where the stone is) remains. And, as local people readily point out, its survival is a godsend: if it wasn't there, the world would be mute, and Blarney pockets rather empty.

At the same time, nothing better encapsulates the basic principles of Irish yoga, or is better calculated to concentrate the mind, than the effort required to kiss the stone. To do so, the intrepid neophyte must first agree to adopt a supine position and then bend backwards over the void, while a pair of strong restraining hands are placed over his or her shins. The options are death or eloquence, though, paradoxically enough, returning survivors are frequently lost for words. In clerically dominated Ireland, kissing a girl in public was frowned upon, but kissing a stone was considered perfectly normal, so happily for all concerned, the practice has continued to this day.

Where the practice comes from is anybody's guess. Most blatherers support the view that it all began with the Lord of Blarney, a MacCarthy, who, being a typical Corkman, despised authority and was determined not to swear allegiance to Queen Elizabeth. At the same time, he wanted to hold on to his land. Pressed by the queen's deputy, George Carew, to accept the idea of tenure from the Crown, he took refuge in evasiveness. As a master of equivocation and procrastination, he is plainly a worthy rival of the fair Scheherazade of the *Thousand and One Nights,* who saved herself from certain death night after night by recounting a succession of yarns, each more entrancing than the other. Making sure to create the impression of willing acceptance of the queen's proposal, MacCarthy deferred an ultimate yes from day to day, gaining in the process a reputation for fair words and soft speech. In the end, the exasperated queen cracked and blurted out: 'This is all Blarney: what he says, he never means!' If one takes 'blarney' to mean evasive talk designed to mislead without causing offence, then that kind of reproach has been levelled at many supposed experts in evasion ever since, all the way from Pinocchio to recent American presidents.

After the rock ordeal, visitors to Blarney Castle may be only too happy to visit the adjacent **Blarney Castle House**, a recently renovated 19th-century Scottish baronial mansion, to view its collection of ancestral paintings, tapestries, and splendid gardens, or to look over the range of woollen and craft goods on display in nearby **Blarney Woollen Mills**.

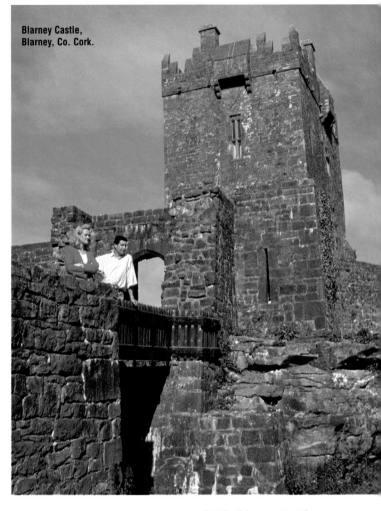

Blarney Castle, Blarney, Co. Cork.

Cóbh

Situated on the south side of Great Island and on the hill above the harbour of Cork, the town of **Cóbh** has played a significant part in maritime history. In September 1838 the steamer *Sirius* left Cóbh to become the first steamship to cross the Atlantic, taking a little over eighteen days in all. The town was also the last port of call for the *Titanic,* which in 1913 took on board 123 passengers here before departing on its ill-fated trip to America. A few years later naval search-vessels were to set out from Cóbh in response to emergency calls from the *Lusitania,* torpedoed by a German submarine in 1915.

The town's original and present name of Cóbh is simply an Irish word for haven. But a change took place after Queen Victoria first set foot here in 1849, and it was known as Queenstown until 1922, when its original name was restored. It had been a British naval base for many years, and remained so until 1938. Long before, in 1776, soldiers were shipped from Cóbh to fight in the American War of Independence, and later to such conflicts as the Boer War and the First World War.

The church that dominates the town is a Gothic-revival building designed by Pugin, Ashlin, and Coleman. **St Colman's Cathedral** took forty-seven years to build and was completed only in 1915, about the time of the *Lusitania* disaster. It boasts a 300-foot spire and a carillon of forty-nine bells—the largest

Cóbh Harbour and Cathedral,
Co. Cork.

of its kind in Ireland. The interior is highly decorated with carved panels of Bath stone and features a floor laid with mosaic, as well as some fine stained-glass windows.

An astonishing 2.5 million people sailed from Cóbh for America between 1845 and 1860. Unfortunately, not all went on to a brighter and better future, and in the late Famine years many thousands died in cramped, sub-human conditions on board what became known as the coffin ships.

In the second half of the 19th century most of the emigrating landless labourers and servant girls setting sail for America would have travelled to Cóbh by train. From the railway station they would have gone to the special jetties of the Cunard and White Star lines and taken tenders to the waiting liners. This part of the port's colourful history is recalled in dramatic fashion in 'The Queenstown Story', a multimedia exhibition in the **Heritage Centre,** where the railway station has been completely refurbished in the style of the era. A touching collection of letters, photographs and other memorabilia relating to emigrants is kept on permanent display, and the detailed passenger lists form a useful archive both for genealogists and for visitors in search of information about their emigrant ancestors.

More scenes from the past can be conjured up at the former **Presbyterian Church,** overlooking the harbour. Here the emphasis is on paintings by famous marine artists, on model ships, and various mementoes of the religious, musical and sporting life of the area. You can also sail into the past with a visit to the **Royal Cork Yacht Club**, the oldest of its kind in the world. Founded in 1720, it continues to stage excellent annual regattas.

Apart from yachting pursuits, Cóbh offers lots of other leisure activities. Its rising terraces of brightly painted houses make a pleasant backdrop to climbing the hill and enjoying splendid views over the neighbouring woods and the land-locked harbour below. You can also stroll to the peaceful **Old Church Graveyard** near the town centre to seek out the last resting-place of many of the *Lusitania* disaster victims. A public monument to the 1,198 people who perished can be found in **Casement Square**.

A short drive from the town is **Fota Island**, just 10 miles from Cork on the Cóbh road, a 16-acre wildlife park owned by the Royal Zoological Society of Ireland. It has more than seventy species of wildlife in open surroundings, with monkeys swinging from tree to tree on lake islands and kangaroos leaping with complete freedom through the park's extensive grasslands. A renowned collection of rare trees and shrubs, many of them sub-tropical, begun in the 19th century and coming from China, South America, the Himalayas and the Far East, is on display in **Fota Arboretum and Gardens**, while a completely new golfing venue, Fota Island Golf Club, set in the midst of a 780-acre estate, adds to the list of fine natural amenities within easy driving distance of Cóbh.

DON'T MISS
- 'I'll do it if it kills me!' Pick up the gift of the gab at **Blarney Castle** by kissing the Blarney stone and risking life and limb.
- See if the newly acquired verbal skills work by talking to the wild animals in the natural habitat of **Fota Island Wildlife Park.**
- Take a look at Cóbh's 19th-century neo-Gothic cathedral, **St Colman's**, the most dominant landmark in the town.
- Visit **Cóbh Heritage Centre** for a record of the port's history and a moving presentation of the trials of early emigrants to America.

ALL-WEATHER OPTIONS
- Visit **Blarney Woollen Mills** and make a winter investment.
- For an explosive time out, take the N22 and visit **Ballincollig Gunpowder Mills** (exhibits, audiovisual display, but no cash and carry!).

Youghal

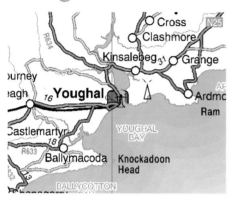

As early as the 9th century, **Youghal** was occupied by the Vikings, and later on it was settled by the Anglo-Normans. The strategic importance of the town led to its being enclosed on three sides by thick walls in the 13th century, with the River Blackwater forming a fourth, natural barrier. Though it traded regularly with the Continent, and from the Middle Ages onwards prospered as one of Ireland's main ports, in later centuries the town's English garrison feared that French and Spanish forces might mount an invasion against it.

Interesting remains of the 15th-century walls and towers with which the town was fortified still remain. They are even more extensive than Derry's city walls, and better preserved. For those energetic enough, a climb to the top of the hill and a seat astride an ancient cannon is an amusing and worthwhile project: the view out over the town, and along the Blackwater seawards, should not be missed at any price.

Pride of place for Youghal's antiquities must go, however, to **St Mary's Collegiate Church**. About the year 400 a wooden church was built on the site by followers of St Declan of Ardmore. But the existing church, originally put up in the early 13th century and restored in the 18th, is one of the few mediaeval churches in Ireland still in regular use. The roof of the nave features 900-year-old beams of Irish oak. The east

window dates from 1498, as does the font in the nave. Distributed at various points within the church are grave slabs and effigies, some of them dating from the 13th and 14th centuries and containing Norman-French inscriptions. The south transept contains an impressive Renaissance monument to the first Earl of Cork, *Sir Richard Boyle*, his three wives, and an equally impressive roster of sixteen children. One of the unique features of the church is the series of holes in the chancel walls, behind which pottery jars have been placed to improve the acoustics and to ensure, no doubt, that every homily preached is picked up by an attentive congregation!

For what it's worth, *Oliver Cromwell* adopted Youghal as his 1649/50 winter quarters in Ireland once the local garrison had declared for the Parliamentarian side. The record of slaughter and pillage he and his soldiers left behind them still lingers in popular imagination in the form of the feared curse of Cromwell. When departing from Youghal the Protector is said to have passed under the **Water Gate**, also known as Cromwell's Arch, in Quay Lane. For the local people, as far as Youghal was concerned, nothing became Cromwell better than his leaving of it.

More affectionately regarded in popular tradition is *Sir Walter Raleigh*, who, though he came to Ireland in 1579 to suppress the Desmond Rebellion and was granted 40,000 acres of Munster land, is supposed to have brought tobacco and potatoes to Ireland from America and planted them at **Myrtle Grove**, his mansion house, which still stands beside St Mary's Church. Why he should be so well thought of is puzzling: by helping to make the potato the staple diet of the Irish people he would have pushed them in the direction of the Great Famine; and by promoting the smoking of tobacco he would have introduced them to perhaps the greatest health hazard of the 20th century. How the tuber and the weed were really introduced into Ireland is the subject of argument. But in the case of the latter at least, the story goes that one day Raleigh lit a pipe of tobacco in the garden under the four yew trees (the English name **Youghal** derives from the Irish name, *Eochaill*, meaning yew-wood) and had a jug of water poured over his head for his pains—an early case of anti-smokers' revenge! Since then the pipe has gone out and Raleigh has departed, but the four yew trees are flourishing.

Lord Mayor of Youghal from 1588 to 1589, Raleigh entertained the poet *Edmund Spenser* in his Elizabethan home, and the first three volumes of *The Faerie Queene* are supposed to have been written in the bay window overlooking the gates of the Collegiate Church. Following Spenser's death, his widow married *Sir Robert Tynte*, and the couple lived together in **Tynte's Castle** in Main Street, a 15th-century tower-house with a device over the door for pouring boiling oil on rebels. Youghal's **Red House**, designed by the Dutch architect Leuventhen and built in 1710 of Dutch red brick for the Uniacke family, stands on the opposite side of the street. Close by, in North Main street, are the **almshouses** for poor Protestant widows, built in 1634 by Richard Boyle and renovated in the early 19th century.

Generally speaking, Youghal has that vaunted Roman quality of history meeting you in the street. And probably the best example of this is the impressive **Clock Gate** straddling the main thoroughfare. A replacement for the original mediaeval **Iron Gate** separating the upper and lower towns, it was built in 1777 and served as town jail until 1837. A four-storey arched red sandstone building, it was quite incapable of accommodating the huge number of people found guilty of revolutionary activity, and for

Clock Tower,
Youghal,
Co. Cork.

a time a policy was instituted of hanging rebels from the windows as an example to the rest of the populace. The film-maker John Huston was in a friendlier mood when he arrived in Youghal in 1954 to film *Moby Dick*. He hanged no-one but dressed the Clock Gate out in clapboard and picket fences instead, to make it look like part of a New England whaling-port. Thirsty and nostalgic film enthusiasts can still catch up on this 1950s Hollywood-style transformation of the town by visiting the **Moby Dick** pub facing the harbour, where photos and memorabilia of the period can be calmly reviewed over a pint.

DON'T MISS
- Don't miss the **Clock Tower**, which up to 1837 served to house the only prisoners in Ireland who had time on their hands (literally).
- Visit **St Mary's Collegiate Church**, by common consent one of the most impressive churches in the country.
- Scale **Youghal Town Walls**, among the best-preserved and most scenic in Ireland.

ALL-WEATHER OPTIONS
- Drive to **Trabolgan Holiday Village**, Midleton, for bowling, swimming and many other sports.
- Visit **Old Midleton Distillery**, Jameson Heritage Centre, for a tour, and a taste, of the local elixir of life.

Kinsale

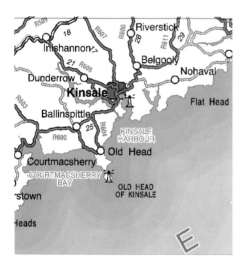

Though Kinsale's origins can be traced back to 1177, its main claim to a place in history is a battle that took place in 1601 between English armies and an Irish-Spanish alliance. Defeat brought to an end the old Irish society; it also paved the way for racial and religious prejudice, and up to the end of the 18th century no Irish or Catholics were permitted to settle within the town walls. Just a year earlier, the Catholic *James II* had landed at Kinsale to begin the battle to recover his throne. After the rout of the Battle of the Boyne in 1690 he returned to the town once more, this time to sail into exile. This was also the lot of the Irish aristocracy who had supported him and were now obliged to flee (the 'Flight of the Earls'), while increasing English influence quickly transformed Kinsale into an important British naval base.

The military function of Kinsale and its history as a garrison are evidenced by two forts facing one another at the harbour entrance. **James Fort**, a representative example of 17th-century military architecture, was built in 1607; it was captured in 1690 by Williamite forces. Opposite it, **Charles Fort**, built in the early 1680s by *William Robinson* (architect of the Royal Hospital at Kilmainham, Dublin), is a classic example of a star-shaped fort. It was besieged in 1690 by the Duke of Marlborough and eventually destroyed in 1922 during the Civil War.

In the town itself, **Desmond Castle**, built as a custom house by the Earl of Desmond in 1500, was occupied by the Spanish in 1601. Then it became known as the French Prison, after a fire in which fifty-four prisoners, mainly French sailors, died in 1747. Later, as a borough prison, it was used to hold captured Americans during the American War of Independence. Since then it has undergone restoration and conversion as an **International Wine Museum**, extolling the virtues of wines produced by the descendants of the exiled Irish leaders who had been forced to flee Ireland and Kinsale in the 17th century.

Round the corner from the Castle is **St Mulrose's Church** (Church of Ireland), built in 1190. Many of its original features survive intact; they include the blackletter inscriptions in Norman-French, the Easter sepulchre, the baptismal font, the carved memorials, and the reredos from the Galway Chapel.

Apart from its fine buildings and houses, its picturesque setting, its reputation as a centre of gastronomic excellence and its renown as a sailing, wind-surfing and deep-sea diving and fishing centre, Kinsale has a few more esoteric strings to its bow. One of the most popular display items in the **Courthouse Museum** is the story of the famous Kinsale giant, *Patrick Cotter O'Brien*, who died in 1806 and was over eight feet tall. What he represented in height the adventurer *Alexander Selkirk* represented in isolation and loneliness. In 1703 Selkirk set sail from Kinsale in the 90-ton *Cinque Ports*, only to find himself marooned for years on a lonely Pacific island, Juan Fernandez Island. Out of his thrilling story and exploits came the inspiration for Daniel Defoe's wonderful novel *Robinson Crusoe*.

Kinsale, Co. Cork.

DON'T MISS

- Don't miss **St Mulrose's Church** with its 12th-century Romanesque doorway and its 16th-century gravestones.
- Visit the star-shaped **Charles Fort**, an interesting 18th-century example of specialised military architecture.
- See the 16th-century tower-house, **Desmond Castle**, which was by turn a magazine, a custom house and then a jail.

ALL-WEATHER OPTIONS

- Shelter from the rain to good effect to watch master craftsmen produce Kinsale crystal at **Kinsale Crystal**, Market Street.
- Visit **Kinsale Silver** in Pearse Street to see beautiful silverwork being made in the studio-workshop.
- Go for a good meal: after all, this is Ireland's gourmet capital.

Inland Cork: Macroom, Mallow & Fermoy

Macroom is a thriving market town, situated to the west of Cork on the Sullane River just above the point where it joins the Lee. In 1654, *Oliver Cromwell* handed over the entire town, and its castle, to *Admiral Sir William Penn*, whose son founded the state of Pennsylvania. Penn subsequently sold the castle to the Hollow Sword Blade Company—proof, if proof were needed, that on occasion the Sword can be mightier than the Penn, yet also ironically appropriate in a second sense, given the futility of the incessant sieges the tower underwent in the 16th and 17th centuries.

The cut and thrust of history is also visible in another, more modern form just a few miles further south, at **Bealnablagh**, where signposts point the way to the spot where *Michael Collins* was killed in an ambush in 1922.

Today Macroom is still dominated by the surviving castle walls and grounds from the Penn era, with old stone arches and guns presenting a striking urban centre. Set close to the Irish-speaking towns of Ballyvourney, Ballingeary, and Cúil Aodha, where Irish dancing and céilí music sessions are held most evenings, the town is renowned for the traditional Irish sport of road-bowling. This is played most Saturday mornings and consists of throwing a 28-ounce solid steel ball, called

a bowl, along a narrow road over a distance of three miles. The winner is the person who completes the distance in the least number of throws. A road-bowling match is called a 'score'. If you're not afraid of a challenge, and fancy a change from marking your golf card, then contact **Mary-Ann's Bar** at Masseytown, Macroom, for further details.

The **Gearagh** (*An Gaorthadh*, 'the wooded river-valley') is one of the area's principal attractions. A wildlife nature reserve, it contains the only post-glacial alluvial oak-forest remains in Europe and features a series of submerged islands where rich woodland flora once bloomed. Rare species of marsh flowers are still present, along with abundant wildfowl, such as whooper swans and kingfishers, and more familiar creatures such as otters, foxes, and badgers.

As well as road-bowling, all manner of recreational activities are available in Macroom, including pitch-and-putt, horse-riding, golf, canoeing on the Sullane River, game-fishing for trout, and coarse-fishing for pike, perch, roach, and bream. In addition to going on walking tours, why not also take a short drive out from Macroom along the R584 road in the direction of **Glengarriff**? This will open up for you some of the most scenic landscape in the country: first the fishing centre of **Inchigeelagh** on Lake Allua, and then, after a short detour, **Gougane Barra**, set among magnificent mountain scenery with twenty different tree species and with brooding cliffs rising high above the lake's dark waters.

North of Macroom, the town of **Mallow** occupies the junction of the Limerick, Cork, Killarney, Waterford and Dublin roads. An excellent hub for the south-west, it is a mere 20 miles from Cork, two hours by train from Dublin, and only one hour's drive from Shannon Airport. Set in the lush Blackwater valley, it caters for all recreational tastes, being well known as an angling and hunting centre, and boasts an excellent golf course as well as a recently erected racecourse.

From 1730 to 1810, Mallow was a famous spa town, but some of the gentry who went there bubbled over a little too much, if one is to judge by the famous song 'The Rakes of Mallow': 'Beauing, belling, dancing, drinking | Breaking windows, damning, singing | Ever raking, never thinking | Live the rakes of Mallow.' Today the town lives from the processing of sugar-beet and punters' money (intermittently) in the spring, summer and autumn versions of the Mallow Races. It has a fortified 16th-century town-house, a picturesque half-timbered clock house, and the abandoned spa well, which, in spite of the worrying absence of rakes, just keeps on gushing.

To the west of Mallow, on the main Cork–Dublin road, is the garrison town of **Fermoy**. The town centre now stands on what was originally the lands of the Cistercian Abbey seized by the Crown and granted by Queen Elizabeth to Sir Richard Greville, a cousin of Walter Raleigh's. As a result of the panic generated by the unsuccessful French invasion of Ireland in 1796, it was decided to create a military base at Fermoy, and a Scotsman, *John*

An Irish lake, Gougane Barra, Co. Cork.

Anderson, provided a site for the barracks, as well as starting up a mail-coach service between Cork and Dublin. In 1797 the first soldiers began to arrive. The largest number of soldiers to be stationed here was probably just before the Battle of Waterloo in 1815. It was at that time that the Duke of Wellington visited the barracks and ensured that a very large contingent left Fermoy to do battle against Napoleon.

To the west of Fermoy all that remains of Edmund Spenser's **Kilcoman Castle** is a single small tower. But it was at Kilcolman—given to the poet for his part in subjugating the Irish of Munster—that Spenser wrote most of *The Faerie Queene*.

DON'T MISS

- Visit the **Gearagh National Nature Reserve** with its ancient forest system, rare plants, and large numbers of wildfowl.
- Make a trip to **Gougane Barra** to enjoy the mountain scenery by the lake where St Finbarr, patron saint of Cork, was once believed to have had his hermitage.
- Make a literary pilgrimage to **Kildorrery** for its links with Elizabeth Bowen, the novelist and short-story writer; recite or read from Spenser's *Faerie Queen* where it was written, at **Kilcoman Castle.**

ALL-WEATHER OPTIONS

- Visit *Prince August Ltd*, Ireland's only toy-soldier factory at **Kilnamartyra**, Mallow.
- Visit **Longueville House**, an 18th-century family hotel and restaurant serving fine white wine grown in its own vineyard!

West Cork: Bandon to Glengarriff

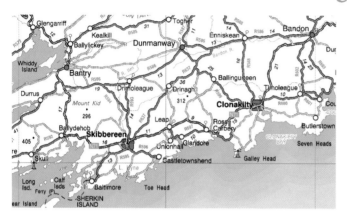

Bandon and **Clonakilty** share the distinction of being founded on land seized from local people and given to English settlers by Richard Boyle, first Earl of Cork, in 1608. But Clonakilty at least turned the tables on its usurpers by giving birth to *Michael Collins*, and the town's **West Cork Regional Museum** drives home the point by graphically illustrating his role in the War of Independence. In recent times the Irishness of Clonakilty has been further accentuated with its growth as a traditional music centre.

But if all you're looking for is a quiet beach, far from the hullabaloo of history, then this busy market town has plenty of those too, as well as a **Model Railway Village**, constructed to preserve the memory of the West Cork Railway and proving an overwhelming favourite with visiting children of all ages.

To the west, between Clonakilty and Skibbereen, lies **Rosscarbery**, site of an ancient monastic school where *St Cillian* was educated before setting out as a missionary to Würzburg. Closer to the sea is **Castletownshend**, once the home of Somerville and Ross, the authors of the *Irish RM* series of books. A pleasant bay set between Rosscarbery and Castletownshend separates **Union Hall**

and **Glandore** from one another. *Jonathan Swift* lived in Union Hall in 1723 and praised it in a Latin poem about the Rocks of Carbery, but in truth Glandore is equally eye-catching.

An Sciobairín, 'the place of the little boats' came into being when Algerian pirates raided nearby Baltimore in 1631 and English settlers fled, setting up two new settlements, which later merged into one. A thriving market town, regarded as the capital of the area known as the Carberies, its inhabitants had clearly no inhibitions about taking on the world. An editorial in the *Skibbereen Eagle* in the 1890s informed all and sundry that the paper was keeping an eye on the Tsar of Russia. If the Tsar was quaking in his boots we do not know about it. Historically, the town was already famous for having produced two battling bishops, one of whom died in 1602 fighting the forces of Queen Elizabeth, while the other dared to take on Cromwellian forces and was hanged in 1650 for his presumption. At a more everyday level, Skibbereen is a favourite port of fishermen and yachtsmen, is close to Lough Ine, the only inland saltwater lake in Europe, and maintains the fine **West Cork Arts Centre**.

Beyond Skibbereen lies **Sherkin Island**, with its marine research station, and Irish-speaking **Clear Island**, the large bird colonies of which make it of great interest to ornithologists. Beyond both these islands is the **Fastnet Rock**, a lighthouse and meteorological station and a western sea-marker in the biennial Fastnet Yacht Race. It is the most southerly point in Ireland.

Both the Mizen and Beara Peninsulas offer exceptional scenery. Seals, gannets and fierce Atlantic storms battle for the suzerainty of Mizen Head in winter, but in summer it can be idyllic. For something different, visit the **Mizen Head Heritage Centre** and cross the suspension bridge between the mainland and Cloghane Island to see the **Fog Signal Station**. Built in 1910, it displays the life of lighthouse-keepers, local marine life and the Fastnet race and has, as you might expect in such a remote and dangerous area, a special section on wrecks. **Ballydehob** and **Schull**, two of the small towns on the peninsula, are both attractive places to visit and stay in and ideal points of departure for walking and climbing in the vicinity.

Bantry is a commercial harbour and fishing-port with one of the most beautiful natural settings of any town in County Cork. Protected by wooded hills at the head of Bantry Bay, it is an ideal base for touring the local peninsulas. In the past it was the chosen target for two unsuccessful landing attempts by French fleets. The first, in support of King James II, occurred in 1689; the second, in 1796, involved General Hoche's expedition. It was on one of Hoche's ships that the revolutionary leader *Theobald Wolfe Tone* stared disconsolately at the Irish coast for a full six days but was thwarted from reaching it by the non-stop storms. As he put it himself, 'We were close enough to toss a biscuit ashore!'

A more successful and durable French invasion is apparent in **Bantry House**, where the furniture is Napoleonic, and Gobelin and Aubusson tapestries, as well as Savonnerie carpets, are on display. But so too are mosaics from Pompeii, and Chippendale and Sheraton furniture, thereby underlining the European character of this brilliantly eclectic Georgian mansion. A **French Armada Exhibition Centre** in the courtyard recalls the events of 1796, and in Bantry itself a museum run by the local history society gathers together and displays interesting items relating to the civic and community life of the town.

Glengarriff, further along the coast and one of the loveliest spots in the south-west, may only be a main street with shops and pubs, but *Queen Victoria* graced the Eccles Hotel here with her presence, and *George Bernard Shaw* wrote part of his play *St Joan* in its dining-room. Palm trees and sub-tropical flowers such as fuchsia and arbutus confirm the mildness of the climate, and **Glengarriff Forest Park**, with its oak, birch, rowan and holly trees and stoats, pine-martens, squirrels, foxes, badgers and the occasional sika deer, is conveniently nearby.

Offshore is the island of **Garinish**, where Shaw completed the play he had begun on the mainland. An exquisite spot, it was turned into a veritable paradise in the 1920s by a celebrated architect and garden designer who integrated a whole range of exotic species such as New Zealand privet, sacred bamboo, magnolias and rare conifers into the Italian gardens, using stone balustrades and Grecian pillars as supports. In 1953 the magnificent ensemble was bequeathed to the Irish people.

DON'T MISS

- Visit the exquisitely furnished **Bantry House** with its Italianite terraced gardens and *1796 Bantry Bay Fench Armada exhibition.*
- Enjoy the miniature paradise of **Garinish**, a magnificently planned Italianate garden with clasical pavilions and sub-tropical plants and flowers from many lands.
- Drive to the **Healy Pass** (R572 west from Glengarriff) for absolutely breathtaking views.

ALL-WEATHER OPTIONS

- Visit **Schull Planetarium** for a 45-minute trip through the stars.
- If the children are going off the rails, bring them to see the **West Cork Model Railway Village** at Clonakilty. It is set in the 1940s, and designed with children in mind.
- Use the time to visit the **West Cork Arts Centre** in Skibbereen, which hosts regular arts events.

TOURING ROUTE

Cork to Killarney via Blarney

Leaving Cork from Lady's Well Brewery, we cross a hill and descend into the Blarney valley. Surrounded by groves of yew and holly—said to have been used by the druids for worship—the massive 15th-century keep of Blarney Castle appears, where it is an essential duty for any active tourist to kiss the Blarney Stone. The McCarthys lost Blarney after the Reformation wars, and the succeeding owners built the fine mansion open to the public close by. The village had a thriving woollen industry until the recession of the 1970s; it is now famed for its shopping facilities.

Continue through Dripsey and Coachford, passing on the way a dam and power station on the River Lee.

Shortly before Macroom we turn off into rougher countryside. Left of us the River Lee flows through a myriad of intertwining channels in a low swampy forest. This ecologically unique area of the Gearagh was once the home of the outlaw *Seán Rua* ('Red Seán') and his faithful dog.

Deep in the mountains lies Gougane Barra, whose monastery was formerly believed to have been founded by *St Finbarr*, patron saint of Cork. He was said to have rid the lake of a monster, and in its flight to the sea it carved out the Lee valley.

We continue through the narrow Pass of Keimeneagh, once leaped over by a stag. Finally we descend to Bantry Bay.

Continue to Glengarriff, where we can take a trip on a boat to the magical gardens on the island of Garinish, then

continue over the dramatic Caha Pass to Kenmare. To pay his soldiers with land, the English dictator *Cromwell* commissioned *Sir William Petty* to carry out the first survey of Ireland. Recognising iron ore in this area, Petty founded the town of Kenmare to work it. A stone circle here can be easily visited on foot.

We now cross Moll's Gap into the Black Valley. At Ladies' View, where *Queen Victoria* of England and her ladies climbed out of their carriages to admire the view, we see the long Upper Lake, which runs out through the Long Range to the two other lakes, Muckross Lake and Lough Leane.

To the left looms Carrauntoohil, Ireland's highest mountain; to the right of this the Gap of Dunloe gives access to the lowlands beyond.

The oakwoods in the valley are a remnant of the ancient forests of Ireland. Notice the moss and ferns growing on the trees. Holly abounds here, and 'strawberry trees' or arbutus, native otherwise to the Mediterranean, grow by the lakeshore. Both are being crowded out by rhododendrons, which are now being burnt away.

Muckross House, a large house on the shores of Muckross Lake, now belongs to the Government. The main rooms are in their original style, while items of Kerry folk crafts are displayed in the basement. The gardens are superb.

Killarney is surrounded by mountains and lakes and has been the main tourist attraction of Ireland since early in the nineteenth century. It has not lost any of its character on that account. The cathedral is a fine work of *Pugin*, the main architect of the English and Irish neo-Gothic.

Killarney lake scene, Co. Kerry.

Poets and Storytellers

Another Killarney lake scene, Co. Kerry.

The image of every second Irishman as poet and storyteller is a stereotype but one that most Irish people are only too happy to subscribe to, because it ties in with their own romantic concept of themselves and corresponds to a deeply rooted notion of what is most fundamental in the national experience. Whether or not, as Yeats claimed, it is necessary to read the poems and stories of a people in order to know them, there is little doubt that the most vital element in their heritage is an oral tradition, which reserved a high place for poetic expression and narrative inventiveness.

The first I of Ireland, the first I of poetic
mythology, chanted:
I am the wind which breathes upon the
sea,
I am the wave of the ocean
I am the murmur of the billows

I am the ox of the seven combats
I am the vulture upon the rocks
I am the beam of the sun.

Taken from a piece of verse ascribed to Aimheirgín and translated by Douglas Hyde, this extract illustrates the nature poetry for which the early Irish were famed, which, in its magnificent pantheism, invites comparison with the work of Wordsworth written well over a thousand years later. Who Aimheirgín really was, and what his life was like, are matters of conjecture, but at least we have some idea of what it meant to be a poet in the age in which he lived.

At first the office of the *file* or official poet was second only to that of the king. Twelve years of instruction in poetic skills were required before he received the degree of *ollamh* and obtained the mantle of crimson bird-feathers and the right to carry a golden musical branch or wand of office. In later times the poets' functions were divided up, with the 'brehons' (*breithiúna*) assuming responsibility for the study of law, the druids put in charge of otherworldly affairs, and the *filí* covering poetry and philosophy.

Early on in their history the Irish saw the spoken word from the point of view of memory and magic and the national language from the point of view of identity. The onus on poets and storytellers was to develop a corpus of myths and verbal formulas that would unite people tribally and provide exemplary models of heroism, valour and grandeur for what was basically a warrior caste. Words constituted an offensive weapon as well as serving to bolster political prestige. Both magical curse-words and satire showed how verbal invective could add to the arsenal of warring chieftains when it came to putting one over on their rivals or enemies. As Spenser had already observed in 1596, poets were so admired in Ireland that 'none may displease them for feare to runne into reproach through their offense and be made infamous in the mouths of all men.'

The ancient Irish had a particular affection for heroic sagas and had professional reciters who accompanied kings to the battle-front (rather like reporters today) and who would afterwards add to the sovereign's renown by including his exploits in their repertoire. The trained memory of the teller and the excellence of his manner of recital were required to keep history alive. But when it came to the audience, what mattered most was whether the heroic saga or historical action made good listening or not. Gradually the poet or storyteller became aware of the need to embellish the truth in order to make his tale or poem more attractive to his listeners. And the most obvious way to ensure this was to resort to variation and inventiveness in cases where the material was already familiar to the audience.

Often this meant pushing a theme or tale back into the realms of myth to give it a supernatural grandeur. And since mythology identifies beginnings, much of the early Irish

concern was with gods and genealogy, with a sacred or heroic history, to magnify ordinary mortals and provide the society of the day with a grandiose pedigree and models worthy of imitation. In common with many emerging peoples, the early Irish wanted to know that at some point in their history they had 'rubbed shoulders with the gods.'

In later years, however, the gods were very far away and, had it not been for oral tradition, might not have survived at all, other than as pen-scratchings on fading parchment in library collections. Towards the end of the 19th century people began to recognise the need to record variants of tales and even local stories before they disappeared. This was the brief of the folklorist, and it encompassed the recovery and popularisation of mythic material preserved in folk-tales. As it happened, the main body of oral literature was found in those areas where Irish was spoken. And the custodian here was the *seanchaí* or local storyteller. It was he who handed on the old stories to new generations with his customary catch-phrase: 'That's how it was, and that's how it'll always be!' In the process he added new twists to the old narratives but also introduced local tales or *seanchas*, illustrative of folk-memory and traditions in his area. On the threshold of the 20th century, traditional storytellers were simple men—farmers, labourers, or fishermen—with amazing memories. They could memorise anything up to two hundred and fifty different stories for instant recitation. Without them the social and imaginative life of dead generations would in many cases have been lost without trace.

At the same time that it imperilled the legitimacy of the past, the decline of mythic and epic material to the level of popular entertainment created a fascinating sub-culture. Most of this recycled material comes under the heading of folklore, and it generated fresh tales and poetry in its own right. It includes such well-known characters as the 'banshee' (*bean sí*), a woman of the Otherworld who wails before a death and whom the

Molly Malone statue,
Grafton Street, Dublin.

professional keeners are said to imitate; the *púca* or 'pook' (supposedly borrowed by Shakespeare for Puck in *A Midsummer Night's Dream*), a mischievous and sometimes nightmarish spirit, linked to the goat; and lastly the leprechaun (*lúchorpán*), originally a water-sprite and now an old and bad-tempered cobbler who has pots of gold stashed away at the end of the rainbow.

One of the first enlightened collectors of folk-tales to recognise both the value and the imaginative force of country stories—even about little people—was Augusta Lady Gregory, who recounts her excitement at discovering that 'the people about me had been keeping up the lyrical tradition that existed in Ireland before Chaucer lived.' She learnt Irish and took Yeats on tours of cottages to hunt down folk-tales that, to her surprise, contained versions of the older mythological cycles. In this way, through books such as *Cuchulain of Muirthemne* (1902)

and *Gods and Fighting Men* (1904), she helped make ancient myths and legends accessible by presenting them in an Irish idiom. As she put it herself, 'I have told the whole story in plain and simple words, in the same way as my old nurse Mary Sheridan used to be telling stories from the Irish long ago, and I a child at Roxborough.' It is no exaggeration to say that without Lady Gregory's work and Yeats's enlistment in it, the Celtic Revival and the Abbey Theatre might not have been as successful as they were.

But the real home of poetry and storytellers—essentially the area in which the native language has survived best and where storytelling was still a living art—was on the Blasket Islands, the Aran Islands and the Irish-speaking districts of Counties Cork and Kerry, Galway, Donegal and Mayo. Peig Sayers, who lived for forty years on the Great Blasket off the Kerry coast, was known as the queen of storytellers for her great skill as a *seanchaí*.

Her reminiscences were dictated to and set down by her son as *Machnamh Seanmhná* ('An Old Woman's Reflections'). Muiris Ó Súileabháin's *Fiche Bliain ag Fás* ('Twenty Years a-Growing') and Tomás Ó Criomhthainn's *An tOileánach* ('The Islandman') are other Blasket Island works that draw on memory and recollection faculties central to the storyteller's performance.

Daniel Corkery gave the name *The Hidden Ireland* to a threatened Irish poetry movement that survived in Munster in the 18th century, in spite of linguistic prejudice and Anglo-Irish indifference. It included poets such as Eoghan Rua Ó Súilleabháin, Aogán Ó Raithile, and Brian Merriman. Impoverished individuals, their poetry is nonetheless rich, aware and critical, and their invective covers the English-speaking, exploiting classes, the tragedy of unmarried women, the misfortunes of Ireland, and the decay of native tradition. All came to a bad end: Ó Raithile was to die in poverty, Ó Súileabháin in the unbearable loneliness of a fever hut, and Merriman abruptly while still in his fifties. But the difficulty of his material situation did not prevent Merriman, for example, from revelling in the ironies of life. Consider, for instance, his major poem and the self-affirmation of his outspoken spinster-heroine vis-à-vis any male candidate for her hand. Her disarming comic verve is one of the great feminist surprises of the astonishing *Cúirt an Mheán Oíche* ('The Midnight Court').

> *A man who's s looking for a wife*
> *Here's a face that will keep for life!*
> *Hand and arm and belly that claim*
> *attention*
> *Each is better than the rest.*
> *Look at that waist! My legs are long,*
> *Limber as willows and light and strong*
> *There's bottom and belly that claim*
> *attention*
> *And the best concealed that I needn't*
> *mention!*

This is a far cry from the 8th-century 'Monk and His Pet Cat', which Robin Flower rendered:

> *I and Pangur Bán, my cat,*
> *'Tis a like task we are at;*
> *Hunting mice is his delight,*
> *Hunting words I sit all night.*

Contrasting preoccupations to be sure, but the portrait of the imprisoned monk and the frustrated spinster make wonderful book-ends with which to measure the distance travelled by Irish poetry and poets between the 8th and 18th centuries.

The clear links between poetry, storytelling and the powerful oral tradition are still visible in 20th-century poets such as the Kerryman Sigerson Clifford, a master of narrative ballad form fused with lyrical emphasis. His magnificent 'Ballad of the Tinker's Daughter' begins like any 'once upon a time' yarn of the traditional kind:

> *When rooks ripped home at eventide*
> *And trees pegged shadows to the ground,*
> *The tinkers came to Carhan bridge*
> *And camped beside the Famine mound.*

Who does not want to hear on—or, in our case, read on? This is narrative suspense infused with magic: the magic of the *filí* of ancient times, weaving a spell through words and rhyme. Even Máirtín Ó Cadhain (1906–70), the greatest of recent writers in Irish, shows just how marked his short-story style is by the time-honoured preamble of the *seanchaí* in beginning 'The Withered Branch':

> *I remember that Sunday night as well as*
> *the night just gone.*

Ireland has always been blessed with poets and storytellers ready and able to give a new twist to time-honoured formulas—Clifford and Ó Cadhain among them. Not surprisingly, in the contemporary world, others like them are still with us. Or, as the *seanchaí* would say, 'That's how it was, and that's how it'll always be!'

Jaunting Car in the Gap of Dunloe, Co. Kerry.

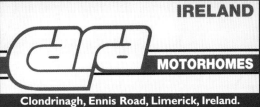

County Kerry

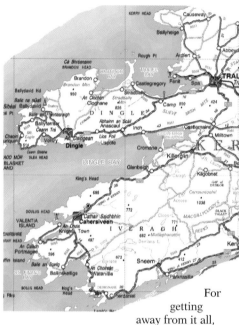

For visitors, it is best to imagine it as four peninsulas: the **Beara Peninsula** (shared with County Cork), the **Iveragh Peninsula** (30 miles long and 15 miles wide), the **Dingle Peninsula**, extending for 40 miles from Tralee to the Blasket Islands, and the most northerly, the **Kerry Head Peninsula**, which is 7 miles long.

The mildness of the weather needs to be stressed. It may rain a lot, but the sun also shines generously, and warmly, and the benign influence of the Gulf Stream permits Kerry farmers to pasture livestock through the winter months and to enjoy all-year-round growth of vegetation. It also makes it possible for tourists to swim from the county's long, sandy beaches and to benefit from the best beauty treatment for dry, city-harassed skin: the soothing touch of warm, moist Atlantic air! Provided one accepts and anticipates the odd rogue shower, it's a climate without extremes, perfect, in fact, for outdoor activity in all seasons.

Of the peninsulas comprising the county, it is probably the **Beara Peninsula** that is the most neglected, because it is the least developed. For those who genuinely want to escape and do their own thing, this is definitely where to go. Most of the untouched and romantic countryside in the area known as **Tuosist**, around **Lauragh**, goes unvisited, and more's the pity. It has some of the finest lakes in the country at **Cloone** and some really striking mountains, few hotels, and brilliant vistas: an ideal place for anyone who enjoys a quiet, undisturbed time, in contrast to a more popular tourist outing such as Killarney.

Not surprisingly, the **Iveragh Peninsula**,

For getting away from it all, County Kerry is the ideal place. In reality, you're not so much getting away from something as going to it: the slow pace of life, the most relaxing and varied scenery in the country, splendid mountains, spectacular lakes, mile after mile of coastline, green-and-yellow chequered hills, slate-coloured cliffs, the kaleidoscopic gaiety of palm trees and sub-tropical flowers and plants, a stunning richness of animals, birds and, saltwater and freshwater fish, acre upon acre of naturally landscaped spaces, hidden and protected by the multiplicity of turns and bends in the jagged coastline of the peninsulas composing the county; and last, but not least, some of the warmest and most charming people anywhere. So don't just get away from it: go to it!

Bordered by Counties Limerick and Cork to the east and by the Atlantic Ocean to the south, west, and north, County Kerry is in the province of Munster and has an area of 1,815 square miles (4,701 square kilometres).

which includes the **Ring of Kerry** and **Killarney**, is the best-known and most travelled of the county's peninsulas. Despite the large numbers of people who visit it, it is still deservedly famous and extraordinarily spoilt by nature in natural beauty.

Smaller but somehow more magical, **Dingle** has a number of distinctive attractions of its own to rival the powerful appeal of the Iveragh Peninsula. Its Irish-speaking district and the Blasket Islands give it the inside track in Irishness, and for an area of its size it boasts the greatest density of archaeological sites in the country.

North Kerry also possesses its own unique strengths, which include the best indoor visitor attractions, good beaches, outstanding golf courses, and first-rate archaeological sites, such as Rattoo Round Tower and Ardfert Cathedral. Here, rolling plains provide a respite from the up-and-down terrain of the rest of County Kerry.

The county has its own special animals. The red deer, a survivor from the last Ice Age over ten thousand years ago, can be found in the hills above Killarney. Japanese sika deer, the only pure breed in the world, are there to provide a contrast. Kerry cattle are reputed to be the oldest breed in Europe and the first developed primarily as milk producers; so if you run into these all-black animals, treat them with the respect they deserve: they're history's first real dairy cow! Last of all, don't forget the Kerry blue: you may need him, one of the finest and most courageous of watch-dogs.

County Kerry also has the widest range of bird habitats in Ireland and an astonishing list of species, which cannot be enumerated here. But if you're in bird-watching mood, try **Blennerville**, near Tralee, for seabirds, and at **Inch** or **Rossbeigh** keep an eye out for the chough. You can enjoy the large population

St Finan's Bay, Ring of Kerry.

of stormy petrels almost everywhere throughout the county, and near **Ballyheige** in autumn watch out for pectoral sandpipers; and if you want to see ringed plover, turnstones, and oystercatchers, the best place is at the fishing village of **Cromane**.

As already mentioned, County Kerry is a botanist's paradise as well. Of special interest are the county's Mediterranean plants, a plant of the saxifrage family known as St Patrick's cabbage, the arbutus, the Kerry lily, fuchsia, and last but certainly not least, the carnivorous greater butterwort, believed by many to be the most beautiful of Irish flowers and found in bogland, where it quietly traps and digests insects as the passer-by admires its innocent, deep-purple flowers.

The Ring of Kerry

Staigue Fort,
Ring of Kerry.

Whether the **Ring of Kerry** begins in Killarney or Kenmare matters little. Both can serve as a point of departure, and the Ring itself can be followed in either direction. Local wisdom argues that the best way to go is to follow the rule of solar ritual and go anti-clockwise. But it should be emphasised that the Iveragh Peninsula is more than a drive; and a simple four-hour spin through the countryside, while better than nothing, will not do the area full justice.

The town of **Killarney**, where most Ring tours begin, originated in the 9th century as a religious site. Early in the 17th century *Sir Valentine Browne* decided to develop a village around Killarney church, and by the 1620s it already comprised forty good English houses. However, the emerging town was largely destroyed during the Cromwellian wars. The existing street layout was the work

of *Thomas Browne* (1726-1795), fourth Viscount Kenmare, and it first became a tourist centre in the middle of the 18th century. Because of its impressive natural setting, Killarney is destined to continue serving as a centre for the numerous tourists who make use of what seems at first glance an over-abundance of hotels, bars, restaurants and cafés for a town of its size.

The most architecturally noteworthy building in the town is **St Mary's Cathedral** (1855), a Catholic church designed by Augustus Pugin in the Early English style. However, the **Franciscan Friary**, built in 1860, is also worthy of notice and contains an admirable stained-glass window by **Harry Clarke**. Opposite the friary is a monument created by **Séamus Murphy** in 1940 to honour Kerry's four best-known poets.

Killarney National Park to the north of

Kenmare is a nature-lover's dream. The lakes are its main attraction, with the highest range of mountains in Ireland, **Macgillcuddy's Reeks**, providing a sumptuous background. **Lough Leane** (5 miles long and with thirty small islands) is the largest; the popular **Muckross Lake** is in the middle; and the **Upper Lake** is peppered with magical islands, each filled with a pleasing variety of trees: juniper, holly, mountain ash, and others. Together, all the lakes and woodlands, including the Muckross and Knockreer demesne and the colourful mediaeval churches and castles, comprise the magnificent park area. The spot is one of incredible horticultural beauty, including rhododendrons, camellias, hydrangeas, azaleas, and magnolias, as well as the arbutus or strawberry tree and oaks, eucalyptus and redwood trees. On the mountain slopes, red deer still roam freely, and in the woods, wild goats and Japanese sika deer share an ideal natural habitat with badgers, foxes, hares, and hawks.

Muckross House, a 65-room mansion built in 1843 now serving as the **Kerry Folk Life Centre**, is the focal point of the national park. It is richly and tastefully furnished on its upper level with oriental screens, Chippendale chairs, and Venetian mirrors, and its ground floor has been transformed into a series of craft workshops and a folk museum. There's also a traditional working farm to see; but the highlight of the estate is the delightful surrounding garden, where, apart from the rhododendrons and azaleas, native strawberry trees make a pleasing display.

Splendid walking areas enliven **Muckross Lake**, providing access to the **Meeting of the Waters**, one of Killarney's main attractions, with, to the left of the **Old Weir Bridge**, an enchanting variety of flowering plants, both native and sub-tropical, including bamboo, arbutus, and magnolia. Nearby, **Torc Waterfall** tumbles decoratively from the wooded sides of Torc Mountain, and on the peninsula separating Muckross Lake from Lough Leane are some of the finest yew woods in Europe, which date back over ten thousand years to the last Ice Age.

Also on the estate is **Muckross Abbey**, founded by *Dónall MacCarthy Mór* and occupied by the Franciscans in 1448. Suppressed at the time of the Penal Laws, the church's surviving ruins include a mid-15th-century nave and choir, a magnificent east window, a wide belfry tower and a south transept constructed in 1500. The striking cloisters have twenty-two arches (a mix of Gothic on two sides and Norman and Romanesque on the others), set about an open court and rendered more dramatic by a giant yew tree supposedly dating from the abbey's beginnings over five centuries ago. Four of Ireland's greatest poets—Feiritéir, Ó Donnchú, Ó Raithile, and Ó Súileabháin— are buried in the abbey grounds.

Lough Leane, the largest of Killarney's lakes, has a splendid backdrop of shelving hills stacked picturesquely behind the lake waters and rising to **Carrauntoohil**, at 3,409 feet (1,039 metres) the highest peak in the country. The main path through the estate leads to **Ross Castle**, which dates from the 15th century and was built by one of the O'Donoghue Ross chieftains. Its four floors, including great hall, parlour, and bedchamber, have been restored, employing traditional mediaeval construction methods. The tower-house is surrounded by a fortified enclosure or bawn. Not only was it the last castle to surrender to the Roundheads during the Cromwellian wars but a legend maintains that the uneasy spirit of its founding chieftain rises from the lower lake on a white horse every first of May.

Across the lake from Ross Castle the island of **Innisfallen** contains the remains of an ancient abbey where *Brian Bóru*, one of Ireland's high kings, is said to have received his early education. The island was also the compilation site for the Annals of Innisfallen, a chronicle of world and Irish history produced between the years 950 and 1380 and now in the Bodleian Library, Oxford.

The **Upper Lake**, the smallest of the three, is held by some visitors to be the prettiest. Sprinkled with neat, generously wooded islands, it is definitely worth seeing. The road running alongside it towards Kenmare continues on up to **Ladies' View**, which provides the best panoramic viewing point of the entire Killarney valley. If in doubt just ask Queen Victoria and her lady companions, whose ecstatic cries on looking down from here gave the spot its name. What they saw, and what any other visitor uttering similar cries can see today, embraces all three lakes, Black Valley and Ross Castle, and the beautiful Gap of Dunloe.

The **Gap of Dunloe** is a tourist institution in itself, especially the spot known as **Kate Kearney's Cottage**. Originally an old coaching inn but now a halting-place for jaunting-cars and travellers before the seven-mile trek or ride to **Lord Brandon's Cottage** on the other side of the Black Valley, its cluster of shops is always packed in the tourist season. Beyond Kate's a road leads up through a narrow gorge created by a glacial breach, Macgillcuddy's Reeks on the right, the Purple Mountain to the left, and imposing cliffs, waterfalls and mountain lakes along the way. Once the Head of the Gap is reached, the track down passes through Gearhameen Valley, a grazing

ground for the ubiquitous red deer, and a fine view opens up of the Upper Lake surrounded by its own oakwoods and set off against the calming beauty of Mangerton Mountain.

The expedition through the Gap can be undertaken on foot, by bike, on horse, or by jaunting-car. At Lord Brandon's Cottage a further and more exciting option beckons: the possibility of taking a boat on the Upper Lake, passing through the Long Range to the Meeting of the Waters under Brickeen Bridge, and actually shooting the rapids on the way back to Ross Castle through Lough Leane.

Another unforgettable view, in an area that is full of them, is that provided by **Aghadoe Hill**, just 3 miles west of Killarney. As well as affording panoramic vistas of lakelands stretching away to a mountain-filled horizon, the hill contains the ruins of a round tower, a castle, and a 12th-century church with an Irish Romanesque doorway and ogham stone on the south wall.

Gap of Dunloe,
Killarney, Co. Kerry.

From Killarney the Iveragh Peninsula runs south-eastwards for nearly 40 miles, with an average width of 15 miles. It contains some of the finest mountains in Ireland, and the coastal route round the peninsula, taken in either direction, comprises the famous Ring of Kerry. Climatic variety accounts for part of its charm, ranging from snow-tipped Carrauntoohil down to gorgeous woodland, desolate bog, and warm, sandy beaches. The 110-mile circuit takes in Killorglin, Glenbeigh, Cahersiveen, Waterville, Sneem, and Kenmare, and so back to Killarney.

As we move anti-clockwise from Killarney, **Killorglin**, situated on the salmon-rich River Laune, is the first town of consequence encountered. Its status as a tourist stop has more to do with the three-day **Puck Fair** held here each August than with any intrinsic virtues. A ritual event involving a large billy-goat dressed out in ribbons and rosettes is the town's great passion and its drawing card for the three-day festival. Each year, in a celebration attended by thousands of people from all over Ireland, as well as foreign tourists, the chosen goat is borne in triumph through the streets and enthroned for a full two days on a raised platform. A great cattle, sheep and horse fair is held during the same period. Why the goat should be king of Puck Fair is anybody's guess. Two explanations have been put forward: the first points to a pagan origin, the second sees it as commemorating an occasion when the stampeding of the animals warned of the approach of Cromwellian forces. Regardless of which version is correct, one imagines the goat requires a little more persuading than that to go along with it all!

After colourful Killorglin comes beautiful **Glenbeigh**, a popular holiday base blessed with a safe and lovely beach (Rossbeigh Strand) and an excellent links golf course at **Dooks**. Nestling at the foot of Seefin Mountain and at the entrance to a ring of mountains where the Beby River flows into Dingle Bay, Glenbeigh is an excellent starting-point for one of Kerry's many fine mountain walks, the 'Glenbeigh Horseshoe', from **Seefin** to **Drung Hill** and affording spectacular views *en route* to Dingle Bay and the Blasket Islands. The **Kerry Bog Village Museum**, just east of Glenbeigh, features traditional 19th-century thatched cottages and a blacksmith's forge.

Further along the road lies **Cahersiveen**, a small town overlooking **Valencia Harbour**. Its most famous son is the 'Liberator', *Daniel O'Connell* (1775-1847), architect of Catholic Emancipation. The ruins of **Carhan House**, his birthplace, can still be seen, and the Catholic church in Cahersiveen was built in 1888 as a memorial to him. Close to the bridge and the town centre, the former barracks of the Royal Irish Constabulary, burnt down during the War of Independence, has been converted into a heritage and tourist information centre. It gives a complete history of the town and its locality, including the **Valencia Weather Observatory**, and also contains a gallery for exhibiting paintings and sculpture by local artists. Near Cahersiveen and joined to it by a bridge is **Valencia Island**, the most westerly inhabited point in Ireland and in Europe, renowned for its deep-sea fishing. It was the chosen site for the laying of the first transatlantic cable in 1857.

Some 9 miles beyond Valencia are the **Skellig Rocks**, one of the outposts credited with helping Christian monastic civilisation survive through the Dark Ages. The **Great Skellig**, an enormous mass of rock rising out of the Atlantic to a height of more than 650 feet (200 metres), which contains the ruins of a settlement built by Early Christian monks, a small church, a larger church, possibly of the 10th century, two oratories, several burial enclosures, and six beehive or corbelled cells. The climb from the lighthouse to the monastery is by stone steps carved out of the bare rock.

At **Portmagee** on the coast, the **Skellig Heritage Centre**, covering the 'Skellig Experience', is a popular visitor attraction. This is an audiovisual centre where the background to the monastic occupation of the island is explained, as well as the life of lighthouse-keepers who worked there between 1820 and 1987. Other topics include the habits of local seabirds and the life of sea creatures in the area.

Waterville, famous as an angling centre,

parades palm-trees and fuchsia to prove it is a famous resort as well. Over the years it has attracted many celebrities, including **Charlie Chaplin** and family, who stayed here regularly at the Butler Arms Hotel and in whose honour the town erected a monument in 1998. Doubly advantaged by its situation on the eastern shore of Ballinskelligs Bay on a strip of land that separates the ocean from magnificent **Lough Carrane**, it provides a choice of seawater and saltwater fishing and some spellbinding walks and views. Linked in legend with the coming ashore of Noah's granddaughter Ceasair in 2958 BC and with the arrival of the Milesians in 1700 BC, the town has four aligned stones, which mutely beg the visitor to accept that either one or the other story is true.

The Iveragh Peninsula's links with Daniel O'Connell surface once more at **Derrynane National Historic Park**, covering over 300 acres of tree-filled land running to the sea along Derrynane. Both the estate and the house on it belonged to O'Connell, who lived and worked here during his political life. The well-preserved house, now a museum filled with O'Connell's personal possessions and furniture, as well as a chapel-room, complete with altar, exudes a powerfully Catholic and 19th-century ethos. Extensive gardens contain plants of many varieties, a ring-fort, and a number of beach and nature trails.

Past the village of **Caherdaniel** is a signposted left turn leading to **Staigue Fort**, one of Ireland's finest archaeological remains. A 2,000-year-old dry-stone fort or 'cashel' built in the form of a circle and enclosing a space 30 yards wide, it has massive walls and was apparently built for defensive purposes, with perfectly fitting interior steps leading to the parapets.

Further along the Ring route, **Sneem** enjoys an appeal attributable to its situation in one of the most scenic parts of the country. The tiny town has a Mediterranean feel to it, not only because of the presence of palms but because of the vivid colours in which the houses are painted. A good fishing location, the town's international outlook is epitomised by an exhibition park with statues and sculptures from all over the world. The two squares contain monuments to *Cearbhall Ó Dálaigh*, former President of Ireland, who lived here, and these have recently been joined on the central green by a memorial to *Charles de Gaulle*, who visited for two weeks; it is sometimes referred to cheekily as 'De Gallstone'!

East of Sneem is the sub-tropical resort of **Parknasilla**, associated with *George Bernard Shaw*, who frequently stayed here. Since Shaw's time Parknasilla's Great Southern Hotel has attracted many overseas visitors, among them *Prince Rainier* and *Princess Grace* of Monaco. But the benign micro-climate of the area has also proved appealing to the general public anxious to enjoy the pleasant woodland walks, safe bathing, magnificent gardens, and lush scenery.

DON'T MISS
- Don't overlook the obvious: see the **Lakes of Killarney**—all of them! Don't just settle for the Ring of Kerry tour: prove you've a head for heights by visiting the unmissable **Gap of Dunloe** as well.
- Visit the **Skellig Experience Centre** which tells the story of the history and archaeology of Skellig Michael's early Christian Monastery. Boat trips operate from the centre to the Skellig Islands.
- Go back in time by visiting the unique 2,000-year-old dry-stone **Staigue Fort**.

ALL-WEATHER OPTIONS
- Visit **Derrynane House**, home of Daniel O'Connell, and see the video of his life in the room where he lived and worked; learn something about the history of Kenmare and the making of needlepoint lace at the **Kenmare Heritage Centre**.
- Go to the **Butler Arms Hotel** in Waterville and examine the fine collection of Charlie Chaplin photographs in a place he stayed in regularly.

Coumeenoole and Slea Head,
Co. Kerry.

Dingle Peninsula

Dingle, the most northerly of the spectacular promontories of County Kerry, stretches invitingly to the west for 30 miles. Between Tralee and Inch runs the Slieve Mish mountain range; this gives way to wild hill and lough country before the mighty peak of Brandon Mountain imposes itself on the horizon as one looks northwards from Dingle. On the western side of the promontory the beautiful coastal plain is covered with a mixture of villages in what is essentially an Irish-speaking area, where traditions, crafts and the art of story-telling also survive. In prehistoric remains the Dingle Peninsula is also one of the richest parts of the country, with more than two thousand prehistoric sites. This fascinating archaeological and linguistic appeal make touring in Dingle, or travelling through it, a marvellous opportunity to learn something new, as well as to enjoy an absorbing holiday experience.

If one approaches the promontory from **Castlemaine**, the **Slieve Mish Mountains** rise up on the right-hand side. Further on, on the inner coast road, is the sheltered seaside resort of **Inch**. Its four-mile beach of firm, golden sand rises up into sheltering dunes where archaeologists have found a wealth of kitchen middens and old habitation sites. In the 18th century, certain elements would tie a lantern to a horse's head when the weather was bad; the idea was to entice mariners to follow a supposed companion-boat or what they might mistake for a welcoming beacon, only to discover too late that they had been tricked into running aground and that their cargo was about to be seized. More recently, the filming of *The Playboy of the Western World* and scenes from *Ryan's Daughter* were carried out here with great co-operation from the local people.

From Inch the road turns inland to **Anascaul**. New arrivals in the village may well be curious to know how or why a South Pole Inn came to be established at Ireland's south-west tip. The answer is that *Thomas Crean* (born 1877–1939), who accompanied Scott and Shackleton on their Antarctic expeditions, was born here. When he came home from sea, he bought the pub and gave it its present name.

Dingle, the next big town on the circuit, has much in common with Kinsale. It is full of gaily painted, well-maintained houses, a lively fishing ambience, and a reputation for good restaurants. A more recent and spontaneous attraction (and one not likely to appear on a menu) is Fungie, a dolphin who strayed into the bay in 1983 and has been winning hearts and minds ever since. The **Dingle Oceanworld** in the town has a life-size model of him and provides valuable background information not just on his movements but on those of many other sea creatures, both local and foreign. The town also contains a Craft Centre with a variety of specialised workshops covering everything from the making of uilleann pipes and violins to more familiar activities such as pottery, hand-weaving, jewellery, leatherwork, wood-turning, and cabinet-making.

As its enclosed natural harbour suggests, Dingle has always been a favoured port of call, especially in the 14th and 15th centuries, when it was Kerry's major port, and in the 16th century, when it was important enough to be a walled town. Later on, its remote situation helped to establish it as a smuggling centre, and at one point in its history it went so far as to mint its own coins. The town's past is very much in evidence at **Dingle Library**, where a large collection of printed material relating to local history is on display, in addition to a permanent Thomas Ashe exhibition, documenting the local man's prominent role in the Easter Rising of 1916.

What follows from Ventry on, all the way to Slea Head, can only be described as an incredible open-air archaeological museum. Here the density of ancient and prehistoric sites and monuments is truly exceptional, beginning with the striking promontory fort of **Dunbeg**. An Iron Age construction set on a 60-foot cliff above the sea, it comprises four defensive walls and, inside these, a stone wall sealing off the promontory. An underground escape passage, situated at the entrance, connects with the interior of the fort, where people and livestock were placed when under threat from rival tribes. Between Ventry and Slea Head a small private museum has recently opened, the **Celtic and Prehistoric Museum**, which boasts a small but beautiful collection of artefacts from the Stone Age up to Viking times, together with fossilised dinosaur eggs and a fully electric sheep!

On the side of **Mount Eagle**, both east and west of Fahan, are over four hundred beehive huts or *clocháns*: circular dry-stone dwellings, most of which were built in pre-Christian times; almost twenty souterrains; and an equal number of incised stones. Such a proliferation of ancient sites dovetails naturally enough with myth and legend, and nearby **Ventry Harbour** is held to be the spot where *Fionn mac Cumhaill* engaged in an epic three-day battle to repel an invasion launched by the King of the World. Fionn, though victorious, was no innocent, having eloped with the wife and daughter of the King of France. A blow-by-blow account of what happened can be read in a 15th-century manuscript now in the possession of the Bodleian Library at Oxford.

The village of **Dún Chaoin** was the setting for the film *Ryan's Daughter*; of the original sets built for the film only the small schoolhouse remains. Most tourists will probably be more interested in the town's **Blasket Islands Heritage Centre**, which displays material connected with the wonderful literary tradition of the islands and also shows the hard farming life, featuring land cultivation undertaken with the spade alone, donkey transport, and fishing by *curach* (a boat of tarred hides stretched over a wooden frame).

Kilmalkedar, Dingle, Co. Kerry.

Winter scene,
Dingle Peninsula, Co. Kerry.

Dún Chaoin is an ideal point of departure for the **Blasket Islands**, as is Dingle. The largest of the islands, the **Great Blasket**, is now a national historic park, where at least some of the dilapidated houses are being restored. If you think you'd like it well enough to stay overnight, bring provisions and a tent: there's no shop and, naturally, no hotel, though the island café serves dinner. A former village at the north-east end was evacuated when its inhabitants were all moved to the mainland in 1953. Today the pleasures offered by the island are those of natural beauty, and reliving a vanished and heroic life-style in imagination as one walks its well-trodden paths.

Further on from Dún Chaoin on the mainland is the delightful Irish-speaking town of **Ballyferriter**, nestling at the foot of the Croaghmarhin mountain. It possesses an excellent heritage centre where prehistoric and Early Christian artefacts are used to illustrate the history and geology of the area. A second centre contains an exhibition of the wild animals and plants of the Dingle Peninsula. North-west of the village stand the remains of **Ferriter's Castle**, birthplace of *Piaras Feiritéir*, one of the last chieftains to hold out against Cromwell's armies.

Also north of Ballyferriter lies **Smerwick Harbour** and the old fort of **Dun an Óir**, where over six hundred Irish and Spanish soldiers surrendered in 1580, only to be massacred by Lord Grey's troops. Close to Ballyferriter, a good idea of what an Early Christian monastery looked like can be had by visiting the recently excavated site of **Reesk**, which dates back to the 4th or 5th century and features beehive huts, an oblong oratory, and a corn-drying kiln, enclosed by a dry-stone wall.

However, pride of place when it comes to Christian monuments must be given to dry-stone **Gallarus Oratory**, just a mile from Smerwick Harbour and one of the best-preserved Early Christian church buildings in Ireland. Thought to have been built some time between the 9th and 12th centuries, its form resembles that of an upturned boat. As good a place to shelter with a friend as to pray (the oratory's snug, and still dry after a thousand years), it measures about 9 feet by 15 feet and has a small window in the east wall and on its west side a narrow door nearly 6 feet in height.

A few miles away at **Kilmalkedar** is a fine rectangular Hiberno-Romanesque church complete with ogham stone and sundial, most of the remains dating from the 12th century. An ancient track leads from here to the top of **Brandon Mountain** and St Brendan the Navigator's Shrine, supposedly the place where the saint saw *Í Bhreasail*, Isle of the Blest, in a visionary moment, after which he voyaged far and wide (some say to America) to find it.

Castlegregory, a small, friendly town on the isthmus separating Brandon Bay and Tralee Bay, is named after Gregory Hoare, a 16th-century chief who built a castle here. Famous visitors to the castle included *Edmund Spenser, Sir Walter Raleigh*, and *Lord Grey*, who, on his way to meet the Irish and Spanish at Smerwick, was received here by Hoare's son, Hugh. But Mrs Hoare objected to receiving the enemy in her home and emptied all the available wine over the cellar floor. Hugh, either mortified at an insult to the prestigious visitors or incensed at the waste of good wine, or both, killed her on the spot. He then showed a superb sense of timing by dropping dead before he could be arrested and tried for murder.

Inland from Castlegregory, two mountains, Stradbally and Brandon Mountain, are separated by the highest pass in Ireland open to vehicular traffic, the **Connor Pass**, a winding, twisting route that climbs and climbs above dark bogs and golden beaches below. The constantly shifting glimpses of mountain slopes and valleys and the distant bays climaxes at the summit, where panoramic views of both sides of the promontory are suddenly revealed in all their glory southwards to Dingle Harbour and northwards to Brandon Mountain, Brandon Bay and Tralee Bay.

Beyond the end of the northern tip of the peninsula, spreading out from Castlegregory, are the Seven Hogs or **Magharee Islands**, one of which, **Illauntaunig**, contains the remains of an Early Christian monastery founded by **St Seanach**. On the site are the ruins of two oratories, circled by a wall, as well as three beehive cells. The village of **Camp**, on the inland route to Tralee, is the best starting-point for the ascent to the fortress of **Caherconree**. On a triangular plateau nearly 1,000 feet (300 metres) high stand the remains of a stone fort. This was the fortress of *Cú Raoi mac Dáire*, a king of ancient Ireland. His wife seems to have had a lot in common with Mrs Hoare of Castlegregory: she spilt things, but with malice aforethought. In a gesture similar to Mrs Hoare's, she poured milk into the local stream, thereby alerting her husband's enemies to his presence in the fort and ensuring that he died at their hands in the shortest possible time. The lesson would seem to be that wasteful women bring death, and that you'd do well to avoid them.

DON'T MISS
- Visit the **Blasket Islands**; if you can't, don't miss the **Great Blasket Island Visitor Centre** at Dún Chaoin, which details the island's heritage and lets you listen to the sounds of keening and crashing waves.
- It's a mortal sin if you fail to visit the Early Christian **Gallarus Oratory**, an absolute jewel of its kind and still in pristine shape after more than a millennium.
- Go to Dingle to meet the toast of the town, a friendly dolphin named **Fungie**—no Disney cartoon, but the real thing!

ALL-WEATHER OPTIONS
- Go to the recently opened **Dingle Oceanworld**, a new aquarium opposite Dingle Harbour, where you can admire fish and other sea-life caught by local fishermen off the Kerry coast.
- Visit **Ballyferriter Heritage Centre** and find out about the area's history and geology through a study of the prehistoric and Early Christian artefacts on display.

North Kerry

At **Blennerville**, on the approach to Tralee, is Ireland's only remaining commercially operated windmill. Constructed in 1780 and recently restored, it now produces five tons of ground wholemeal per week. A guided tour is supported by an audiovisual and hands-on demonstration.

Blennerville is also the terminus for the **Tralee-Blennerville Steam Railway**. A mile of the former Tralee and Dingle Light Railway, which closed in 1953, has been relaid, and locomotive no. 5 (restored by a team from the North Yorkshire Moors Railway), along with two coaches from Bilbao, have been operating here since January 1993. A novel attempt to build a replica of the *Jeanie Johnston*, a triple-masted passenger ship that carried emigrants to Baltimore, New York and Québec at the time of the Great Famine, is being made in a local shipyard. It is hoped that it will retrace the original routes and mark in this way the Famine's 150th anniversary before returning to a permanent berth at Blennerville.

Tralee, Kerry's county town, was founded in the 13th century by the Anglo-Normans and takes its name from the River Lee, which flows into Tralee Bay. By the 12th century Tralee had emerged as a fortified town and was the seat of the Earls of Desmond. In 1580 it was burnt because of a revolt against Queen Elizabeth, and in 1587 she granted it to *Edward Denny*. The association of the Denny family with the town continued for over three hundred years. The town became a borough in 1613 but was largely destroyed during the wars of the 17th century. Much of the town's existing architecture dates from the 18th century.

Modern Tralee began to take shape in the 19th century, when Day Place, Staughton's Row and Prince's Quay were added. Denny Street was completed in 1826, and the recently restored courthouse was built in 1835. The Tralee Ship Canal (1846) and the arrival of the railway (1859) opened it up for trade and commerce and laid the basis of the town's prosperity. The establishment of an institute of technology, and the opening of a regional airport at **Farranfore**, just 10 miles from the town, have also contributed to its continuing development.

At the **Ashe Memorial Hall** the mediaeval town and the Anglo-Norman Fitzgeralds are the subject of an audiovisual presentation entitled 'Geraldine Tralee', which carries visitors through a partial reconstruction of the time in specially equipped cars with multilingual commentary. Upstairs the **Kerry County Museum** uses local artefacts and audiovisual techniques to convey a clear picture of the countryside north of Tralee and its history. Tralee is also home to **Siamsa Tíre**, the national folk theatre, which makes use of local tradition and its own resources of music, song and dance to celebrate the ancient seasonal festivals and rural way of life. The theatre itself is built in the form of a ring-fort, with a round tower providing access to the upper levels, so that the architecture effectively reinforces the traditional focus of performances within it. On a more contemporary note, leisure activities are well provided for with the multi-million-pound **Tralee Aquadome**, which features a wide range of indoor water pursuits. A few miles down the road at nearby Fenit, reputed birthplace of **St Brendan**, is **Sea World**, an aquarium filled with representative sea creatures from all round the coast of Ireland. Tralee also has its own horse and greyhound racing tracks and a Gaelic football stadium.

Before leaving the Tralee area, make sure to visit **Ardfert**, 5 miles to the north-west, for its partially restored mainly 15th-century cathedral. Originally the site of a monastery founded by St Brendan the Navigator in the 7th century, it later became the headquarters of the Anglo-Norman church in Kerry. The cathedral retains an Irish Romanesque doorway with fragments of an arcade on each side and stylish lancet windows. The south transept houses an exhibition dealing with the church's historical background. In the graveyard are a number of ancient tombs and a 5th-century stone carved with ogham characters. Nearby is the late 12th-century **Temple na Hoe** (Temple of the Virgin) and 15th-century **Temple na Griffin** (Temple of the Griffin), which on its north wall window-jamb carries an image of two winged dragons with crossed necks, apparently an emblem of evil devouring itself. Down the road from the cathedral, **Ardfert Friary**, a Franciscan house, was founded in 1253 by **Thomas Fitzmaurice**, the first Lord Kerry. It has a well-preserved tower and chancel.

Ballybunnion Beach, Co. Kerry.

The South

Blennerville,
Co. Kerry.

Up the coast from Ardfert are the splendid beaches of **Banna** and **Ballyheige**. The five-mile Banna Strand was used in the filming of *Ryan's Daughter* in 1968, but a more poignant memory is evoked by the memorial to *Roger Casement* at the entrance to the strand. This was where Casement landed from a German submarine on 21 April 1916 with arms for the Easter Rising. He was found in an ancient ring-fort a couple of miles from Ardfert and arrested. Later the British authorities tried and hanged him. The fort where he hid is signposted 'Casement's Fort'.

Eastwards and inland from Tralee, the market town of **Castleisland** was once the power base of the Earls of Desmond. It is known today for its distinctive red marble, much favoured in local construction projects. Not too far from the town is the recently discovered **Crag Cave**, a limestone cave system with brilliant clusters of stalagmites and stalactites casting eerie shadows through dark, hollowed-out areas that run for almost four miles and are traversed by their own rippling underground streams. A thirty-minute guided tour is time well spent, especially for younger visitors.

The attractive town of **Listowel**, on the River Feale, is the first large centre encountered between Tralee and Tarbert. Its main landmark is the ruined 15th-century **Fitzmaurice Castle**, set in its fine central square. The town is dominated by two facing neo-Gothic churches, **St John's** (Protestant) and **St Mary's** (Catholic). St John's was deconsecrated in 1988 and today houses a theatre, arts and heritage centre and the local tourist office. In the south-west corner of the main square is the Listowel Arms Hotel, where many historic figures, including *Daniel O'Connell, William Makepeace Thackeray* and *Charles Stewart Parnell*, stayed on occasion. It is from the hotel's upper window that Parnell is reputed to have made his famous declaration, 'No man has the right to set a boundary to the march of a nation.'

Listowel is justifiably proud of its literary traditions. *Maurice Walsh*, author of *The Quiet Man*, lived here, and the writer *Bryan MacMahon* was headmaster of the local boys' national school. But probably the town's most famous son is *John B. Keane*, author of *Sive* and *The Field*, whose name is also associated with one of the town's best-known events, the **Writers' Week** held in June each year. The other event that galvanises local energies is the annual **Listowel Races**, held in the third week of September.

At one time the town was a terminus in the world's first monorail system. Called the Lartigue Railway, after the Spanish engineer who brought it into being, the system ran successfully from 1888 to 1924 and linked Listowel and Ballybunnion. A more recent international connection, the **Garden of Europe**, begun in 1995 to coincide with the commemoration of the ending of the Second World War, is close to **Childers Park**. It consists of a monument made from railway sleepers and chains and is dedicated to those who died in the holocaust. It is set among gardens where thousands of shrubs from all over Europe symbolically recall the innocent victims of a campaign of genocide.

West of Listowel are a series of long sandy beaches and promontory forts, running from Ballyheige along the coastline northwards to Ballybunnion. At the estuary's most westerly point, **Kerry Head**, stand the remains of two stone forts, built over two thousand years ago as promontory defences against attack from the sea. All that's left today are semicircles of stone wall no more than 3 feet high, with 60-foot cliffs behind them.

Further up the coast at **Knappogue North**, **Ballyduff**, is the **Rattoo Heritage Museum**. It contains local archaeological finds and houses exhibits covering the history of the area in all ages, including a Bronze Age ferry-boat carved from a split oak trunk. On the other side of Ballyduff is **Rattoo Round Tower**, an exceptionally well-preserved round tower dating from the 10th or early 11th century. The ruins of a 15th-century church mark the spot where an earlier abbey, founded in 1200 and taken over by the Augustinian order after two years, was burned to the ground in 1600.

Ballybunnion, the next town of consequence, is essentially a seaside resort with several fine beaches, hot seaweed baths, and an extensive network of caves. The 30-foot wall of the 16th-century **Fitzmaurice Castle**, standing on the promontory at the end of the main beach, has become the town's most recognisable landmark. There are fine views from the ruin to Loop Head and the Dingle Peninsula. At its mid-point, the cliff-top walk opens up on a 12-foot-wide blowhole that, though fenced off, still permits one to view and hear the sea crashing on the rocks 100 feet below. In the 13th century an O'Connor chief discovered that his nine daughters had plans to elope with his sworn enemies, the Normans. Furious at what he considered their betrayal, he hurled them one by one to their death through this terrifying gap in the cliffs. To this day the place is known as Nine Daughters Hole.

However, for those who prefer eighteen holes to nine daughters, Ballybunnion has one of the best links courses in the world, beloved in particular of **Tom Watson** and played over on an epic Saturday, 5 September 1998, by that renowned bunker specialist, **Bill Clinton**.

On the road from Ballybunnion to Ballylongford lies the village of **Astee**. Nothing special, you may think, until you find a pub bearing the familiar name of Jesse James. The father of the notorious outlaw was born here, and later emigrated to Missouri. It was in that state, also on 5 September (1847), that the great trouble-maker himself made his entrance into the world, all barrels blazing.

Northwards from **Ballylongford**, a farmland village beyond Astee, lie the striking Gothic ruins of **Lislaughton Franciscan Friary**, built in 1478 by *John O'Connor Kerry*. Despite centuries of neglect, the walls of the friary are still in good condition, and a number of attractive windows and well-preserved *sedilia* make viewing worth while. To the west of Ballylongford stands **Carrigafoyle Castle**, main seat of the O'Connors. The castle stands over 60 feet high, but only three of its walls are standing as a result of the destructive assault launched by Cromwellian forces in 1649.

Tarbert, on the northern shore, apart from being the ferry-port providing access to County Clare, is also a favoured spot for shoreline fishing. **Tarbert House**, built about 1730, displays a fine collection of Georgian furniture, including one of the best examples of an Irish Chippendale mirror.

Golf

Teeing-off at Ashford Castle, Cong, Co. Mayo.

In Ireland's fields, the golfing grows. 'There is surely no finer place in the world in which to play the greatest of games,' *Nick Faldo,* winner of three Irish Open Championships, once said of Ireland. It is estimated by the Department of Tourism, Sport and Recreation that by 2005, when the Ryder Cup is held in Ireland, over 500,000 people a year will visit the country specifically to play golf.

The Irish affinity for golf, as traditional as the passion for horse-racing, is steeped in the sport's well-documented lore, and you have to go back almost a hundred years to find out when the famous Portmarnock links hosted its first tournament. Golf aficionados still associate the Portmarnock and Woodbrook clubs outside Dublin with the Irish Open in the 1970s, when television first transmitted images of legendary golf figures such as *Jack Nickalaus* and *Seve Ballesteros* to a global audience. The magic of the Nickalaus name continues to resound in Ireland. The six-times US Masters champion and winner of a staggering seventy-one US Tour events designed the spectacular course at Mount Juliet in County Kilkenny. Indeed not many new eighteen-hole golf courses in Ireland have been designed without the expertise and invaluable contribution of professional golfers: the Ryder Cup heroes *Christy O'Connor Junior* and *Philip Walton* designed Galway Bay Golf and Country Club and St Helen's in County Wexford, respectively.

The description that comes to mind about Irish golf courses is 'testing'. Oozing acres of charm, with spectacular views of a seascape panorama at one hole and a verdant valley bisected by a rotating column of sunlight at the next, the average Irish golf course is paradise gained. The drawn beauty of the championship course in Ireland has been immortalised by some recent famous Irish Opens at Mount Juliet and the Druid's Glen in County Wicklow, where giants of the modern game, such as *Colm Montgomerie*, have plied their trade with distinction. Unlike the cradle of the game, St Andrews, Irish golf courses do not set out to intimidate the golfer but to titillate—but be warned: the beauty of an Irish golf course is as deceptive as the Irish charm, and no one hole is remotely the same as another.

No country has such a concentration of golf courses as Ireland, the diversity of whose terrain is reflected, for example, in the marvellous turf surface of the Ballyferriter club on the Dingle peninsula or the natural sand dunes of the Portsalon links in north Donegal. The development of courses at a pace unequalled in Europe has been accompanied by the construction of new hotels, club houses and amenity facilities to complement many famous existing establishments, which nestle in the radiant landscape, from the quaint hospitality of the 32-bedroom Bushmills Inn in a County Antrim village that is home to the world's oldest distillery and is close to the Bushfort course, where Scotland is visible on a clear day, to the modern 110-bedroom Castlerosse Hotel in the heart of County Kerry, replete with pool, gym, sauna and restaurant and adjacent to quality golfing in Killarney. Ireland's richest reservoir of history is celebrated and preserved in hotels well known to travelling golfers, like the Edwardian Aberdeen Lodge and Victorian Court Hotel in Dublin or indeed the Old Inn in Crawfordsburn, County Down, with records dating back to 1614.

Records of a different nature will be the hot topic among the international fraternity of golf-lovers when the Ryder Cup comes to Ireland in 2005. In 1999 we witnessed the intensity of the Ryder Cup confrontation between Europe and a jubilant America on a level almost unprecedented since the biennial event began in 1927. The eyes of the sporting world will be firmly focused on the K Club in County Kildare for an event that has a tendency to almost exclusively immortalise the selected venue—think of the Belfry and Valderrrama—such is the interest in the drama that unfolds over eighteen precious holes.

The hosting of golf's most celebrated team competition takes place during a golden age of the sport in Ireland, when over £200 million has been invested in golf as an industry to ensure that facilities are second to none. The Department of Tourism, Sport and Recreation estimates that 250,000 overseas golfers visited Ireland in 1998, four times the figure of ten years ago. The Government introduced an eight-year programme of promotion, culminating in the Ryder Cup matches in 2005, which represents one of the most intensive and sustained tourist promotions ever undertaken. Meanwhile the Junior Ryder Cup has been scheduled for the K Club in 2001. To borrow a phrase from the great poet Rupert Brooke: in whatever country our golfing visitors pursue their sport, some corner of a foreign field will remain forever Ireland.

Leaving Killarney, take the T20 road to Farranfore, turn left on the R561 to Castlemaine, and head for Inch to start the tour of the Dingle Peninsula. We follow the Slieve Mish Mountains, stretching along the peninsula as far as Brandon Mountain. Inch Strand, a long, dune-backed beach, is a favourite with walkers and swimmers.

Continue along the coast road, with fine views to Anascaul, where the South Pole pub is named after *Thomas Crean,* who took part in Scott's ill-fated Antarctic expedition in 1912.

Continue past Minard Castle on the right, the largest fortress on the peninsula, and the dry-stone circular fort. On the left, Anascaul Lough at the foot of Slieve Mish offers great views and good fishing. Continue via Lispole, with its colourful pub fronts, to Dingle, situated on Dingle Harbour, home of the resident wild dolphin Fungie. Boat trips are available.

A former trading port with America, Dingle is now an active, well-protected fishing port at the head of the bay and an 'ecological' tourist centre in the heart of the Irish-speaking district of County Kerry. Pubs, seafood restaurants, boutiques and art galleries abound. In the Old Presbytery in Main Street is a permanent exhibition on the archaeology, ethnology and history of the region.

Leave Dingle and follow Slea Head Drive via Ventry Bay, a naturally protected bay with excellent beaches.

On the left is Burnham, the former residence of *Lord Ventry.* Legend had it that the hero *Fionn mac Cumhaill* rebuffed an attack by *Dáire Donn,* King of the World, who landed in the bay. Between Ventry and Slea Head we find an astonishing concentration of ancient monuments, notably the 5th-century *clocháns* or dry-stone beehive huts of the Fahan group. (Permission is required from the landowner to visit the site.) Nearby is Dunbeg Fort, an Iron Age stone fort on the tip of the promontory.

Continue around Mount Eagle and the abrupt cliffs of Slea Head, from where we can admire spectacular views of the Iveragh Peninsula and the Skellig Rocks. Further on we discover the now uninhabited Blasket Islands, home of the islanders until 1953, among whom figure such

TOURING ROUTE
Killarney to Tarbert via Dingle

writers as Tomás Ó Criomhthainn, author of *An tOileánach* ('The Islandman') and Peig Sayers, who wrote *Peig*. In 1588 two Spanish Armada ships sailed between Dunmore Head and the Great Blasket Island before being shipwrecked on the treacherous rocks. Continue to Dún Chaoin, the village where the Blasket Islanders settled.

The Blasket Islands Heritage Centre welcomes visitors to an exhibition on island history and culture. Smerwick Bay has excellent beaches, while Irish-speaking Ballyferriter is the main village on the peninsula. Continue on to Gallarus Oratory, a perfectly preserved 8th-century chapel with dry-stone corbelled roof, characteristic of Early Irish Christian architecture. Nearby at Kilmalkeder is an example of a 12th-century chapel and a rare two-storeyed mediaeval building called St Brendan's House. Return to Dingle and continue back via Anascaul and Camp, with its splendid views over Castlegregory and Tralee Bay, to Tralee.

Tralee is the county town of Kerry (16,980 inhabitants), best known for its Rose of Tralee festival held each September. Nearby Fenit is one of the principal ports of County Kerry, now a yachting centre, from where *St Brendan* was believed to have sailed in the 6th century to discover America. Ardfert was an important monastic city in the 6th century founded by St Brendan, with a ruined 13th-century cathedral and earlier Romanesque chapels, and Ardfert Abbey, founded in 1253 for the Franciscans by *Thomas Fitzmaurice*, Lord of Kerry.

From here we take the N69 road to Listowel, a busy market town best known for its annual Writers' Week held each May, with a series of conferences and theatrical representations. Continue to Tarbert on the Shannon Estuary for the Tarbert–Killimer car ferry to Kilrush and Ennis in County Clare.

Old village at Dún Chaoin, Dingle Peninsula, Co. Kerry.

Traditional Music and Dance

Martin Hayes, traditional musician.

FIRST STEPS

The harp (*cruit* in Irish) is the earliest musical instrument mentioned in Irish literature. After 1700, harpers and musicians lost the aristocratic patronage they had enjoyed up to then and became itinerant performers dependent on the hospitality of the so-called big houses and Ascendancy landlords. *Ó Cearúlláin* (Turlough O'Carolan) (1670–1738), perhaps the greatest of Irish harpers, lived through this period of decline but, eclectic in taste, mixed Irish and non-Irish airs and produced a wide range of compositions, from baroque to vernacular dance music.

With the eclipse of the harper, the piper stepped into the breach. The now familiar *uilleann* (elbow) pipes represent an Irish variation on the bagpipe. Uilleann pipes rely on a bag filled by a bellows, a chanter or melody pipe, and the addition of regulators, in contrast to the blow-pipe technique of the war-pipes that preceded them. As played by

Séamus Ennis, Willie Clancy, Liam O'Flynn and *Paddy Maloney,* the uilleann pipes had a massive impact on folk music and took on an increasingly important solo role in ensemble performances.

Traditional musicians also make use of the fiddle, generally thought to have made its entry as early as the 17th century (but not necessarily for the playing of traditional music), the flute, the tin whistle, the accordion, melodeon and concertina, and the *bodhrán* or frame-drum. Guitar, banjo and bouzouki are late entries to the fold.

Sometimes, of course, there are no instruments at all, and the unaccompanied singing known as *sean-nós* (old style) is seen by many purists as the most authentic part of the Irish musical tradition.

In the case of Irish dancing, critical emphasis is often placed on its uniqueness. But it is not unique at all. Of the two words for 'dance' in Irish, *damhsa* and *rince,* the first comes from the French *danse,* while the latter is a borrowing of the English *rink.* As for the dances themselves, Irish reels have a Scottish ancestry, the hornpipe is of English origin, and the Irish set-dance (eight measures of music are called a *step*) derives from quadrilles performed at the French court. But if one takes any national music or dance tradition in any European country, a multiplicity of influences and sources is visible. What the Irish adopted they made their own, and the real shapers of Irish dance were the late 18th-century dancing-masters who travelled from village to village accompanied by a piper or blind fiddler and imparted their skills to their pupils while devising ever new and more intricate steps.

OPPRESSION

Under English rule, any manifestation of cultural difference on the part of an Irishman was regarded as potentially seditious. Queen Elizabeth started the ball rolling by decreeing that bards and harpers were to be executed on the spot and yet at the same time

professed herself in private exceedingly pleased with Irish tunes and country dances. King Henry VIII, having decided that harps and organs were inciting the natives to revolt, outlawed them, and referred to a prevailing assumption that Irish musicians were spreading a talent of Irish disposition and conversation among the gentlemen of the English Pale. And so it went.

But apart from the catastrophic reverses in battle that typified Irish luck on the battlefield, the last and most sinister oppressor of Irishmen in their daily lives and, by extension, of Irish music and dancing was *Phytophthora infestans*. In its destructive effect on Irish lives and fortunes, the fungus that produced the potato blight and set off the Great Famine can best be compared to the AIDS virus and its decimation of talented artists in this century. Those musicians who survived the Famine years and stayed on found themselves singing songs of death and destitution, loss and lament, while those who went away took their music and their memories with them.

REPRESSION

With so much already stacked against them, you would think that Irish music and dancing had more than enough to contend with. Not so. Where English oppression and the Famine left off, Irish repression took over. True, the Gaelic League, founded in 1893, had the avowed goal not just of bringing back Irish but of reviving Irish culture in general. But it went about it in a rather narrow way. It was the League that sponsored the first *céilí* in 1897, but at the same time it frowned on step-dancing as a suspect, imported cultural form. And wherever step-dancing was carried on, parish priests aided and abetted the League by restricting arm movement in dancers, favouring the stiff upright stance and effectively banishing Eros to Limbo. In 1935, to make matters worse, Éamon de Valera introduced the Public Dance Halls Act, which banned country house dances, as well as all-night jazz dancing in unlicensed halls. And crossroads dancing fared no better. Even the establishment in 1951 of the annual *fleá cheoil* (music festival) did little to disturb the puritanical 'hear no evil, see no evil' ethos that prevailed throughout 1950s Ireland.

EXPRESSION

But suddenly, and unexpectedly, one man appeared on the scene and ended this crisis by transforming traditional music from within. In 1960 *Seán Ó Riada* composed the score for *Mise Éire,* a documentary on the 1916 Rising. Such was the success of the film that he became a celebrity overnight. Next he worked in 1960 with a traditional music group, *Ceoltóirí Chualann,* to produce and perform another score, this time for a film version of *The Playboy of the Western World.* The new sound won universal acclaim at the concert-hall level, and Ó Riada quickly integrated classical forms, harmonies and improvisations into the traditional music. Solo statements, duets and trios livened and enhanced ensemble playing and paved the way for a redefinition of what was both possible and permissible within the traditional canon. Soon the *Chieftains* were launched; other innovative groups, such as *Planxty, Stocktons Wing* and *Clannad,* followed, and today the Willie Clancy Summer School, held each July in County Clare, ensures consolidation of the progress made. With Ó Riada, traditional Irish music had attained an expressive freedom and versatility undreamt of under the old dispensation. The only question remaining at the time was: could the same thing happen in dance?

Against all the odds, it did. And in conjunction with the Chieftains. Of course, it was heresy to those brought up with the early *sean-nós* dance style in mind: close form and posture, legs kept together, no high kicks, little or no turning, and obviously no travelling! Who would dare challenge this paradigm of rigidity? The answer in two words was *Michael Flatley,* who, by breaking most of the rules in the *sean-nós* style sheet, lit up the rather dull step-dance scene with all the brilliance of a meteor. His talents as a dancer and flute-player were already known to the Chieftains, who integrated him into their performances on world tours. But it was the 1994 Eurovision Song Contest interlude performance of 'Riverdance' that showed how magnificently Irish dance had come of age as an entertainment, spectacle and, indeed, flexible art form.

FOOT-NOTES

As the entire world knows, Irish traditional music has always had one grandstand day when the entire universe wears green and the world's population stamps to an Irish beat: St Patrick's Day, celebrated by natives and non-natives alike. But because of the incredibly rapid growth of interest in Celtic music and dancing, from the first impact of exiled Irish in the Appalachian communities of the United States to the more recent phenomenon of foreign groups, both amateur and professional, playing Irish music in concert halls and pubs, the span of interest throughout the world is no longer one day but the entire year.

While it was to be expected that America and Australia, with their large communities of expatriates, would perpetuate the Irish folk tradition and even contribute to it, who could possibly have predicted the appearance of a Swedish band called *The James Gate,* a *Dóchas* band in Prague, the *Kyle na no* from Italy, *Ashplant* in Denmark, the *Hair of the Dog* in the Netherlands, *Deoch an Dorais* in Germany, the *Inishowen* in Grenoble, or *Shantalla* in Belgium? Add to this the fact that Irish musicians themselves have carried on the tradition of the itinerant harpers of the Ó Cearúlláin era by travelling, not from house to house but anywhere and everywhere— musical missionaries spreading the gospel of Irish rhythms to fresh converts in every corner of the globe.

During the folk and traditional revival of the

Early 20th century — set dancing on the Blasket Islands, Co. Kerry.

1960s and 1970s, groups such as the *Dubliners, Planxty*, the *Chieftains, Dé Danann, Christy Moore, Davy Spillane* and *Van Morrison* broadened the scope of Irish music enormously. *Planxty* merged Balkan bouzouki rhythms with uilleann piping; other groups assimilated American folk, Cajun and African melodic and instrumental influences that took straight trad in totally new directions. This broadening continues apace. Even *Altan,* the most talked-about group to come out of Ireland in a decade, deeply rooted as it is in Donegal authenticity, produces compositions marked by the drive of Scottish music, and with a bouzouki added. Increasingly, home-grown Irish music can only be fully understood against a global background, even if, as Turgenev says, art must be parochial in the beginning to be cosmopolitan in the end.

Inspired by American inventiveness, Irish dance has also moved forward. The current production of *Dancing on Dangerous Ground*, an Irish dance spectacular inspired by mythology's great lovers, Diarmaid and Gráinne, and starring *Jean Butler* and her new dance partner *Colin Dunne,* has been described as the raunchiest Irish dance show yet. But even at a less ambitious level of basic instruction, the audience for Irish dancing has expanded far beyond these shores, and in the most unlikely places. *Patricia Kilalea,* for example, an Irish dance specialist, is at present teaching fifty boys and girls the rudiments of Irish dance in Dubai. The students are mainly Irish but include a good number of Dutch and Russian pupils as well.

With all these astonishing changes from a purely Irish tradition likely to increase further, and a new millennium and St Patrick's Day almost upon us, God knows what kind of beat we'll be tapping our heels to next year. Only one thing is certain: the whole world's invited!

The West

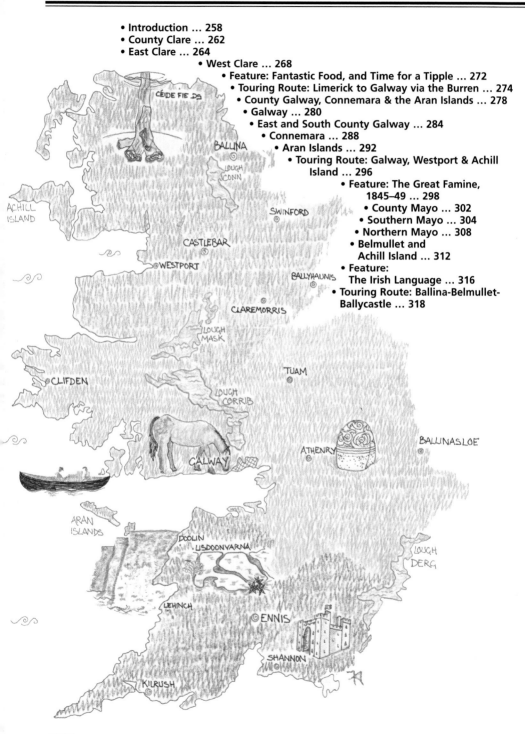

CÉIDE FIELDS

BALLINA

LOUGH CONN

ACHILL ISLAND

SWINFORD

CASTLEBAR

WESTPORT

BALLYHAUNIS

CLAREMORRIS

LOUGH MASK

CLIFDEN

TUAM

LOUGH CORRIB

BALLINASLOE

ATHENRY

GALWAY

ARAN ISLANDS

DOOLIN

LISDOONVARNA

LOUGH DERG

LEHINCH

ENNIS

SHANNON

KILRUSH

View from Clare Island,
Co. Mayo.

The West

As a recent film title reminds us, the idea of 'into the west' is synonymous with romantic escape and adventure. In the film the efforts of an impoverished Dublin teenager to retain possession of an abandoned horse trigger off a flight westward. This motif strikes a natural chord with an urban population holding on to childhood memories of Galway holidays punctuated by glimpses of Connemara ponies. For most people the western counties are first and foremost havens of mountain, beach and lake recreation and, at a second remove, taken collectively, a quintessential Irish-speaking source of national character and identity. For Dubliners, holidays in County Galway, Clare or Mayo have the added dimension of informing them experientially about their own Irishness—an attribute threatened by the levelling effect of a standardised urban existence. In other words, a Dubliner's trip to the west is no different in kind from that of Irish-Americans in search of their beginnings, in that it involves a return to the 'roots'.

To a large extent, the strength of this extraordinarily attractive and diverse region lies in exactly that: roots, survival, and character. It is an area where the colourful landscape can be rich, spectacular and savage by turn, or again stony, hard, and desolate (one thinks of the Burren plateau, or the young fisherboy perched on the island cliff-tops in O'Flaherty's *Man of Aran*). Even a remembered visit is enough to stamp the mind with powerful images of survival, millennial endurance, and asceticism—summoning up in the process the entire historical record of simply being there, and pulling through. Wasn't this in fact what happened once Cromwell informed the natives of Ireland of their simple choice, 'To Hell or to Connacht,' thereby setting in motion the westward displacement of those strong-willed patriots who refused to accept the idea of submission to English rule.

The romantic notion of 'westerners' as independent spirits and radical custodians of Irish identity and values owes much to decisions taken in one of the most crucial and painful periods of Irish history. From the 16th to the 19th century, the west suffered severe poverty, with most people making a precarious existence from subsistence farming or fishing. Life was bleak and hard, rendered worse by the stony, infertile nature of much of the land and the disastrous advent of the Famine. But times have changed, and the popularity of the area with tourists from Ireland and abroad has given the people fresh pride in their major inherited assets: a hardy, positive character, loyalty to the native language, and a passion for music.

To a generation brought up on instant mass-media culture and quick fixes, the revelation of another world—of tradition, of difference, of continuity, involving spontaneous communal participation in such activities as céilí dancing and folk music—comes as a breath of fresh air. Who could have foreseen that consumer-age children would turn out to be the latest enthusiasts of such traditional pursuits as fiddle and bodhrán sessions in rural pubs—homely milieus light-years away from the neon disco-lands of the metropolis. But such is increasingly the case, especially in the Clare and Galway areas where the poor, the excluded and the expelled native Irish have won their own late victory over adversity and taken up position centre stage.

County Clare is bounded to the north and south by Galway Bay and the Shannon Estuary; to the east its extension ends with the immense Lough Derg, and to the west it finds its limits in the Atlantic. To the north the countryside is stark and empty, characterised by the plateau of the Burren, but on the coast, cliffs at Loop Head in the south give way for a space to seaside towns and sandy beaches, such as Lehinch, only to reappear in spectacular form in the Cliffs of Moher. Very different scenery typifies the east of the county, where the tranquil waters of Lough Derg permit clear unobstructed views of the Tipperary mountains.

County Galway, the second-largest county

Ballynahinch,
Co. Galway.

The West

in Ireland, is divided in two by Lough Corrib, which also defines a major landscape difference: that between eastern inland and western coastline terrain. The eastern side of the lake is made up of arable farmland, while on the western side lies Connemara, a rugged landscape fashioned out of rock and water, soaring mountains, and limpid lakes. The Aran Islands represent a continuation of Connemara, both in scenic starkness and in cultural attachment to Irish language and traditions. The city of Galway—independent, lively, and prosperous—mediates all the county contrasts as fishing-port, cultural mecca, and booming cosmopolitan fun-spot.

County Mayo—the third-largest county in Ireland—stretches from Lough Corrib and Killary Harbour in the south to Killala Bay and the barony of Erris in the north and from Achill Island, Clew Bay and the Mullet peninsula in the west to Counties Sligo and Roscommon in the east. It has one of the lowest population densities in Europe and has suffered for many years from correspondingly high levels of emigration. With the exception of Broad Haven, the north coast is made up of a succession of cliffs, while inland, bog prevails, and the central area is dominated by the Nephin Beg range of mountains. The larger towns are in the southern plains of the county.

As this summary physical description suggests, the west cannot be spoken about in monolithic terms, even if it is rightly considered a region. The astonishing diversity of its landscape means that each area has its adherents. Painters and solitary souls drawn by the sparsely populated, abandoned look of western Galway, with its bog, lough and mountain panoramas and its soft, pastel sky-colourings, can vanish without trace into Connemara to enjoy an 'out-of-time' experience. Those of a more sociable and epicurean frame of mind will head instead for the fun-filled music pubs of the region and focus on the city of Galway for its restaurants and lively cultural and festival scene; while those in search of Irish and archaeological riches will make a trip to the Aran Islands, or the Craggaunowen Project, and delight in the perennial simple things like hundreds of little stone walls and wind-bent, solitary trees that confer on the region its timelessness and unpretentious charm.

Or again they may choose to head off to the Céide Fields, at the northern tip of County Mayo, where the excavation of boglands has revealed primitive dwellings, megalithic tombs and prehistoric boundary walls built over five thousand years ago. These were eventually abandoned and covered over by turf, long before the Egyptian pyramids were even thought of! And let us not forget that for the devout the west has its magical, visionary appeal, containing as it does the largest Marian centre in Ireland at Knock, as well as the foremost ancient monastic centres of Clonmacnoise and Clonfert and the penitential and pilgrim mountain of Croagh Patrick. Also very special, the haunting grey limestone slabs of the Burren draw amateur geologists and botanists, especially in early spring, when the unrelieved lunar landscape suddenly acquires exquisite splashes of colour as the wild flowers return and the miracle of growth from the tiniest of rock crevices is replicated on a massive scale. Finally, those restless individuals who cannot conceive of landscape without a turbulent sea and a limitless horizon will undoubtedly head to the windswept fastnesses of Moher to experience the thrill of sheer cliff-face plunging into the raging Atlantic—the ideal location for reciting Byron, or striking the pensive attitude of Caspar David Friedrich's sea-gazer on a headland!

The region's exceptional attractiveness is visible from what's on offer for tourists: undisturbed and stunning areas of peace and natural beauty; an opportunity to hear Irish spoken as the community language; an immensely rich heritage of music, song and dance, available throughout the three counties; unsurpassed access to leisure-time activities of every kind, including boating, fishing, horse-riding, sailing, water-skiing, scuba-diving, surfing, golfing, mountain-climbing, and walking; a chance to explore geological, archaeological and botanical phenomena unique in their genre—all in a shower-drenched and sun-drenched environment of utter relaxation.

**Twilight on Killary Harbour,
Co. Galway.**

County Clare

A magnificent fresh-water resource, the largest and most majestic river in Ireland, and thousands of miles of unfettered sea, stretching to America— the spectacular borders of County Clare show both how spoilt and how undervalued it is in its aquatic variety. But totally unseen, under an age-old stretch of limestone rock, lies still more water: the trapped underground run-off of rain that has cut its way through the karst surface, widening lines created by the process of Ice Age marking and the glacial melt, which plays its part in producing microclimatic surprises favouring the appearance of a wholly unexpected profusion of floral life.

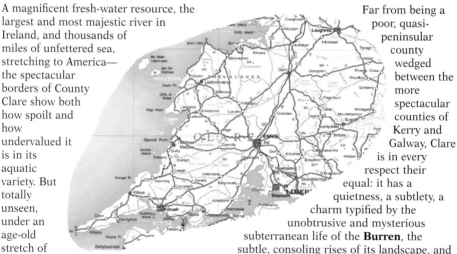

Far from being a poor, quasi-peninsular county wedged between the more spectacular counties of Kerry and Galway, Clare is in every respect their equal: it has a quietness, a subtlety, a charm typified by the unobtrusive and mysterious subterranean life of the **Burren**, the subtle, consoling rises of its landscape, and the meticulous craft of its many gifted fiddle-players—music personified and shy delight in their low-key, unrivalled expressiveness.

Although it has already been discussed as part of the Shannon region, it is worth recounting the crucial place that **Lough Derg** occupies on County Clare's eastern

Doonagore Castle, Doolin, Co. Clare.

flank. One of the largest of Ireland's lakes, comprising 50 square miles, it constitutes a superb leisure water-park where cruising, sailing, windsurfing, water-skiing and quality angling can all be pursued. Over and above the attractions of Lough Derg itself, the lakelands of east Clare provide a chance to enjoy fine scenery and holiday activities of the same kind, but in still calmer and cheaper surroundings.

While County Clare has no metropolitan centre to rival the cities of Galway or Limerick, its county town, **Ennis**, with its narrow and winding streets, is a busy market town with a good deal of character and plenty of music pubs. In the Middle Ages its friary was a thriving university, with up to six hundred students still enrolled towards the end of the 14th century. Recently it was chosen by the Government as a pilot town for the development of internet and other computer-related facilities among the local population. It is an unassuming, relaxed urban centre situated at the crossroads between the west and south-west, and an ideal base from which to explore County

Clare in depth.

Apart from the magical qualities of its landscape and people, the 'Banner County' (so called, it is said, from the participation of its sons in the Battle of Ramillies in 1706) is renowned for a variety of other reasons as well. As the 'Banner' tag suggests, County Clare is a very historic place: aside from its evident ties with *Éamon de Valera*, who represented the county for many years in Dáil Éireann, and *Daniel O'Connell*, who successfully contested a Clare seat in 1828, the county has a wealth of prehistoric vestiges, Norman castles, and monastic sites.

The longest-serving church in the country, dating from the year 969, is situated at **Tuamgraney** in the east of the county and is still open to visitors. The **Craggaunowen Project** in mid-Clare recalls life in the county from the Bronze Age to the Middle Ages, and the role of crannóg construction in lake-based communities in early Ireland. The legacies of the past are still visible in the 12th-century **Ennis Abbey** and the mediaeval abbey at **Quin**. And, as many former visitors can testify, nightly mediaeval banquets at **Knappogue** and **Bunratty Castle** re-create ancient life in a festival of Irish music, dancing, and song. In County Clare, the past is alive, and it is alive with music.

Music is in fact one of the most imperishable assets of an area that is also affectionately referred to as the 'singing county'. In recent times the main centre for tourists in search of the best in traditional music has been **Doolin**, a small seaside village that in the summer attracts hundreds of tourists, fans of Clare's heritage of song, dance, and instrumental music. But there are many other places—such as **Milltown Malbay**, **Scariff**, **Tulla**, **Killaloe**, **Feakle**, **Spanish Point**, **Quilty**, **Lehinch**, **Ballyvaghan**, and **Lisdoonvarna**—where impromptu music and dancing sessions provide an opportunity for Clare men and women to show what they are best at, while also providing a chance for visitors to test their own dancing or musical skills in front of sympathetic and appreciative onlookers.

East Clare

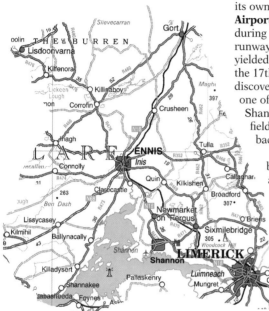

its own right. Those who land at **Shannon Airport** may be intrigued to learn that during the construction work for the main runway, two forts were excavated and yielded proof of habitation in the region in the 17th and 18th centuries. However, the discovery of a stone axe-head at **Tullyglass**, one of the townlands taken over by the Shannon complex, pushes the earliest field evidence for activity in the area back nearly four thousand years.

Transatlantic flying into Ireland began in 1937 at **Foynes** with the arrival of a Pan-American plane from Newfoundland after a $12\frac{1}{2}$-hour flight. Soon aircraft were flying regularly into the newly constructed airport; and following a break in traffic during the Second World War, service resumed in September 1945 when a Pan-American Skymaster touched down after a $7\frac{3}{4}$-hour flight from Gander. But the airport, which benefited from the fact that the limited range of aircraft necessitated a fuelling stop, began to experience difficulties as soon as longer-range planes were introduced. To compensate, local points of appeal have been created. **Bunratty Castle** and **Knappogue Castle** banquets, **Bunratty Folk Park**, the **Craggaunowen Centre** and the Rent an Irish Cottage scheme, along with the building of a 10,000-foot runway, form the spearhead of a strategy to ensure that tourists continue to come to County Clare.

Situated half way between the lower sections of east and west Clare, **Ennis** (population 16,000) is the main town in the county. A busy market centre straddling the River Fergus, its narrow and winding streets give it a distinctly mediaeval feel, though it is now the chosen site for an innovative technological project whereby local people have been supplied with computers to prepare the public for the information and

Dominated by the River Shannon, Slieve Bernagh Mountains and Lough Derg, east Clare is a superb outdoor activity area and one of the best places in the country for hunting, shooting, and fishing. To the south-east the county is low-lying and unspectacular by comparison with the lake region north of Killaloe or the impressive Atlantic coastal scenery, but its closeness to Limerick makes it easily accessible, and it possesses its own tourist appeal in the shape of such proven attractions as **Bunratty Castle and Folk Park**, **Cratloe Woods House**, and the Bronze Age reconstruction of **Craggaunowen**. (Some of the important features of east Clare—Bunratty Castle, for example, and Killaloe—have already been examined as part of the Shannon region and will not be discussed in great detail here.)

Shannon is County Clare's newest town. With a population of over 8,000 people, it is not only the site of the world's first duty-free airport but an important industrial site in

Craggaunowen,
Quin, Co. Clare.

communications challenges of the future. Ennis contains a 19th-century cathedral, a monument to *Daniel O'Connell*, and a mediaeval monastery, **Ennis Friary**, founded in 1242 by the O'Briens, kings of Thomond. Now in ruins, it contains a number of interesting sculptures and decorated tombs. Of these the best is the 15th-century MacMahon tomb, with its well-crafted alabaster carvings of the Passion. The O'Connell monument is especially appropriate in a county that, despite the ban on Catholic MPs, returned *Daniel O'Connell* by such a huge majority that it proved impossible to prevent him taking his seat in the House of Commons in London. Ennis was also the place where *Charles Stewart Parnell* made his famous speech in 1880 advocating the use of the boycott against landlords. And finally, *Éamon de Valera* was the TD for Clare from 1917 to 1959. A bronze statue outside the courthouse records his connection with County Clare, as does the **De Valera Library Museum** in Harmony Row, a small but fascinating local history centre. Less fascinating and more forbidding, the austere cathedral at the end of O'Connell Street seems architecturally out of character with the general friendliness of the townspeople and the Clare consensus that small is beautiful.

Apart from its historical connections, Ennis is a great music centre and has two annual festivals, the **Fleá Nua** and the **Guinness Traditional Music Festival**, the first in May and the second in November. But even outside festival times the town maintains a high standard in folk music, and good sessions of Irish music, Cajun and rock can be enjoyed in local pubs and clubs throughout the year.

To the east of Ennis, **Quin** is an old-world village with a well-preserved Franciscan friary, founded in 1433. Monks continued to live here up to the 19th century. Beside the friary is the 13th-century Gothic church of *St Finnéan*.

Just 2 miles south-east of Quin is **Knappogue Castle**, an enormous town-house built in 1467 by the McNamaras. They constructed no less than forty-two

castles in this part of County Clare from about the year 600 to the middle of the 15th century. Happily, the immense walls at Knappogue are intact, and many of the rooms have been skilfully restored, with their carved 16th-century oak fireplaces and furniture. Less of a piece with the more ancient elements in the castle are the 19th-century additions, set off by anachronistic furniture and crystal. However, the general effect is imposing, and provided one is not too concerned with period niceties, the castle is admirably suited to its present role as staging-place for mediaeval banquets. Incidentally, one reason the castle survived for so long is that *Cromwell* used it as his headquarters in the 17th century, thereby safeguarding it from the destructive fate of similar castles elsewhere.

Dromoland Castle and the town of **Newmarket-on-Fergus** lie to the south below Knappogue Castle. Constructed in 1826, Dromoland is situated in 550 acres of parkland by the River Fergus. It is now a top-class hotel, with its own 18-hole golf-course at the disposal of its guests. Newmarket-on-Fergus owes its name to Lord Inchiquin, who named the local racecourse after the horse-racing centre in England. In the grounds of his neo-Gothic mansion, Dromoland Castle, is the most extensive hill-fort in Ireland, **Moghane Hill-Fort**, with several acres of ground encompassed within its treble walls. It is supposed to have been the site of a prehistoric walled village and a meeting-place in about 500 BC. The ramparts of the fortification are 23 feet thick in places, but low-lying. A magnificent find of elaborate gold Bronze Age adornments was made near here in March 1854, but many were later sold off cheaply, or melted down for the value of the metal. But some casts were made, and these have been preserved in the Royal Irish Academy.

Sixmilebridge, a pretty village to the west of Newmarket, grew up around a crossing-place on the O'Garney River. As early as 1664 the first rapeseed-oil mills were established here, and Dutch artisans later improved and rebuilt the existing facility. The village benefited from a steady river trade; and ships from Amsterdam sailed up the river almost as far as Sixmilebridge in the 17th and 18th centuries, returning to Holland with cargoes of oil from the mill. Today the village is an architecturally picturesque complex with three squares and a green; with the decline in river trade and the closing of the railway link, its survival is tied increasingly to tourism and local initiatives.

Scarriff, to the north-east towards Lough Derg, is a small angling and market town, charmingly situated near the shore of Scarriff Bay and especially popular with fishermen, who use the town as a base for fishing the River Graney, the Shannon, and nearby Lough O'Grady, 2 miles to the west. Scarriff and neighbouring **Tuamgraney** have grown so much since the 1950s as to become almost one town, yet each retains its separate identity. Five miles north-east of Scarriff is **Mountshannon**, another fishing centre and the main port for trips to **Holy Island**.

Of the other villages within striking distance of Lough Derg, Tulla and Feakle are among the prettiest. **Tulla** grew up around *St Mochulla's* monastery and is a small commercial centre. Wedge-shaped gallery graves are numerous in the vicinity,

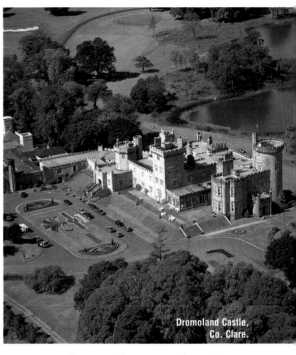

Dromoland Castle, Co. Clare.

as are the ruins of various castles and tower-houses and interesting caves called 'taumeens', formed by the action of an underground river eroding an open gorge. **Feakle** is an agreeable, secluded village set on the southern slope of the Slieve Aughty Mountains.

DON'T MISS

- Don't miss the unique opportunity to visit **Cratloe Woods** to see the last inhabited example of an Irish longhouse—a type of building that has almost disappeared. The 17th-century house belongs to a descendant of Brian Bórú and contains family portraits and other works of art, as well as a collection of antique farm machinery.
- Don't miss **Knappogue Castle**, which dates back to 1467 and was painstakingly restored by an American couple and transformed into a splendid venue for mediaeval banquets and Irish historical evenings. Well worth a visit, even during the day.

ALL-WEATHER OPTIONS

- Reduced to despair by the glowering black skies? Then look in on Bunratty Barn, part of the **Bunratty Folk Park**, where you can see cheerful local women prepare a piping-hot Irish stew and scrumptious griddle bread while you relax and wait for the sun to come up in the yeast!
- If you're mesmerised by the sparkling resemblance between a rain-drop and a sequin, then perhaps you should see **Quin**, especially its elegant **Franciscan friary**. The effort of climbing the spiral staircase will be suitably rewarded by the cheering vista of the cloister, and some mint-fresh countryside!

West Clare

Most of south-west Clare has already been touched on in relation to the Shannon system, and so attention will be concentrated here on what lies northwards from Kilkee.

In the late 19th century, **Kilkee** became popular as a seaside resort for Limerick families, and the town still retains a democratic appeal and character based on entertainment arcades, fast-food outlets, and a fine sandy beach. It offers safe swimming both off the beach and in the *pollock holes*, natural swimming-pools found in the **Duggerna Rocks**—a sort of natural reef to the south of the strand. With its wide range of diversions and sports, including diving, snorkelling, scuba-diving, good trout fishing and golf links, as well as a small **Heritage Gallery**, it remains an ideal family resort.

Above Kilkee, along the coast, is the fishing village of **Doonbeg** (*An Dún Beag*, 'the small fortress'), where a Spanish Armada ship, the *San Estebán*, was wrecked on 20 September 1588. Those who survived at sea did not do so on land and were hanged at Spanish Point, 2 miles to the west of Milltown Malbay. **Doonbeg Castle**, now in ruins, was a fortress of the MacMahons and later of the O'Briens. **Quilty**, a village with an excellent sandy beach and boats to hire for sea angling, is a seaweed production centre. Another Armada ship, the *San Marcos*, was wrecked off nearby **Mutton Island**. The headland above Quilty, **Spanish Point**, is named in memory of the dread events of 1588, when so many ships from Spain foundered or were wrecked in the area.

Opposite Spanish point is **Milltown Malbay**, a popular holiday resort but in recent years more famed for its Willie Clancy Summer School, held in the first week of July and named after one of the

greatest uilleann pipers the country ever produced. Beyond Milltown Malbay is another extremely popular resort, **Lehinch**, favoured with an excellent beach that—provided the weather is right—is a fine place for surfing. If you don't surf you can play golf on its excellent championship course. And if you neither surf nor golf you can go for a swim, or explore the pleasant surroundings on foot. Two miles inland is the old town of **Ennistimon**, with its unpretentious 19th-century church and single main street lined with colourful shops. Situated close to the Cullenagh River, it is an excellent centre for traditional music, and good brown trout-fishing is available in the vicinity.

Further northwards the coast curves towards **Hag's Head** and the town of **Liscannor**. To the west of the town, **Clahane Beach** is a favourite place to

Cliffs of Moher,
Co. Clare.

swim. From Liscannor the coast road leads to the spectacular **Cliffs of Moher**, which run for nearly 5 miles. Following the cliffs on foot, from O'Brien's Tower down to Hag's Head, makes for a dramatic walk. Part of the walk was blocked off with Liscannor

stone by **Cornelius O'Brien** (1801–57), the local landlord, who apparently had the look-out tower constructed to make a favourable impression on some lady visitors. But the splendid views over the Aran Islands, Galway Bay and the hills of Connemara may

Poulnabrone Dolmen,
The Burren,
Co. Clare.

have impressed them even more than his tower!

Just a few miles from the cliffs is the celebrated village of **Doolin**, traditionally a small fishing village with a sandy beach but nowadays famous as a place of pilgrimage for traditional music lovers—a solid reputation based on no more than three pubs. From Doolin a ferry runs to the Aran Islands.

Corrofin, on the road from Ennis to the Burren area, is set in the heart of the Clare lakelands on the banks of the River Fergus, near the shore of Lough Inchiquin. It began to acquire prominence when **Máire Rua Ní Bhriain**, who married a Cromwellian to save lands for her son, lived here after her eviction from **Lemaneagh Castle**. At the end of the 17th century a small Huguenot colony was established in Corrofin. **Inchiquin Castle**, built in the 15th century on the north shore of the lake, is in a ruinous condition, but part of the old castle tower can still be seen, and a good portion of the banqueting hall is intact. The recently restored **Ballyportry Castle** was occupied in 1580 by **Mathúin Ó Briain** and appears to have escaped the ravages of war and time. Corrofin is an ideal spot for anglers, being close to the **Clare Heritage Centre**, which runs a service helping visitors to trace their roots.

On the route northwards from Ennis to Corrofin is **Dysert O'Dea**, site of a monastic settlement founded by **St Tóla** in the 7th century and the scene of a famous battle in 1318, when the O'Briens vanquished the de Clares of Bunratty and thereby prevented an Anglo-Norman takeover of the county. A ruined 12th-century Hiberno-Romanesque church with an ornately carved south-facing doorway, decorated with grotesque animal heads and human faces, brings the period quickly into perspective. The archway, with its row of twelve stone heads, is intriguing; and the **White Cross of Tóla**, carrying high-relief carvings of Christ and a bishop and a depiction of Daniel in the lion's den, is also well worth seeing. A museum and archaeology centre are accessible in the nearby **O'Dea Castle**; you can follow this up by setting off on the trail of twenty-five sites of historical and archaeological interest identified within a 2-mile radius of the castle.

A few miles above Corrofin is **Killinaboy**, a village that contains a ruined church from the 11th century. For most visitors the main point of interest is not the church but the grotesque figure over the south door of a woman exhibiting her genitalia. The carving, of the kind known as a **sheela-na-gig**, may have been intended as a warning to monks of the seductive power of women, or else simply constitute some form of fertility symbol.

DON'T MISS

- You'll lose face, like the cliffs, if you don't view **Moher**, one of the most majestic sights in Ireland. Five miles of dramatic cliff-top son et lumière, superb views on all sides, and to crown it all the great spectacle of the sea in all its moods, orchestrated by the incessant wheeling and screaming of birds.
- Swimming or playing golf at **Lehinch** are both exceptional experiences. Lehinch has a marvellous sandy beach in a protected bay, with welcoming Atlantic water warmed by the Gulf Stream as well as one of the best and most demanding links courses in the country. Strike while the iron's hot!

ALL-WEATHER OPTIONS

- Visit the **Clare Heritage and Genealogical Centre** in **Corrofin** to get an absorbing multidisciplinary introduction to the past three hundred years of the area's history. A central exhibit, Ireland West, 1800–1860, covers the Famine years, emigration, and the Land War. An on-the-spot genealogical service is also available.
- If you don't dig the rain then at least see the spade with which Parnell turned the first sod for the **West Clare Railway**: it's on show at the **De Valera Museum and Library** in **Ennis**, along with lots of other interesting exhibits relating to Ireland's famous leaders.

 'Don't forget to pick up your Global Refund Tax Free Shopping Cheques as you shop.' *www.globalrefund.ie* GLOBAL REFUND™

Fantastic Food, and Time for a Tipple

After a good night out there are perhaps few things more satisfying than tucking in to a full Irish breakfast the next morning. A bowl of porridge followed by a fully garnished plate of mushrooms, soft black and white pudding, sausages, rashers and eggs, and toast, washed down by lashings of hot tea, creates an aroma that whips up a fierce appetite that is sated as quickly. A meal in itself, the Irish breakfast is unrecognisable in comparison with its Continental counterpart, but it is a great opportunity to sit around a table and discuss the fun from the night before and make plans for the day ahead.

Lunch is a more understated affair but no less tasty for that. Hot soup followed by lavish servings of thick home-baked bread topped with fresh cottage cheese, again washed down with copious amounts of tea, regularly found in the comfortable environs of a local pub, is a great way to break up a hectic schedule.

Come evening time, and diners seeking out authentic fare are spoilt for choice. Irish stew is something of a national dish and readily found on most menus. Consisting of diced meat, most likely beef or lamb, with a rich mix of vegetables and a good stock, it has in many ways taken over from its poorer relation, coddle, a thick soup containing just about anything edible, once common in Dublin. Bacon and cabbage is another favourite with natives and visitors alike.

Surprising as it may seem, the potato remained popular after the Great Famine, and even today Irish people have not lost their taste or appetite for this humble root vegetable. Boiled, baked, roasted, chipped, or mashed, it continues to command pride of place at meal time, most commonly with lamb cutlets or slices of prime roast beef. Another, more traditional method of serving it is in the form of boxty or potato bread, a special potato pancake that is experiencing something of a revival in recent times.

As an island nation, Ireland's diet naturally features sea-food, especially in coastal villages and towns. Mussels, oysters, cod and crab are just some of the many species cultivated from the seas around the country. Inland, the majestic salmon, with its stunningly serene flavour, is a popular fish dish, and a taste of the first catch of the season will set you back thousands of pounds, such is its pedigree.

Diet gurus tell us that 'we are what we eat.' If this is true for the individual, then it also holds at a national level. In an alarming age of food scares and debates about genetically modified food, Irish farm produce retains that essential and natural link with the land. It may not be 'delicate' in the same way as *haute cuisine,* but it is this unadulterated earthiness, a sense that it has come from the locality, that gives it its character and appeal.

All this talk of food conjures up the image of Sancho Panza, the squire in Cervantes's book *Don Quixote,* pleading with his knighted master to 'quench this confounded thirst that plagues our throats ten times worse than hunger did our guts.' If the Irish are fond of a tipple, then it is because their native drinks are of a very high quality and embody the easygoing outlook that good things should happen at their own pace. Indeed this approach to time is arguably the greatest ingredient in the art of drinking. It takes time, some might say practice, to come to a full appreciation of the taste of a distinctive stout like Murphy's. It takes time—no less than 119.5 seconds—for a pint of Guinness to settle properly, and to rush the process is to do this popular drink an injustice. Whiskey, a traditional chaser to a sup of the black stuff, must under

Oysters and Guinness.

Irish law be stored in oak vats for at least three years, and in reality it is often kept much longer to give it its smooth and distinctive flavour. In fact a good whiskey, like wine, is critically measured by its age.

Cider, an alcoholic drink distilled from apples, also requires no small amount of patience in the making—so much so that one Irish producer, Bulmer, proclaims that nothing is added to the drink but time itself. Other drinks, like the luxury beverage Bailey's Irish Cream, demand to be drunk at a decadently slow tempo, not a drink to be rushed. The Irish understand this implicitly. Brendan Behan, for example, was fond of saying, 'Hold your hour and have another,' while another toasting cheer runs, 'May you be in Heaven half an hour before the Devil knows you're dead.'

Limerick to Galway via the Burren

Leave Limerick by the N18 road, driving by **Cratloe Woods House**, the only surviving example of an Irish long-house still used as a residence, and continue on past **Bunratty Castle**, seat of the O'Briens, with the possibility of a stop for a visit to the surrounding **Folk Park** or a mediaeval banquet in the evening. Continue on through **Shannon**, the second-largest town in the county, and then past **Newmarket-on-Fergus** to **Ennis**, an old town with narrow winding streets, well worth lingering in. From Ennis proceed by the N85 in the direction of colourful **Ennistimon**. Here the road bends left towards **Lehinch**, a popular seaside resort developed in the 19th century, providing a range of entertainment and now boasting a demanding championship golf course and a blue-flag beach for swimming. From Lehinch take the R478 towards **Liscannor**, a fishing-village famous for its slate, set half way between Lehinch and the Cliffs of Moher and associated with *John Holland*, inventor of the submarine. Further along the road are the spectacular **Cliffs of Moher**, with their extensive bird colonies of kittiwakes, petrels, and puffins. After the Cliffs of Moher the R478 begins its swing to the right, passing **Lisdoonvarna** (with its mineral springs and annual bachelor contest) before starting to double back on itself as the R476 in the direction of **Kilfenora**, where two well-preserved high crosses flank the late Romanesque cathedral. The **Burren Display Centre** in Kilfenora explains the flora, fauna, butterflies and rock of the

area, and Kilfenora itself boasts four 12th-century crosses, as well as the 12th-century church of *St Fachtna*, a small building with a square tower. The R476 from Kilfenora then becomes the R480 and runs on past **Lemaneagh,** an O'Brien castle with a tower dating from 1480 and home to the strong-willed *Máire Rua*, before reaching the Burren itself. Naked bedrock stretches in every direction round plants that survive from before the Ice Age, such as maidenhair fern, which mix here with alpine plants from the Later Stone Age. **Poulnabrone** (*Poll na mBrón*, 'the hole of sorrows'), a portal tomb from the Later Stone Age with a huge capstone, dominates the landscape. Another, somewhat later neolithic grave, **Gleninsheen Megalithic Tomb**, lies about half a mile further on.

Continuing northwards, the R480 joins the N67 before entering **Ballyvaghan**, the Burren's harbour, where you can rent an Irish cottage. The N67 then continues along the edge of the bay, past **Kinvarra**, a charming fishing village at the head of the bay. On a small promontory beside the bay is the castle of **Dún Guaire**, where mediaeval banquets also serve as an occasion for introducing tourists to Irish culture in the broadest sense—dance, music, song, and literary readings. Some of the most famous beds of native oysters consumed enthusiastically by gourmets from around the world at the Galway Oyster Festival lie near **Clarinbridge**, a village reached after the N67 merges with the N18 to become the N6. From Clarinbridge the N6 leads to Galway. Soon after the Norman castle at **Oranmore**, the road reaches the outskirts of **Galway**.

The Burren,
Co. Clare.

Fishing at Kylemore Lake,
Co. Galway

EXPERIENCE THE PAST ...
REALISE YOUR DREAM

Holiday at Clomantagh Castle in Kilkenny, where the medieval meets the Georgian, in a restored towerhouse with farmhouse attached ... For a different perspective, stay at a Lighthouse in Wicklow ... Live the fairytale at Ballealy Cottage near Lough Neagh in Co. Antrim ... Reign supreme in our Miniature Castle at Annes Grove in Co. Cork ... Enjoy the grand life at our townhouse in Dublin ... Step back in time and experience a unique holiday by the seashore in Donegal.

*All our houses are
faithfully restored and
celebrate our
architectural heritage.*

THE IRISH LANDMARK TRUST
Tel: + 353 1 6704 733
E-mail: landmark@iol.ie

County Galway, Connemara & the Aran Islands

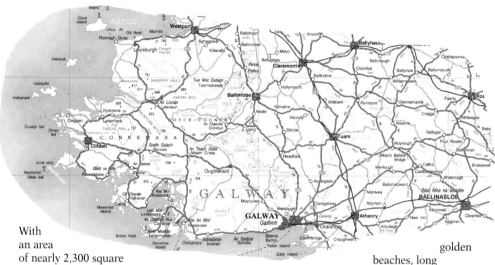

With an area of nearly 2,300 square miles, County Galway is the second-largest county in Ireland. To the north it is bounded by Counties Mayo and Roscommon, to the east by Counties Roscommon and Offaly, and to the south by Counties Clare and Tipperary. In physical relief it runs from the desolate mountain and lake, bog and river terrain of **Connemara** in the west to the low-lying banks of the **River Shannon** and **Lough Derg** in the east. In fact the eastern two-thirds of County Galway form part of the central lowlands. But here the extensive plains comprise rich pastureland and feature large farms lying in generously wooded landscapes, with thriving market towns and neat villages within easy reach. This largely flat eastern section of the county is cut off from the dramatic coastline on the west by **Lough Corrib**, a vast expanse of water dotted with islands, and then by the **Maamturk Mountains**, a range with many summits that reach over 2,000 feet in height.

Most visitors feel that **Connemara** contains the best of the county's scenery—a painter's landscape of impressive mountains, golden beaches, long stretches of bogland and bleak lakelands, with twisted trees permanently angled back by unrelenting winds from the Atlantic. Much further out to the west, in the Atlantic, the **Aran Islands**, tied administratively to County Galway but geologically an extension of County Clare's Burren area, make the agriculturally unrewarding task of working with a limestone surface even harder to bear by throwing up a tough, uncompromising climate dominated by wind and rain. In both Connemara and the islands the conditions of existence are among the most difficult to be found anywhere in Ireland; but for those not obliged to make a living here, the wild and unspoilt beauties are immensely satisfying after long exposure to the feckless comforts of city life.

These remote and economically challenging places enjoyed a less constantly oppressive English domination than many other parts of Ireland, and the survival of Irish as the community language is in part due to the lack of sustained setlement and

Boat on Moyrus beach in Connemara.

exploitation by English forces here at the country's limit. One bonus of this imperial neglect is the fact that its people have successfully preserved their language, traditions, and culture. Today even the previously remote Aran Islands are quickly accessible by air and ferry, and the danger is no longer that of isolation but of conquest in a friendlier form, as tourists in excessive numbers threaten to swamp the limited facilities.

Galway, the joyous capital of the county, first showed up on a map of *Ptolemy's* almost two thousand years ago. However, the groundwork for its present urban appearance was laid by the Anglo-Normans in the 13th century. In succeeding centuries, regular trade links with France and Spain helped it develop quickly, and prosperity followed. With a population of nearly 60,000 people, and a modern university catering for 6,000 students, the city plays a vital role in the social, business and artistic life of the county.

In more recent times the Galway area has become home to multinational corporations and high-tech industry, and unemployment has plunged in a remarkable way. For anyone familiar with previous levels of hardship, the changes in recent years seem nothing less than miraculous.

Apart from Galway, the towns of the county possess their own dynamism and charm, often based on traditional rural values. **Ballinasloe**, for example, hosts a large horse fair each October. **Clifden**, the 'capital of Connemara', relies on its

magnificent situation, high above an Atlantic inlet and with the striking framework of the **Twelve Pins** range behind it. **An Spidéal**, on the other hand, draws on the fact that it is an Irish-speaking village to impress itself on the visitor's attention, while the curach races held here each summer give an impressive stamp of authority to its fidelity to traditional values.

Arguably the best point from which to begin any visit to the county is in the city of **Galway**, where, as Galwegians proudly say, 'the traditional and the modern sit comfortably side by side.' It is unlike any comparable city of its size, in that the ebullience, good humour and appetite for fun visible in a public place such as **Eyre Square**, and the characteristic of Galway people in general, has nothing tired or cynical about it. Indeed it serves as a perfect introduction to the sanguine, open-hearted way of being that is typical of people in the rural areas as well. Whether it's shopping, music, pub life, or restaurants, there's lots to enjoy in the city, and a period of joviality is a pleasant prelude to the quieter, more measured but no less enjoyable cornucopia of pleasures awaiting the visitor to the county at large.

Galway

Galway is a tribal, and cosmopolitan, county town with enough communal feeling to give it a warm, caring ethos and enough urbanity to rival larger but less dynamic centres. Being at one and the same time profoundly Irish and economically secure, its credentials for

Morans of the Weir, Kilcolgan, Co. Galway.

being both Irish and progressive are indisputable and mean that it defers in nothing to Dublin, preferring instead to deepen its specific urban identity in a joyous and self-assured way.

Galway is one of Europe's fastest-growing cities and Ireland's fourth-largest, with a population of 57,000 people. Economic growth has in no way affected its reputation as a lively and friendly place, and the spin-off of sponsorship and subsidy money has helped improve its standing in the performing arts, with a pronounced emphasis on drama. The oldest theatre, the **Taibhdhearc**, which stages plays in Irish, was associated with *Walter Macken* and *Siobhán McKenna*. In 1995 the city's largest playhouse and entertainment facility, the **Town Hall Theatre**, was opened, and since then it has played host to such diverse companies as the **Abbey Theatre**, the **Royal Shakespeare Company**, and the **Druid Theatre Company**. The Druid, with *Gary Hynes* as director, recently established an international reputation for Galway theatre by performing *The Beauty Queen of Leenane* by Martin McDonagh in New York, to critical acclaim.

Galway forms a natural gateway to **Connemara**, one of the most attractive areas in the west, but can equally well serve as a point of departure for excursions to the Burren. But the city is not merely a crossroads for travellers moving on to scenic splendours elsewhere: it is a place to stay, or to linger in, in its own right. And though it can be walked round in half a day, there is something in the air, in the streets, in the talk and music of the busy restaurants and pubs that makes seasoned travellers want to remain here as long as possible. So much the better if this urge happens to coincide with the Arts Festival Week at the end of July, or Galway Race Week, also towards the end of July, or the Galway Oyster Festival at the end of September: you'll simply double your enjoyment of the city!

Galway began as a fishing village where the *de Burgos* built a castle in 1226. Fourteen families later established a hold over the city and became known as the 'Tribes of Galway'. Together they composed a powerful Anglo-Norman presence in the midst of the native Irish, whom they attempted to subdue with the help of hostile edicts such as *'no uninvited "O" or "Mac" shall show his face in Galway's streets.'* Galway's loyalty to the English crown over the centuries led to its downfall when *Cromwell* appeared on the scene. He bombarded the city until it was forced to surrender in April 1652, after nine months of siege. In the process an important wine trade with Spain came to an end, and Cromwell's *coup de grâce* spelt commercial

Spanish Arch,
Galway.

disaster for the city, which went into decline until its recent spectacular revival. Formerly a 'borough', Galway became a city in 1985.

Everything that happens in Galway begins in **Eyre Square**, the small park at the centre of a traffic interchange. Sometimes used as a performing space, it contains a rather simplistic and old-fashioned statue of *Pádraig Ó Conaire*, the short-story writer. The park also contains a sculpture by *Éamonn O'Doherty* evoking the sails of the traditional Galway sailing boats known as hookers. The rusted metal of which these sculptures are composed is of a piece with the pair of cannon from the Crimean War also on display in the square but is at odds with the Ó Conaire statue. Not far away, impressive lengths of mediaeval walls uncovered during excavations have been integrated into the new **Eyre Square Shopping Centre**, creating an agreeable sense of historical continuity between the past and the present.

Lynch's Castle, to the south-west of the square, is generally considered the first mediaeval town-house. It belonged to what was for three centuries Galway's most influential family. The house—which now, suitably enough, serves as a bank—dates from the 15th century and has a decorative façade, containing carved panels, gargoyles, and a lion devouring its prey.

A more romantic monument is the **Spanish Arch** (originally called the 'Blind Arch'), situated near the harbour. A 16th-century structure used to protect ships as they unloaded their cargoes of wine and brandy, it is a reminder of the time when Galway rivalled London and Bristol as a port for the Continental trade. At one point the city had extensive walls, including fourteen towers, but they were destroyed first by Cromwell and then by time's no less ruthless hand. Close to the Spanish Arch is

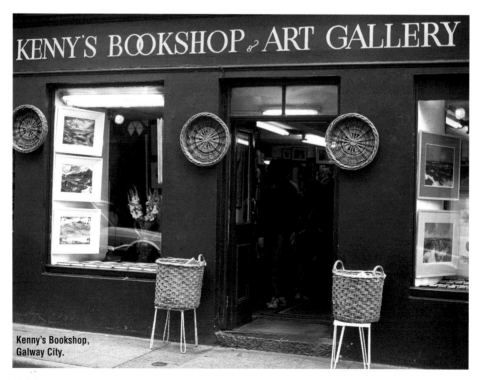

Kenny's Bookshop,
Galway City.

the small **Galway Museum**, which houses artefacts from the old fishing village of the **Claddagh**—today just an area of suburban housing over the bridge at the western end of the city.

The celebrated 'Claddagh ring'—a traditional design of gold wedding-ring with two hands holding a heart surmounted by a crown, deriving from a Roman design popular throughout Europe in the Middle Ages—was once widely worn by the people of the Claddagh. If you buy any of the countless reproductions available, remember to wear the ring with the heart pointing upwards towards the arm if you are married.

From the Spanish Arch it is a short walk over the river to the **Salmon Weir Bridge** and across to the **Cathedral of Our Lady Assumed into Heaven and St Nicholas**. A rather unprepossessing thirty-year old edifice, monstrously self-important in virtue of its considerable mass, its lack of grace and elegance is sufficient comment on the abuse of a challenging site. By contrast, the mock-Tudor lines of **University College** behind the cathedral induce a sense of relief; and the **Church of St Nicholas** in Market Street, the largest mediaeval church in Ireland, built in 1320 (and used as a stable by Cromwell), creates a comforting feeling of delight. Dedicated to the patron saint of sailors, it has a number of fine carvings and discreet gargoyles; the ludicrous legend that *Christopher Columbus* stopped in at the church on his way to America may add some imaginative colour to your visit.

Close to St Nicholas is the **Nora Barnacle House Museum**, where Joyceans come to worship. Once the home of *James Joyce's* wife, the museum contains copies of correspondence between the couple and documents connected with their links with Galway.

Salthill, a busy seaside resort just outside Galway, is treated as a suburban extension of the city by day-trippers. A good-natured but honkytonk atmosphere prevails; at night, club and disco activity take over from middle-class hotel and family pursuits. The promenade is a favourite place among local people for a daily stroll. Here's a tip if you're there to do likewise and to watch the sun go down on Galway Bay: kick the wall at the end of the walk. It's what Galwegians do and have done for generations, and it may save you from being identified straight away as a 'blow-in'!

DON'T MISS

- Don't miss the **Church of St Nicholas**, Galway's most significant mediaeval building, where (if you believe it) you'll tread where Columbus went to pray, admire a crusader's tomb, and, on the strength of both, dream of the discovery of America and the loss of Jerusalem—a full programme for the day ...
- Don't miss **Eyre Square Shopping Centre**—not for wall-to-wall carpeting but for wall-to-wall urban enclosure: the unique and surprising integration of the ancient city walls into a contemporary merchandising complex; at least you'll have something to bang your head against if you don't like the prices!
- **Turoe Pet Farm and Leisure Park**, Loughrea. This centre incorporates the Turoe Stone, a rare national monument dating back to the 2nd or 1st century B.C.

ALL-WEATHER OPTIONS

- If you find the weather's bad in Galway, why not go to china—Galway's china, the **Royal Tara** on Monivea Road. The casting of bronzes and the production of hand-painted bone china are made all the more enjoyable by this 17th-century house that was formerly the home of the Joyces, one of the celebrated Tribes of Galway.
- If you'd still like superb views, even when it's raining, why not visit the **Galway Crystal Heritage Centre** on Dublin Road, which is in fact much more than that. Splendid vistas of Galway Bay from the balcony, an introduction to Galway boat-building methods, a history of Galway families, the work of early Irish artists and of course a demonstration of glassworking skills by experienced craftsmen make this an unforgettable experience.

East and South County Galway

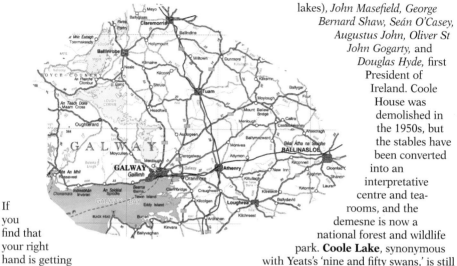

lakes), *John Masefield, George Bernard Shaw, Seán O'Casey, Augustus John, Oliver St John Gogarty,* and *Douglas Hyde,* first President of Ireland. Coole House was demolished in the 1950s, but the stables have been converted into an interpretative centre and tea-rooms, and the demesne is now a national forest and wildlife park. **Coole Lake**, synonymous with Yeats's 'nine and fifty swans,' is still as it was when he wrote his memorable tribute to it. Background material on Lady Gregory and the Celtic Revival can be consulted at **Kiltartan Gregory Museum** to the north of Gort.

If you find that your right hand is getting longer than your left, don't worry! It's your giving hand, according to local tradition. In any event, you'll have a great deal in common with *Guaire,* the 7th-century Connacht chief who built a fortress at **Gort**.

Situated 20 miles south of Galway, **Gort** lies in a natural gap between the Slieve Aughty mountains and the Burren. In the early 19th century *Viscount Gort* laid out the main lines of the town, concentrating on wide streets and a spacious square. But today most people associate the town with *William Butler Yeats,* a man brought up on fairy stories like those recounted above, who lived just 4 miles away at **Thoor Ballylee**. Yeats bought this tower in 1917 for £35 and spent his summers here until 1929, after which it fell to ruin. It has been completely restored and now houses an interpretative centre on Yeats's life and works. An audiovisual presentation traces the history of the tower and the Yeats connection.

Just outside Gort, to the north on the Galway road, is **Coole Park**, the former residence of *Lady Gregory,* one of the founding members of the Abbey Theatre. Guests who stayed here included Yeats (many of whose poems evoke its woods and

About 3 miles south-west of Gort, the ruins of **Kilmacduagh Monastic Settlement** comprise an 11th to 12th-century round tower that leans dangerously in Pisa fashion, a cathedral, which is a 14th or 15th-century rebuilding of an earlier church, an oratory dedicated to St John the Baptist, and various small chapels. The cathedral is roofless but contains a number of good carvings.

Kinvarra is a delightful fishing village in the south-east corner of Galway Bay. Its small harbour contains a number of Galway hookers, and on a promontory to the north, at the head of the bay, stands the restored 16th-century castle of **Dún Guaire**. It was put up in 1520 and was later taken over by *Oliver St John Gogarty,* though now it specialises in guided tours and mediaeval banquets, with readings from Irish literature, and singing and dancing.

Doorus House, at the head of the peninsula, was formerly a lodging-place used by *Yeats* and *de Maupassant,* and this in fact

Dún Guaire Castle,
Kinvarra, Co. Galway.

is where the idea of a national theatre was first discussed. Today it is a youth hostel. **Clarinbridge**, on the main Galway–Limerick road, is a small place but a temple of oyster worship. Every September, Clarinbridge pubs are filled to overflowing with Guinness, and oyster enthusiasts come to swallow more than a few of each.

On the north shore of **Lough Derg**, 15 miles east of Gort, is the busy market town of **Portumna.** The ruins of **Portumna**

Priory, a mainly 15th-century Dominican edifice, stand close to the shore, and not far away is the early 17th-century **Portumna Castle**, now being restored by the Office of Public Works. Just 3 miles north-west of Portumna is **Derryhivenny Castle**, a well-preserved tower-house, built in 1653; and on the Loughrea road about 6 miles from Portumna is **Pallas Castle**. Both of them are well worth seeing.

A market town by the edge of Lough Rea,

285

and in many respects similar to Portumna, **Loughrea** is nonetheless smaller, and the lake it borders on is also smaller than Lough Derg, and less scenic. A Carmelite monastery founded by *Richard de Burgo* in the 13th century still stands here and is well preserved. The town is also notable for **St Brendan's (Catholic) Cathedral**, or rather for the way in which its stained-glass windows (by *Sarah Purser* and others) illustrate developments in ecclesiastical art about the turn of the century. Next door to it in Dunkellin Street is **Loughrea Museum**, which contains a variety of ecclesiastical items, from 12th and 13th-century carvings to 16th-century gold chalices and 17th-century vestments and crucifixes. On the secular side, it provides a record of the development of the Gaelic Athletic Association. About 5 miles north of Loughrea is a spiral-covered rounded pillar, the **Turoe Stone**, decorated in a manner reminiscent of the La Tène style and the finest example of its kind in Ireland.

Ballinasloe, the main town in east Galway, situated on the River Suck, caters for fishermen but has made its mark on rural Ireland thanks to its October Horse Fair, as well as its Angling Week. **St Michael's Church** contains stained-glass work by *Harry Clarke* and *Albert Power*. To the south-west of the town is **Aughrim**, site of the victory of the forces of *William of Orange* over the followers of *King James II* in 1691 and the bloodiest battle ever fought in Ireland. A **Battle of Aughrim Interpretative Centre** exists to explain what happened, and signposts from the centre lead to the battle site.

Five miles to the south of Ballinasloe the well-preserved ruins of **Clontuskert Abbey** date from the 14th century, though the original abbey was founded in the 9th century. The unusual West Door, dating from 1476, has carvings depicting figures of the saints, various creatures, and a rather puzzled mermaid.

Set half way between Galway and Ballinasloe, **Athenry** is probably better known for a song associated with it, 'The Fields of Athenry', than for any special tourist attractions it has to offer. The castle, built in 1240, dominated the southern approach to Athenry, and not too far away from it stands the ruined **Dominican priory**, also constructed about that time.

A few miles to the south-west of Athenry, **Moyode Castle** is a large ruined house with an ancient castle standing in its grounds. It was here in 1770 that the first steps were taken in forming what is now the Galway Blazers Foxhounds. In 1916 the house was taken over for a time by *Liam Mellows*, the socialist revolutionary later executed for his part in the Civil War. Not too far away is a town whose name suggests that it cannot decide which side of the fence it's on, **Claregalway**—not connected with County

Kinvarra Harbour, Co. Galway.

O'Connor kings of Connacht. Its strong suit is a fine 12th-century cross in the town square and the 12th-century **St Mary's Cathedral**. This has been largely rebuilt, though it retains a sandstone chancel-arch from the original edifice. Tuam's **Little Mill**, a working corn-mill near the town centre, functions as a museum and heritage centre, providing evidence of the town's industrial past, as well as tourist information.

Five miles to the west of Tuam, wooded **Knockma Hill** is reputed to be the home of *Fionnbharr*, king of the Connacht fairies, and one of the supposed burial places of *Méabh*, legendary queen of Connacht. The summit is filled with prehistoric remains. Also of interest in the area, and situated just outside the angling town of **Headford**, is **Ross Errilly Abbey**, an unusually complete and well-preserved 14th-century site, founded by the de Burgo family. The cloister is intact, and the surrounding buildings illustrate in detail the workings of a mediaeval friary, giving a general sense of the way in which day-to-day existence was interwoven with religious observance. Many of the buildings were wrecked by Cromwellian forces in 1656.

Clare but distinguished thus from other places of the same name. Near it are the interesting remains of a **Franciscan abbey** from the 13th century.

A larger town, **Tuam** (*Tuaim*, 'burial mound') may not be inspiringly beautiful, but it is certainly not deathly. It began as a 6th-century settlement founded by *St Iarlaith* and in the 12th century was the seat of the

---

DON'T MISS

- Don't miss **St Brendan's Cathedral** in Loughrea. A must for amateurs of art and in particular of stained glass, the church is not striking from the outside but is celebrated for the Celtic Revival *vitraux* within. Produced by *Sarah Purser* and her Túr Gloine workshop in Dublin, the windows provide a brilliant introduction to a movement that, beginning in 1903 and attracting the great *Evie Hone*, was the dominant force in leaded-glass design and craft up to 1957.
- Don't miss **Thoor Ballylee**, a 16th-century tower-house that Ireland's greatest poet bought, renovated, and lived in for long periods. Filmed material is available to fill you in on the details of his life, and various editions of his works are on display, with first-class readings of some of the poems transmitted to almost every room in the building

ALL-WEATHER OPTIONS

- Though **Coole House** has gone, the converted stables of **Coole Park** provide invaluable background information on *Lady Gregory*, who jointly founded the Abbey Theatre and was *Yeats's* confidante—site of great historical and literary significance associated with a cultivated woman and patron and with her friend the poet.
- A castle in excellent condition is a rarity in Ireland. **Dún Guaire** is one, which means you have a good roof over your head if the rain comes down, and you move through rooms where *Oliver St John Gogarty* (*James Joyce's* companion in the Martello tower) once lived and composed poetry. It has a long history, from being a 6th-century king's residence to a venue for mediaeval banquets. Displays on every floor make it an intriguing architectural and historical experience.

Connemara

Connemara is that section of county Galway west of the city, beginning at **Oughterard** and bounded by **Lough Corrib** on the east, the Atlantic to the west, and **Killary Harbour** to the north. It is an area dominated by two mountain ranges, the **Twelve Pins** and **Maamturk Mountains**, and embraces some of the most beautiful and dramatic scenery in Ireland. A powerful contrast of rock and bogland, towered over by rugged mountains, is part of the appeal, but not the full story. Magical small lakes that shimmer with the least sign of luminosity, sparklingly pure rivers, rain-fed waterfalls that cut neat paths through the upland slopes and, on the coast, unspoilt white beaches, countless rocky islands and remote inlets and creeks all add to the enchantment.

Oughterard (*Uachtar Ard*, 'upper height') is a charming town situated on a small river, the Owenriff. It prides itself on being the natural gateway to Connemara; it is also one of the premier fishing centres in the country, because of its proximity to Lough Corrib. Surrounded by trees and with the Twelve Pins providing an imposing background, it is made up of Georgian houses built alongside a few surviving thatched cottages. **Aughanure Castle**, a 16th-century building on a rock island 3 miles to the south-east of the town, was the main O'Flaherty

stronghold and considered one of the most formidable of its type at the time when *Cromwell* laid siege to Galway. The castle, which has been restored, is now open to the public. **Lough Corrib**, which forms a natural divide between east and west Galway, is one of the largest bodies of fresh water in Europe. The last link in a chain of lakes stretching from Lough Carra in County Mayo, it is certainly the largest lake in Ireland, drained by the River Corrib, on which Galway is built. One of its 360 islands contains **Inchagoill**, an Early Christian monastic settlement, and a Romanesque church with a fine doorway and accomplished carvings. It also contains an obelisk with a very early Old Irish inscription, which some claim is the oldest Christian inscription in Europe. The island can be reached by boarding the *Corrib Queen* at the Oughterard Pier.

The 'Western Way' from Oughterard leads to **Maam Cross**, a village known as the Piccadilly Circus of Connemara and famed locally for its annual Bogman's Ball, at

Roundstone Harbour, Connemara, Co. Galway.

which wheelbarrows of turf are used to light fires, and steaks are cooked on shovels.

Recess, set among superb lake and mountain scenery, is one of the beauty spots of Connemara. Situated in the shadow of the Twelve Pins, it has quarries for green Connemara marble and is extremely popular with anglers. Beyond Recess the **Lough Inagh** valley is also extremely attractive, flanked as it is by Derryclare and Inagh loughs. At the northern end of the valley is the equally striking **Kylemore Lake**, with its 19th-century **Kylemore Abbey**, a neo-Gothic edifice in white granite and grey limestone, built for a wealthy English businessman but now run as a girls' boarding-school by a group of Benedictine nuns. The grounds and part of the building are open to the public.

Leenane (*An Líonán*, 'the sea inlet') stands at the head of the narrow inlet of Killary Harbour and is a good base for fishermen and mountain-climbers. It recently became practically a household name when it was chosen as the location for the film *The Field*, based on the play by *John B. Keane*, and because it features in the title of *Martin McDonagh's* drama *The Beauty Queen of Leenane*. The **Leenane Cultural Centre**, overlooking the harbour, contains a **Sheep and Wool Museum** where carding, spinning and weaving and the use of natural dyes are all demonstrated.

Clifden, the largest town in Connemara and often referred to as its capital, was founded at the beginning of the 19th century by a local landlord, *John D'Arcy*; but it is large only by comparison with the villages surrounding it, and its population is only about 1,000 people. Its greatest asset is its situation, set astride the Owenglen River, open to the mountains and the Atlantic and encircled by the magnificent Twelve Pins. It is the centre of Connemara pony breeding, and one of the best times to visit it is when the Connemara Pony Show is in progress in August.

To the south of the town, on the Ballyconneely road, visitors may wonder what a 14-foot aeroplane wing carved in limestone is doing sticking out of the bog. It's a memorial to the exploits of Alcock and Brown who on 15 June 1919 flew a tiny plane from Newfoundland to Ireland in 6 hours and 12 minutes and landed in the Derrygimlagh Bog near Clifden at the end of their pioneering transatlantic flight.

Clifden,
Connemara,
Co. Galway.

Another equally striking local attraction is **Dan O'Hara's Homestead**, about 5 miles east of Clifden off the main N59 road, a pre-Famine farm and heritage centre incorporating a prehistoric lake-dwelling dating back to 1500 BC, a 5,000-year-old neolithic tomb, a prehistoric tomb, and a farm homestead. The centre faithfully reflects the farming life of the middle of the 19th century, with local people demonstrating traditional tilling and farming methods.

Also well worth a visit is the **Connemara National Park**, situated on the Clifden–Westport road at **Letterfrack**, a village founded by Quakers. Connemara ponies and Irish red deer roam through

5,000 acres of scenic mountains, bogs, and grassland, and the well-organised exhibition centre contains displays and audiovisual presentations to familiarise visitors with the variety of birds and animals in the park. North of Letterfrack on the Renvyle Peninsula, the **Oceans Alive Visitor Centre** has an aquarium, museum, and organised sightseeing cruises.

North-west of Clifden is **Cleggan,** a fishing village nestling at the head of **Cleggan Bay** on Connemara's Atlantic coast. The area around the town is blanket bog, an especially acidic turf in which few plant species can survive, but those that manage to do so end up forming a vegetation not found outside Ireland.

Cleggan is the departure point for ferry services to the islands of Inishbofin and Inishturk. **Inishbofin**, 6 miles off the County Galway coast, is a compact island—4 miles long by 2 miles wide—that is surprisingly rich archaeologically and geologically, as well as offering some splendid scenery. Made up of some of the oldest rocks in Ireland, it also has an extensive bird life, covering corncrakes, corn buntings, and a large number of seabirds. In the 7th century *St Colmán* founded a monastery here, and some remains have survived. In the course of the 13th century the O'Flahertys relinquished ownership of the island to the O'Malleys, and in the 16th century it was occupied by *Don Bosco*, a Spanish pirate who was an ally of *Gráinne Ní Mháille*, the pirate-queen. Then the island was taken over by the Cromwellians, who built a barracks where they incarcerated monks and priests. A promontory fort, **Dún Ghráinne**, and Bosco's ancient castle overlooking the harbour are among the principal surviving monuments. Inishbofin has over two hundred permanent residents, two hotels, a pub, and several bed-and-breakfasts and guest-houses and is a good holiday location for fishing, sailing, and swimming.

From Connemara's southern coast the road runs in a roundabout way back to Galway, from Clifden through **Roundstone**, a fishing village at the foot of the Errisberg mountains. Lobster boats and curachs rest at anchor in the small harbour, while just south of the village is the Industrial Development Authority's craft centre and various factory shops turning out bodhráns, flutes, tin whistles, and pottery. The road between Roundstone and Galway passes through Irish-speaking areas, and this is where *Patrick Pearse*, one of the leaders of the 1916 revolution, chose to build a cottage, thereby demonstrating his commitment to the Irish language and culture. Many of his plays and poems were written here, and the **Patrick Pearse Cottage** is open to the public during the summer months. Further along the coast, **An Cheathrú Rua** is well known for its fine beaches, one of which, the **Coral Strand**, is entirely made up of shells and coral fragments. Half way between An Cheathrú Rua and Galway is **An Spidéal**, a lively little town with an excellent craft centre and some good pubs. Set in the heart of an Irish-speaking district, it has a fine sandy beach.

DON'T MISS

- **Connemara National Park**, a conservation area of great natural splendour encompassing the **Twelve Pins** and the valley of **Glanmore**. The **Visitor Centre** provides useful information on the fauna and flora of the park as well as a display covering 10,000 years of Connemara. In high season it's even got a botanist who'll provide a $2\frac{1}{2}$-hour guided walk. Unmissable.
- **Kylemore Lake** and **Kylemore Abbey and Walled Garden** form an irresistible double feature. The lake views reveal images of Connemara at its magnificent best; and after touring it, what summer ending could you ask for than to meet a set of beaming and welcoming Benedictine nuns, running a convent boarding-school in a 19th-century neo-Gothic Abbey that was once owned by a Connemara-loving Englishman. To their credit, the nuns have kept large sections of the abbey open for public viewing.

ALL-WEATHER OPTIONS

- At the first sign of rain, show some craft or, better still, let others show it. Head for **Ceardlann an Spidéil**, a group of small shops in An Spidéal where woodworkers, sculptors in stone, potters, weavers and jewellery-makers produce their wares in front of their customers.
- If the weather's getting your goat, then visit **Roundstone Musical Instruments** (at the IDA craft centre), where you'll see the real thing—goatskins—being stretched to make bodhráns.

Aran Islands

Think of the three Aran Islands as three large-scale segments of intractable Burren limestone tossed into the raging Atlantic with, on each island, a small population of hardy, independent people, fiercely proud of their wonderful traditions. The availability of aircraft and high-speed motor-boat connections have vastly improved levels of creature-comfort. But in times gone by, when they endured dark and storm-filled winters, cut off from the mainland for long periods by tempestuous seas, they must at times have harboured their own gloomy and reductive thoughts. The point, though, is that they developed the human qualities needed to triumph over stark, unpromising conditions of existence; and it is this capacity to survive in adversity that makes the islands so fascinating and so different for the visitor. A feature of the appeal of the islands is the chance of exploring this and other differences that set the Aran Islanders apart from everybody else.

One can begin by saying they are different by virtue of their attachment to Irish and to an oral tradition where the conservation of age-old stories, legends and music is a natural part of life. They are different by virtue of their heroic battle for sustenance, visible in the tiny fields separated by dry-stone walls and fertilised with the help of seaweed, and only large enough to

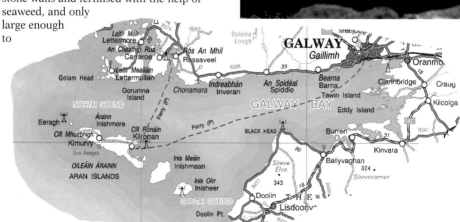

Inis Meáin, Aran Islands.

accommodate one or two sheep or cattle. They are different again by virtue of their upturned beetle-shaped *curachs*, frames of wooden laths covered with tarred canvas and with three single seats for the team of three oarsmen. They are different also by virtue of their independence of spirit and self-sufficiency, illustrated by their ability to spin and weave their own clothes, with their characteristic waistcoat of unbleached wool (*báinín*), rugged tweed trousers held in place by a gay multicoloured belt (*crios*), and formerly also rawhide shoes without heels for the men and black woollen shawl and red flannel skirt for the women. To visit any

of the islands is to become aware of the successful preservation of a culture and language that have resisted the bulldozing standardisation of the 20th century.

The largest of the three islands is **Árainn** (sometimes called **Inis Mór**), which is about 8 miles in length and has a year-round population of about 900 people. The dominant impression is of Burren limestone with high cliffs, and views to the mountains over on the mainland. **Cill Rónáin,** where the ferry berths, is the focus of activity, but the main centre of interest is the spectacular prehistoric fort of **Dún Aonghasa**, perched on the edge of cliffs plunging over 300 feet

293

The West

An Atlantic sunset.

into the Atlantic. It consists of three concentric enclosures ranged by thick walls of stone and completed by an intimidating *chevaux de frise*—a series of sharp upended rocks planted at strategic intervals around the fort to dissuade would-be invaders from advancing any further. Excavations in the area indicate activity round the fort from the late Bronze Age (100–700 BC) up to the 5th century AD.

Another fort with an equally majestic setting is that of **Dúchathair** ('black fort'), also placed on the edge of cliffs, which lost its eastern gateway into the sea in the 19th century. Its entrance (just a foot from the sheer drop) is unlikely to tempt those without a head for heights. Inside are the remains of four *clocháns* or beehive huts.

Two other strongholds exist in the middle of the island, **Dún Eochla** and **Dún Eoghanachta,** each impressive in its own right. The first is drum-like, with walls 15 feet thick enclosing dry-stone huts, the second a circular construction with buttresses added at some time in the 19th century. The ruins of **Caisleán Aircín** (sometimes erroneously called 'Arkin's Castle'), probably built by *John Rawson*, to whom the islands were granted by *Queen Elizabeth I* of England, stand in the small bay of **Cill Éinne**. A garrison was kept here during the 17th and 18th centuries and gave rise to the mischievous rumour that Aran people are really descendants of Cromwellian soldiers!

Christianity came to the islands in the 6th century, and a good number of Early Christian remains exist. The 12th-century ruins of **Teampall Chiaráin** (St Ciarán's church) are in a field not far from Cill Rónáin , with St Ciarán's well alongside. A particularly appealing and tiny 9th-century oratory is set on the hill behind Cill Éinne. Called **Teampall Bheanáin** (St Beanán's church), it dates from the 6th century, has steep gable ends, and is thought by some to be the smallest church in Europe. At the island's southern end is **Teaghlach Éinne**, a 12th-century church associated with *St Éanna* (Enda) and supposedly the spot where he is buried.

The **Aran Heritage Centre** in Cill Rónáin provides a good briefing on the cultural traditions and landscape of the islands.

Inis Meáin ('middle island') measures 3 miles by 2. The least-visited of the three islands, it was nonetheless the one favoured by both *J. M. Synge* and *Patrick Pearse* for the purpose of improving their Irish, and it acquired some recent publicity as a result of Martin McDonagh's drama *The Cripple of Inis Meáin*. About 300 people live here. As befits a smaller island, Inis Meáin has a scaled-down version of Dún Aonghasa called **Dún Chonchúir** (*Conchúr* was possibly a brother of *Aonghas*), except that it was constructed inland. Not too far from

the fort is **Teach Synge** (Synge's house), the thatched cottage where Synge spent his summers between 1898 and 1902; and a sheltered spot on the western cliff overlooking Gregory's Sound has been called **Cathaoir Synge** (Synge's chair), because it was the dramatist's contemplative favourite during his stint on the island. A smaller stone fort, **Dún Fearbhaí**, stands on high ground overlooking An Córa. The 8th-century chapel **Cill Cheannannach** is at the eastern end of the island. The little church of **St Mary Immaculate**, constructed in 1939, contains some excellent *Harry Clarke* windows, personalised for the islanders by the inclusion of local scenes in the Christian context.

Inis Oírr ('eastern island'), the smallest of the three, can be covered on foot in a single afternoon. Its most outstanding ruin is **Caisleán Uí Bhriain** (Ó Briain's castle), atop the only hill on the island. Periodically engulfed in sand, the 10th-century **Teampall Chaomháin** (St Caomhán's church) is each year equally regularly disinterred, just in time for the saint's feast day on 14 June. West of the main pier is **Cill Ghobnait** (St Gobnait's church), founded by a woman in flight from an enemy she'd encountered on the mainland. The **Inis Oírr Heritage House**, a stone-built thatched cottage, contains a collection of locally relevant photographs, as well a craft shop and café.

TOURING ROUTE

Galway, Westport & Achill Island

Leave Galway by the N17 road in the direction of Tuam. At **Claregalway** the ruins of a de Burgh castle show up on the left, and on the right a 13th-century Franciscan friary. **Tuam** is the ecclesiastical capital of Connacht. What is now the Church of Ireland cathedral here was founded in 1130 by *Toirealach Ó Conchúir,* but only the chancel with its triplet window and chancel arch survive from this period. The shaft of the high cross in the nave probably belonged originally to the market cross in the square. Both bear an inscription to Ó Conchúir and to a contemporary abbot. The market cross, signed by a Leinster artist, resembles the high cross of Glendalough. From Tuam the N17 continues on to **Knock**. When *Pope*

John Paul II visited Ireland in 1979 it was primarily to go to Knock for the centenary celebration of the apparition of the Virgin Mary, St Joseph and St John the Evangelist at the church here. Today the basilica (affiliated with San Maria Maggiore in Rome) welcomes huge numbers of pilgrims, most of whom have arrived in the country through the airport north of the town.

At Charlestown leave the N17 and take the N5 in the direction of **Castlebar**, the county town of Mayo, with a large square and tree-lined mall. Its greatest moment historically is still remembered here, the day of the 'Castlebar Races' in 1798, when *General Humbert* and his mixed French and Irish force routed the British army. *John Moore* was thereupon proclaimed President

Hill walking near Newport,
Co. Mayo.

of the Republic of Connacht, a presidency that ended a week later when Humbert was forced to surrender at Longford. Next on the route is **Westport**, an 18th-century gem with a gracious tree-lined mall and formal octagon. From Westport head north towards Newport on the N59. On the left, **Westport House** has magnificent collections, including the long-missing pillars from the tomb of Atreus in Mycenae (the originals now in the British Museum). At Newport the neo-Romanesque Catholic church is worth visiting to see the magnificent stained-glass window by *Harry Clarke*. Glaciers once covered this part of County Mayo and, following the thaw, left swarms of little gravel-hills everywhere; they are strung out into **Clew Bay** as

innumerable islands. The route passes **Carrigahowley House**, where the 16th-century chieftain *Gráinne Ní Mháille* divorced her husband by shouting 'I dismiss you' as he tried to enter their home. Nearby are the ruins of the Dominican **Burrishoole Abbey**.

At this point the road crosses the bridge at Achill Sound to **Achill Island** and the R319. Basking sharks surface here in June after winter hibernation in the mud-flats offshore. The most effective way of catching them is still to net them and then harpoon them from a curach. **Keel Strand** is the longest of Achill's beaches. Further west, amethysts are sometimes found on the southern slope of **Croaghaun**. To the north is another superb beach at **Doogort**.

The Great Famine, 1845–49

Anne Moore statue, Cóbh, Co. Cork.

food producers. The conflict provided a large export market for tillage products at premium prices. It was at this time that the potato, a high-yielding and reliable foodstuff, ideally suited to the Irish climate, became the staple diet of the majority of the population. However, with the end of the wars in 1815 this sector went into decline, to be replaced by the grazing of livestock. Large tracts of land were opened, and tens of thousands were made unemployed. Reliance on the cheaply and readily grown potato increased further for many.

The system of land-holding also played a part in the way the famine affected the country. The region west of the Shannon and counties such as Kerry, Cork and Donegal were hardest hit. Ulster, with its industrial base and reliance on cattle rather than tillage, escaped the worst ravages of the famine, as did the rich plains of the east coast.

The population had been growing for at least fifty years before the famine, thanks to the potato; and the most rapid demographic changes took place in the poorest regions. As family sizes increased, the land was divided and sub-divided again between siblings, making it increasingly difficult for a larger population to make a living out of the same amount of existing but ultimately less productive land.

Irish history is no stranger to tragedy and upheaval, but without doubt the Great Famine of the middle of the 19th century was the greatest disaster to visit the country in modern times. While the immediate causes of the famine struck suddenly and without warning, the conditions that allowed it to devastate the country to such a massive extent were laid out decades before 1845.

The Napoleonic wars were a boon for Irish

Apart from large commercially driven farms, all classes in the farming community were susceptible to severe changes in crop production. Some segments of the population, such as the *spailpíní*—migratory workers or cottiers who rented 'conacres' from other farmers—had no other resources at their disposal. The famine in effect wiped out these landless people.

The effects of the blight were first noticed in 1845, but a higher than normal harvest and the fragmented spread of the disease meant that its impact would not take hold immediately. The following year, however, saw less seed planted, and the disease became more prevalent in the potato crop. The harvest of 1846 was almost completely destroyed, removing at a stroke the staple diet of the majority of the population. It also meant that very little seed could be put away for the 1847 season; and food became so scarce that this year became known as 'Black 47'. The next two years would see further crop failures through the epidemic spread of the disease. Bad weather over these years contributed to the crop failure and the hardship suffered by the people.

Landlords, many of them wealthy and absentee English businessmen, continued to demand rent from farmers, despite the fact that no harvest was gathered.

Some estimates put the population at approximately eight million at the beginning of the famine. Less clear are the statistics of those lost in the catastrophe. However, by the mid-point of the century at least one million had died of hunger, malnutrition, and disease, while another one million had emigrated. So traumatic was the this demographic blow that it was not until the 1960s that the population would once more begin to show signs of growth.

In some places entire villages were wiped out; and, dotted around the countryside, a number of mass graves can still be found. When the land failed its people and they in turn lost confidence in it, emigration became the only hope for many. Chartered vessels offered millions the hope of escape to the 'new world'— America. However, conditions on these ships were so primitive, and so many people were crammed into them, that the long journey was exacerbated again by hunger, malnutrition, and disease; so many died on the journey that these vessels became known as 'coffin ships'. Once established abroad, a family member would save the fare for the rest of the family to make the same trip.

Prospects were bleaker for those who stayed behind. The workhouse was the final refuge of those who could no longer afford to pay their own way, and it was perhaps the most hated institution of that time. Spouses were separated from each other, and parents from their children; conditions were so bad that disease and death followed thousands of them into these institutions.

The ramifications of the famine went deep to the heart of Ireland at an economic, social, religious and political level. Whereas the desire for self-determination had been a peaceful campaign of mass appeal, led by **Daniel O'Connell**, the second half of the century would be marked by violent struggle and secret societies. The Fenians, forerunners of the Irish Republican Brotherhood, which would spawn the Irish Republican Army (IRA), were born shortly after the end of the famine during the 1850s. Support for these groups would continue to attract assistance from sympathetic overseas Irish communities. At home, social order broke down, and protest crimes became commonplace. Evictions were particularly emotive events, when the local community would often be in confrontation with the constabulary. Many of the Protestant landlords were eventually replaced by the Catholic aristocracy as religious intolerance squeezed this community out. Security of tenure became the catch-cry for farmers, who no longer wanted to rent their farms but to own them. The Irish language, generally spoken at the time, lost a huge number of speakers and became associated with poverty.

The Great Famine was therefore both a natural and a human disaster, a conspiracy of politics and economics as well as nature that would ironically set Ireland on the path that has led to the country we know today.

BORD FÁILTE IRISH TOURIST BOARD
INFORMATION CENTRES

IRELAND
Bord Fáilte - Irish Tourist Board
Baggot Street Bridge, Dublin 2
Tel: + 353 1 602 4000
Fax: + 353 1 602 4100
Email: user@irishtouristboard.ie
www.ireland.travel.ie

NORTHERN IRELAND
Bord Fáilte, 53 Castle Street
Belfast BT1 1GH
Tel: + 44 28 9032 7888
Fax: + 44 28 9024 0201
Email: info@irishtouristboardni.com
www.ireland.travel.ie

Bord Fáilte
44 Foyle Street, Derry
BT48 6AT
Tel: + 44 28 71 369501
Fax: + 44 28 71 369501
www.ireland.travel.ie

EUROPE

BELGIUM
Irish Tourist Board- Bord Failte
Avenue de Beaulieulaan 25/12
1160 Brussels
Tel: + 32 02 673 9940
Fax: + 32 02 672 1066
Email: info@irishtouristboard.be
www.ireland-tourism.be

BRITAIN
Irish Tourist Board
Ireland House, 150 New Bond Street
London W1Y OAQ
Tel: + 44 20 7493 3201
Fax: + 44 20 7493 9065
Email: info@irishtouristboard.co.uk
www.irelandtravel.co.uk

DENMARK
Det Irske Turistkontor
"Klostergaarden"
Amagertorv 29B,3
1160 København K
Tel: + 45 33 15 8045
Fax: + 45 33 93 6390
Email: info@irske-turistkontor.dk
www.irland-turisme.dk

FINLAND
Irlannin Matkailutoimisto
Embassy of Ireland, Erottajankatu 7A
PL33, 00130
Helsinki
Tel: + 358 9 608 966
Fax: + 358 9 646 022
Email: failte@netlife.fi
www.irlanninmatkailu.com

FRANCE
Office National du Tourisme Irlandais
33 rue de Miromesnil, 75008 Paris
Tel: + 33 1 53 43 12 12
Fax: + 33 1 47 42 01 64
Email: info@irlande-tourisme.fr
www.irlande-tourisme.fr

GERMANY
Irische Fremdenverkehrszentrale
Untermainanlage 7
D60329 Frankfurt am Main
Tel: + 49 69 92318550
Fax: + 49 69 92318588
Email: info@irishtouristboard.de
www.irland-urlaub.de

ITALY
Ente Nazionale del Turismo Irlandese
Via Santa Maria Segreta 6
20123 Milano
Tel: + 39 02 8690541
Fax: + 39 02 8690396
Email: info@turismo.irlandese.it
www.irlanda-travel.com

SPAIN
Oficina de Turismo de Irlanda
Paseo de la Castellana 46, 3 Planta
28046 Madrid
Tel: + 34 91 577 17 87
Fax: + 34 91 577 69 34
Email: ireland@ran.es
www.turismodeirlanda.com

NETHERLANDS
Iers Nationaal Bureau voor Toerisme
Spuistraat 104
1012 VA Amsterdam
Tel: + 31 20 530 6050
Fax: + 31 20 620 8089
Email: info@irishtouristboard.nl
www.ierland.nl

NORWAY
Irlands Turistkontor
Karenlyst alle 9A, Postboks 295
Skøyen, 0213 Oslo
Tel: + 47 22563310
Fax: + 47 22543120
Email: ciaran.delaney@online.no
Email: unni.ellingsen@lysline.no
www.visit-irland.com

PORTUGAL
Delegacao de Turismo Irlandesa
Embaixada da Irlanda
Rua da Imprensa a Estrela 1-4
1200 Lisboa, Portugal
Tel: + 351 1 392 94 40
Fax: + 351 1 397 73 63
www.ireland.travel.ie

SWEDEN
Irlandska Turistbyran
Sibyllegatan 49
PO Box 5292
10246 Stockholm
Tel: + 46 8 662 8510
Fax: + 46 8 661 7595
Email: info@irlandskaturistbyran.a.se
www.irlandsinfo.com

SWITZERLAND
Irland Informationsburo
Neumühle Toss
Neumühlestraße 42
CH-8406 Winterthur
Tel: + 41 52 202 69 06
Fax: + 41 52 202 69 08
Email:
irishtouristboard.ch@bluewin.ch
www.ireland.travel.ie

NORTH AMERICA

Irish Tourist Board
345 Park Avenue, 17th Floor
New York, NY 10154-0180
Tel: 1 212 418 0800
Fax: 1 212 371 9052
Email: info@irishtouristboard.com
www.irelandvacations.com

SOUTH AFRICA

(Physical Address)
Irish Tourist Board
c/o Development Promotions
Everite House, 7th Floor
20 De Korte Street
Braamfontein - Johannesburg 2001
South Africa

(Postal Address)
PO Box 30615
Braamfontein 2017
Tel: 011 339 4865
Fax: 011 339 2474
Email: devprom@global.co.za
www.ireland.travel.ie

NEW ZEALAND

Irish Tourist Board
Dingwall Building, 2nd Floor
87 Queen Street, Auckland
Tel: + 64 9 3798720
Fax: + 64 9 3022420
Email: patrick.flynn@walshes.co.nz
www.ireland.travel.ie

AUSTRALIA

Irish Tourist Board
5th Level, 36 Carrington Street
Sydney, NSW 2000
Tel: + 61 2 9299 6177
Fax: + 61 2 9299 6323
Email: itb@bigpond.com
www.ireland.travel.ie

JAPAN

Irish Tourist Board
Ireland House 4f
2-10-7 Kojimachi
Chiyoda-ku
Tokyo 102-0083
Tel: + 81 3 5275 1611
Fax: + 81 3 5275 1623
Email: bfejapan@oak.ocn.ne.jp
www.ireland.travel.ie

Looking for accommodation?

From castles to cosy cottages, one number has it all

+800 668 66866

+ denotes international access code in the country where the call is made eg. 00800 UK, 011800 USA)

Instant access to available accommodation ross the country and on the spot booking service or Hostels, B&Bs, Hotels, Farm Houses, Country ouses, Guesthouses and Self-Catering premises.

resireland
+800 66866866
operated by Gulliver infores

resireland
IRELAND'S RESERVATION SERVICE

resireland is a credit card reservation service with access to thousands of properties throughout Ireland, all of which are officially approved by the Irish Tourist Board and the Northern Ireland Tourist Board. You can now have all your accommodation needs catered for by contacting resireland.

How do I make a reservation?

Online Booking

reservations can be made on-line through the Tourism Brand Ireland website www.ireland.travel.ie. Choose the tab "make a booking" for connection to resireland booking service.

Freephone

Freephone numbers operate in USA, Canada, United Kingdom and Ireland.

Calling from the USA/Canada Call 011 800 668 668 66
Calling from the United Kingdom/Ireland Call 00 800 668 668 66

Reservation lines are open 7 days a week and our multilingual travel advisors will be delighted to process your booking.

email

reservations@gulliver.ie

For personal callers in Ireland the service is also available in the major Tourist Information Offices.

A standard booking fee and deposit applies to all transactions.

operated by Gulliver InfoRes

County Mayo

the country, and pilgrims still climb to its summit each year. However, **Mweelrea**, to the north of **Killary Harbour**, at 2,687 feet is the highest mountain in Connacht. And to complete the list of superlatives there is **Achill Island**, the largest island off Ireland's coast, now connected to the mainland by a bridge, accessible yet still largely unspoilt.

County Mayo has marvellous salmon and trout fishing, some of the loveliest scenery in the country—in particular around **Lough**

In the historical record, **County Mayo is** a relative newcomer, as it became a county only in the 16th century, when *Queen Elizabeth's* Lord Deputy in Ireland, **Sir Henry Sidney**, set about shiring the province of Connacht. Its name, *Maigh Eo*, 'plain of the yew trees', refers to the diocese associated with *St Colmán* and his monks at a place now known as **Mayo Abbey**.

With a landmass of over 1,900 square miles, the county is bordered by the Atlantic on the north and west, by Counties Sligo and Roscommon on the north-east and east, and by County Galway on the south-east and south. It contains the largest expanse of bog in the country (200 square miles), running east and north from **Lough Carrowmore**, and some splendid lakes, imposing mountains, and high cliffs. Towards the east it is made up of limestone plains, but in general the landscape is dominated by the low peaks of **Nephin** (2,648 feet) and **Croagh Patrick** (1,854 feet). The latter is Ireland's holy mountain, from the folk belief that *St Patrick* spent time here. On it stands the highest church in

Furnace and **Lough Feragh**—and a portfolio of outdoor pursuits that include rock-climbing, windsurfing, hill-walking, pony-trekking, water-skiing, and swimming—something for everybody. But for those who prefer to book themselves a seat in Heaven, the village of **Knock**, with its famous shrine to the Virgin Mary, has its own international airport, with reduced fares for pilgrims. It is also popular with couples from all over the world who come to get married here. Then there is **Westport**, an elegant Georgian town planned by **James Wyatt**, which in summer stages the International Sea Angling Festival and the Westport Horse Show and is renowned for the festive atmosphere of its streets and pubs throughout the tourist season.

The most universally attractive side to County Mayo is the overwhelming impact of its scenic beauty ('Mayo is magic!' declared an entranced *Tony Blair* on his visit to **Cong**

Croagh Patrick,
Co. Mayo.

in 1998). But this enjoyment can be carried a stage further by a 'reading' of the landscape to find out historically what lies behind it. The recently instituted **Céide Fields Visitor Centre** set up by the Office of Public Works is perfect in this regard, as it provides a detailed explanation of the archaeology and geology of this north Mayo area. Not only are there magnificent views from the top of Céide Hill but the hill itself and the surrounding area constitute the most extensive Stone Age monument in the world. Under this beautiful landscape of bog and heather the work of excavation has revealed the existence of a wheat and barley-farming community whose stone walls and farm buildings have now been rescued from oblivion after millennia of neglect. Dating back over five thousand years, this is the oldest enclosed landscape in Europe. Mayo is indeed magic!

Despite its tourist assets, County Mayo suffered in the past from wholesale emigration. In the mountain communities of the north and west the farms have

traditionally been small, and the law of primogeniture meant that a large number of young men were forced to emigrate to England to supplement their meagre incomes. Today the trend is being slowly reversed. Agricultural activity geared to the export market, an increased emphasis on tourism and steady industrial growth account for the change. For the intending visitor, the simplest way to sum up the spell cast by County Mayo is to remember that this is *Quiet Man* country, where *John Wayne* (whose own ancestors came from these parts) and *Maureen O'Hara* cinematographically introduced the west of Ireland to a world audience. In addition to the stunning scenery shown in the film, County Mayo has thirteen blue-flag beaches, wonderful golf courses, and world-record fishing venues. And when it comes to outstanding personalities, it's also high on local colour, with a list that includes the 'pirate queen', *Gráinne Ní Mháille*, who, when she wasn't plundering merchant ships, lived at **Rockfleet Castle**.

303

Southern Mayo

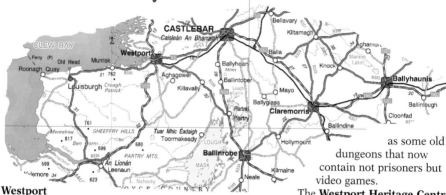

as some old dungeons that now contain not prisoners but video games.

Westport

is one of the few Irish towns that was planned, rather than haphazardly coming into being. Designed by *James Wyatt* and *Richard Cassel* in the 18th century, it has a graceful tree-lined boulevard known as the **Mall** and a central square known as the **Octagon**, where a country market is held each Thursday morning. Set at the head of one of Europe's greatest fishing grounds, **Clew Bay**, it is by far the most attractive urban centre in County Mayo. The Continental tourists who return here year after year obviously think so too, corroborating the positive impression the place made on the English writer *William Makepeace Thackeray* when he first visited it in 1842.

One of the principal drawing-cards of the area is stately **Westport House**, a mansion designed by Cassel in 1730 and later added to by *Thomas Ivory* and *James Wyatt*. Built on the site of a castle belonging to the pirate-queen *Gráinne Ní Mháille*, it is a rectangular three-storey edifice furnished with magnificent late Georgian and 19th-century furniture and containing a fine collection of silver and bric-à-brac. Family portraits by *Pie* and *Reynolds*, a Holy Family by *Rubens*, one of *J. M. Synge's* violins and a collection of old Waterford glass are all on display. The lovely Chinese wallpaper on the first floor is over two hundred years old. Superbly situated close to a lake, the house has its own zoo-park in the grounds, as well

The **Westport Heritage Centre** on Westport Quay provides a useful insight into the historical background of the area, as well as displaying documents and artefacts illustrative of the lives of famous people associated with County Mayo. It includes the spinning-wheel presented by the people of Ballina to *Maud Gonne MacBride*, the revolutionary beloved of *Yeats* who married *John MacBride*. Among other notables dealt with are the infamous *William Joyce*, 'Lord Haw-Haw', who lived near Ballinrobe and broadcast propaganda for Nazi Germany during the Second World War, and *Grace Kelly*, whose grandfather lived near the road to Castlebar before he emigrated to the United States.

Just over 6 miles west of Westport, off the Louisburgh road, is the 2,500-foot **Croagh Patrick**, Ireland's holy mountain. Its perfect conical peak towers over Clew Bay and the entire western coastline, and on the last Sunday of each July ('Reek Sunday') thousands of pilgrims, many of them barefoot, make the two-hour climb through rocky terrain to the summit, where, above the south precipice, people once believed *St Patrick* rang his bell and the terrified snakes of Ireland plunged to their death. Recent excavations suggest that the area was inhabited by prehistoric settlers, who have left megalithic tombs, standing stones, burial mounds and ring-forts behind them.

Louisburgh (*Cluain Cearbán*, 'Cearbán's meadow'), a pleasant fishing village 12 miles

Westport,
Co. Mayo.

from Westport, got its English name from Louisburgh, Nova Scotia. The town is surrounded by superb sandy beaches and is close to **Roonagh Pier**, the departure point for ferries to Clare Island and Inishturk. Its broad terraced streets preserve something of its 18th-century origins, and it acts as the focal point of a wonderfully scenic area stretching from Killary Harbour in the south to the Owenree river in the north and from the coast to the Erriff valley in the east. The **Granuaile** [*Gráinne Ní Mháille*] **Heritage Centre** in the town provides the background to the history of the O'Malleys and their territory and gives extensive coverage to the life and times of the colourful pirate-queen. A Great Famine display recalls the unsuccessful trek of six hundred local people in 1849 to **Delphi Lodge** on the shores of Finn Lough in search of relief. Built in the 1840s as a fishing-lodge, the lodge was named after the Greek site by a member of the Browne family of Westport. The Brownes converted to Protestantism to avoid the effects of the Penal Laws and were rewarded with a title at the time of the Act of Union in 1801. The second marquis was a friend of Byron's and presumably animated,

like him, by classical and humanitarian virtues; but not on this occasion. The starving petitioners were brusquely turned away, and many of them died on the return journey. Lest it be forgotten, this sad episode is commemorated annually in the Great Famine Walk.

The road from Louisburgh through the Doo Lough valley passes through spectacular lake and mountain scenery on its way towards Killary Harbour.

Just above Lough Corrib in County Galway and below Lough Mask in County Mayo and perched on a narrow isthmus separating the two is the village of **Cong** (*Conga*, 'isthmus'). One of its most impressive sites is the ruined **Augustinian Long Abbey,** founded in the 12th century by *Toirealach Ó Conchúir*, King of Ireland, who, having failed to defeat the Normans, retired here for his final years, dying in the abbey in 1198. The Cross of Cong, a 12th-century decorated processional cross, now one of the treasures of the National Museum in Dublin, was made in County Roscommon for the abbey on his orders. A guest refectory and the monks' 12th-century fishing house remain. One curious feature of the latter was

Doolough,
Co. Mayo.

the arrangement whereby a bell rang in the kitchen when a fish was caught in the net lowered through a hole in the floor. A 12th-century cross, marking the completion of the abbey, still stands in the town centre.

For cinema-goers, however, the town's greatest claim to fame is that it was the setting for the film *The Quiet Man* (1956), starring *John Wayne* and *Maureen O'Hara*. The **Quiet Man Heritage Centre** contains reproductions of the furniture and costumes used in the film, as well as photographs of *Barry Fitzgerald* and *Maureen O'Hara* and other memorabilia.

Ashford Castle, a Gothic Revival mansion, now functions as a luxury hotel.

Ballinrobe, near the eastern shore of Lough Mask, is an excellent angling centre. Its Catholic church, **St Mary's**, has no less than nine beautiful stained-glass windows by *Harry Clarke,* and the town is also the site of

the **South Mayo Family Research Centre**. About 2 miles south-west of the town is the great stone fort of **Cahernagollum**, and further on the **Killower Cairn.**

Northwards above Lough Mask and set close to Lough Conn are the towns of **Partry** and **Ballintubber.** Four miles beyond Partry a road on the right leads to **Ballintubber Abbey**. The abbey was founded in 1216 by *Cathal Ó Conchúir,* King of Connacht, near the site of a church supposedly built by *St Patrick* in the 5th century. Suppressed by *King Henry VIII* and destroyed by *Oliver Cromwell* in 1653, it remained roofless for a long time, but despite this, local people continued to attend Mass here in large numbers. Known as 'the abbey that refused to die', it is the only one of its kind in Ireland, in continuous use for over 780 years. Completely restored in 1966, its interior contains a video display and

and served originally to link the mountain-top with Cruachan, seat of the kings of Connacht. Not far from Ballintubber, on the N84 road, is a new interpretative centre, the **Celtic Furrow,** providing information on the festivals and seasons of the megalithic farmers.

In 1879 some people claimed they saw the Virgin Mary, St Joseph and St John the Evangelist on the gable of the parish church at **Knock**. Ever since then the town has exerted a fascination for millions of believers as a place of pilgrimage. *Pope John Paul II* made it the focal point of his visit to Ireland in 1979. The major focus for visitors is an enormous basilica opened during the Pope's visit that accommodates 20,000 people. **Knock Folk Museum**, an interpretative centre, supplies background information on rural Knock in 1879 as well as documents relative to the apparition.

Castlebar, the county town, began as a settlement around the 11th-century de Barry family castle and received a charter from *King James I* of England in 1613. But its greatest historical moment came in 1798 when *General Humbert's* French forces routed the English army under *General Lake,* an engagement known ever since as the Races of Castlebar, because of the rapidity of the English withdrawal. The town itself has good shopping facilities, and the **Linenhall Arts Centre** has a programme of arts performance throughout the year. The tourist information office is in the same building.

interpretative centre. Pilgrims on their way to Croagh Patrick pass by Ballintober, along the path known as **Tóchar Phádraig** ('St Patrick's causeway'), in honour of the saint; but in fact the route pre-dates Christianity

---

DON'T MISS
- Whether you're Pagan or Christian, **Croagh Patrick** will be the climb of a lifetime.
- **Ballintubber Abbey** and nearby **Moore Hall**, birthplace of *George Moore*, one of Ireland's greatest writers.

ALL-WEATHER OPTIONS
- Visit **Westport House** and admire the doors made from Jamaican mahogany and the marble staircase installed by Italians; if the children get impatient, there's a small zoo in the old walled garden.
- Make a trip to **Louisburgh Folk and Heritage Centre** to learn about the O'Malleys, a prominent family in the area. And since children of all ages love pirates, the high point will be the life of the great pirate-queen herself, *Gráinne Ní Mháille.*

Northern Mayo

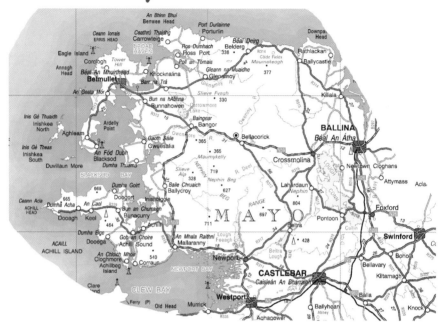

Newport, situated close to Nephin Beg mountain on the north-east corner of **Clew Bay**, is a well-known fresh-water and deep-sea angling centre. One of its most salient features is the imaginative conversion of a disused seven-arch viaduct dating from 1892 into a park walkway spanning the Newport River. It is also notable for the neo-Romanesque **Church of St Patrick** (1914), which has a number of *Harry Clarke* windows, of which the centrepiece is a magnificent Last Judgment in blues, greens and reds set dramatically above the high altar. Reflecting the interests of visitors and local people alike in fishing as a business and leisure pursuit, a **Salmon World Visitor Centre** on nearby **Lough Furnace** provides details on the salmon's life-cycle, as well as showing how a fishery is maintained.

The area surrounding Newport contains a number of historic monuments, one of the most memorable of which is the 15th-century **Burrishoole Abbey**, a Dominican priory. The church is topped by a tower and

comprises a nave, chancel, and south transept. Of the cloisters, only the east wall remains. Built on flat rocks beside an inlet of the sea, **Carrickahowley Castle**, a 15th-century tower-house, also known as **Rockfleet**, belonged at one point to *Gráinne Ní Mháille*. The castle has been partly restored, and a flight of wooden steps and a spiral staircase enable visitors to see the rather restricted conditions in which the pirate-queen lived.

Situated on the banks of the River Moy, east of Lough Conn and Lough Cullin, **Foxford** is a small market town and angling centre with a famous woollen-mill. In Famine and post-Famine times the local people suffered from enormous deprivation because of the repeated failure of the potato crop. Evictions became commonplace, and these led to the founding of the Land League in 1879 by *Michael Davitt* to combat landlordism and to find some remedy for rural injustices. He lived in a cottage at **Strade**, between Foxford and Castlerea,

Nephin Mountain,
Co. Mayo.

where the **Michael Davitt National Memorial Museum** is now established. As part of her personal efforts to find a solution to unemployment difficulties, a Sister of Charity called *Mother Agnes Morrrogh Bernard* set up a woollen-mill at Foxford in 1892 called the Providence Mills. Providence certainly provided, and today the mill has an impressive visitor centre that fills in the background to the entrepreneurial vision of this unusual and gifted businesswoman.

At the top of Lough Conn, **Crossmolina** serves as a base for fishermen anxious to try their luck on the lake or on the River Deel and for walkers or hikers with enough energy to explore the Nephin mountain area. The **North Mayo Family Research and Heritage Centre,** about half a mile outside the town, is worth a visit, as it acts as a museum of rural history by providing a display of agricultural machines and demonstrations of traditional crafts. By the way, if you want to 'forge' a new career for yourself and make your own good-luck horseshoes, try the five to ten-day blacksmith course offered by the centre!

Ballina is the birthplace of Ireland's first woman President, *Mary Robinson*. With a population of 7,000 people, it is the largest town in County Mayo and is closely associated with salmon and trout-fishing. While the centre of the town lacks distinction, there are some pleasant quayside walks beside the River Moy. It is a convenient place in which to shop for provisions (especially smoked salmon) as well as a base from which to travel in north Mayo, and it contains its fair share of good pubs and restaurants. On the east bank of the Moy the 19th-century **Cathedral of St Muiredach** (*Muiríoch*) stands next to the ruins of a late 14th-century Augustinian friary. Near the railway station is a portal tomb supposedly marking the burial-place of four foster-brothers who found education too demanding and murdered their tutor, *Ceallach*, a 6th-century bishop. In an equally uneducated act of retribution, Ceallach's brother hanged all four on the opposite side of the river.

Killala (*Cill Ala*, 'church of St Ala') takes its name from a 5th-century foundation supposedly established under St Patrick's patronage. Tradition affirms that the Church of Ireland cathedral is built on the site of the first Christian church, where *Muiríoch* was invested as first bishop of the town. But Killala's place in history was assured later when the French chose to stop here after landing in support of the United Irishmen with a force of 1,100 men in 1798. After taking Killala, Ballina and Castlebar they were defeated by *Lord Cornwallis* a few weeks later at Ballinamuck in County Longford, bringing to an end an exciting and revolutionary period in Mayo and Irish history, preserved in local memory as 'the year of the French'.

Further along the north Mayo coast, past Ballycastle, are the **Céide Fields**, one of the most exciting prehistoric discoveries of recent years. Brought to light as the result of turf-cutting activity, the Stone Age landscape of fields, places of habitation and megalithic tombs had been completely covered with blanket bog. Dry-stone corrals and dwellings with flint tools and pottery were laid bare by excavation. The fields have been mapped out over a 6-mile area and were worked and maintained 5,000 years ago by farmers who were contemporaries of the people who built the Boyne Valley tombs. The **Céide Fields Visitor Centre** provides information on the geological characteristics of the terrain and the growth of the bog as well as a summary of the site's archaeological significance.

Beyond the Céide Fields, on the west coast and about 25 miles from Achill, is **Bangor Erris**, one of the old Norman baronies. The Erris area is one of the most sparsely populated and loneliest tracts of landscape in Ireland. Little evidence of human activity marks the scenery, which unfolds in slopes of brown heather, rising into high bare hills and rocky escarpments whipped by merciless winds. The most eye-catching sight here is **Moista Sound**, a narrow chasm shut in by sheer cliff-faces, which seem about to touch 100 yards overhead. A demanding and challenging walking route called the **Bangor Trail** begins in the town and takes its course through the Nephin Beg mountain to Newport.

Cliff scenery,
north Mayo.

DON'T MISS

- Even if you're not religious, you must be curious! **Knock Shrine** has attracted millions—why not you? Go and see this extraordinary monument of Irish Catholicism and learn something of its history in the **Knock Folk Museum**, where permanent displays also cover many other local passions and pursuits. **Our Lady's Domain** is a carefully landscaped parkland, a botanical bower of bliss and a place of retreat as well.

- The recently uncovered monument to successive communities and generations of farmers, the **Céide Fields** is one of the most astonishing and fascinating large-scale archaeological finds of the last few decades. These ancient Mayo men wrote in the landscape, and thousands of years later the lines they left in the soil are still waiting to be read by you, today's visitor.

ALL-WEATHER OPTIONS

- When it's cold and wet, it's nice to think of something warm! Visit **Foxford Woollen Mills**, where you can see rugs and tweeds being made—just for you, the freezing visitor! Opened in 1992, the **Historical Woollen Mill Tour** will transport you back in time to how things were in Foxford in the 1890s. More than a factory, it's a lesson in resourcefulness and survival, starring an Irish Sister of Charity.

- **The Michael Davitt Museum** in Strade is a good bad-weather place. Archive material, photographs and documents are devoted to this giant of 19th-century Irish politics, a man who was born in the town and is buried in the graveyard of the modern church. Davitt's two dominant interests, the Land League and the GAA, are well covered, and the centre contains books by and about him.

Belmullet and Achill Island

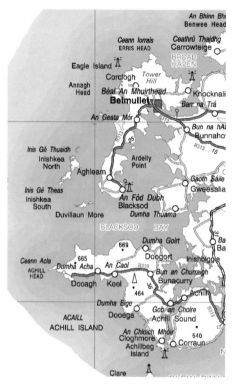

completely stripped of vegetation, while the eastern, more sheltered side, overlooking the landlocked inlet of **Blacksod Bay**, has some good beaches. Other promontory forts are situated at **Doonaneanir** and **Portnafrankach**.

Off the peninsula are the **Duvillaun Islands**, the **Inishkea** islands, **Inishkeeragh**, **Inishglora** and **Eagle Island**. **Inishglora** is the legendary island where the ringing of St Patrick's bell announcing the arrival of Christianity released the Children of Lir from the spell cast on them by their wicked stepmother. Immortal in their swan shape, the bell 'mortalised' them once more, and they came ashore blind, enfeebled, and close to death. **Inishkea** is associated with a rather similar exemplary tale, that of a woman who, turned into a heron for her infidelity, lived out a lonely banishment for a thousand years. **Inishglora** has the ruins of a dry-stone chapel linked to *St Brendan the Navigator,* and **Blacksod Bay** covers the remains of *La Rata Encoronada,* one of the largest of the galleons belonging to the Spanish Armada, which went aground and was burnt by its crew at the height of the storms that swept Ireland in September 1588. At the tip of the peninsula is the 12th-century church of **St Dervila**. Near the church is **St Dervila's Well,** said to be good for curing eye trouble.

Three great mountains dominate **Achill Island**, which is joined to the mainland by a bridge. They are **Slievemore**, **Croghaun**, and **Minaun**, all of which are over 2,600 feet in height. The village of **Achill Sound**, close to the bridge to the mainland, is the main supply and shopping centre and is a useful point of departure for exploring the southern part of the island. To take in some of the best scenery, follow the main road round the island, known as the Atlantic Drive. **Keel,** south-west of Doogort, is a popular resort and an excellent base for water sports and boat hire. It has a magnificent 2-mile sandy beach that curves away to the base of the Minaun cliffs. Eroded by the sea, the 'Cathedral Rocks' provide a phantasmagoria

Belmullet, a small seaside town set on the isthmus between Broad Haven and Blacksod Bay, is the key to the windswept Mullet peninsula. Its life revolves around fishing and agriculture and, in particular, the annual sea angling festival. A town originally planned by *William Carter,* a local landlord anxious to create a home market for produce, it can be extremely busy on market days, but the peninsula itself is a desolate and lonely expanse of territory.

At **Doonamo Point**, on a clifftop site, are the remains of a prehistoric promontory fort with a great wall that stretches across the neck of the headland and embraces three *clocháns* and the ruins of a circular fort. Facing it on stark **Eagle Island** is a lighthouse, more than half a mile out to sea. The western coast of **Mullet Peninsula** is

Evening light in Co. Mayo.

Beach at Doogort,
Achill Island, Co. Mayo.

of weird shapes and forms, and the cliffs are actually higher than the more celebrated Cliffs of Moher. At the island's western tip is **Croghaun**, with the cone-tipped Slievemore mountains to the north.

Doogort, a popular holiday and fishing village on the lower slopes of Slievemore, has a contentious background. Its more modern section, known as the 'Settlement' or the 'Colony', was founded in 1834 by a Protestant clergyman, with the aim of converting Catholics to Protestantism. The reward for so doing was food, clothing, and shelter. The proselytising zeal of the clergyman went beyond acceptable bounds for the local people when, in the Famine period, children were won over with offers of soup and bread. As a result of the public outcry, the 'Mission' was forced to close down.

Desertion, abandonment, eviction, emigration and decay form a persistent motif in Achill history. Apart from the doomed colony, the lower slopes of Slievemore also have a deserted settlement that formerly was occupied only in the summer, when flocks were brought to the upland grazing areas. This kind of seasonal encampment, involving nothing more than temporary dwellings, was called a 'booley' (*buaile*) village. A hope exists that some of the surviving ruins may be restored and an interpretative centre established.

Boats can be hired at Doogort pier to visit the **Seal Caves**, apertures cut out by the sea under the quartzite mountain from which, on a sunny day, tiny masses of mica chips can flash out unexpectedly.

At the southern end of the island, close to Achill Sound, is the well-preserved **Carrickkildavnet Castle**, an elegant 15th-century tower-house that once belonged to *Gráinne Ní Mháille*. On the shore of the sound are the restored ruins of **Kildavnet Church**, established in the 17th century and with Irish annotations on its Stations of the Cross as a reminder that this was an Irish-speaking district until quite recently.

Set in the entrance to Clew Bay is **Clare Island**, where *Gráinne Ní Mháille* had her fortified headquarters, a tower-house. The castle, situated at the eastern end of the island, has been altered considerably since it passed into the hands of the Coastguard Service. She herself is believed to be buried in a tomb in the small 13th-century **Clare Abbey** in the same area, now in ruins. Her motto, 'Invincible on land and sea,' scrawled on the wall in Latin, has a hollow ring to it today. The one hotel on the island serves sea anglers, scuba-divers and yachtsmen, and the island can be reached by boat from **Roonagh Bay**, near Louisburgh.

Below Clare Island, **Inishturk** has small farms and a population of 90 people, many of whom live from fishing. With a pretty harbour and beach at **Portadoon**, the island is only 3 miles by $1\frac{1}{2}$ miles in size. Nearby uninhabited **Caher Island** has a small roofless church encircled by twelve stone crosses, and legend associates it with *St Patrick*.

DON'T MISS
- From Doogort get a boatman to take you on a voyage of discovery to the **Seal Caves** to admire the extraordinary variety of grotesque forms produced by the ocean's prodigious creative energy.
- Go hang-gliding from the **Minaun Heights**, one of the best places for the sport in Ireland.

ALL-WEATHER OPTIONS
- Visit **Achill Island Crafts Centre** in Bullsmouth in the north-east of the island for a look at products representative of local skills in pottery and weaving.
- Even if you can't be out of doors because it's pouring, drop in on the **Activity and Leisure Centre** on the road to Keel to plan for the better days ahead.

The Irish Language

Imagine you have software for an advanced computer, and this software provides access to over two thousand years of archives containing vital information relative to your background and identity. You wouldn't want to throw it away, would you?

Well, that's the situation of those trying to preserve and promote Irish—the modern descendant of the language spoken continuously in Ireland from at least 300 BC and constituting an invaluable intellectual and emotional interpretative tool for a new generation of Irish men and women coming to terms with their own history and its bearing on contemporary reality.

Both English and Irish belong to the Indo-European family of languages; but whereas English belongs to the West Germanic branch, Irish forms part of the Celtic branch. It is closest to Gaelic (spoken in Scotland) and Manx but has affinities with Welsh, Cornish, and Breton—all of them Celtic languages that came to the fore in Britain and Ireland as a result of the expansion of the Celtic-speaking peoples round 500 BC.

Following the introduction of the roman

alphabet by Christian missionaries some time after the 5th century, the ground was laid for the gradual development of Irish in written form, though it was not until the 11th century that the first manuscripts were written in Irish by monks adapting Roman uncial lettering to the vernacular. But, as one of the few countries spared the onslaught of the Roman legions, Ireland managed to retain a language and a linguistic outlook rooted in the thoughts and feelings of western Europe in pre-Roman times. Also, when Latin was introduced by the monks (in contrast to experience with the vernacular on the Continent) it never became a rival to Irish in the production of literature, and the latter remained the privileged vehicle of Irish thought and expression.

The Irish language came through the Anglo-Norman conquest of the 12th century relatively unscathed. But the 16th-century Tudor colonisation proved disastrous. Many of the native Irish were deprived of their lands, which were handed over to English and Scottish settlers. Then, in 1649, Cromwell invaded the country; and in the early 18th century the anti-Catholic and anti-Irish Penal Laws prepared the way for the final overthrow of the native tongue. Evictions and the mass emigration of poor Irish-speaking families as a result of the Great Famine in 1845–9 further weakened the language, and by the end of the 19th century it had largely retreated to the mountainous areas of the western seaboard—a situation that, broadly speaking, persists today.

But despite the efforts of successive English governments to extirpate it completely, Irish managed to survive. In 1893 *Douglas Hyde* and *Eoin MacNeill* founded the Gaelic League, and soon Irish-speaking districts obtained permission to pursue a bilingual policy, though it was not until 1922, following the establishment of the Irish Free State, that Irish was taught as a school subject throughout the country. Official policy then aimed at establishing Irish as the vernacular; and while this has not been achieved, census figures from 1946 onwards indicate an increasing proportion of the population having proficiency in Irish, with the figures for 1991 showing a surprising million people in the Republic, and 140,000 in the six counties, claiming a working knowledge of the language.

The traditional Irish-speaking regions—collectively known as the *Gaeltacht*—are the jewel in the crown of the language revival policy. These pockets of cultural survival are found in Counties Cork, Kerry, Galway, Mayo, and Donegal, and in them the language of everyday expression is Irish. Not only that but the Gaeltacht has shown its cultural worth by producing important writers such as *Ó Criomhthainn, Ó Cadhain,* and *Mac Grianna*. Unfortunately, most of these areas are economically poor, and, despite Government support, people living in them associate English with jobs and affluence, and migrate in large numbers to English-speaking parts of the country.

But both the Government and language enthusiasts remain optimistic about the prospects for a general revival of the language. Various steps taken, in public and private, have created this positive mood. In 1953 a private company, Gael-Linn, was set up and financed the first widely distributed feature film in Irish. The company continues to flourish and since that time has produced a steady stream of records, films, and television programmes. In 1981 BBC Radio Ulster began broadcasting Irish-language radio programmes. Weekly newspapers and literary magazines in Irish exist. There is a wide and rapidly increasing network of Irish-language schools; and the arrival of a contemporary Irish-language television channel, TG4, has broadened interest considerably.

Every language is an interpretation of the world, and therefore valuable in itself. Bearing this in mind, persevering with Irish makes sense. In the long term, it needs to be taken from the *'cúpla focal'* (few words) that many people now enjoy to the point where it can gradually become the everyday language of a sizable proportion of the population.

TOURING ROUTE
Ballina-Belmullet-Ballycastle

Leave Ballina by the N59 road, passing by Lough Conn and, after it, Nephin Beg mountain on the left. Then the road passes through the little country town of **Crossmolina** and on to **Bellacorick**, with the cooling-tower of its turf-burning power station. It also has a musical bridge; you'll know you've reached Bellacorick if you see people rubbing large pebbles against the stone-capped parapets. These emit a dull sound when struck, with each block producing a different tone. The game is to try to orchestrate the diverse tones in a free composition! Local tradition says the bridge will never be completed, and whoever tries

to do so will die. Don't play with fate; pursue your route to **Bangor Erris**, an angling centre for the Owenduff River and Carrowmore Lough.

From Bangor Erris leave the N59 and continue northwards along the R313 past Attavalley to **Belmullet**, the key to the bleak and exposed Mullet Peninsula, which extends northwards to Erris Head and southwards to Blacksod Point. The minor road going north-west leads to **Doonamo Point** and the remains of Doonamo Fort, while the R313 swings around in a southerly direction. Stay with it, driving south. On your left, off the Mullet Peninsula, the

Inishkea Islands come into view and, once the end of the peninsula is reached, the **Duvillaun Islands**. (At Blacksod Bay it's possible to hire a boat for the trip to **Doogort** on Achill Island.) Complete the small looped road section at the tip of the peninsula, returning northwards through Binghamstown to Belmullet. From Belmullet take the R313 and then branch off at the R314, heading north-east through Barnatra and on to **Glenamoy.** (One option is to take a road to the left at Glenamoy Bridge; it leads to **Portacloy**, a small cliff-enclosed harbour. **Benwee Head** on the west looks onto immense cliffs offshore, the **Stags of Broadhaven**—seven sections of sheer cliff face rising 100 yards from the sea and forming one of the most dramatic features of this coastal area.)

From Glenamoy proceed to **Belberg** and the ensuing North Mayo coast with its spectacular ocean views. A short distance after Belberg appear the **Céide Fields**— archaeologically the largest prehistoric farming site in the west. Following the Céide Fields, **Ballycastle** affords a fine view of **Downpatrick Head** to the north. Near the head are a number of 'puffing holes' and the lonely, detached rock of **Doonbristy,** reminding viewers of the Atlantic's fury. A little further along the R314 is **Killala**, once believed to have been founded by *St Patrick* and also famous as the landing-place of the French force under *General Humbert* in 1798. (Another small detour is possible here for those interested in antiquities who can take the slightly longer coast road back to Ballina in order to view the remains of **Moyne Abbey** and **Rosserk Abbey,** both of which have interesting features.) From Killala the road leads back to Ballina.

View in the Nephin Mountains, Co. Mayo.

The North-West

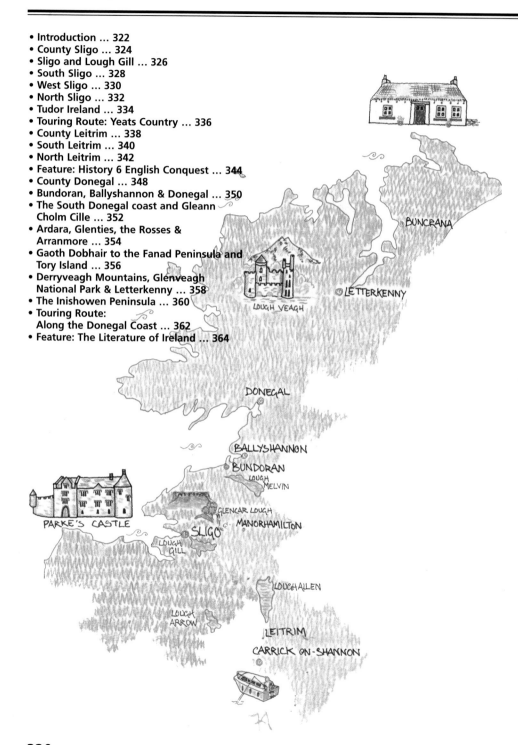

Knocknarea Mountain,
Co. Sligo.

North-West

Every area, like every county in Ireland, offers the traveller something different, something wonderful, something magical—because Ireland is different, wonderful, and magical! But if you are the sort of traveller who needs open spaces, needs time and yet needs to feel wanted, the three counties of the north-west will each extend the hand of hospitality against a background of uncrowded natural beauty.

Each of the three counties covered in this section tells its own individual story, and yet, like members of an extended family, they share a similar history—a history that has marked their landscape and shaped their people. They all share the mighty Atlantic Ocean, though limited to a mere 2 miles in the case of County Leitrim. Mountains and lakes spread throughout the three counties, not only affording much delight to the beholder but also offering a natural playground for those who cannot resist the lure of water or the challenge to rise above sea level.

Like so much of the west coast, Counties Leitrim, Sligo and Donegal have suffered from the ravages of famine and emigration: populations decimated, their sons and daughters scattered to the four corners of the world. Left behind are the reminders: uncrowded roads and natural beauty left unspoilt and for the most part untouched by humans.

County Leitrim is often overshadowed by better-known and larger counties, but small can be beautiful, and this is certainly true of 'Lovely Leitrim'. Lying between Counties Donegal and Sligo, this county has two distinct areas, divided by the first of Ireland's three great lakes, **Lough Allen**. To the south of Lough Allen is a gentle, undulating *drumlin* landscape, filled with lakes and rivers. This part of the county is for the angler and boatman; cruisers can now make their way into Lough Allen, or travel on to discover the waters of County Fermanagh by way of the **Shannon-Erne Waterway**, reopened in 1994. Small towns

and villages tell the story of the Celt and the settler. North of the great lake you have the mountains and glens, which offer excellent hill-walking and pot-holing, or simply the beauty of nature for those who simply want to drive off the beaten track. The cultural visitor is catered for in County Leitrim by a variety of local museums and big houses, such as **Lough Rynn House and Gardens** and **Parke's Castle** on Lough Gill.

County Sligo has so much to offer the visitor that it is difficult to know where to begin. Not only has the county the mountains, lakes, rivers and forests that one comes to expect in Ireland but it also has the powerful Atlantic Ocean shaping and moulding its coastline. For visitors interested in those who came before us, this county is littered with ancient monuments: court tombs, portal tombs, souterrains, and ring-forts. Even the most uninterested visitor cannot but be impressed by the 40,000 tons of rock on the 1,000-foot-high **Knocknarea**. Immortalised for ever by *William Butler Yeats*, Ireland's greatest poet, majestic Sligo has been the inspiration for many a creative spirit.

We have divided County Sligo into four areas, which take their point of reference from the county town. The first area concentrates on the town itself and the neighbouring Lough Gill. Perhaps the most famous of Sligo's lakes, **Lough Gill** will live up to your expectations, and it will not require much imagination to see what it was that inspired Yeats to write his best-known poem, 'The Lake Isle of Innisfree'.

To the north of Sligo we have the rugged limestone mountains, dominated by the sheer rock face of **Benbulbin** towering above the small church of **Drumcliff**, and again we are reminded of Yeats and how he chose his final resting-place here in his beloved County Sligo. There is much to see in north Sligo and, as is the case throughout most of the county, there are lots of opportunities to pursue a wide range of activities.

The scenery in west Sligo is quite varied, affording coastal cliffs and beaches, mountains, bogland, and secluded lakes. In contrast, for our fourth area we travel inland, but nevertheless excellent views can be had of the rest of the county from the **Curlew Mountains**. This is also an area rich in archaeological remains and where mythological stories of the brave and fearless abound.

Benbulbin, Co. Sligo.

Majestic Sligo has something to offer everyone, from the lover of nature and wildlife enthusiast to the beach-goer, the historian, and the visitor who simply wants to relax in a peaceful setting soaking up its rich cultural past.

Some would say that the best part has been kept until last, because **County Donegal** is truly a place apart! Some would go as far as to say that dramatic Donegal is the most beautiful county in Ireland. With a vast rugged coastline set against a background of mountains and moors, County Donegal is wild and beautiful, full of possibilities for the enthusiastic visitor undaunted by a little bit of wind and rain and with the time to travel the winding uncluttered roads, visit the local museums, or get to know the local people over a pint or two.

Significantly larger than either of the other two counties in this region, County Donegal is divided into six areas, each with its own individual character and personality. Beginning on the Sligo border, the Bundoran-Ballyshannon-Donegal area is a gentle introduction to the county and hardly indicative of what is to come. Moving west from **Donegal**, the principal town in this part of the county, we come to the magnificent **Slieve League** cliffs of south Donegal and **Gleann Cholm Cille**. *St Colm*

Cille is to County Donegal what *St Patrick* is to Ireland; and in this, his valley, even 1,400 years after his death you cannot fail to be touched by his presence.

In the third area—that of Ardara, Glenties, the Rosses, and Arranmore—you have reached the wild and rugged Donegal you may have been expecting. Here, where the people have long struggled to survive, they have been surrounded by scenery often described as spectacular. The fourth area we look at is from **Gaoth Dobhair** to the **Fanad Peninsula** and **Tory Island**; and again words such as 'magnificent', 'dramatic' and 'fascinating' spring to mind when you travel through this region. Irish-speaking and proud, the people of these areas will welcome any who make the effort to travel this far.

The final two areas are **Glenveagh National Park** and **Letterkenny**, and the **Inishowen Peninsula**. Both these areas have so much to offer that it is scarcely possible to cover everything.

The north-west is a place that offers visitors the opportunity to really get away from it all and do whatever it is they enjoy doing. Whether you are a golfer or a pub-goer, a hill-walker or a coach tour visitor, whether you are an antiquarian or a water sports expert, the north-west has something for you.

County Sligo

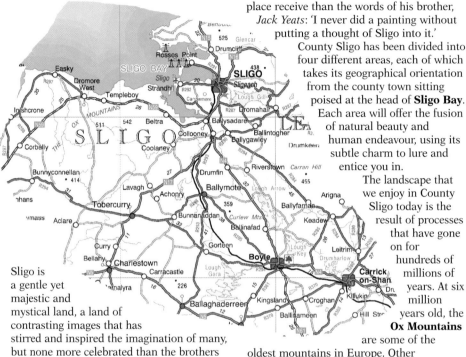

place receive than the words of his brother, *Jack Yeats*: 'I never did a painting without putting a thought of Sligo into it.'

County Sligo has been divided into four different areas, each of which takes its geographical orientation from the county town sitting poised at the head of **Sligo Bay**. Each area will offer the fusion of natural beauty and human endeavour, using its subtle charm to lure and entice you in.

The landscape that we enjoy in County Sligo today is the result of processes that have gone on for hundreds of millions of years. At six million years old, the **Ox Mountains** are some of the oldest mountains in Europe. Other mountains, such as **Benbulbin** and the **Bricklieve** range, appeared much later— about three hundred million years ago. A crucial element in the formation of County Sligo's landscape was the various ice ages that crossed Ireland during the last 200,000 years. The last ice age melted around 10,000 years ago, carving out valleys such as **Glencar** and **Sligo Valley**, and the melting waters helped to form lakes such as **Lough Gill** and the **Glencar Lake**.

Historically, the region began with the mesolithic (Middle Stone Age) hunter-gatherers who settled around **Lough Gara** over six thousand years ago. The arrival of the neolithic (Late Stone Age) era brought the first farmers to this area, and evidence abounds throughout the county from this period.

Whereas the mesolithic and neolithic people are remembered for how they

Sligo is a gentle yet majestic and mystical land, a land of contrasting images that has stirred and inspired the imagination of many, but none more celebrated than the brothers Yeats: Jack and his unique style captured for posterity on canvas, William and his creativity expressed in words 'dropping from the veils of the morning.'

With its mountains, lakes, rivers, forest and the omnipresent Atlantic Ocean, County Sligo combines natural beauty with the ancient stones of history. It has the greatest concentration of megalithic monuments in Ireland. It was here that the mythical lovers *Diarmaid and Gráinne* made their way when pursued by the heroic *Fionn mac Cumhaill*. And it was on the enchanted and enigmatic **Benbulbin** that Diarmaid was killed when the bristles of a wild boar pierced his heel— his only vulnerable spot.

It is not without reason that *William Butler Yeats* called this the 'Land of the Heart's Desire,' which inspired in him some of the best and most evocative poetry of the twentieth century. No better accolade can a

Kesh,
Co. Sligo.

honoured their dead, the Celts, who arrived much later—about 300 BC—have left behind monuments commemorating how they lived. County Sligo is rich in *crannógs* (artificial islands), ring-forts, stone forts (enclosures around the dwelling-place), and tribal hill forts.

The Early Irish church left its mark on County Sligo, just as it did on the rest of Ireland, and nowhere can that be better appreciated than on the small island of **Innishmurray**. The introduction of the European monastic orders such as the Franciscans and the Dominicans coincided with the arrival of the Anglo-Normans. The importance of these monastic establishments is evident from the extensive ruins they have left behind in places such as the town of **Sligo**. But the Anglo-Normans failed to make any lasting impression on the region, and those who did settle here integrated well with the indigenous population.

In the middle of the 17th century many changes occurred with the Cromwellian plantation of north Connacht. The names of English settlers now begin to appear as local landowners. The 17th century was generally a turbulent period throughout the country. Yet at the same time we see the new merchant-landlord class developing trade and industry in the region, improving its economic life.

This all changed dramatically with the Great Famine of 1845–50. County Sligo, like so much of the western seaboard, suffered from a dependence on one crop; death and emigration took their toll, decimating the population and leaving many with no option but to take their dreams and aspirations with them to a new country.

Today County Sligo has a population of 55,000. Agriculture is still an important element of economic life, but new industries, such as telecommunications, pharmaceuticals and computers, are finding a willing, hard-working and educated work force seeking to get on in life. Local initiatives also reflect the optimism the people of County Sligo are feeling towards their future.

325

Sligo and Lough Gill

Situated at the head of Sligo Bay, **Sligo** is the county town and the largest town in the north-west area. A lively, prosperous town, it has endured much because of its strategic position on the Garvoge River. It is an excellent base from which to tour, with the majestic Benbulbin to the north, the mystical Knocknarea to the south, and the magical Lough Gill to the east.

The first recorded mention of Sligo was in the year 807, when the town was sacked by some marauding Vikings. The arrival of the Anglo-Norman *Maurice Fitzgerald* in 1245 was marked by the building of a castle, nothing of which, unfortunately, remains. In 1252 Fitzgerald established a **Dominican friary** in the town, which flourished until it was destroyed by fire in 1641; it has recently been restored and is now open to the public.

Sligo, like its surrounding county, lies in the shadow and in the glory of the creative genius of the poet *William Butler Yeats* and the painter *Jack Yeats*. In the **County Library** in Stephen's Street the **Municipal Art Gallery** displays drawings and paintings by Jack Yeats, and the **Yeats Memorial Museum** in the same building houses a collection of memorabilia of W. B. Yeats. Included in the collection is Yeats's Nobel Prize medal of 1923; when he was informed he had won it he replied by asking simply how much money he would receive!

There is more, however, to Sligo, both artistically and culturally, than the omnipresent Yeats family; and every summer the Sligo Arts Festival features the best in music, theatre, and street entertainment. Also of interest in the town are the two churches: the 18th-century Church of Ireland **Cathedral of St John the Baptist** and the 19th-century **Catholic cathedral**.

Within an hour's walk of Sligo you will find **Lough Gill**, which you can also reach by road if you choose. The lake, which is just 5 miles in length (or a 24-mile round trip) has often been compared for beauty to the better-known Lakes of Killarney. Surrounded by wooded mountains, it is best seen and enjoyed by boat, which can be arranged locally. The most famous of the islands on the lake is **Inisfree**, immortalised by a homesick Yeats in his poem 'The Lake Isle of Inisfree'. From the small **Cottage Island** you get a view of **Dooney Rock**, again immortalised in words by Yeats in his poem 'The Fiddler of Dooney'. On **Church Island** you will find the ruins of an Early Christian monastery founded by *St Lómán* in the 6th century. Establishing a place of worship on an island was very typical of the early Irish church, which opted for a contemplative life in harmony with nature.

Near Lough Gill is the **Cairns Hill Forest Park**. The hill itself is nearly 400 feet high and is capped by two pre-Christian cairns. According to legend, the two cairns mark the graves of *Omra* and *Romra*, who fought and died over the beautiful *Gille*. Gille drowned herself when she heard what had happened to Omra and Romra, and it was the tears from her grief-stricken nursemaid that formed Lough Gill.

Tobernalt, near the lake and below Cairns Hill, is a place of great peace and tranquillity. Here, close to the **holy well**, a crude stone altar stands where Mass was secretly celebrated during Penal times. Water from the holy well is said to possess curative powers, and many come every year on Garland Sunday (the last Sunday in July) to continue the rituals of traditional belief.

On the north shore of Lough Gill at **Half Moon Bay** there is a lovely forest walk

Yeats statue, Sligo.

not open to the public), was built in 1731 for the Wynne family by *Richard Cassel*, the architect of Leinster House in Dublin, Westport House in County Mayo, and Powerscourt House in County Wicklow.

In the **Deerpark Forest** you will find the remains of a megalithic court tomb, a wedge tomb, and a stone cashel with a souterrain, all thought to be built by the same group that built the Creevykeel court tomb.

East of Lough Gill and near the village of Dromahair are the ruins of **Creevelea Friary,** the last Franciscan monastery to be founded in Ireland before the suppression of the monasteries by *King Henry VIII* of England. Founded by the O'Rourkes in 1508, it displays many fine examples of stone sculptures, especially one of St Francis himself with the stigmata.

Parke's Castle on the lakeshore is a 17th-century fortress, open daily to the public. It was built by *Robert Parke* in 1620 on the site of an earlier O'Rourke castle; the O'Rourkes of Sligo were dispossessed of their lands by the new planters at this time.

through the **Hazelwood Estate**, where you will find among the trees a unique set of outdoor sculptures by Irish and foreign artists. The manor house attached to the estate, **Hazelwood House** (unfortunately

---

DON'T MISS
- The **Dominican Friary** in Sligo
- A cruise with the **Wild Rose Water** on **Lough Gill**
- **Hazelwood** Forest Park **Sculpture Trail**
- A walk in the **Deerpark Forest Park**
- A **Walking Tour of Sligo**
- **Carrowmore Megalithic Cemetery**
- **Yeats Country cycle tours**

ALL-WEATHER OPTIONS
- **County Museum & Library** in Sligo
- Visit to the **Cathedral of St John the Baptist**
- **Parke's Castle** on Lough Gill
- Visit the **Cat & Moon Gallery**
- An evening at the **Yeats Candelit Supper**
- An evening at the **Hawks Well Theatre**
- **Niland Gallery**
- **Lissadell House**
- **Drumcliffe Church and Visitor Centre** – where WB Yeats is buried

South Sligo

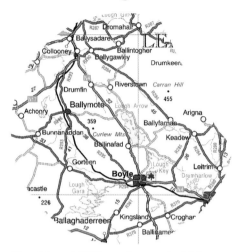

The rising of 1798, a milestone in Irish history, is commemorated by the **Teeling Monument** in the village of **Collooney**, 7 miles south of Sligo. *Captain Teeling* won his place in history when he came to the aid of the combined Irish-French force under *General Humbert* at the Battle of Carricknagat. Victory, however, was short-lived, and their defeat was sealed once the soldiers reached Ballinamuck in County Longford. **Markree Castle**, also in Collooney, is home to one of County Sligo's most powerful Anglo-Irish families, the Coopers. The castle itself, which dates from the 17th century, is now open to the public and offers luxury accommodation and restaurant facilities.

In south Sligo you will find an incredible concentration of megalithic and neolithic reminders in the area surrounding **Lough Arrow**. The **Heapstone Cairn** on the north shore of Lough Arrow is, according to tradition, the burial place of *Ailill*, brother of the illustrious *Niall of the Nine Hostages*; once High King of Ireland, he is strongly associated with the neighbouring county of Donegal. In the nearby **Moytirra** area more Stone Age and Bronze Age tombs are found, all of which suggests that the area was at one time well populated.

Overlooking Lough Arrow and close to the Heapstone Cairn you seee the ruins of the Dominican priory founded in 1507 and known as **Ballindoon Abbey**. The roof is gone and the interior has been used for burials, but otherwise it is in a well-preserved state.

At the southern end of the lake and on the hill above the village of **Ballinafad** on a fine day you can enjoy splendid views of the county: **Knocknarea** and **Benbulbin** to the north, **Lough Arrow** to the east, and the **Ox Mountains** to the south.

In the often-neglected Bricklieve Mountains and also overlooking Lough Arrow you will find the **Carrowkeel Passage Tombs.** This cemetery from our distant past comprises fourteen cairns, some portal tombs, and over fifty pieces of stone foundations. The graves have been dated to the later Stone Age—between 2500 and 2000 BC. One cross-shaped tomb with a dry-stone corbelled roof allows the setting sun to penetrate into the chamber on the longest day of the year—in contrast to the more famous Newgrange passage tomb, where the light enters the burial chamber at sunrise on the shortest day of the year.

Also of interest in the area are the seventeen small caves to be found on the side west of **Keshcorran Hill**, where legend tells us that *Diarmaid*, the infamous lover of *Gráinne*, lived at one time. On the summit of Keshcorran is another passage tomb, and superb views of the surrounding area.

Back on the R293 road and south of Collooney, **Ballymote** is best known today as a centre for anglers, offering some excellent coarse fishing. Historically the town developed around a 14th-century castle, which is now crumbling into obscurity but was once the strongest fortification in all of Connacht. It was here in 1391, within the walls of the now ruined Franciscan friary, that the Book of Ballymote was complied which gave us the key to the *ogham* writing, which was used

Carrowkeel Passage Tombs, Co. Sligo.

on standing-stones throughout the country from the 4th or 5th century.

Continuing south from Ballymote you come to the market town of **Tobercurry**, where you will encounter more archaeological remains. The town has had long associations with traditional music and also boasts one of the oldest amateur drama festivals in Ireland, dating back to 1944. **Gurteen**, 10 miles south-east of Tobercurry, is considered by many to be the centre of traditional music in County Sligo.

Not too far away, the 16th-century **Moygara Castle,** once the principal fortress and home of the O'Gara family,

affords excellent views, particularly to the south. **Lough Gara,** further south, is dotted with many artificial islands, known as *crannógs,* which were exposed when the lake was drained in the 1950s.

Back on the Sligo road and heading north of Tobercurry you will pass a hill called **Knocknashee** (*Cnoc na Sí,* 'hill of the Otherworld') on your left. It is here that the 'little people' are said to gather once a year to celebrate the passing of another year. We mortals can enter into this world by visiting **Gilligan's World**, 'a land of the imagination' that has been created here at the foothills of Knocknashee.

DON'T MISS
- A drive around **Lough Arrow**
- Go fishing on **Lough Arrow**
- Visit to **Ballindoon Abbey**, Ballindoon
- Visit to **Ballymote Castle**, Ballymote
- A walk around **Carrowkeel Passage Tomb Cemetery**
- A look at the **Keshcorran Caves**
- Visit to **Ballinafad Castle**, Ballinafad

ALL-WEATHER OPTIONS
- Visit to **Coleman Heritage Centre**, Gurteen
- Go to **Gilligan's World**, Knochnashee
- An evening of music in a singing pub in **Tobercurry** or **Gurteen**

West Sligo

In search of a good bracing walk? Head 5 miles west from Sligo to **Strandhill**. Alternatively, you can opt to walk, at low tide, out to **Coney Island**. It is said that a sea captain from this area took the name with him when he went to America, and gave it to the pleasure island near New York. The island attracts many different types of birds and is popular with ornithologists.

Overlooking Strandhill and visible from Sligo is **Knocknarea**, or, as it is sometimes called, Queen Méabh's Grave. On its summit at 1,078 feet (329 metres) is a cairn made up of 40,000 tons of rock put here by neolithic farmers. Legend claims that the warrior chief *Méabh* of Connacht was laid to rest here. Knocknarea, like Benbulbin—that other limestone mountain to the north—stirred *Yeats's* creative imagination. Knocknarea is the place of which *Oisín* speaks to *St Patrick* in 'The Wanderings of Oisín':

> *And passing the Firbolgs' burial-mounds*
> *Came to the cairn-heaped grassy hill*
> *Where passionate Maeve is stony-still …*

More ancient monuments are to be found 3 miles away at the **Carrowmore Megalithic Cemetery**, one of the largest of its type to be found in western Europe. In the 19th century there were up to 150 tombs here, but sadly today only 40 remain. A typical tomb is surrounded by a circular kerb of big stones, has a large burial chamber with a roof cap, and would have contained cremated bones. An exhibition centre is open here during the summer months, but you are free to wander around the area and contemplate what life might have been like back in 4000 BC.

Moving on from this area, you head south-west towards **Ballysadare.** Situated at the head of the bay, it's a good place for traditional music and salmon-fishing. The Owenmore River makes its way over shelving rocks to create some picturesque cascades in the town. The ruins of a 7th-century monastery founded by *St Feichín* of Fore are to be found further downstream on the river bank.

Heading away again from the coast and towards the village of **Coolaney** you will pass the Holy Well at **Tullaghan**, which claims to be the source of eternal youth. Local legend tells us that *Gamh* ('ox'), servant of *Eireamhón*, was slain at this spot and in his memory the mountains were named *Sliabh Gamh* or, in English, **Ox Mountains**. Gamh's head was then thrown into a well on the mountain, which thereafter gave forth both sea water and fresh water.

Stay long enough to take the waters from this well and you are promised eternal youth! Otherwise, take the road with the romantic title of **Ladies' Brae**, which takes you through the Ox Mountains and alongside the Owenmore River. This road eventually leads you back to the N59 and through the villages of **Templeboy** and **Dromore West.** In Dromore West visit **Culkin's Emigration Museum** and discover how one *Daniel Culkin* helped those in the area who had no prospects but emigration.

Heading away from the mountains and back towards the Atlantic Ocean, you will arrive at the town of **Easky** (*Iascaigh*, 'place abounding in fish')—though today it is better known for its surfing than for its fishing. Two fine martello towers remind us

Rosses Point,
Co. Sligo.

of the fear that existed at the beginning of the 19th century that Bonaparte was planning to invade Ireland, until he became preoccupied elsewhere.

A mile south of Easky is the unusual **Split Rock**. Legend tells us that the mighty *Fionn mac Cumhaill* tried to throw this rock into the sea from the top of the Ox Mountains, and when it fell short he was so enraged that he struck the rock and it split in two. According to local people, dare to go through the rock three times and it will close in on you!

The last town before you cross into neighbouring County Mayo is **Enniscrone**, a popular seaside resort. First a 3-mile walk along the lovely sandy beach, then treat yourself to a relaxing and energising seaweed bath in **Kilcullen**'s 19th-century bath house: you will emerge, if not with the promise of eternal youth then at least with the feeling of total rejuvenation!

DON'T MISS
- A walk up **Knocknarea**
- A visit to **Carrowmore Megalithic Cemetery**
- Go fishing in **Ballysadare**
- A drive through **Ladies' Brae**
- Go surfing at **Easky**
- A round of golf in **Enniscrone**

ALL-WEATHER OPTIONS
- Visit to **Kevin's House,** Strandhill
- Visit to **Carrowmore Visitors' Centre**
- **Culkins Emigration Museum** in Dromore West
- An afternoon at **Waterpoint**—all-weather waterpark in Enniscrone
- A **Seaweed Bath** in Enniscrone
- **Nolan's Castle** in Enniscrone

North Sligo

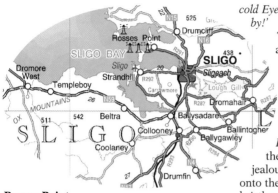

Rosses Point,
5 miles from **Sligo**, is a holiday resort that is slowly expanding to become part of the greater Sligo area. Here two magnificent sandy beaches offer safe swimming; County Sligo Golf Club has an eighteen-hole championship course; and Sligo Yacht Club at Deadman's Point has played host to many national and international sailing events. **Coney Island** can be viewed from Rosses Point and reached at low tide from **Strandhill** at the opposite side of the bay; it is said to have given its name to the New York pleasure island of the same name.

Heading north from Sligo, we come to the small Church of Ireland church of **Drumcliff**. This was built on the site of an early monastic settlement founded by the celebrated *St Colm Cille* in the year 575. A 10th-century high cross and the lower portion of a round tower are all that remain from that period. Drumcliff, lying under the shadow of **Benbulbin**, is better known as the last resting place of *W. B. Yeats*. In the graveyard beside the church, where his great-grandfather served as rector for thirty-five years, Yeats is buried together with his wife, *George*. He died in January 1939 in the south of France, at the age of seventy-three, and it was only in 1948, in accordance with his wishes, that his body was re-interred in his beloved Sligo. On a simple and uncomplicated headstone read the last lines of the epitaph he penned for himself: '*Cast a*

cold Eye | *On Life, on Death.* | *Horseman pass by!*'

Towering 1,730 feet (527 metres) above the small church and graveyard is the majestic and memorable **Benbulbin.** Named after the fabulous monster *Gulban*, the mountain, like so many places in Ireland, has been associated with the mythical lovers *Diarmaid and Gráinne.* According to the legend, Diarmaid, fleeing from the jealous *Fionn mac Cumhaill*, was lured onto the mountain, only to die when the bristles of a wild boar pierced his foot—his only weak point. There are some good walking possibilities in the area, but do be on the look-out for dangerous clefts and bog-holes.

East of Drumcliff is **Glencar Lough.** Fed by the Differeen River and surrounded by steep-sided mountains, this unspoilt area is where the 50-foot **Glencar Waterfall** will guarantee an impressive display, especially after heavy rain.

To the north-west of Drumcliff, **Lissadell House** is a fine example of Greek Revival architecture. Built in the 1830s for the Gore-Booth family, it is still their home but is open to the public during the summer months. An eminent family with much to their credit, the best-known member was *Constance Gore-Booth*, later *Countess Markievicz.* Constance was one of the leaders of the 1916 Rising, the first woman to be elected to a seat in the British House of Commons, and later Minister for Labour in the first Irish government. Yeats, a regular visitor to the house, immortalised both Constance and *Eva*, her sister, in his poem 'The Winding Stair'.

County Sligo, like so many places on the west coast, was visited by the ill-fated Spanish Armada. In 1588 three Spanish ships foundered near **Streedagh Beach** in a place now known as **Carraig na Spáinneach** ('Spaniards' rock'). Today the area has been nicknamed 'Little Bavaria' because of the number of Germans who have chosen to settle in the area.

Further along the road in the direction of Bundoran is the remarkable **Creevykeel Court Tomb**, which is claimed to be the best example of a classic court tomb in Ireland. The tomb, which has two main burial chambers, was built by a Stone Age farming community who settled in this area between 3000 and 3500 BC.

Past Creevykeel and on to the sandy beaches of **Mullaghmore**, where you can hire a boat to take you out to the island of **Innishmurray**. Described as a museum of Christian antiquities, it was inhabited up to 1947, when the last fifty people living on the island were moved to the mainland. With very little arable land, the economy of the island was based on *poitín*, the illegally distilled spirit, which had a ready market on the mainland. On the island you have the remains of three churches, beehive cells, and over fifty cross-inscribed graves, all from the monastery founded by *St Molaise* in the 6th century. A visit to the island is well worth the effort but is only possible in fine weather, because of the lack of a harbour.

Before leaving the Mullaghmore area, a walk around the headland will bring you near to **Classiebawn Castle**, built in 1874 and until 1979 the home of the late *Lord Mountbatten*.

Creevykeel Court Tomb, Co. Sligo.

DON'T MISS
- Coastal route **Drumcliff** to **Mullaghmore**
- Boat trip to **Innishmurray** (weather permitting)
- Visit to **Yeats Grave** and **Drumcliff Church**
- A round of golf or a quick dip at **Rosses Point**
- Drive around **Gleniff Horseshoe**
- Visit to **Creevykeel Court Tomb**

ALL-WEATHER OPTIONS
- Visit to **Lissadell House**
- **Glencar Waterfall** (at its best after a good shower of rain!)

Tudor Ireland

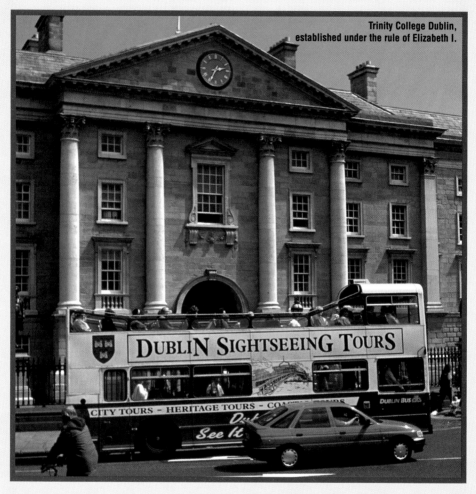

Trinity College Dublin, established under the rule of Elizabeth I.

Henry VIII reigned as King of England from 1509 until 1547. He was a new kind of king, restless, ambitious, and anxious to bring all his territories under his own centralised rule. This had serious implications for Ireland, where local customs and usages had existed for centuries, untouched by English ways. English was not widely spoken, and English common law was unknown outside the Pale. In the daily life of most people, the English connection was entirely theoretical, hardly to be thought about at all.

Henry began the process that ended all that, and did so in the most spectacular manner possible, by breaking the power of the Kildare Fitzgeralds. *Garret Óg Fitzgerald,* ninth earl of Kildare, had succeeded his father, the Great Earl, as Lord Deputy in 1513. For twenty years things went on much as they always had. Occasionally he had to go to London to give an account of himself to the king; but he always returned to Ireland to resume his position. In

1533 Garret Óg was summoned once more to London. He told his son Thomas—known to history as *Silken Thomas*—to make a show of force if he were to be dismissed. Not only was Garret Óg dismissed but he was clapped in the Tower of London. Silken Thomas duly made the show of force his father had suggested. Its purpose was the traditional one: to demonstrate to the king that Ireland was ungovernable without the Kildare interest. It was never intended as a rebellion against the crown itself. Even in the balmy days of the Great Earl that option was never considered.

Henry's response, however, was not a judicious retreat and accommodation with the Fitzgeralds of Kildare. Garret Óg died in the Tower, and Henry sent over an English army to deal with Silken Thomas. It crushed his forces in short order. Thomas and his leading followers were sent to London and beheaded on Tower Hill. The hands-off policy of the English crown in Ireland that had persisted all through the Middle Ages was at an end.

In the meantime, Henry VIII had no male heir. He was only one generation removed from the end of the Wars of the Roses; the need to secure the dynastic succession obsessed him. He wanted to divorce his wife, Catherine of Aragon, and marry the younger Anne Boleyn. When the Pope refused him a divorce he broke with Rome and appointed himself head of the Church of England. The break with Rome was not doctrinal. Henry considered himself a Catholic to his dying day; but the new church organisation provided a vehicle for those who wished to import the Lutheran reformation to England. Gradually, as the 16th century wore on, the Reformation established itself in England.

But not in Ireland. Most Norman and Irish families remained loyal to the older faith. This was not a uniquely Irish phenomenon: many of the more remote parts of England itself resisted reform. Again it was largely a matter of distance and the innate conservatism of remote places.

In the meantime Henry had consolidated his victory over the Fitzgeralds of Kildare by strengthening royal government in Dublin. Direct rule through the Lord Deputy, based in Dublin Castle, replaced devolved rule through powerful local magnates. English armies were quartered in Ireland. Henry introduced the English system of land tenure to replace Irish land law, though in practice the two systems ran confusingly in parallel for over a century. He declared himself King of Ireland, the first English monarch to do so (his predecessors had contented themselves with the title 'Lord of Ireland').

The twin legacy of Henry was centralisation and reformation, a revolution in both church and state. Ireland resisted both. Henry's daughter, *Elizabeth,* who reigned from 1558 to 1603, gradually tried to advance both causes. There were now three distinct interest groups in Ireland. First were the ancient Irish families, now known as the Old Irish. The successors of the Normans, most of whom stayed Catholic like the Old Irish, were called the Old English. Finally there were the New English: settlers and planters who were given grants of Irish land in the hope of securing the countryside loyally for the crown. They were Protestant to a man, and included such distinguished Elizabethans as the poets *Sidney* and *Spenser.*

Provincial wars gradually weakened the older interests. First the Fitzgeralds of Desmond launched a series of rebellions against the crown in the 1570s and 80s. They were crushed with great devastation and suffering. In the 1590s the Old Irish redoubts of central and western Ulster rebelled in the conflict known as the Nine Years' War. Despite Spanish aid—too little, too late—they were finally defeated in 1603.

The wars of the late 16th century weakened both the Old English and Old Irish interests. In the north the defeat was so complete that the land was cleared for the fateful Plantation of Ulster. Thousands of English and Scottish planters were settled on lands confiscated from the defeated Irish. It was the most successful and enduring of all English plantations in Ireland. The planters were the antecedents of the Ulster Protestant community of today.

TOURING ROUTE

Yeats Country

We begin our tour from the town of **Sligo**, situated at the mouth of the Garvoge River and surrounded by mountains: **Benbulbin** (1,726 feet) and **Truskmore** (2,116 feet) to the north, the **Ox Mountains** to the east, and **Knocknarea** (1,079 feet) to the south.

We leave Sligo and go left on the R282 towards Sligo Abbey. Shortly afterwards we join the R286 to catch our first glimpse of beautiful **Lough Gill** and the Garvoge River. We also see part of the Hazelwood estate. **Hazelwood House** is one of the largest Georgian houses in the country, and the estate can be entered from the northern shore of Lough Gill. About 200 yards further on we find the entrance to the car park of **Cairns Hill Forest Walk**. Two hills here, Belvoir and Cairns, are crowned by stone cairns of the passage tomb type.

Continuing on our way, we take a short detour at the next right turn to the **Holy Well**, signposted Tobernalt. This was an important ancient assembly site of the *Lúnasa* festivities, in honour of the Celtic god *Lú*, who gave his name to the autumn festival and the month of August. The well water is credited with many cures.

Returning to the lake road and turning right, we soon notice **Dooney Forest Walk** and nature trail. Walking along the lakeshore and up a steep climb, we get some magnificent views of Lough Gill and the mountains surrounding it. Short detours can be made off the main Dromahair road to **Cashelore** stone fort and to the lakeshore to get a close view of the lake isle of Innisfree, immortalised in the poem by *W. B. Yeats.*

On arrival at Dromahair we note that we are now in County Leitrim. **Dromahair** is a pretty village resting in wooded surroundings on the banks of the Bonet River. Not far from the village we find a prominent rock plateau from whose lofty heights Lough Gill and its islands provide a breathtaking view. Also worth visiting at Dromahair is **Creevelea Abbey**, founded in 1508 and situated on the left bank of the Bonet River.

We continue along the eastern shore of the lake and head through the picturesque and wild countryside of north Leitrim to

Manorhamilton, a modest country town. From here we make our way on the R260 towards Kinlough through the valley of **Glenade**. Famous for its rare scenic beauty, this wild and rugged district has captivated many a traveller. Here we are in 'sheep country'.

Shortly after **Kinlough**, which is a major angling centre, we reach **Tullyhan**, County Leitrim's only seaside resort, lying on the coast overlooking the broad Atlantic, where the three counties of Donegal, Leitrim and Sligo meet.

We turn towards Sligo southwards on the N15, and a few yards before Creevykeel crossroads we note the signpost and entrance to **Creevykeel** court tomb. Built between 3000 and 3500 BC, this is the finest example of a classic court tomb with full court in Ireland.

From Creevykeel crossroads we take a detour to **Mullaghmore**, where we find a fabulous sandy beach running for 2 miles. In the background, towering above the beach and village, is the majestic **Classiebawn**

Castle, former home of *Lord Mountbatten.* Lying off Mullaghmore is the island of **Innishmurray**, uninhabited since 1947. It is the most southern breeding ground of the eider duck.

Returning to the N15 road, we travel to Cliffony and then to Grange, shortly after which we leave the main road yet again to visit Lissadell. **Lissadell House** was once the home of the Gore-Booths, who included *Sir Henry Gore-Booth* (1843-1900), the Arctic explorer, and *Constance Markievicz* (1884-1927), a leader in the 1916 rising. *W. B. Yeats* stayed here and referred to Lissadell many times in his writings. Lissadell is open to the public in summer, and the estate is now a forestry and wildlife reserve.

Rejoining the main N15 road at Drumcliff, we pause at this picturesque village nestling beneath Benbulbin. It is here, in a lonely churchyard, that we find the tomb of *W. B. Yeats* (1865-1939), poet, patriot, and Nobel Prize winner. We recognise his tomb by the now famous epitaph of his own composition:

Cast a cold Eye
On Life, on Death.
Horseman pass by!

While in Drumcliff—an important Christian monastic site founded by *Colm Cille* in the year 575—we visit the round tower and see the 10th-century high cross, the only one known to occur in County Sligo.

We return to Sligo via **Rosses Point**, a favourite seaside resort with two magnificent sandy beaches, situated 5 miles from Sligo.

Lake Isle of Inisfree, Co. Sligo.

County Leitrim

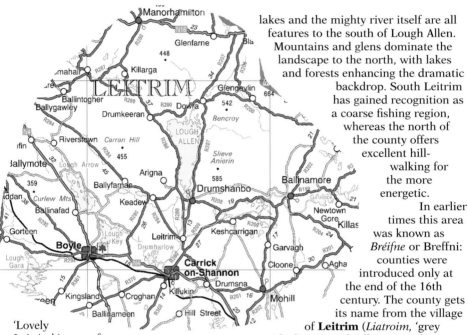

lakes and the mighty river itself are all features to the south of Lough Allen. Mountains and glens dominate the landscape to the north, with lakes and forests enhancing the dramatic backdrop. South Leitrim has gained recognition as a coarse fishing region, whereas the north of the county offers excellent hill-walking for the more energetic.

In earlier times this area was known as *Bréifne* or Breffni: counties were introduced only at the end of the 16th century. The county gets its name from the village

'Lovely Leitrim' is one of those counties that has never had the confidence to promote its own beauty and charm, and it has been left to a few discerning visitors to discover and enjoy it. With a population of a mere 25,000 and very little industry, County Leitrim is not only beautiful and charming but also unspoilt.

The county is long and narrow in shape, stretching 50 miles from the border with County Longford in the south-east to the Atlantic Ocean in the north-west. The county is divided by **Lough Allen**, the first of the three great lakes on the River Shannon; the river itself rises nearby in the neighbouring County Cavan. Land in County Leitrim is generally ill suited to agriculture, and in recent times parts of the county have been planted with trees that grow quickly and effectively in the poor soil. Broken, rugged countryside with smaller fish-filled

of **Leitrim** (*Liatroim*, 'grey ridge') on Lough Allen, once the stronghold of the mighty O'Rourkes. Their place in the history books was assured when, in 1152, the king of South Leinster, *Diarmaid Mac Murchú*, eloped with *Dearbhorgaill*, the wife of *Tiarnán Ó Ruairc*. This led to the Anglo-Norman invasion of 1169, the beginning of a long and fraught relationship between Ireland and England.

But Breffni was not affected at first by the Anglo-Norman invasion, and the Irish way of life lasted until the plantations of the 15th century. The O'Rourkes did support the O'Donnells and the O'Neills in the nine years' war against the encroaching English power, and they were at the Battle of Kinsale in 1603, when the death knell marking the end of traditional Irish society was sounded. They are also remembered in history for offering refuge to the O'Sullivans Beare after their forced exile from the Glengarriff peninsula in

Glencar Waterfall,
Co. Leitrim.

County Cork in 1602.

County Leitrim was eventually colonised in 1622, when the various O'Rourke estates were seized and given over to English and Scottish planters. The plantation brought about dramatic and irrevocable change. Towns such as **Carrick-on-Shannon** and **Jamestown** were established as fortified strongholds to control the crossings on the Shannon. **Manorhamilton** was settled by a Scottish planter called Hamilton.

As in so much of Ireland, the population of County Leitrim was almost annihilated in the Great Famine of 1845–50. Before the famine the population of the county was over 155,000, whereas today it is approximately 25,000. However, the land that has caused so much hardship for those who farmed it is now offering space to those who enjoy an activity-based holiday, be it fishing, boating, walking, or golfing. Tourism continues to grow in this region and certainly offers the best potential for arresting the population decline that has haunted County Leitrim for so long.

South Leitrim

Lough Allen is the natural divide between north and south Leitrim—two areas of obvious differences. South Leitrim starts with the county town, **Carrick-on-Shannon**, one of the principal bases for pleasure cruises on the **River Shannon**. The town dates its origins to the plantation of *King James I of England* at the beginning of the 17th century. During this time the place was garrisoned, and the native Irish were excluded for a long time from settling in or near the town. Today it attracts not just the pleasure cruises but also the angling fraternity, who are well catered for.

Of interest to the visitor is the rather curious **Costello Chapel**. Said to be the second-smallest chapel in the world, it was erected in 1877 by *Edward Costello,* a local businessman, for his wife on her untimely death.

The **Ballyconnell–Ballinamore Canal** was reopened in 1994, connecting the Shannon waterways with Lough Erne in County Fermanagh, and it has proved to be an enormous success, doing much to attract visitors to this part of the country. The canal was completed in 1860, towards the end of the canal-building boom, and was in use for a mere nine years; the introduction of the railways meant that, along with many others, the canal was no longer viable. But

130 years later the growth in the leisure market was recognised and thanks to the reopening of the Shannon–Erne Waterway, an area that has suffered much from emigration and unemployment has been greatly revitalised. Just south of Carrick-on-Shannon is the attractive village of **Jamestown**, which again dates from the 17th-century plantation. Continuing on your way, and staying close to the meandering River Shannon, your next village, **Drumsna**, is encountered on a hilltop overlooking the river. In the graveyard *Surgeon Parke,* who accompanied *Stanley* on his expedition to the Congo, is buried. The novelist *Anthony Trollope* spent some time here as postmaster. And if that wasn't enough, *Robert Strawbridge,* who went on to establish the Methodist church in America, was born in Drumsna in 1732.

This area south of Lough Allen is dotted with lakes and small hills or 'drumlins' and, sparsely populated, offers a wonderful retreat from the pressures of modern living. The picturesque villages of **Dromod** and **Roosky** on the Roscommon border retain an old-world charm. **Lough Bofin** and the nearby **Lough Boderg** and **Kilglass Lake** are well known for their wildlife sanctuaries and, of course, excellent fishing. **Lough Rynn** is surrounded by lands acquired by the Earls of Leitrim in 1750, and the estate and house, built in 1832, are now open to the public during the summer. Within the grounds there is a walled garden, sawmills, a farmyard, an arboretum, a greenhouse, and terraced gardens, which can all be enjoyed by the visitor.

Mohill was once the site of a 6th-century

Cruising the Shannon–Erne Waterway, Co. Leitrim.

abbey founded by *St Manchán,* but today it is better known as a centre for coarse angling. The town also remembers a person who became one of traditional Ireland's most celebrated composers. *Toirealach Ó Cearúlláin* (1670–1738) lived here for some time, and a sculpture in the main street commemorates his stay here. He was one of the last of the musicians of the old society, which came to a dramatic end with the plantations of the 16th and 17th centuries and the introduction of English ways.

As you travel further east, the parish of **Carrigallen** marks the convergence of three provinces: Ulster, Leinster, and Connacht. The beautiful lake district of **Garadice** is a short distance from **Ballinamore** on the road from Carrigallen.

The village of **Fenagh** is a short distance from Ballinamore and is noteworthy for its historical associations. Two church ruins stand on what is believed to be the site of a monastery founded by *St Colm Cille* in the 6th century. In the graveyard there is a mausoleum dating from the 17th century; and a prehistoric portal tomb stands in a field beside the village.

Finally, half way between Carrick-on-Shannon and Drumshanbo, we have the one-street village of **Leitrim** (*Liatroim,* 'grey ridge'), from which the county gets its name. A portion of the wall belonging to the old **O'Rourke Castle** is all that is left to remind us of this once strategic stronghold.

DON'T MISS
- **Hire a cruiser** for a weekend or longer
- Do a two-hour boat trip on the **Shannon-Erne Waterway**
- Spend some time **fishing!**
- Try some Wild West Style horse riding at **Drumcoura City Western Tour** in Ballinamore

ALL-WEATHER OPTIONS
- Visit the **Costello Chapel** in Carrick-on-Shannon
- Visit **Lough Rynn House and Gardens**
- Visit the **Cavan & Leitrim Railway Museum** in Dromod
- Spend an evening at the **Corn Mill Theatre** in Carrigallen

North Leitrim

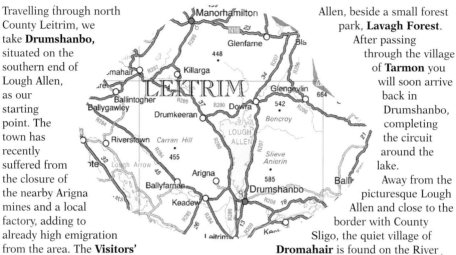

Travelling through north County Leitrim, we take **Drumshanbo,** situated on the southern end of Lough Allen, as our starting point. The town has recently suffered from the closure of the nearby Arigna mines and a local factory, adding to already high emigration from the area. The **Visitors' Centre** will give you a good insight into local life, and for the energetic the 30-mile (48-kilometre) **Leitrim Way** begins here.

A sombre but beautiful body of water, **Lough Allen** was formed by the melt-water of dissolving glaciers. Shaped like a triangle, it is 7 miles long and 3 miles wide. The recent reopening of the **Lough Allen Canal** now makes it possible for cruisers to enter Lough Allen and to enjoy its many bays, islands, and fishing areas.

North of Lough Allen, in the village of **Dowra,** traces of the **Black Pig's Dyke,** an ancient earthwork dividing Ulster from Connacht, are still visible. This fortification is mentioned in the great mythological histories of Ireland, where it played an important role in dividing the two provinces.

Continuing the drive around Lough Allen, close to Dowra you will find **Corry Strand,** an amenity area scenically situated on Lough Allen. The most important island in Lough Allen is **Inishmagrath,** where the ruins of an early ecclesiastical settlement can still be seen. The neighbouring village of **Drumkeeran** is also situated on Lough

Allen, beside a small forest park, **Lavagh Forest**. After passing through the village of **Tarmon** you will soon arrive back in Drumshanbo, completing the circuit around the lake.

Away from the picturesque Lough Allen and close to the border with County Sligo, the quiet village of **Dromahair** is found on the River Bonet. Here you can see the ruins of **Breffni Castle,** where the powerful O'Rourkes once resided. It was from here that *Dearbhorgaill* eloped with the King of Leinster, *Diarmaid Mac Murchú,* in the 12th century, and in doing so changed Irish history utterly and irrevocably. Mac Murchú, on finding himself outlawed by his neighbouring chiefs, sought help from *King Henry II* of England, an invitation that was accepted by *Richard de Clare, Earl of Pembroke,* also known as *Strongbow*; and so began the Anglo-Norman invasion of Ireland.

Close to Dromahair is **Lough Gill.** Here we have a fine example of a 17th-century fortified plantation manor-house, **Parke's Castle,** which has been extensively restored and is open to the public. Beautifully set on the banks of the River Bonet and on the Leitrim-Sligo border we have the 16th-century Franciscan **Creevelea Abbey.** This was one of the last abbeys to be founded in Ireland before *King Henry VIII* dissolved all the monasteries in England and Ireland.

Centrally situated in the northern half of County Leitrim, **Manorhamilton** (*Cluainín,* 'little meadow') is the other main town in

Lough Rynn House and
Gardens,
Co. Leitrim.

the county, after Carrick-on-Shannon. It derives its English name from the manor-house built here in 1638 by *Sir Frederick Hamilton,* one of many who received lands originally belonging to the O'Rourkes during the plantations of 1622.

From Manorhamilton there is a choice of roads. Travelling north-west by way of **Lurganboy** you come to **Glencar Lake**. At the eastern end of the lake the **Glencar Waterfall** is particularly impressive, and the drive along the lakeshore boasts some of the loveliest scenery in Ireland. Heading north out of Manorhamilton there is a delightful drive to Lough Melvin by way of the River Bonet. The landscape here is wild and rugged, dominated by steep, often cliff-like limestone hills. The village at the end of the valley, **Kinlough**, has an interesting

museum, worth a visit if you have the time. **Tullaghan** is County Leitrim's only seaside resort, on a coastal strip a mere 2 miles long, sandwiched between Counties Sligo and Donegal.

To return to Manorhamilton, take the route by **Rossinver** along the shores of **Lough Melvin**. Famous for salmon and trout fishing, the lake marks the border between Leitrim and the neighbouring County Fermanagh. South-west of Lough Melvin is the village of **Kiltyclogher**, where there is a memorial to *Seán Mac Diarmada,* one of the leaders who was shot by firing squad for his part in the rising of 1916.

North Leitrim has much to offer, especially for those who are looking for somewhere different, somewhere that is waiting to be discovered.

DON'T MISS
- Walk **The Leitrim Way** from Drumshanbo to Manorhamilton
- Pay a visit to **Creevelea Abbey**
- Drive around **Glencar Lake** and visit **Glencar Waterfall**
- Visit **Eden Plants**—an organic herb garden near Rossinver

ALL-WEATHER OPTIONS
- Visit the **Sliabh an Iarainn Visitors' Centre** in Drumshanbo
- Visit **Parke's Castle** on Lough Gill
- Visit the Manorhamilton **Castle Heritage Centre**
- **Drumkeerin Heritage Centre**
- Visit **Kinlough Folk Museum**

Call the USA direct   Just call 1-800-COLLECT

English Conquest

us gevegt van Koning William tegens den gewesen Koning Iacobus, in I

Battle of the Boyne, 1690.

The Plantation of Ulster, which began in 1607, meant that English and Scottish settlers were given grants of land in Ulster that had formerly belonged to Irish lords defeated in the wars of the late 16th century. The Plantation established a Protestant bridgehead in the north. Moreover, unlike previous efforts at plantation further south, it established people in numbers on the land. The new settlers were hardy, determined, and loyal to the new Protestant order in England. They brought advanced agricultural skills to what had been the most traditional part of Ireland; they cleared woodland, built towns, and gradually established a flourishing agricultural and trading economy.

The southern part of Ireland in the early 17th century remained overwhelmingly in Catholic ownership. The land stayed in the hands of the Old English and Old Irish; but the government in Dublin was exclusively New English. The consequent uneasy accommodation between the different interests was finally resolved in the most brutal manner in the 1640s. First, Catholics in Ulster rose in rebellion against their new masters. Many settlers died horribly (though the numbers were later much exaggerated for propaganda purposes). The rebellion drew Ireland into the confused series of English civil wars between *King Charles I* and Parliament. Since the king was a moderate Anglican, reasonably indulgent towards Catholics, and the Parliament was uncompromisingly Protestant, Old Irish and Old English alike rallied to the royal cause. But the king lost and was beheaded in London in January 1649. Parliament was triumphant in England, and the monarchy was replaced by a republic, the English Commonwealth. Its leading figure was *Oliver Cromwell.*

Cromwell landed near Dublin in July 1649 to settle things once and for all with the Irish. In the first place, he wanted revenge for the murders committed in Ulster in 1641. Secondly, he wanted to bring the whole country finally under English control.

He succeeded spectacularly on both counts. He was a military commander of exceptional ability, and his progress through Ireland was rapid. He massacred the garrisons at Drogheda and Wexford *pour encourager les autres,* actions that shocked even contemporary opinion, less squeamish about such matters than we are. Though Cromwell spent less than a year in Ireland, he established the basis for final victory, which his lieutenants accomplished after his departure. By the early 1650s, for the first time in history, all of Ireland was safely in the control of English power.

Cromwell exacted a high price from the losers, Old English and Old Irish alike. Firstly, he made no distinction between them: he simply lumped them together as Catholics and therefore rebels—a significant moment, this, for he was the first person to treat Irish Catholics as a unitary group, undifferentiated by national origin. Catholics in the wealthy east and south were dispossessed in huge numbers and their lands transferred to new English settlers. These new men were usually either soldiers or investors who had fought in or financed Cromwell's Irish campaign. The dispossessed were either transferred to poorer lands in the west, shipped abroad, or reduced to the status of merchants. Many emigrated to offer their services to the Catholic monarchs of Europe.

The Cromwellian plantation established the class later known as the Protestant Ascendancy, which was to remain in place until the early 20th century. In the meantime Cromwell's Commonwealth did not survive his death in 1658, and two years later the Stuarts were restored in the person of *King Charles II.* The new king left Cromwell's Irish arrangements in place: it was too dangerous to do otherwise. In 1685 he was succeeded by his brother, a Catholic. Hopes rose for a restoration of the old order; but Protestant England was profoundly suspicious of a Catholic king. Within three years James was overthrown in a *coup d'état* politely known as the Glorious Revolution. He was replaced by his son-in-law, *William of Orange,* a Protestant.

The subsequent war between William and James was fought out in Ireland. It really became a sideshow in a larger European war against the France of *Louis XIV,* whose client James was in effect. William won the war, through his decisive victories at the Boyne (1690) and Aughrim (1691). Protestant Ireland was saved; the Catholic interest was prostrate. The way was open for the new victors to breathe more easily.

The result was the gilded world of Ascendancy Ireland. The long peace of the 18th century produced the conditions needed for a flowering of the arts and for the creation of a new civic order. Its fruits were most vividly seen in the rebuilding of Dublin as a Georgian city of exceptional coherence and elegance. Provincial towns flourished as well. Fine country houses, no longer fortified against attack, were built all over the country, none more splendid than Castletown House in County Kildare. The Royal Dublin Society was founded in 1731 to promote the arts and sciences. All this was the achievement of the Anglican Ascendancy—barely 10 per cent of the population—and it was a magnificent achievement. But it was built on the exclusion of the vast majority, Catholic and Presbyterian alike. And just when everyone thought that ancient antagonisms and hatreds were buried for ever in the stability of the new order, they burst forth again in a new form.

345

Mount Errigal,
Co. Donegal.

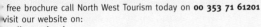

County Donegal

Wild and rugged, dramatic and beautiful, County Donegal has always been a place apart—a well-kept secret! A stronghold of Celtic civilisation, its relative inaccessibility left it untouched by the Viking and Anglo-Norman invasions. Separated from the rest of Ulster by partition in 1922, its only connection with the rest of the Republic is a narrow strip of land.

Donegal was never the coveted land of the new settler: the land, for the most part poor and infertile, was left for the indigenous Irish, who struggled and grew strong against the elements. The independent-minded people of Donegal reflect the rugged landscape that has moulded their identity.

Geography, they say, makes history, and certainly County Donegal has inspired its men and women to express their creativity in word and song, in politics and sport, at home and abroad. The people of Donegal are proud of where they come from, and this pride can be shared by those

who take the time to discover the charm and magic of this place. The weather, like the countryside, is ever changing, and the best advice is to take it as it comes: don't fight it, enjoy its diversity, and your experience will be all the richer. It does rain in County Donegal—for where there are mountains there is rain—but it's a fresh rain, soft and gentle, enhancing the scenery, invigorating the soul.

Surrounded on three sides by the Atlantic Ocean, County Donegal's coast is indented with inlets, loughs, headlands, peninsulas, and beaches that are legendary—golden sands stretching for miles. The Caledonian mountains, extending from Scandinavia through Scotland

to Ireland, created a plateau-like wall running through the county from north to south. Quartzite peaks, such as **Errigal Mountain**, emerged later, dramatically enhancing the landscape. The last Ice Age, ten thousand years ago, carved out valleys such as Gleann Cholm Cille, and the melting ice created lakes such as Lough Finn. People have inhabited this part of the country from as far back as 5000 BC, leaving behind evidence not of how they lived but rather of how they honoured the dead. Throughout County Donegal you will come across examples of the court tombs, passage tombs, portal tombs and wedge tombs of the mesolithic and neolithic people. With the Iron Age and the arrival of the Celts, the archaeological evidence shifts from honouring the dead to buildings for the living. The greatest archaeological survival from this period is the magnificent **Grianán of Aileach** hill-fort, where the 5th-century High King of Ireland *Niall of the Nine Hostages* held sway.

It was Niall's son *Conall* who gave the county its earlier name, *Tír Chonaill* ('land of Conall'): Donegal (*Dún na nGall*, 'fortress of the foreigners') was a 16th-century innovation. Conall's brother *Eoghan* received land on what is today the **Inishowen Peninsula**, spreading later into the surrounding area of modern County Tyrone (*Tír Eoghain*, 'land of Eoghan').

Christianity arrived in Ireland some time before the 5th century; and Ireland's most celebrated native saint was to come from what is now County Donegal. (*Patrick*, let us not forget, was a Briton.) The son of a nobleman, *Colm Cille* (sometimes known by the Latinised name *Columba*) founded monasteries throughout Ireland; but his most famous legacy is to be found in Scotland. Not only was his monastery on the island of Iona an important centre of learning but it was also there that the famous Book of Kells may have been written by the descendants of Colm Cille.

The Viking period came and went without leaving any visible reminders; similarly, the Anglo-Norman invasion failed to effect any significant change in this area. The watershed in the history of Donegal was the 'Flight of the Earls' in 1607. Reluctant to accept English rule, and despairing of any future, the powerful Irish chiefs of the O'Neills and O'Donnells left for Spain, marking the end of an era and of traditional Irish society. Subsequent plantations changed much of Ulster, the effects of which are still being dealt with today

Before the Great Famine of 1845 the population of County Donegal was over 300,000; today, 150 years after that calamitous event, it is 129,000. Famine and emigration have taken their toll, and reminders litter the countryside. County Donegal has always maintained strong ties with Scotland, and even today many local people would consider Glasgow to be their capital city rather than Dublin!

County Donegal is somewhere special, and to miss out on coming here is to miss a unique and spectacular part of Ireland. Take our advice: make time—don't deny yourself a memorable experience!

Bundoran Strand, Co. Donegal.

Bundoran, Ballyshannon & Donegal

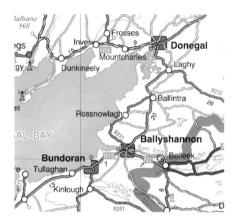

Crossing over the border from County Sligo into County Donegal, the first place you will encounter is one of Ireland's oldest seaside resorts, **Bundoran.** For those looking for 'all the fun of the fair', this town has it all, with its amusements, arcades, and the new water sports centre, all open during the summer months. Once the **Great Northern Hotel** served the rail passengers coming to holiday in Bundoran; today its main attraction is the eighteen-hole championship golf course.

Near the hotel, a fine cliff walk leads out to the **Fairy Bridges**, a natural causeway fashioned over thousands of years by the Atlantic Ocean. Also of interest is the **Puffing Hole**, which impressively ejects water, especially during rough weather.

Bundoran is only 4 miles from the next town, Ballyshannon. Along this road you will see the army's Finner Camp, where some fine earthen ring-forts can still be identified, and also the ruins of the 15th-century **Finner Church** and **Graveyard.**

A short detour from Ballyshannon takes you to **Belleek** in County Fermanagh, famous for its china and pottery. A visitors' centre is open here all year round, where you can visit the factory and see the potters at work.

Strategically positioned on the River Erne, **Ballyshannon** has been in the past an important centre. According to folklore, *Parthalán* landed on the island of **Inis Saimer** in the estuary, where the River Erne meets the Atlantic, 3,500 years ago, and in doing so launched the first colonisation of Ireland.

The bridge crossing the River Erne marks the birth of the Bard of Donegal, *William Allingham,* in the town in 1824, with the following carved in stone: *Here once he roved, a happy boy | Along the winding banks of Erne; | And now, please God, with finer joy, | A fairer world his eyes discern.* His grave is marked in the local Protestant church, from which you can enjoy marvellous panoramic views over the town and its surrounding hills. Ballyshannon is also noted for being the birthplace of the legendary blues guitarist *Rory Gallagher,* who died in 1995.

A few miles from Ballyshannon are the scant remains of a 12th-century Cistercian abbey, the **Abbey of Assaroe**, a centre of learning and piety for over four hundred years. On the river bank at the rear of the graveyard stands a grotto-like cave known the **Catsby**. It was here that Mass was celebrated during the Penal Laws of the 18th century. During this time Catholics faced imprisonment or death for practising their faith. On the shore edge of the abbey is **St Patrick's Well**; bless yourself with its water three times and your prayer for a cure will be answered! Past the abbey is the **Watermills**, a visitors' centre with a coffee and gift shop, a display centre, and a working water-mill.

Five miles on from Assaroe is **Rossnowlagh**, with its magnificent beach over 2 miles long, where you can take time to relax, unwind, and perhaps even enjoy a dip in the Atlantic. A mile to the north of Rossnowlagh is a conspicuous mound called **Glasbolie Fort**. This earthen rampart, according to local tradition, is the burial place of a 6th-century High King of Ireland.

Leaving the coast behind you, and before you make your way into the town of Donegal, you may feel the need to make a

The North-West

detour to **Lough Derg**, famous for 'St Patrick's Purgatory'. A visit here is not for the sightseer, nor for the faint-hearted. Legend tells us that *St Patrick* spent forty days praying and fasting on the island in the lake, expelling the evil spirits that infested it. Today thousands of pilgrims come every year between 1 June and 13 August to continue the tradition of self-sacrifice and penance. Pilgrims spend three days and nights without sleep or food, other than black tea and dry toast, while praying and making circuits of the basilica barefoot. The Lough Derg pilgrimage is said to be one of the most demanding and difficult pilgrimages in Europe.

Lough Derg Pilgrimage Centre, Co. Donegal.

But perhaps you don't feel you've sinned enough to make a detour to Lough Derg; and so on to **Donegal**, which, despite its name, is not the county town (Lifford in the east of the county can lay claim to that title). In the centre of the town, known as the Diamond, stands an obelisk on which the names of the *Four Masters* are inscribed. These were four Franciscan monks who, between 1632 and 1636, wrote down the history of Ireland from 2242 BC to AD 1616. They called their 1,100 pages *Annála Ríochta Éireann* ('Annals of the Kingdom of Ireland'), but they have come to be known as the Annals of the Four Masters. Written during a time of great strife, the work was carried out because it was feared that the ancient records of Ireland might be lost for ever; and what an invaluable legacy it is has become!

Donegal was once home to the powerful O'Donnells, and their imposing castle standing on the banks of the River Eske has recently been restored and is open to visitors. And during the summer months you can be adventurous and enjoy a water cruise around **Donegal Bay**.

North-east of Donegal and worth a visit is **Lough Eske**. At the southern end of the lake is an old wooded estate, now in the hands of Coillte (the Forestry Commission), but they are pretty relaxed about visitors. Get to the lake and make your way to the western gate of the estate, pass the farmyard, and look out in the nearby hedgerows—and there, tucked away, should be a massive cauldron. This is a **famine pot**, made in England and shipped to Ireland during the Great Famine, when it was filled with Indian maize and used to feed the starving people in the area—a stark reminder of times past.

DON'T MISS
- Do the cliff walk in **Bundoran**
- A swim at **Rossnowlagh** or catch the Surfing Championships here in August
- Take a **water cruise** on Donegal Bay
- Have a walk around **Lough Eske** and visit **Ard-na-Mona Gardens**
- Visit **Lough Derg**—for serious visitors only
- Surfing at **Donegal Adventure Centre**, Bundoran

ALL-WEATHER OPTIONS
- Visit to **Waterworld** in Bundoran
- A visit to the **Watermills** at Assore Abbey
- Do a guided tour of **Donegal Castle**
- Visit **Donegal Parian China** exhibition centre in Ballyshannon
- For rail enthusiasts visit **Donegal Railway Heritage Centre**
- **Donegal Craft Village**

'Don't forget to pick up your Global Refund Tax Free Shopping Cheques as you shop.' www.globalrefund.ie

 GLOBAL REFUND

The South Donegal coast and Gleann Cholm Cille

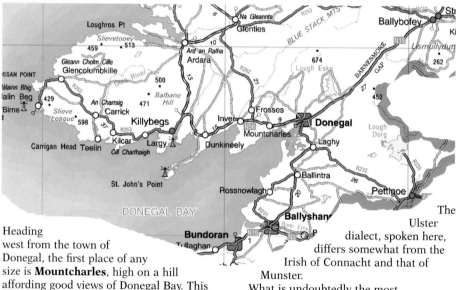

Heading west from the town of Donegal, the first place of any size is **Mountcharles**, high on a hill affording good views of Donegal Bay. This is the birthplace of the historian and novelist *Séamus MacManus*. But let us not linger too long, for we have much to see. Four miles down the road, **Inver** is a good place for sea and river fishing. *Thomas Nesbitt*, the inventor of a whaling harpoon, was born near here in 1730 and is buried in the local graveyard. From **Dunkineely**, the next village, a narrow peninsula rarely more than half a mile wide juts out into the sea, terminating in **Saint John's Point**, where stands a lighthouse. Fine views of **Donegal Bay** can be enjoyed from the road.

Killybegs is Ireland's most important town when it comes to the fishing industry. The waters here abound in herring, cod, plaice, whiting, and ray, and the harbour with its flotilla of trawlers and fish-processing plant bears testimony to this. We move on to discover the rugged and romantic Donegal that awaits us. The subtle change in the signposts reminds us that we are now entering an Irish-speaking area.

The Ulster dialect, spoken here, differs somewhat from the Irish of Connacht and that of Munster.

What is undoubtedly the most remarkable sight in County Donegal, **Slieve League** is approached by way of the fishing village of **Teelin**. Towering 2,000 feet above the crashing waters of the Atlantic Ocean, these cliffs will leave you breathless in more ways than one. The fantastic face of the cliff glows with the mineral tones of its complex geological formation. On a good day the view from the summit is sublime, with its magnificent combination of sea, cliff, and mountain scenery. Make the effort to get to the summit: it is said that from the top you will be able to see a third of Ireland.

A continuously changing landscape is one of the many charms of County Donegal, and nothing comes more as a surprise than **Gleann Cholm Cille** ('Colm Cille's valley'). *Colm Cille* ('dove of the church') was the name taken by Ireland's most illustrious 6th-century saint. This is a place of historic magnitude and unique tranquillity. Colm Cille, born at Gartan in 521, was banished

Gleann Cholm Cille,
Co. Donegal.

from Ireland for copying the manuscript of *Finnéan* of Moville and died on the Scottish island of Iona in 597. Ironically, it may have been on Iona that the followers of Colm Cille created the Book of Kells, one of the most copied Irish manuscripts there is. So much for the high king Diarmaid's famous judgment, 'To every cow its calf, and to every book its copy.'

Today St Colm Cille's associations with the valley are celebrated on his feast day, the ninth of June, when pilgrims come to walk barefoot what is known as *'an Turas'* or the Pilgrim's Way. Three miles long, it takes in the circumference of the glen and ends up at the **Holy Well**, where an enormous pile of stones left by pilgrims bears testimony to the numbers who have, over the centuries, come to pay homage to St Colm Cille.

In this century another man of the cloth left his mark on the glen, in a different way. In the 1950s *Father James McDyer,* the parish priest, established a rural co-operative in an attempt to combat depopulation and the steady stream of emigration from the district.

Artists, writers and those simply looking for a break are attracted to the glen. The Welsh writer *Dylan Thomas* is remembered for renting a cottage for several weeks and then disappearing early one morning without settling his bill!

Near the glen is the village of **Malinbeg**, from where you will come to what must be one of Ireland's most beautiful beaches, **Trabane** (*an Trá Bhán,* 'the white beach'). In a landlocked bay, the strand is crescent-shaped and protected from the winds by high cliffs—a perfect sun trap. A swim here will leave you glowing, with a feeling of well-being and an appetite for more!

Suitably refreshed, you can now walk back to **Malinmore** to discover a large number of prehistoric tombs, or visit the Folk Museum in the village of Gleann Cholm Cille.

DON'T MISS
- A walk on **Slieve League**
- Walk St Colm Cille's **Pilgrim Way**
- A swim at **Trabane**
- Visit the portal tombs at **Malinmore**
- Do a PADI Diving Course at **Malinmore Adventure Centre**

ALL-WEATHER OPTIONS
- Visit the **Ulster Cultural Institute,** Gleann Cholm Cille
- Visit the **Folk Village & Museum,** Gleann Cholm Cille
- Learn Irish for a week or a weekend at **Oideas Gael**
- Visit the **Gate House** in Carrick

Ardara, Glenties, the Rosses & Arranmore

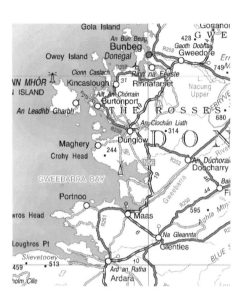

To get to **Ardara**, the next town, you have the choice of travelling directly from the fishing port of **Killybegs** or—after spending some time in **Gleann Cholm Cille**—taking the scenic route through the **Glengesh Pass**. A modest signpost after the alpine-like Glengesh Pass and before Ardara does not prepare you for the spectacular **Mahera Caves**. Impressive and dramatic, these sea caves disappear into the side of the mountain for what seems like an eternity. Local folklore tells us that in the 17th century over a hundred people fleeing from Cromwellian soldiers sought refuge in one of the caves. A light spotted from afar led to all but one, who hid on a high shelf, being massacred. On a practical note, do take care if you go exploring the caves, as some of them do flood with the changing tides.

County Donegal's spectacular scenery can all too easily bring on a thirst that needs to be satisfied, and there is no better place to do this than in the picturesque village of **Ardara**. Such is the selection of pubs in the main street that it's a wonder the local people manage to remain sober at all! Awarded the title of 'heritage town', Ardara has a tradition of hand-woven tweed and hand-knitted jumpers. An interesting museum in the renovated Law Courts is to be found down by the bridge.

The nearby village of **Glenties** was the birthplace of the author *Patrick MacGill*. MacGill's books give a unique insight into the reality of life as it was for the labourers and small tenant farmers in west Donegal at the beginning of the 20th century. To be surrounded by so much beauty was little consolation for those struggling to put food on the table and keep a roof over their head. MacGill captures the world of those travelling every spring to Scotland for the potato-picking season, or going to England to work as labourers on the roads—working to send money home for those who depended on it for their very existence. Glenties itself is situated where two valleys converge, a well-kept place and four-times winner of the Tidy Towns award. The local museum presents a fascinating record of the history of the village and the surrounding area.

Heading away from Glenties you come to the village of **Finntown**, set beside the picturesque **Lough Finn**. Legend tells us that the lake was named after *Finna*, sister to *Fergoman*—she was drowned in the lake trying to save her brother. This is a wild, desolate but delightful area to explore. Be warned, though: the lack of signposts can often be upsetting, so make sure you have a good map!

North from Ardara, the twin towns of **Narin** and **Portnoo** are surrounded by magnificent sandy beaches. **Doon Fort**, on an island in nearby **Doon Lough**, is easily reached by boat and is worth the detour. It is an important archaeological site but one that is relatively unknown and rarely

Glengesh Pass,
Co. Donegal.

disturbed by visitors.

All around this area you will enjoy the ever-changing mountains, bogs, lakes, and omnipresent Atlantic Ocean. The **Rosses** is a vast expanse of rock-strewn land and stony soil, dotted with over 120 lakes. It was here that *Paddy Gallagher—Pat the Cope*, as he became known locally—pioneered the co-operative movement, seeing it as a way forward for impoverished rural communities and an alternative to emigration. In 1906 he founded the Templecrone Co-Operative Agricultural Society, and today Co-Op Supermarkets are to be fund throughout the Rosses.

From the fishing village of **Burtonport** a 20-minute ferry will take you across the strait to **Árainn Mhór** or Arranmore—also known as Aran Island (not to be confused with the Aran Islands in County Galway). There are no gardaí stationed on the island, so the local pubs have to worry about closing hours only when a late-night ferry is spotted coming from the mainland. A few roads crisscross the island, but the main villages are to the south and south-east, where they are protected from the Atlantic winds. Like most of County Donegal, the island offers perfect walking country, and for anglers, **Lough Shure** holds rainbow trout in abundance.

To visit County Donegal and not mention *Daniel O'Donnell* is like going to Rome and not mentioning the Pope. Daniel O'Donnell, from the village of **Kincasslagh**, is one of Ireland's musical heroes. The other notable musical export from County Donegal is of course the world-famous group Clannad and singer-musician *Enya*; their father runs a pub in the village of **Crolly**, and it would not be unknown for one of the family to participate in one of the sessions held nightly in the pub. Crolly's other claim to fame is its 'Crolly dolls', which were once a household name throughout Ireland.

Dunglow, the main town in this area, is a lively and bustling town where the Donegal equivalent to Miss World is held on the August holiday weekend. From Dunglow a walk or drive out around **Crohy Head** will not disappoint.

DON'T MISS
- Drive through the **Glengesh Pass**
- Visit to the **Mahera Caves**
- A drive to through the **Rosses**
- Take a trip to Doon Island to see **Doon Fort**

ALL-WEATHER OPTIONS
- A visit to the **Ardara Heritage Centre**
- See Donegal tweed being made at **Triona Design**
- A visit to the **Muc Dhubh Historic Railway** in Finntown
- A visit to **St Connell's Museum** in Glenties

Gaoth Dobhair to the Fanad Peninsula and Tory Island

This area of County Donegal takes in just some of the coastal inlets and peninsulas for which the county is famous. **Gaoth Dobhair** (Gweedore) is a quite densely populated Irish-speaking area.

The villages of **An Bun Beag** (Bunbeg) and **Doirí Beaga** (Derrybeg) lie a few miles west of the village of Gaoth Dobhair, and there are excellent sandy beaches nearby.

From here there is a wonderful journey around **Bloody Foreland**, the headland between Gaoth Dobhair and An Fál Carrach, which must be travelled to be appreciated. Contrary to expectations, the name of the headland probably comes from the spectacular shades of red that colour the rocks as the sun sinks into the west, rather than in memory of some great battle. It is interesting to see as one travels along the Donegal coasts that many of the older houses have stones projecting from underneath the eaves, so that ropes could be tied down over the roofs to protect the dwellings from wild Atlantic storms.

The two Irish-speaking villages of **Gort an Choirce** (Gortahork) and **An Fál Carrach** (Falcarragh) are good places from which to climb Donegal's other famous mountain, Muckish; you will be rewarded with magnificent views from the top!

Dunfanaghy, a small town 7 miles from An Fál Carrach, is the gateway to the peninsula of **Horn Head** (a name derived from the shape of the cliffs, which resemble a double horn). Projecting straight into the crashing Atlantic, Horn Head rises sheer from the sea to a height of 620 feet (219 metres). Close to the head is a signal tower used by the coast-watching service during the Second World War. In late May and June this area attracts vast numbers of sea birds, who come here to nest and breed on the cliff edge. Every variety of wildfowl is to be found here, including shellcrakes, stormy petrels, sea parrots, guillemots, gannets, speckled divers, shags, puffins, and gulls in their thousands.

Lying 7 miles from the shore and visible from Horn Head is **Toraigh** or Tory Island, which can be reached by taking the ferry from Maheragroarty pier, An Bun Beag, Portnablagh, or Downings. The island must be visited if one is to begin to understand why this remote crag, $2\frac{1}{2}$ miles long and $\frac{3}{4}$ mile wide, should hold such an attraction for its inhabitants. The island has apparently been inhabited since prehistoric times, and various attempts by the Government to resettle the inhabitants have proved futile. The present population of about two hundred people lives mainly from fishing and a growing tourist industry. The islanders have gained a new recognition through the Tory Island school of painters. In the late 1950s, encouraged by *Derek Hill*, four islanders began to paint. Knowing little about art and with the most basic equipment, they went on to give a new meaning to 'primitive art'. This artistic tradition has been maintained and continues to excite international interest.

St Colm Cille, once believed to have

banished rats from the island, founded a monastery in the 6th century that flourished as a centre of learning up to the time of *Queen Elizabeth I* of England. Today there is little to see here apart from the remains of a round tower.

A worthwhile diversion along Donegal's northern coast is **Doe Castle**, which stands on a low rocky promontory jutting into **Sheephaven Bay**. The MacSweeneys, mercenary soldiers brought from Scotland by the O'Donnells, gained possession of the castle in 1440, and it was inhabited up to the end of the 19th century. Plans are afoot to open the castle to the public.

No traveller to County Donegal should fail to leave time for the famous 'Atlantic Drive'. This is a fascinating 9-mile drive around the Rossguill Peninsula, which commands an ever-changing panorama of some of the finest romantic scenery in the country.

On the Fanad Peninsula the western route has some patches of excellent scenery, but the eastern side is much more interesting. If you have the time, the complete Fanad Peninsula scenic tour is a 50-mile circuit and is well signposted.

Ballymacstocker Bay, Co. Donegal.

DON'T MISS
- A drive around An Bun Beag **Bloody Foreland**
- Do a sailing course in **An Bun Beag**
- Visit to **Doe Castle**, Sheephaven Bay
- Drive the **Atlantic Drive**
- Pay a visit to **Tory Island**

ALL-WEATHER OPTIONS
- **Dunfanaghy workhouse**, Dunfanaghy
- Visit to the **Gallery**, Dunfanaghy
- Go see the **Derryveagh Crystal** in An Fál Carrach
- Visit **Mhicí Mhic Gabhann** in Gort an Choirce
- Visit the **Flight of the Earls Museum** in Rathmullan on the Fanad Peninsula

Derryveagh Mountains, Glenveagh National Park & Letterkenny

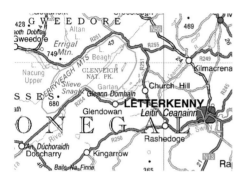

Hidden behind the Derryveagh and Glendown mountains, **Glenveagh National Park** is like an oasis in a desert of bogs and moorland. On land acquired by *John George Adair* in 1857, the park covers nearly 25,000 acres. During the 19th century Glenveagh was the scene of some of the worst evictions to afflict the tenants of County Donegal; but today the park is a haven of tranquillity and beauty.

In 1870 **Glenveagh Castle** was built by Adair on the shores of Lough Veagh, and it was improved considerably by his wife following his death in 1885. In 1932 the estate passed into the hands of the McIllenny family, who, among other things, made their fortune from tabasco sauce. The McIllenny era marked an end to the misery previously associated with the estate and ushered in a period of glamour. Throughout his time as owner of Glenveagh Castle, McIllenny entertained on a lavish scale, playing host to *Greta Garbo, Cecil Beaton,* and *Lady Sarah Churchill,* to name just a few. Eventually McIllenny opted to leave Glenveagh and presented the castle and gardens to the nation in 1983; it is now run and managed by the Heritage Service.

Within the national park is the highest peak in the Derryveagh mountain range, **Errigal Mountain**. It has a height of 2,466 feet (752 metres); but what makes it unique it its conical quartzite peak. Errigal has often been described as a miniature Fujiyama. If you are prepared to climb the mountain you will be rewarded with a view that, on a clear day, is said to extend all the way from the Twelve Pins of Connemara to the mountains of western Scotland.

On the edge of the national park is **Lough Gartan**. Serene and beautiful though it is, it would not rate a mention had it not been for the fact that *St Colm Cille* (also associated with **Gleann Cholm Cille**) is believed to have been born here in the year 521. The supposed birthplace is marked by a huge cross, close to which is the 'Flagstone of Loneliness': if you lie on it, tradition tells us, all your sorrows and troubles will disappear. The **St Colm Cille Heritage Centre** on the lake is largely devoted to following the saint's life and the impact the early Irish church had on the Continent.

But perhaps you are not religiously inclined nor prone to superstitions; so let us move on to visit the once-upon-a-time home of the English artist *Derek Hill*. Derek Hill joined with Henry McIllenny in a spirit of generosity by bequeathing to the state his home, **Glebe House**, and his complete art collection, which included names such as *Kokoschka, Renoir, Braque, Picasso,* and *Dégas*. Hill, himself an artist of repute, was also the inspiration behind the now world-renowned Tory Island painters.

Letterkenny (*Leitir Ceanainn*, 'hillside of Ó Ceanainn'), the largest and most populous town in County Donegal, takes its name from the local chieftains here before Norman times. **St Eunan's Cathedral** is a fine building and worth a visit. Evidence of Letterkenny's importance is confirmed by the recent opening of a high-technology theatre here.

While we associate the Inishowen Peninsula and east Donegal with the

Glenveagh Castle, Co. Donegal.

O'Neills, most of what we know today as County Donegal was dominated by the O'Donnells. Near Letterkenny we find **Carraig an Dúin** or the 'Rock of Doon', where the O'Donnell chiefs were inaugurated. The last great chieftain to be inaugurated here, in 1603, was *Niall Garbh O'Donnell*, cousin of the more famous *Red Hugh O'Donnell*. Near the rock is the **Holy Well of Doon**, where pilgrims have been coming since Penal Law times. An amazing collection of bandages, pieces of clothing, Rosary beads and medals lies in evidence of the powerful belief the local people have in the curative properties of its water. Legend tells us that the 'Little People' live here at Doon Rock and that the King of the Fairies, *Fionnbharr,* holds court here!

Fourteen miles to the south of Letterkenny are the twin towns of **Stranorlar** and **Ballybofey**—alike in beauty but rivals in trade. **Lifford**, the county town, is strategically situated at the junction of the Rivers Mourne and Finn.

DON'T MISS
- **Glenveagh National Park**
- Go to **Carraig an Dúin** (Rock of Doon)
- Climb **Errigal Mountain**
- Pay a visit to **Millbridge Open Farm** in Convoy

ALL-WEATHER OPTIONS
- Visit **Glenveagh Castle & Gardens**
- Visit to **Glebe House & Gallery**
- Visit to **Saint Colm Cille's Heritage Centre**
- Visit the **Dunlewy Centre** at the foot of Errigal Mountain
- Visit **Newmills Corn & Flax Mills**, Letterkenny
- Visit the **Donegal County Museum** in Letterkenny
- Visit the **Seat of Power Visitors' Centre** in Lifford

'Don't forget to pick up your Global Refund Tax Free Shopping Cheques as you shop.' www.globalrefund.ie

GLOBAL REFUND™

The Inishowen Peninsula

the might of the English crown, when they departed Ireland in search of help from Spain. The year was 1607, the month was September, and in history this eventful moment is recorded as the Flight of the Earls. But Spain did not come to Ireland's aid; and soon afterwards there began the Plantation of Ulster, the effects of which are still being felt today.

The ubiquitous *St Colm Cille* also made his way here, and in the village of **Fahan** the ruins of an old Protestant church mark the site of the abbey founded by him in the 6th century. **Carndonagh** deserves a mention, if not for the 7th-century cross—said to be the oldest standing cross in Ireland—then surely for the fact that its school is the largest in Ireland, with over 1,700 pupils.

A visit to the Inishowen Peninsula would not be complete if you did not make it to the most northerly point, **Malin Head**. At a mere 266 feet above sea level, Malin Head is of no great height; but looking out onto the Atlantic from this, Ireland's most northerly point, leaves you with the feeling that it was worth the effort. On the nearby shores there are tons of what are known as 'Malin pebbles', and semi-precious stones such as coral, jasper, opal, agate, topaz, amethyst and crystal have also been found.

There is so much to see on this peninsula that mere words can hardly do justice to all its majestic splendour; but make time to travel through the **Gap of Mamore**, where *Méabh*, the warrior queen of mythological Ireland, is said to have been laid to rest.

Buncrana, the chief town of the peninsula, is a seaside resort that has suffered greatly in recent times with the closure of the 'Fruit of the Loom' clothing factory. **Greencastle**, on the western shore of the peninsula, deserves a mention if only for the local Church of Ireland church, **St Finian's**, where the 'east end of the church faces west'. The Bishop of Derry, who built

The 'Ring of Kerry' of the north—the Inis Eoghain 100—is a well-kept secret left for the discerning and adventurous traveller to discover. Stretching out between the waters of **Lough Foyle** and **Lough Swilly** to become Ireland's most northerly point, the **Inishowen Peninsula** embraces all that is best in County Donegal.

Much of Donegal's past can be traced back to a former High King of Ireland, *Niall of the Nine Hostages*. Inishowen is no exception, for in the 5th century *Eoghan*, son of Niall, was made first lord of the peninsula by his father. Eoghan's descendants later spread from the Inishowen Peninsula into what is today County Tyrone (*Tír Eoghain*, 'the land of Eoghan'). Eoghan's brother *Conall* became first lord of what is now County Donegal, and this area west of Inishowen became *Tír Chonaill* ('the land of Conall'). The descendants of Conall became the O'Donnells, and those of Eoghan became the O'Neills. These two powerful families stood united in their Irish traditions until they were no longer able to hold out against the church in the 18th century, is said to have built the entrance porch of the church in such a way as to be able to view it by telescope from his palace at **Downhill** across the bay. If he didn't like the looks or number of his congregation, he didn't bother to attend!

Our final journey takes us to another site of prehistoric associations. The **Grianán of Aileach** was built about the year 1700 BC and is perhaps the most remarkable of all the prehistoric antiquities of Ireland. It was a seat of the O'Neills, chiefs of Ulster; and it was used as a fortress up to the 12th century, when it was sacked by the O'Briens of Clare. Three concentric ramparts encircle a stone *cashel* with a 17-foot wall that is 13 feet thick at the base. The Grianán was extensively and sensitively restored in the 1870s. Apart from its historic importance, the view from the battlement is wonderful, with a memorable panorama of Lough Swilly to the left and Lough Foyle to the right.

The Grianán of Aileach, Co. Donegal.

DON'T MISS
- A visit to the **Grianán of Aileach**
- Go all the way to **Malin Head!**
- Have a swim at the **Five Fingers Strand**
- Go to see the high cross in **Carndonagh**

ALL-WEATHER OPTIONS
- A visit to **Doagh Isle** Vistors' Centre
- Visit to **Guns of Dunree Military Museum,** Buncrana
- Visit the **Irish National Knitting Centre** in Buncrana
- Visit the **Tullyarvan Mill** in Buncrana
- Visit the **Vintage Car Museum** in Buncrana
- Go to see the **Greencastle Maritime Museum**

TOURING ROUTE

Along the Donegal Coast

Our tour begins from the town of **Donegal**, situated at the mouth of the River Eske as it flows into Donegal Bay. Our journey first takes us out along the northern shore of Donegal Bay on the N56 to **Killybegs**, a major centre for the fishing industry. From here we make our way further along the bay to **Kilcar**, a centre for the hand-woven tweed industry, and then on to **Carrick**, set on good land above Teelin Bay. Carrick is an excellent base for climbing the spectacular **Slieve League**, which rises some 1,970 feet (600 metres) from the sea, forming the highest marine cliff in Europe.

We travel on to **Gleann Cholm Cille**, where the soil becomes poorer but the scenery nevertheless remains breathtaking. The valley is named after *St Colm Cille* of Iona. Worth visiting is **Beefan** half a mile away, an early ecclesiastical site. Our next stop is **Ardara**, an important centre of Donegal hand-woven tweed and hand-knits produced from a thriving cottage industry.

Continuing on the N56 road, we travel to **Maas** on Gweebarra Bay. This area is dotted with magnificent sandy beaches. We make our way northwards to **Dunglow**, known as the capital of the Rosses. This is a lake-strewn and rock-strewn district, with houses dotting the poor soil.

On to **Gaoth Dobhair** and **Dunlewy**, lying under the shadow of Errigal Mountain. This road offers remarkable scenic beauty by Loughs Nacung and Dunlewy into the Derryveagh Mountains, with Errigal's white quartzite cone rising like a miniature Fujiyama.

From Dunlewy we take the national park road and visit **Glenveagh National Park**, lying deep in a gorge formed by geological action at the base of high surrounding ridges. **Lough Veagh** is a beautiful long, narrow lake running along the bottom of the gorge for some 5 miles, surrounded by mountains and woodland. A castle is strategically placed to offset the natural beauty.

Leaving the national park we travel to **Creeslough** at the head of Sheephaven Bay, and continue on towards **Carrigart**. At **Doe Castle** we pause and admire this 15th-century keep of the MacSweeneys, which is protected by the sea on three sides and by a deep *fosse* on the fourth. Nearby we see **Muckish**, at 2,000 feet (610 metres) Donegal's third-highest peak and not an easy one to climb. **Carrigart** is situated on an inlet of Mulroy Bay, and in the sandhills between it and Downings there are many prehistoric habitation sites where numerous objects of the Bronze Age have been found.

Horse-riding on the strand at Bundoran, Co. Donegal.

Downings, famous for its tweeds, is a fine village in an idyllic setting looking out onto the waters of Sheephaven Bay.

Leaving Downings and returning to Carrigart, we travel along Mulroy Bay to **Milford** and **Ramelton**. Turn 3 miles left on the R247 road to Rathmullan, site of the 'Flight of the Earls' in 1607, when O'Neill and the other chieftains sailed into exile in Italy. Continuing along the western shore of Lough Swilly we arrive at **Letterkenny**, the most populous town in the county.

To reach the Inishowen Peninsula we take the western road from Letterkenny to **Buncrana**, the N13. Our first stop is **Manorcunningham** on the east of the River Swilly estuary. From here we make our way northwards for approximately 5 miles before turning off for a 1-mile uphill drive to the **Grianán of Aileach**, a stone fort enclosed within three earthen banks, the site of a tumulus and an ancient approach road.

From the Grianán we return to the N13 road and continue to **Fahan**, where we find a few traces of **St Muran's Abbey**. Travelling along the eastern shore of Lough Swilly from Fahan we arrive at **Buncrana**, a seaside resort and excellent shopping centre.

The road north climbs through beautiful vistas of sea and mountainside to the **Gap of Manore**. We descend to **Clonmany** to view the waterfall nearby at **Glenview**. Veering due east at Ballyliffen we travel to **Carndonagh**, an important ecclesiastical site dating from the 5th century. Half a mile away we find **St Patrick's Cross**, which expert opinion holds to be the oldest standing cross in Ireland.

Leaving Carndonagh we go through comparatively good land to reach the village of **Malin**, the most northerly settlement in Ireland. On the nearby Hill of Dean is a well-preserved monument called the **Temple of Dean**. Eight miles further on we reach **Malin Head**, where spectacular seascapes are offered out to the wild Atlantic Ocean.

Returning by way of the coast to Culdaff, we spot several fine sandy beaches that are safe for bathing. Two miles south of Cloncha is the impressive shaft of **St Boden's Cross**, rising to a height of 13 feet. **Moville** on Lough Foyle was once a port of call for transatlantic liners but has found a new role as a leisure centre.

The drive between Moville and Muff takes us along the western shore of Lough Foyle, looking onto Derry. From Muff, a small border village, we make our way back to Letterkenny by way of Newtown Cunningham and Manorcunningham.

The Literature of Ireland

Oscar Wilde (Sculpture),
Merrion Square, Dublin.

If one includes its oral and mythic components, then up to the end of the 17th century the term 'literature of Ireland' refers to the oldest European vernacular literature and denotes Irish-language literature. But after this, with the gradual winding down of spoken Irish, it's a question of a new language, English, and of how those speaking and writing it—conquerors and conquered—interrelate historically, politically, and imaginatively.

The coming of the 18th century marked a shift in emphasis from an Irish nation to one dominated by an Anglicised world view and signalled the blossoming of Anglo-Irish culture and society. Some would even argue that in this period the London stage could not have survived without *Farquhar, Congreve, Goldsmith,* and *Sheridan.* Politically the star is *Burke*; philosophically, *Berkeley,* and in the novel the delightful *Laurence Sterne.* But the greatest luminary of this distinguished Anglo-Irish age remains the incomparable *Jonathan Swift.*

Yet at the same time that emigrant Anglo-

Irishmen were entertaining sophisticated English audiences with drawing-room comedies rich in innuendo, the Irish language was refusing to lie down. It threw up a masterpiece in *Cúirt an Mheán Oíche* ('The Midnight Court') by *Brian Merriman*—a Rabelaisian parody of the *aisling* or vision-poem that comes closer to Swift in tone, spirit and satirical verve than do many of his own English-language contemporaries. Add to this *Eibhlín Dhubh Ní Chonaill's* 'Lament for Art Ó Laoire', judged the greatest love poem ever written in Irish, and it is clear that, despite the decline in the language's fortunes, great works were still being written in it.

From the 18th century on, paradox and irony characterise the mutual relations of the Gaels and the Anglo-Irish, and much of subsequent literary history is a record of how writers on each side of the divide deal with this complex sense of difference, both here in Ireland and in England.

At the beginning of the 19th century *Maria Edgeworth* wrote *Castle Rackrent,* a novel designed to interpret an Anglo-Irish landed family and its native retainers for the English. The poet *Thomas Moore* similarly attempted to adapt Irish airs to English drawing-rooms but succeeded only, according to *Hazlitt,* in converting 'the wild harp of Erin into a musical snuff-box.'

At the end of the same century *Wilde* and *Shaw* exploited the ambiguities inherent in being Anglo-Irish in an English context. But to most of the native Irish they were 'West Britons' (i.e. always looking to England), while to the English they were highly entertaining gadflies wearing green jackets—until, that is, the first had the bad taste to insist on being recognised sexually and the second the effrontery to demand that people pay attention to him politically.

For *Yeats,* things were more difficult. A prime mover in the Celtic Renaissance, he was obliged, for the sake of appearances, to keep one foot in a peasant cottage in County Sligo, even as he placed the other in his London rooms.

Joyce's solution was more radical: 'A plague on both your houses!' Repulsed by the suppurating version of Catholic morality in the Ireland of his time, and nationalist enough to defend his personal freedom against an imperialist power, his move to the Continent was logical in its simplicity. Independent of cliques and socio-historical pressure groups, he masterminded his own revolution in literature through *A Portrait of the Artist, Ulysses,* and *Finnegans Wake,* charitably including English and Irish as two of the many contributing languages admitted in his final work. *Beckett,* on the other hand, cut through the umbilical cord of English and, aspiring to a Gallic nativity, affected French for important first drafts. Despite this, no rebirth occurred, either for himself or for his characters; and, like Yeats, he ended up paying a backhanded tribute to the Irish peasantry. Yeats's own work with the Abbey Theatre led to plays called *The Countess Cathleen* and *Cathleen Ni Houlihan,* while Beckett chose Murphy, Malone (dies) and Molloy—native Irish family names—as titles for his novels.

In recent drama, *Friel, Murphy, Barry* and the three 'Macs'—*McGuinness, McPherson,* and *McDonagh*—constitute the major forces at work. In the novel, *McGahern, Banville* and *Patrick McCabe* are top of the heap, while *Derek Mahon* and *Séamus Heaney* are possibly our best poets. Writing, like Friel, from a Catholic and nationalist Ulster background, the latter has suffered from pressure to make artistic statements with political resonance. But Heaney is an artist of rare integrity and independence. His award of the 1995 Nobel Prize for Literature recognised a body of literary achievement that is singular and outstanding.

In total, four Irish writers—Yeats, Shaw, Heaney, and Beckett—have received the Nobel Prize; and even if Joyce, the greatest of all, never did, the record still indicates a remarkable achievement for a small country.

Northern Ireland

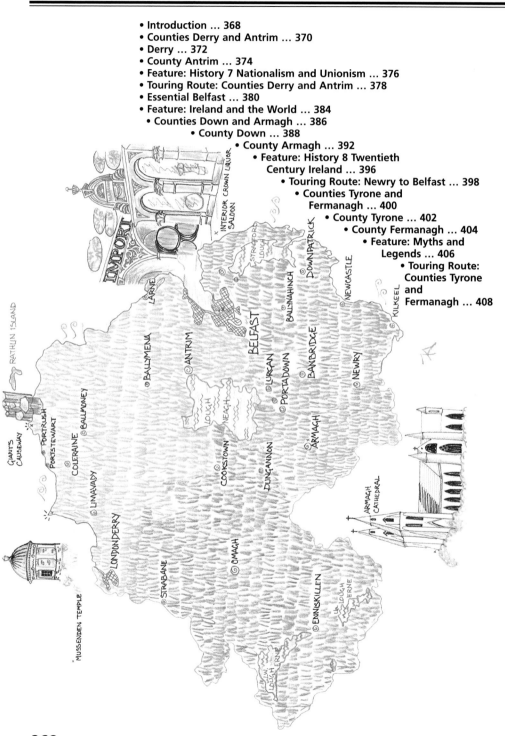

Giant's Causeway,
Co. Antrim.

Northern Ireland

*"Nature is a foolish place to look for
inspiration in, but a charming one in which
to forget one ever had any."*
—Oscar Wilde.

Oscar Wilde's schooldays on the beautiful
shores of **Lower Lough Erne** in County
Fermanagh may well have inspired him—as
could any of the breathtaking scenes that are
to be found along the coast, in the lush glens
or wild moors that make up Northern
Ireland. Stretching 85 miles from north to
south, with a tiny population of some $1\frac{1}{2}$
million, the six counties have much to offer
the visitor.

Though still suffering from years of
negative publicity, tourism has improved
dramatically since the ceasefires, and the
curious who travel here are not
disappointed. Passing through energetic
towns and areas of tilled fields and fertile
land, they meet a warm welcome, a keen
smile, and the humour that sharpens the
softest edge. While more acclaimed regions
might acknowledge their guests with a shrug
of ennui and a rattle of change, Northern
Ireland's finest locations flaunt their jewels
with an eye to the past—and a glimpse of
tomorrow. There's the splendid north Antrim
coastline and the fabled **Giant's Causeway**,
making into the sea its giant steps. Or vast
Lough Neagh, which holds in its waters the
angler's dreams. Layers of the past can be
revealed in ancient tombs and blessed wells.
Castle ruins and stately homes recall some
of those who at one time ruled; now, in these
precarious days of peace, an uncertain
history is being made. Politicians and
strident voices struggle to acknowledge the
other's view, but for the people life goes on,
though dividing walls still stand.

Northern Ireland is separated from the
Republic by a 250-mile hedge-strewn border.
Crossing was once quite formidable, when
checkpoints could block one's journey and
British army watchtowers cast their
shadows. Today your passage north might be
marked by nothing more significant than

paying in pounds sterling at a frontier petrol
station. Though patrols are still evident in
certain places, they have been greatly scaled
down, and travel around the excellent
network of roads is easy. Along minor routes
a farmer driving cattle is more likely to slow
progress than any more sinister delay. Road
signs are many and clear and show distances
in miles. Should you go astray, local people
are ever willing to advise, eager to offer
visitors an alternative view of their too-
famous region. The huge investment in
tourism has supported this, and
international investment has also
contributed to rebuilding and development.
There have been considerable changes since
the ceasefire of 1994; but away from the
main centres and back on a country lane
with its fuchsia or yellow gorse, it can
sometimes seem that time has stood quietly
still.

In 1998 the majority of people voted
overwhelmingly in favour of the Belfast
Agreement, which established a framework
for their future government. Though more
specific details remain unclear, nothing
could have been more lucid than the call for
peace and a way forward that would
acknowledge all traditions.

Nowadays there are numerous festivals
and venues for the sounds, visions, theatre
and song that are so much a part of
everyone's life. The actor *Liam Neeson,*
singer *Neil Hannon* of the Divine Comedy,
artist *Basil Blackshaw* and poets *Séamus
Heaney* and *Medbh McGuckian* are among
the artists who speak with pride of their
northern origins. The blues man *Van
Morrison* has sung famously of Hyndford
Street and Cypress Avenue, the lilting words
that recall his Belfast birth. These people
may be renowned; but in this part of the
world, which is well used to the media
spotlight, the scathing northern wit
maintains little reverence for any icons.
Comedians like *Patrick Kielty* and the *Hole-
in-the-Wall Gang* have turned on their heads
the staunchest of views and often provided

much-needed relief. Locally too the humour is sharp and the dialect can be strong, just like the tea that's served with the Ulster fry for breakfast.

Offering a more sophisticated cuisine are the chic restaurants of **Belfast**, including Cayenne, run by the television celebrities *Jeanne* and *Paul Rankin*. Recent years have seen countless eating places spring up, serving a range of food to increasingly discerning diners. But pubs probably remain the preferred meeting place, where the Guinness or Caffrey's flows and the local whiskey, Bushmills, glints golden in the glass.

While newcomers to Northern Ireland may, understandably, have questions regarding their safety, a visit to any of the excellent tourist centres will reassure you with advice. You may be tempted to keep to coastal or rural regions, but it is only by moving through the cities and towns that you can get any real sense of people's lives and times. Not only are holiday-makers encouraged but the landscapes of this region are being marketed to attract the film-maker. The strong character and the sense of drama through its people make it an ideal location.

But you don't have to be in films to see that. You can find out for yourself what it is that makes this small corner of western Europe so different. Northern Ireland has lost many years but is endeavouring to make them up. Take time when you get here and learn to tune in to the heartbeat of this unique place. Its rhythms will reverberate long after in your memory, making you eager to return.

City Hall, Belfast.

Counties Derry and Antrim

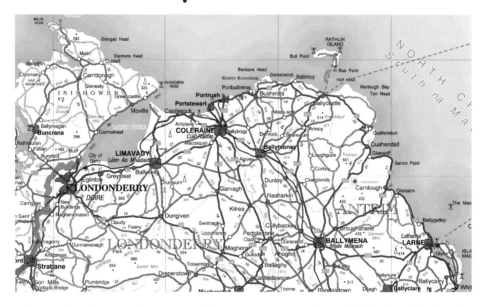

O Danny boy, the pipes, the pipes are calling,
From glen to glen, and down the
mountainside …

The words of the 'Derry Air' resound around the globe in sports stadiums, pubs, and concert halls. When *Jane Ross* first noted it down from a travelling player in Limavady in 1851, she little realised that it would become Ireland's favourite song. Its words recall another time, when musicians wandered through hill and glen, given patronage by the Irish chiefs, who held court in the adjacent counties of Derry and Antrim.

Joined by magnificent coastlines, which attract today's visitors, one county is just a giant's step away from Scotland, while the other is parted from the Republic by laws of man. And in between is 'the fishy, fruitful Bann' of *Edmund Spenser* ('The Faerie Queene', 1596), once carrier of oak and elm from ancient wood for the building of new towns by planters' rules. Travelling from the verdant **Glens of Antrim** by the **Giant's Causeway** inland to the plantation towns and on to the now vibrant walled city, one

traverses paths touched by legend and strife. When the native chiefs were ousted, the musicians were left by the wayside; but somehow the music survived, in fiddles and harps, drums and pipes, which told of loss and gain on every side.

The much-loved city of **Derry** has been famous too long for all the wrong reasons. These days it is the city of a Nobel Peace Prize winner, a jazz festival and film festival, and one in which giant British retail chains have been investing tens of millions. Looking out over the River Foyle from the grey 17th-century walls, you can get a sense of a past that has left the city scarred. History recalls a time when the chieftain *Calgach* ruled the oak groves of *Doire* up to the era of monastic rule of *St Colm Cille* and his men. Later settlers from London imposed their identity and their name, creating the county and city of 'Londonderry', under siege in 1689, when apprentice boys shouted 'No surrender' and slammed shut the city gates against the forces of *King James II*. Inside the uncompromising walls, the people starved until 'a handful of chickweed cost a penny, a quart of horse blood cost a shilling and rats fattened on corpses the same.'

Centuries later the call for civil rights was heard, as one side protested against injustice and inequality. The city title became through time a touchstone of one's political views. Media personnel stumbled over the problem, often opting for both names to avoid offending, while street signs showed convenient weathering long before winter winds had blown. In this place where the once formidable military presence has been scaled down considerably, carnivals and festivals celebrate. Multimedia vies with dance music, a new population has grown up; and while contentious marches persist, the warm and soft-spoken people of Derry are determined to make their own history.

The neighbouring county of Antrim (*Aontroim*) is surrounded on three sides by magnificent coasts. Visitors have long followed this route of unspoilt beauty, from the 'air of comfort and neatness' observed by *W. M. Thackeray* in **Portstewart** to the upper shore of **Belfast Lough**. Where the Giant's Causeway stands like a number of gigantic columns tumbled out into the waves, the high points have yielded panoramic vistas to centuries of dreamers

pondering this arrangement of stones. Today's tourist can pass easily through villages and towns along the north-eastern edge, places where the Troubles did not often reach and where golden beaches follow sun-kissed strand. Inland are the magical glens, the nine valleys that touch like a giant hand across the range of hills lying between **Ballycastle** and **Larne**.

Folklore is rich in these places, where small communities lived isolated for years, cut off by the absence of road or transport. Even after the A2 road was blasted out of the chalky cliffs, linking villages with distant towns and cities, Irish language and music persisted, passing on history in story and song. Industry touched on inland towns where linen once wove its way. Now **Lisburn** tells the linen yarn, and much of mid-Antrim is agricultural, with dialect overtones of the Scottish Hebrides as you wander 'roon the toon'. Modern tastes can opt for waterskiing at **Ballymoney** or perhaps feasting on the past at a mediaeval banquet in **Carrickfergus**. Though castles, many in ruins, stand testimony to a troubled past, the *fleánna*, fairs and festivals throughout recall old ways but newer times as the people of County Antrim welcome the guest to their abundant and varied county.

Derry at night: River Foyle.

Derry

The Guildhall, Derry.

Derry, the walled city

Derry's beginnings are often traced back to *St Colm Cille*, who founded a monastic community here in 546; but archaeological evidence suggests that there were inhabitants here at least two thousand years earlier. In 1311 the Anglo-Norman *Richard de Burgo* was granted these lands by *King Edward II* of England. The skeleton on the city's coat of arms is thought to refer to a later de Burgo's imprisonment of an insubordinate nephew who subsequently starved to death. It was here that some of the earliest civil rights marches of 1967 and 1968 took place, led by, among others, a schoolteacher named *John Hume*. Now a member of the European Parliament, he received the 1998 Nobel Peace Prize along with David Trimble of the Ulster Unionist Party.

Successive attempts by English rulers to suppress the local chieftains, following their initial efforts against *Shane O'Neill* in 1566, led ultimately to *King James I* offering the land to English and Scottish settlers in 1609. The city of London was given the power to settle the area, which it did by rebuilding the town within a mile-long sturdy wall accessed by four main gates. During the siege of 1688–89 against *King James II*, who wanted to restore his authority, the Protestants within these walls withstood bombardment and starvation for 105 days. By its end, some seven thousand had died, but in the meantime *William of Orange* had organised his army on the Continent and returned to victory at the Battle of the Boyne, leading to a Protestant ascendancy in Ireland throughout the 18th century. The siege cry of *No surrender* features to this day on banners during the 12th of July celebrations.

While iron gates made it impossible to walk the circuit of the walls until the mid-1990s, nowadays it is possible to walk most of the way around, passing 17th-century cannons that alternate with modern cast-iron figures representing peace and reconciliation. Standing at **Butcher's Gate** and looking out on the Catholic **Bogside**, you get a view of Free Derry Corner with its oft-repainted sign. Once the end wall of a row of old houses, it recalls the people's resistance to the police and army during the late 60s and early 70s. The houses were later demolished, and a grassy park now spreads over the hillside. The **Bloody Sunday Memorial** to the right is dedicated to the thirteen unarmed civilians shot by the British army during a protest march in 1972.

Of the numerous cultural events now taking place in Derry, the **Two Cathedrals Festival** celebrates **St Eugene's (Catholic) Cathedral** in the Bogside and **St Columb's (Protestant) Cathedral** (1628) inside the walls. The city's oldest Catholic church is the **Long Tower**, said to be on the original site of *Colm Cille's* monastery and now containing most of the artefacts relating to the saint, including a kneeling stone.

In Derry it is hard to avoid the past. The **Tower Museum** tells the city's history up to the present day, while the Apprentice Boys' Hall houses the **Siege Exhibition**. On the other side of the first Derry Presbyterian Church is the **Calgach Centre**, telling a Celtic story, and you can trace your own origins in the genealogy centre. But right up to date are the lively coffee bars and restaurants of **Shipquay Street**, which climbs up from the gate through the city, leading to the **Diamond**. A craft village sells tweeds and linen. Just outside the gates is the beautiful restored **Guildhall**, seat of local government.

Bombed twice in 1972, it has fine stained-glass windows, which were given new life in 1984.

Leaving the city

The River Foyle is crossed here by two bridges: the double-decker iron **Craigavon Bridge** by the *Hands Across the Divide* sculpture and the **Foyle Bridge**, which virtually bypasses the city. One person who intended to bypass but didn't, mistaking Derry for Paris, was *Amelia Earhart,* the first woman to fly the Atlantic solo. She landed in 1932 in a field on the north edge, where a cottage exhibition centre recalls her bravery. Inland, the **Roe Valley Country Park** stretches on each side of the peaty Roe River, which echoed to the sound of clattering water-mills in linen times. Today's visitor can see the weaving-shed museum and the watch-towers that overlooked the river banks where linen was laid out for bleaching by the sun. Ghosts of the O'Cahans haunt the place where a dog leaped across the river at **Dogleap Rock** to bring allies to their rescue. **Limavady** (*Léim an Mhadaidh,* 'the dog's leap') became the leading linen town of the county. Music is in the air of this town, and also over in **Dungiven**, a place noted for its traditional sessions. The ruined **Priory** here preserves the fine mediaeval tomb of *Cúmhaí na nGall Ó Catháin,* who died in 1385.

Dramatic views are offered from the road through the Sperrin Mountains over the **Glenshane Pass**. At the foot of the pass is **Maghera**, with unusually winding streets that date it to pre-Plantation times. The old church stands on the site of a 6th-century monastery.

A bishop's view

When the eccentric 18th-century Bishop of Derry, *Frederick Hervey,* wanted to improve access to his palace at **Downhill**, north of Limavady, he built a road over Binevenagh Mountain. This offers a spectacular view across the shell-covered Blue Flag strand to **Magilligan Point**. A martello tower stands guard as gliders from Bellarena cruise on the swirling air currents.

Above the salmon-rich Bann estuary is the market town of **Coleraine**, given by *King James I* to Londoners in 1613, now home to the **University of Ulster**. A walk around the town's pedestrianised centre would give little idea of its proximity to Ireland's oldest known settlement at **Mount Sandel**, south of here. In May up to 70,000 people watch the more contemporary sight of the 'North-West 200' motorcycle race. It passes the 3-mile golden beach at **Portstewart** (*Port Stíobhaird*), where fiery sunset skies inspired *Jimmy Kennedy* to write 'Red Sails in the Sunset'.

DON'T MISS

- Explore the city of **Derry** and contemplate the past and present from the look-out points along the ancient walls.
- Learn the story of Derry, from Colm Cille to the present, in the Museum in **O'Doherty's Tower**.
- Why did **Amelia Earhart** land in Ireland? Find out at the exhibition centre north-west of the city.
- Follow in the steps of the O'Cahan chiefs in the **Roe Valley Country Park**, where the linen industry is remembered in the Visitors' Centre and surrounding area.
- Enjoy the view from the curious **Mussenden Temple**, perched on the edge of a cliff, a short walk from the ruined bishop's palace at Downhill.

ALL-WEATHER OPTIONS

- Shop for souvenirs and support local craftworkers at the **Craft Village** in **Derry**.
- Trace your Irish roots at the genealogy centre or the origins of the Celtic warrior Calgach at the **Fifth Province**.
- The Nobel Prize winner Séamus Heaney is celebrated at **Bellaghy Bawn**, where you can learn about his life and work.

 'Don't forget to pick up your Global Refund Tax Free Shopping Cheques as you shop.' www.globalrefund.ie

GLOBAL REFUND™

County Antrim

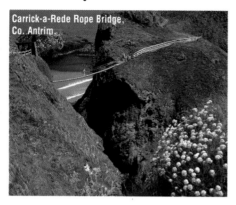

Carrick-a-Rede Rope Bridge, Co. Antrim.

The north Antrim coast and the Giant's Causeway

The family resort of **Portrush** (*Port Rois*) is situated on **Ramore Head**, which juts out into the Atlantic. The **Dunluce Centre** will interest small nature enthusiasts, but the rolling waves are also attracting surfers. At the **Countryside Centre** the geology of the fossil-rich cliffs, weathered into caves and arches, is explained. **Dunluce Castle**, now a romantic ruin hanging on the edge of a crag, originated as a Norman fortification, later becoming the stronghold of the MacDonnells.

The visitor will be revived by the spirit of **Bushmills** (*Muileann na Buaise*), the site of the world's oldest licensed distillery. Though it was first officially distilling in 1608, 13th-century records tell of soldiers being fortified with *aqua vitae*, otherwise *uisce beatha*—the water of life.

Have a 'wee snifter' in the 1608 Bar before moving on to the North's number 1 tourist attraction, the **Giant's Causeway**. Publicity for this phenomenon began as far back as 1693 from a Royal Society publication. Later, paintings by *Susanna Drury* brought the geological phenomenon to fame on the Continent. Scientists vied with each other to explain its origins, while mythology suggested that *Fionn mac Cumhaill* wanted stepping-stones to the Island of Staffa, where a particular female giant lived. Nineteenth-

century tour guides perpetuated these myths with names like the Organ Pipes and Chimney Tops. All is explained in the visitors' centre, and a superior view of this world heritage site can be had from the clifftop at Hamilton's Seat by **Benbane Head**.

The coastal path continues round to the ruins of **Dunseverick Castle**, possibly a stronghold as long ago as the Iron Age. *St Patrick* is said to have visited here, and it also has associations with Ireland's oldest love story, 'Deirdre of the Sorrows'. Between the sand-duned strand of **White Park Bay** are the picture-postcard villages of **Portbradden**, with Ireland's smallest church, and the limestone harbour at **Ballintoy**. The stout-hearted will brave a bridge of ropes and slats at **Carrick-a-Rede**, swaying 80 feet above the water to cross to the salmon fishery at the small island, where razorbills swirl fearlessly overhead.

Ballycastle and Rathlin

Ballycastle (*Baile an Chaistil*) marks the end of the Causeway coastline. The town's Ould Lammas Fair, commemorated in song, dates back to 1606 and still has sheep and pony sales, while the quintessential items of dulse (dried seaweed) and yellow man (hard toffee) are sold readily. Ballycastle is a lively resort, with plenty of music, particularly during the **Fleá Amhrán agus Rince** (Festival of Song and Dance) each June and the **Northern Lights** celebration of culture in late May. *Marconi* and his assistant established wireless contact here with Rathlin Island in 1898. The town was at one time a seat of the epic MacDonnell family, whose bodies are contained in a vault in easterly **Bonamargy Friary**.

The Antrim glens and coast

The nine Glens of Antrim run 'from glen to glen' between steep headlands down to the sea, an area of outstanding beauty with white sandy beaches, towering cliffs, and tranquil glens. The route from **Ballycastle** to **Larne** is one of the most scenic in Europe. From vantage points along the coast you can enjoy uninterrupted views of the Mull of Kintyre and beyond. Lush and green is **Murlough Bay**, past the stone cross memorial to the revolutionary *Roger Casement*, a native of County Antrim. Travel on past **Torr Head**, where *Shane the Proud O'Neill* was killed, and along the wild fuchsia and honeysuckle road to the National Trust village and beach of **Cushendun** and the brown **Glendun**. The Glens are rich in story: here the Children of Lir swam in the ancient sea of Moyle; and the legendary warrior *Oisín*, son of *Fionn mac Cumhaill*, is said to be buried on the slopes of Tievebulliagh mountain.

The centre of the Glens is picturesque **Cushendall**, with its **Curfew Tower** built to confine 'idlers and rioters'. A cliff path from the beach leads to the ruins of the 13th-century **Layde Old Church**, another MacDonnell burial place. Inland is **Glenariff**, 'Queen of the Glens', which *Thackeray* called 'Switzerland in miniature'. Its Forest Park is filled with wild flowers and includes **Ess-na-Larach Waterfall**.

Mid-Antrim

Leaving the Glens and heading through the flat agricultural landscape to Slemish Mountain, the next stop is **Ballymena** (*an Baile Meánach*), a town originally of seven towers and a busy 370-year-old market. The town offers golf, a small museum of local history, and a barracks housing the Museum of the Royal Irish Regiment.

Around Belfast

Deer roam about **Randalswood Forest**, as far as the lough shores. The Presbyterian church of **Randalstown**, dating from 1790, merits a look before the nature reserve at **Shane's Castle**. There is also the remarkably intact 10th-century round tower in **Steeple**

Park. This is all that remains of the monastery that was founded by *Aodh*, reputedly a follower of St Patrick, on the banks of the Six Mile Water. Back in the town, in **Pogues Entry**, is the 18th-century mud-floored cottage of the author *Alexander Irvine*.

Lovers meet at **Doagh**, north of the water-driven spade mill at **Templepatrick**. Surrounding views compensate for the scramble up to join hands through the ever-popular **Hole Stone**. In the distance the port of **Larne** is terminus for the fastest sea crossing to Stranraer in Scotland. Crumbling **Olderfleet Castle** and the 19th-century **Chaine Memorial Tower** link this town with its past.

On to **Carrickfergus** (*Carraig Fhearghais*), childhood home of *Louis MacNeice* and noted for its brilliantly positioned Norman castle overlooking the harbour, where *William of Orange* landed in 1690 on his way to the Boyne. It now revels in mediaeval banquets, as well as the **Lúnasa Fair** of the 1st of August. Some ultra-modern attempts to re-create the past include the Knight Ride, a monorail trip through a thousand years. **St Nicholas's Church** contains a monument to the Earls of Donegall and several stained-glass windows. Outside the town is the **Andrew Jackson Centre** in a reconstructed 18th-century cottage near the site of the American president's parents' original home. American soldiers were trained in Carrickfergus during the Second World War and are remembered here. From the town it is a short drive along the lough shore back to Belfast.

South of Belfast, the industrial town of **Lisburn** grew rich on the linen industry, as recalled in street names like Linenhall Street and Market Street.

DON'T MISS

- Visit ruined **Dunluce Castle**, with its thousand-year-old souterrain and original cobbled yard.
- See the **Giant's Causeway** and follow in Fionn mac Cumhaill's footsteps around this world heritage site.
- Brave the line of ropes and slats that is **Carrick-a-Rede Rope Bridge** across to the island.

ALL-WEATHER OPTIONS

- Sample the 'water of life' in the world's oldest licensed distillery at **Bushmills**.
- Take the **Knight Ride** through time and learn the history of Carrickfergus.
- Find out about the industry that wove its way into Northern Ireland at the **Irish Linen Centre** in Lisburn.

Nationalism and Unionism

Daniel O'Connell addresses a public meeting.

The story of modern Ireland begins in the late 18th century. Catholics gradually began to agitate for the removal of civil disabilities, which they had suffered for most of the century. They could not bear arms; they could not own property on the same terms as Protestants; they could not own a horse worth more than £5; they could neither practise law nor hold a commission in the army, nor sit in Parliament. British attitudes to Catholics gradually softened with the passage of time, and one by one these disabilities were either lightened or removed altogether, and by the end of the century the only major demand left unfulfilled was the right to sit in Parliament.

The British change of heart came under pressure from the American Revolutionary war. Concessions to Catholics achieved two ends: they made recruiting in Ireland easier, and they made it less likely that civil disturbance would require the army to be weakened in America to keep order in Ireland. Later on, the series of long wars between England and France in the wake of the French Revolution had a similar effect.

The French Revolution shook Ireland, as it shook most parts of Europe. New concepts of popular sovereignty, of republicanism and of civic equality spread quickly, especially among the middle class. The result was the formation of the Society of United Irishmen in 1791, dedicated to the creation of a common Irish citizenship among people of all religious denominations in Ireland. It later evolved into a republican separatist society, aiming at complete independence from Britain.

In 1798 a rebellion organised by the United movement was almost foiled by government spies but went off at half cock. The most serious outbreak was in County Wexford, where over 25,000 people—most of them civilian non-combatants—died in less than a month. Other brief outbreaks in Ulster and Connacht were less bloody. The Ulster rebellion was mainly a Presbyterian affair, reflecting the democratic instincts of parts of the Calvinist north against the Anglican Dublin Ascendancy. The Wexford rebellion, by contrast, was a confused mixture of French revolutionary idealism and an older indigenous sectarianism. Horrible atrocities were committed on both sides.

The British government, locked in a lethal struggle with Napoleonic France, decided to abolish the Irish Parliament and effect a full union between the two countries. On 1 January 1801 the Kingdom of Ireland ceased to exist and Ireland became part of the new United Kingdom. Thereafter it became the aim of the growing Catholic campaign in Ireland to repeal the Union—either through a form of home rule or through outright independence—while Protestants, thoroughly frightened by the events of 1798, became the Union's most ardent supporters.

In the first two decades of the 19th century, modern Irish nationalism developed out of the demand for Catholic Emancipation. This meant the removal of the last major civil disability, the right to sit in Parliament. Under the leadership of *Daniel O'Connell,* a new kind of mass politics brought the weight of numbers to bear on a reluctant British establishment. The demand was conceded in 1829. O'Connell then moved on to campaign for the repeal of the union. He was less successful in this ambition, though abolishing the union became the central nationalist demand for the rest of the century.

O'Connell died in 1847, by which time Ireland was in the throes of the Great Famine, in which the population of 8 million was reduced by a quarter. A million people died and a million fled on emigrant ships. The last major subsistence crisis in western Europe was caused by the total failure of the potato crop, the nutritious staple on which the Irish poor depended. And it was the poor who bore the brunt of the horror. The British government did less than it might have done to relieve the appalling suffering: there is no doubt that some elements in London regarded the Famine as divine retribution on the Irish and a providential opportunity to clear the land of its excess population.

The Famine was a trauma that lay like a silent shadow over Irish life for generations. Many of the old landlords were ruined along with their tenants and cottiers. By the same token, many of the Catholic middle class were untouched. Indeed the welter of Catholic church-building that was largely financed by that class went on apace through the 1840s and 50s.

It was the Catholic survivors of the Famine and their principal instrument of social control, the Catholic Church, to whom the second half of the century belonged. Catholic education spread throughout the community. A campaign for land reform produced a succession of agrarian campaigns and outrages from the 1870s on. Finally, the old demand for the repeal of the union was renewed. The catchphrase was now 'home rule', and the leader—ironically a Protestant landlord—was *Charles Stewart Parnell,* an enigmatic genius.

Parnell forged an alliance with Gladstone's Liberal Party. The result was a Home Rule Bill that was only narrowly defeated in the House of Commons in 1886. In the meantime a number of Land Acts had greatly advanced the position of tenants at the expense of the Ascendancy landlords. The land question was finally settled in 1903 by the introduction of a wholesale tenant purchase scheme. This established an independent owner-occupier system, and the old estates were broken up. In short, it was the undoing of the Cromwellian land settlement.

The steady march of nationalism dominated Ireland outside Ulster. That province, however, had a very different history. It had been relatively unscathed by the Famine. Instead, it participated fully in the Industrial Revolution that swept across much of north-west Britain. Belfast became one of the boom towns of the century, a centre of engineering, shipbuilding, and heavy industry. Its population increased eighteen-fold between 1823 and 1896, and by the outbreak of the Great War it was bigger than Dublin. The local Protestant majority was firmly opposed to home rule, on two grounds: firstly, because they feared for their future in a country with an overwhelming Catholic majority; and secondly, because they associated their new-found industrial prosperity with membership of the United Kingdom, the largest and richest economy in the world. It was as if nationalism had created unionism, its irreconcilable opposite. The twin fortunes of these opposed traditions would dominate Ireland in the 20th century.

Drive away from **Derry** across the two-tiered iron Craigavon Bridge, noting the sculpture *Hands Across the Divide* as you leave the historic city. Travelling on the A2 road along the edge of the River Foyle, go through the plantation town of **Ballykelly** and on to the linen town of **Limavady**, situated on the Roe River. To the tune of 'The Derry Air', noted down by *Jane Ross,* who lived in one of the surviving Georgian houses at number 51 Main Street, turn onto the B201 road from the A2, and continue for a mile before turning left.

You are now on the scenic **Bishop's Road** across **Binevenagh Mountain**, built by the flamboyant *Bishop Hervey* to improve access from his palace at **Downhill**. Stop at the **Bishop's View** for a panoramic view

across to the golden strand at **Magilligan Point**. Rejoin the A2 at Downhill, where a roadside gateway marks the entrance to the demesne, and continue on to the town of **Coleraine**, seat of the University of Ulster. The popular seaside resort of **Portrush** is renowned for its prestigious international golf championships. North of the town, on the peninsula of **Ramore Head**, we have a magnificent panorama stretching from **Rathlin Island** to the **Inishowen Mountains** in County Donegal.

Our tour continues along the north Antrim coast to the tiny resort of **Portballintrae**, from where we see the spectacular ruins of **Dunluce Castle**, built by *Richard de Burgh* in 1300 and later held by the MacDonnells. On to **Bushmills**, the village celebrated as site of the world's oldest licensed distillery, where the

TOURING ROUTE
Counties Derry and Antrim

378

famous Black Bush is produced. At **Causeway Head** on the B146 road we can continue by foot or minibus to the **Giant's Causeway**, an impressive and curious rock formation composed of over 37,000 basalt columns in several groups forming a natural amphitheatre.

Continue along the coast past the ruined **Dunseverick Castle** and the wild waters of **White Park Bay**, through **Ballintoy** and on to **Ballycastle**, situated at the foot of **Glenshesk Valley**. Boat trips are available to **Rathlin Island**, a thinly inhabited botanical, ornithological and geological paradise that provided a retreat for Scotland's *Robert Bruce*. He hid in a cave here in 1306 at the nadir of his fortunes prior to his return to Scotland. A more recent sanctuary was offered to the tycoon *Richard Branson,* whom the islanders rescued when his transatlantic balloon landed off shore. He subsequently underwrote an activity centre at Church Bay. From **Ballycastle** we follow a beautiful narrow coast road, passing a memorial to *Roger Casement*, patriot and native of County Antrim, who sought German help in liberating Ireland of English domination and was found guilty of high treason in 1916. On to the picturesque village of **Cushendun**, with its Cornish-style cottages and beach.

The A2 road passes by the foot of the legend-filled **Glens of Antrim**. In Glenaan at the foot of **Tievebulliagh** stands a stone circle said to contain the tomb of *Oisín,* Celtic warrior and poet. From the delightful resort of **Cushendall**—a perfect base for excursions into the Glens—take a right turn for the B14 towards Ballymena and then follow the A43 through **Glenariff**, the most attractive of the nine Glens, to **Waterfoot** at the foot of **Glenariff Forest Park**. In summer Feis na nGleann, a joyous folklore festival of music and dance, takes place here. Continue on the winding coast road, past the **Garron Tower** from Famine times, to the charming harbour village of **Carnlough** (where *Winston Churchill* briefly owned a hotel) and on to **Glenarm** at the head of the valley. The 17th-century castle of the Earls of Antrim is clearly visible across the river.

After a stop at **Carnfunnock Country Park** to see the walled garden and maze, our road curls through **Blackcave Tunnel** towards the port of **Larne**. Pass through the busy town and make for the mediaeval town of **Carrickfergus**. The remains of the strategically positioned castle on the edge of the lough demand a visit, especially during the *Lúnasa* fair in the month of August. But for those less historically oriented, sailing and other water sports as well as the futuristic 'Knight Ride' are on offer. And from this commuter town it is a short drive along the shores of the Lough back to **Belfast.**

Dunluce Castle, Co. Antrim.

379

Essential Belfast

Belfast has origins as far back as the Stone Age, when people gathered cockles from the Lagan shores. In 1177 a settlement grew up around the castle built nearby by *John de Courcy*. Being situated at the entrance to **Belfast Lough**, it was frequently contested, until the lands reclaimed from the sea were granted to *Sir Arthur Chichester*, Governor of Carrickfergus and Earl of Donegall, in 1603. In spite of settlers from Devon and Scotland, it remained a village until significant expansion began with the late 17th-century arrival of French Huguenots, who provided a boost to linen-making. They were followed by Presbyterians who imported power-driven cotton machinery, heralding the arrival of the Industrial Revolution. While much of the rest of Ireland remained without knowledge of the whirr of machinery, Belfast grew to become a major industrial town, with linen and rope manufacture and shipbuilding; and the population exploded during the 19th century to reach 400,000 by 1925. Today, though many have moved to outlying areas to escape the political unrest, the population is some half a million people living within 10 miles of the centre.

Donegall Square

The centre of Belfast is undoubtedly **Donegall Square**, dominated by the enormous white Portland stone building of **City Hall**. Built in Classical Renaissance style, it was completed in 1906 on the site of the former White Linen Hall to mark Belfast's new status as a city.

At ground level, various memorials hearken back to times past, including statues of *Queen Victoria*, *Edward Harland* and the war veteran *James Magennis* and a stone commemorating the American Expeditionary Force that arrived in Belfast in 1942. The **Titanic Memorial** recalls the doomed liner and the gallant men who perished on it—not a reference to the stars of the *James Cameron* film, which has rekindled huge interest in the ship and inspired Belfast City Council to designate

the 15th of April 'Titanic Day'.

Around the Albert Clock

At the bottom of High Street stands the subsiding **Albert Memorial Clock** of 1867. Lanyon made his mark on this area with the ornate **Queen's Bridge**, the **Northern Bank** (1852), now First Trust, the grand renovated **Custom House**, with its sculpted pediment of Neptune, Britannia, and Mercury, and the nautical **Sinclair Seamen's Church**.

This redeveloped area around **Clarendon Dock** is part of a programme of improvements that include a riverside walk and the **Lagan Lookout Visitor Centre**. Here one can view the Weir and the giant cranes of Harland and Wolff's shipyard, founded in 1862 by the Yorkshireman *Edward Harland* and *Wilhelm Wolff* from Hamburg.

We head upstream along Oxford Street towards the magnificent **Waterfront Hall**, opposite the neo-classical **Courts of Justice**. The spaceship contours of the Waterfront are almost dwarfed by the towering structures of the Hilton Hotel and British Telecom. Nearby is the sympathetically restored **St George's Market**. Off Russell Street is the red-brick **St Malachy's (Catholic) Church**, with its dazzling fan-vaulted ceiling. Past meets present at the Robinson Patterson architectural office, an imaginatively redeveloped warehouse in Clarence Street.

The cathedral quarter

The Donegall Street area is one of the most historic districts in Belfast. The Belfast Buildings Preservation Trust, established in 1996, aims to rescue historic buildings and give them new life and relevance. One of its projects is the restoration of **St Patrick's Church and School** in Lower Donegall Street. Other buildings of interest in this quarter are the **Exchange Building** (1769), the oldest public building in the city, and the **Ulster Bank** (1860), with its elaborate carvings of Britannia, Commerce, and

Donegall Place
from City Hall,
Belfast.

Northern Ireland

Justice. Also of note are the **Northern Whig Building** and the **War Memorial Building**, which offers a permanent exhibition about Northern Ireland during the Second World War.

The imposing **St Anne's (Protestant) Cathedral** was built in 1898. A more lively detour can be made to the **North Street Arcade**, a 1930s shopping area that houses an eclectic range of shops, including a café, a tattooist's, a gallery, and cobblers.

Towards the Golden Mile and university area

In a city with such a history of strife, the Gothic **Presbyterian Assembly Rooms** on the corner of College Square have ironically been given over to the consumer gods of the Spires Shopping Mall. Opposite is the Georgian **Royal Belfast Academical Institution** (the 'Inst') of 1814, set on lawns, many of which were sold off because of debts and on which was built the **Belfast Institute**—the 'College of Knowledge'. In

Great Victoria Street, around the corner from the Ulster Unionist Party offices, is the sumptuous **Cirque and Grand Opera House**. Along the much-altered Great Victoria Street you meet the **Dublin Road**—the 'Golden Mile'—with its variety of restaurants, shops, and pubs. Draft and Overdraft are for once not to be avoided: these are the bronze figures tacked on to the front of the Ulster Bank building in Shaftesbury Square, which marks the beginning of the university area.

Queen's University, designed by *Charles Lanyon* in 1849, has long held a strong reputation. Queen's caters for about eight thousand students, many of whom live in the surrounding streets of terraced red-brick houses, the 'Holy Land'. A particularly fine terrace is the Georgian **University Square**, now owned by the university.

We leave the world of books for the **Botanic Gardens**, where *William Thomson, Lord Kelvin*, inventor of the Kelvin scale of

Stormont Parliament Buildings, Belfast.

temperature, stands just inside the gate. A huge variety of plants, from fuchsia and begonia to lush tropical species, makes the renovated 19th-century bulding an essential visit. Through the fir trees is the **Ulster Museum**, which has a unique collection of treasure, including gold jewellery from the shipwrecked Spanish Armada vessel *La Girona,* as well as displays on Irish history.

A left turn out of the gardens will bring you into the prosperous **Malone Road** area. The North Gate of the gardens brings you onto tree-lined **Botanic Avenue**, Heaney's Boul' Mich' (Boulevard San Michel in Paris). Among the bookshops, art cinema and coffee bars, visitors can find much to distract them in this distinctly European-flavoured area.

Divided Belfast

Belfast's 'Living History' tour offers visitors the chance to view for themselves the places that have for so long been etched in our memories. No mere fifteen minutes of fame for these streets, which have flashed continuously around the world as bombings ripped them apart and shattered the lives of their inhabitants. Today a walk—or trip by black taxi—up the **Falls Road** or down the **Shankill** can offer some insights into hard-held views, while the citizens go about their business. Red, white and blue kerbstones or green, white and orange ones run along neat rows of terraced houses that have replaced the 19th-century slums. These houses may look the same; but where one gable is emblazoned with republican figures of resistance and slogans promising *saoirse* (freedom), in another street King William on his horse rides triumphant, while masked paramilitaries declare *No surrender.* Continuously updated and repainted, these murals have become as much a part of the streetscape as any more traditional art form and are a living history worth seeing.

Arts, galleries, and artists

When the Cirque and Grand Opera House reopened after its restoration in 1980 it signalled a revival of evening entertainment in the city. Mercury and Shakespeare have survived on the outside, while the gold-leaf cherubs within have witnessed the talents of

Sarah Bernhardt and *Orson Welles.* Nowadays Belfast hosts several arts festivals, including the Belfast Festival at Queen's, the summertime Féile an Phobail (West Belfast People's Festival), the FLAME month of world music during the Belfast Civic Festival, and the Cinemagic International Film Festival for the Young in December. Numerous pubs, such as the **Empire**, provide live music; the historic **Ulster Hall** offers music among other events; and the **Waterfront Hall** promises the latest facilities for the world-class acts that perform here.

Theatrical venues include the **Lyric**, where *Liam Neeson* performed in his early days; the **Crescent Arts Centre** in the university area; and the **Civic Arts Centre**.

As well as its wealth of street art, Belfast boasts many artists, including *Basil Blackshaw, Tom Carr,* and *T. P. Flanagan.* There are several art galleries, principally the **Ormeau Baths Gallery** in Ormeau Avenue. Originally the public baths, it opened as the city's premier visual arts space in 1995. The **Old Museum Arts Centre** and the **Engine Room** have temporary modern art exhibitions. Some of the work of the Belfast-born artists *Sir John Lavery* and *William Conor* can be seen in the Ulster Museum.

Outside in Belfast

When the city gets too much for them, the people of Belfast take to the hills. A popular climb up the Napoleon's Nose of **Cave Hill**, past the neolithic caves to the fort at the top, rewards the energetic with fine views.

The Lagan Valley, along the old canal route, offers wildlife and ancient monument, passing over bridges and along river banks.

The peaceful old mill village of **Edenderry**, hidden away on a river bend, resounds to marching feet and Lambeg drums on the 12th of July, when Orangemen gather here in an open field. Yet more ancient ways are suggested by the **Giant's Ring** portal tomb a short walk away.

Other green oases include the **Ormeau Park**, one of the city's largest, and further out the 80-acre **Redburn Country Park**. To the east are the rolling parklands of **Stormont**, site of Northern Ireland's former Parliament.

Ireland and the world

St Patrick's Day Parade, O'Connell Street, Dublin.

From a purely geographical point of view, Ireland is a modestly sized island with a small and dispersed population and with limited mineral resources. Isolated on the periphery of the European continent and 6,000 miles east of America, it is not a strategically important location. Yet it has forged a sphere of influence that belies the physical attributes of what at first appears to be a very unexceptional country. The causes, varied and diverse, have culminated through the ages to achieve this effect.

Christianity arrived in Ireland some time before the 5th century and quickly became the religious creed of the people. As is clear from the examples of Glendalough and Clonmacnoise, monasticism proved to be a popular expression of religious practice in Ireland. Such was the success of this model that it was exported to the Continent, as Irish monks travelled throughout lands thrown into disarray by the barbarian invasions of the Dark Ages. At a time when Christianity was under fire, Irish monks are credited with the founding of major religious centres in Europe, such as *St Fursa* at Péronne in France and *St Colmán* at Bobbio in Italy. It is from this era that Ireland wins its reputation as the 'island of saints and scholars.'

In the 16th, 17th and 18th centuries, when Catholicism in Ireland was experiencing persecution, the link with the Continent was rekindled. An Irish College was established at Paris in 1587, and another thirty around the continent followed in order that Irish priests could train for their vocation.

It was not just men of God who turned to the outside world. The 'Wild Geese'—exiled Irish mercenaries—were active in the armies of Europe up to the end of the Napoleonic wars. Throughout the centuries Irish revolutionaries would turn to Catholic countries such as France and Spain in their attempts to overthrow English rule at home. Despite a ban on doing so, hundreds of Irish people went to Spain to fight on both sides of the civil war in the late 1930s. Tens of thousands more fought in both world wars on the side of the British forces, while at the same time the IRA was trying to solicit the support of Germany in their bid to oust the British from Ireland.

Irish writers have also established a presence in the world. **James Joyce,** for example, has been called the first European. In his life he lived in Trieste, Zürich, Rome and Paris as well as Dublin. Other artists, such as **W. B. Yeats** and **J. M. Synge,** as well as Joyce's contemporary **Samuel Beckett,** also chose to live in Paris. For them it was a conscious cultural and artistic decision to remove themselves from the Anglo-American world in favour of a new world outlook.

Once Ireland had gained independence it went about establishing its national identity and actively strengthening diplomatic ties. Ireland's position on neutrality during the Second World War may not have gone down well with **Winston Churchill** but won near-universal acclaim for **Éamon de Valera** in his address on the autonomy of small states to the League of Nations. From this point on Ireland would begin to assume a role in world affairs with a distinct voice. In 1955 Ireland was admitted to the United Nations, playing an active role in peace-keeping missions since 1958 around the world. In Third World countries, Ireland has a strong tradition of providing bilateral aid and humanitarian volunteer workers. A founder-member of the Council of Europe in 1949, Ireland would eventually become a full member of the European Economic Community in 1973. In 1999 the Government controversially ratified Ireland's involvement with the 'Partnership for Peace' programme, which is a part of NATO operations, an organisation Ireland has traditionally steered away from.

Yet it is emigration, more than any other factor, that has secured Ireland's standing in the world. Some 40 million Americans claim some Irish ancestry, and of these about a quarter claim only Irish roots. In Australia—once the destination for transported prisoners from Ireland—almost 30 per cent of the population are thought to be of Irish descent. Approximately a million people of Irish birth are estimated to live in Britain, a figure that can be multiplied many times over when second and third-generation Irish are taken into account. At present there are no clear statistics relating to their numbers, but the recognition of the Irish as a national minority for the purposes of the census in 1999 should help realise the full import of England as a traditional destination for emigrants.

The legions of Irish emigrants had a profound effect on those countries they went to. In the United States they were first employed in manual labour, but it was thanks to their efforts that major rail routes and the modern cities were built. Their children, naturalised citizens, climbed the social ladder, becoming a powerful force within their various countries. **John F. Kennedy,** a descendant of an emigrant from County Wexford, is a good example.

The nature of Ireland's relationship with the rest of the world in modern times has evolved in new and exciting ways. Because of developments such as the International Financial Services Centre, Ireland is now recognised as a world-class participant alongside London, New York, and Hong Kong. Over a thousand 'blue-chip' multinational corporations have selected Ireland as their European base of operations, and strong efforts are being made to establish the country as the 'e-commerce' hub of Europe. Such is the growth of the economy, one of the leading economies in the OECD, that people from around the world are being drawn to the 'Celtic Tiger'.

Popular culture is also at an all-time high. The staging of the MTV Europe awards in 1999 in the Point Depot, Dublin, was symbolic in more ways than one. Normally staged in cities such as Paris, London, or Milan, it recognised the musical achievements of groups such as U2 and Boyzone. The Point was also the stage from where the largest production of Irish music and dance, 'Riverdance'—itself a global phenomenon—was first introduced to the world.

Bound by its restrictions as a small island nation, Ireland has learnt how to overcome and even exploit its limitations to become something of a world force.

Counties Down and Armagh

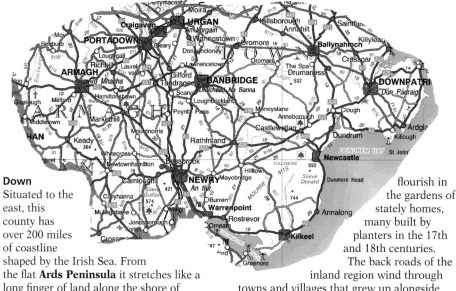

Down

Situated to the east, this county has over 200 miles of coastline shaped by the Irish Sea. From the flat **Ards Peninsula** it stretches like a long finger of land along the shore of **Strangford Lough** to the purple-and-grey granite peaks of the **Mourne Mountains** and inland to the Georgian splendour of **Hillsborough**. Though associated by legend with *St Patrick*, this immensely varied county has uncovered secrets of prehistoric times that suggest a culture in existence long before the arrival of Christianity in the 5th century.

This is drumlin country, where little hills of boulder clay left over from the Ice Age pervade the landscape, while cairns and portal tombs stand tall in fields. The exposed nature of its coastline and proximity to Britain meant that it was subjected to frequent invasion from Vikings and Normans and, later, planters from Scotland and England. Many of the Early Christian churches were destroyed, though there remain several sites that confirm the status of the county during the Dark Ages as 'a light of northern Europe'. Historic castles, many now in ruins, stood defence along the eastern peninsula, while in sheltered parts the mild climate allows rare plants to flourish in the gardens of stately homes, many built by planters in the 17th and 18th centuries.

The back roads of the inland region wind through towns and villages that grew up alongside tributaries of the Rivers Bann and Lagan around the linen industry, which reached its peak during the 18th century. Rich in land, County Down farmers of today explore such diverse activities as ostrich farming and daffodil cultivation. Along the coast, seaside towns and picturesque fishing villages provide opportunities for golfing, sailing, birdwatching, and walks along golden sandy strands, while trails through the Mourne Mountains, which 'sweep down to the sea,' follow in smugglers' footsteps. The sheltered shores of **Strangford Lough** offer sanctuary to hundreds of marine species and birds. In recent years, as people have sought to escape the main centres of political unrest, the population of several towns has increased and with it leisure and transport facilities, all of which go towards making a visit to County Down both pleasurable and memorable.

Armagh

The varied scenery of County Armagh, the smallest county in Ulster, ranges from the

Mount Stewart House and Gardens, Co. Down.

reclaimed wetlands on the peaty shores of **Lough Neagh** to the orchard regions around **Loughgall** and **Portadown**, filled with pink blossom in springtime, the rivers that once turned the wheels of flax mills, the lush **Clare Glen**, down to the mountainous Ring of Gullion and the forest park. The venerable town of **Armagh** has been the ecclesiastical capital of Ireland since the Middle Ages. However, its much older heritage stems from pre-Christian times, when the ancient people of Ulster ruled for six centuries from their hilltop fort at **Eamhain Mhacha**, till it was burned by forces from Tara in the 4th century. The area was supposedly ruled by *Macha*, a legendary warrior queen who, according to the Annals of the Four Masters, ruled from 658 BC until her death seven years later. Christian influences came to dominate with the building of an Early Christian stone church, attributed by legend to *St Patrick*.

The county moved into the industrial age with the development of the linen industry, which helped to shape the social and cultural life of parts of Northern Ireland and was centred on what is now called the Linen Homelands, to which **Lurgan** and **Portadown** both belong. The **Newry Canal** provided the means of transporting linen to the Irish Sea and north to the coast through Lough Neagh. A birdwatchers' heaven, the lough shores are home to thousands of wildfowl. Excellent fishing country, it is threaded by the Rivers Blackwater and Bann, which yield salmon as well as the unique species of lake trout known as the dollaghan.

The county has suffered throughout the years of the Troubles, with strong political beliefs being maintained and manifested through parades as well as the fortified police stations and British army posts still visible throughout the region. Armagh is a beautiful county, and great efforts are being made to boost tourism in this ancient region.

The cathedral town of **Newry** lies between the Mourne Mountains on the east and Slieve Gullion to the south-west, where the tribes of Leinster met the Northmen during the days of the Fianna legend, resulting in the town being destroyed several times in battles for control of the north. Close to the border with the Republic, Newry's fortunes have been mixed, but its location at the Gap of the North has given it a place in history both past and present.

County Down

Bangor and the Ards Peninsula

The **Ards Peninsula** (*an Aird,* 'the point') stretches 23 miles from the 'peaked hill' of **Bangor** to **Ballyquintin Point**. A busy commuter town, Bangor is a popular seaside resort for holiday-makers and day-trippers. The town itself originates from the era of *James Hamilton,* a 17th-century Scottish settler. Early Bangor can be seen in the fragment of wall near **Bangor Abbey** parish church, with its 15th-century tower and 17th-century octagonal spire.

In the dormitory town of **Holywood** (*Ard Mhic Nasca*) east of Bangor are the ruins of a 16th-century Franciscan monastery and a 70-foot mast known as the maypole. Allegedly, when a Dutch ship ran aground in 1700 on May Eve the mast was cut down and used as part of the celebrations.

The **Ulster Folk and Transport Museum** is set in the beautiful parkland estate of **Cultra Manor**. This extensive open-air museum gives impressions of rural and urban Irish life over the past few hundred years. The transport museum houses the Irish Railway Collection and examples of the Dandy Horse, the Velocipede, veteran motor cars, and a 1982 De Lorean gull-wing stainless steel car. Aircraft exhibits include the full-scale model of the monoplane used by *Harry Ferguson,* the first Irish person to fly.

The North Down Coastal Path will bring you to **Crawfordsburn Country Park** or the beach at **Helen's Bay**. The 17th-century **Old Inn** at Crawfordsburn was the honeymoon venue of the Belfast-born writer *C. S. Lewis* (1898–1963) and his American wife. On a hilltop towards Newtownards stands the three-storey **Helen's Tower**, with *Browning's* inscription of *Lady Helen Dufferin's* 'fair countenance'. In 1994 the Somme Heritage Centre opened here to commemorate local men killed in the First World War, while a replica, the **Ulster Memorial Tower**, was erected on the Somme battlefield. The summit at **Scrabo Hill Country Park**, with

its **Memorial Tower** from 1857, offers some excellent views of Strangford Lough; and the **Ark Open Farm** opposite has rare breeds of sheep, cattle, and poultry.

Strangford and Lecale

The 15-mile stretch of water known as **Strangford Lough** is a maritime nature reserve, of world importance for its wildlife. It is a refuge for seals, particularly at its southern end; and tens of thousands of seabirds winter here.

Arriving in the old fishing village of **Killyleagh** (*Cill Ó Laoch*), you see the fairy-tale turrets of **Killyleagh Castle** come into view, built in the 12th century by *John de Courcy*; the turrets were added in the 1850s. The naturalist *Sir Hans Sloane* grew up in Killyleagh, and his collection was the basis for the founding of the British Museum in London. The eastern lough shore passes the 18th-century **Mount Stewart House and Gardens**.

To the north-east the village of **Carrowdore** is the resting place of the poet *Louis MacNeice* (1907–63) and also the venue of the annual 'Carrowdore 100' motorbike race.

In **Grey Abbey**, an antique-shoppers' haven, stands one of the most complete Cistercian abbeys in Ireland, set in mature parkland. The monks practised herbal remedies in the romantic physic garden here, which has been re-created. Passing on through the fishing village of **Kircubbin** you come to **Portaferry**, where you can visit the 'Exploris' aquarium and marine biology station. The remains of a tower-house can be seen in **Castle Lane**.

Donaghadee is a seaside town with a lighthouse that used to be linked by a regular sea service to Portpatrick in Scotland. Some celebrated visitors included *John Keats,* who complained of the local people's objections to 'my mode of dress.' Not so deterred was *Peter the Great* of Russia, who stopped at **Grace Neill's Inn**

(1697–98). Undoubtedly adding to the pub lore, the writer *Brendan Behan* was given the job of painting the lighthouse after the Second World War. **Drumawhey Junction** at **Donaghadee** has an extensive passenger-carrying miniature railway.

The **Copeland Islands—Big Isle**, **Lighthouse**, and **Mew**—are accessible by boat from Donaghadee. These uninhabited places covered in spring turf are left to the rabbits, birds, and flowers, while summer brings weekend visitors. **Cross** is a bird sanctuary and observatory where flocks of Manx shearwaters nest. Less homely were the ten thousand Williamite soldiers who landed with *Marshal Schomberg* in 1689 in **Groomsport**, where two of the 18th-century **Cockle Row** harbour cottages are still intact.

A five-minute journey across the **'Narrows'** brings you to **Strangford** ('violent fjord') on the **Lecale Peninsula** (*Leath Chathail*, 'Cathal's half'), where the sea traffic was controlled by the tower-houses on each shore.

The fishing village of **Ardglass**, with its new marina at **Phennick Cove**, was once the busiest port in Ulster. Still noted for its herrings, it had a row of fortified buildings around the harbour between the 14th and 16th centuries.

Patrick's Country

The **Ballynoe Stone Circle** and **Rathmullen Mote** are both situated on the maze of little roads leading to the county town, **Downpatrick** (*Dún Pádraig*, 'St Patrick's fort'). A statue of the saint stands on top of the nearby **Slieve Patrick**. In 1176 *John de Courcy* claimed to have brought the remains of the saints *Colm Cille* and *Bríd* here; and it was he who added *Patrick* to the town's name. It was once believed that the saint is buried on the great hill at Downpatrick, or alternatively under the cathedral, and a huge granite slab was placed on the hill in 1900 to protect it from pilgrims removing handfuls of earth.

Downpatrick Cathedral is a kind of conglomeration of centuries of churches that were continuously plundered. Today's building is an 18th and 19th-century

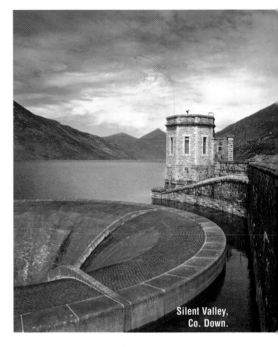

Silent Valley, Co. Down.

reconstruction. Some fine Georgian dwellings stand in the **Mall** leading up to the cathedral, particularly the **Southwell School** of 1733. The **County Museum and St Patrick's Heritage Centre** were formerly the county jail. A signposted way from the museum leads to the **Mound of Down** earthworks, while across the River Quoile are the ruins of **Inch Abbey**, a 12th-century Cistercian monastery where Irishmen were refused entry.

The Mournes

Red, purple, and grey, the **Mourne Mountains** are a 15-mile long range that fills the south-eastern corner of County Down, between Newcastle and Rostrevor. Driving through the granite mountains is possible only from the fishing port of **Kilkeel**, up 1,200 feet, overlooking **Spelga Dam**, before descending to **Hilltown**. Old tracks thread a way through this region along the smugglers' route of **Brandy Pad**, which begins at **Bloody Bridge**, site of a massacre in 1641. The **Great Mourne Wall**, built around the reservoir in the glacier-formed **Silent Valley**,

'St Patrick's Grave',
Co. Down.

scales fifteen mountains and provides a steep guide to Slieve Donard (2,796 feet), named after St Dónart, who lived in a stone cell on the top.

Following the coastline, you come to the village of **Annalong**, which has an 1800s water-powered corn mill. The premier port of **Kilkeel** has a Nautical Centre, and the ruined church of its name is in the busy town centre. To the west the **Kilfeaghan**

portal tomb has a 35-ton capstone, while the ruins of **Greencastle** stand formidably at the entrance to **Carlingford Lough**. The castle was vacated in the 17th century after 350 troubled years.

Along the shores of Carlingford is the small 19th-century resort of **Rostrevor**, where the mild climate encourages palm trees and mimosas. An obelisk stands to its most famous son, *Robert Ross*, who captured

Washington in 1814 and burnt the White House. Behind the town, in **Kilbroney Forest Park**, stands the **Cloghmore**. This enormous boulder was either carried by an Ice Age glacier to the mountain or thrown by the great *Fionn mac Cumhaill*. **Warrenpoint** is a picturesque resort arranged around the large Diamond, and the nearby **Burren Heritage Centre** gives information about the area. Travelling inland through **Hilltown**, the small roads off to the right lead to **Gowards portal tomb** and a large fairy thorn, immune from cutting for fear of bad luck.

Mid-Down

The Brontë homeland is centred on Drumballyroney Parish School, just past **Rathfriland**, where *Patrick Prunty* (later Brontë), father to *Charlotte, Anne, and Emily*, taught. Patrick was the son of *Hugh Prunty*, a storyteller, and it is thought that many of the stories of Ireland heard by the sisters gave them ideas for their novels. **Banbridge** (*Droichead na Banna*) is the industrial centre of this area and gateway to the Linen Homelands region. The town's **Ferguson Linen Centre** is the only producer of double damask linen in the world. **McConville's Flax Farm**, a water-powered scutching mill and the former Banford Bleach Works near **Gilford** give an insight into this one-time thriving industry.

Ulster's most famous Stone Age monument, the impressive **Legananny portal tomb**, stands on the slope of **Slieve Croob** on the road to the agricultural centre of **Ballynahinch**. This valley was the scene of the last battle of the United Irishmen, some of whom are buried in **Saintfield**. Nearby are the magnificent **Rowallane Gardens** and the natural lough of **Ballykeel Lough Erne**, stocked with trout. To the west the Georgian **Market House** and **Court House** grace the town of **Hillsborough**, where the Hillsborough agreement was signed. The house has seen many negotiators pass through the magnificent wrought-iron gates, which were taken from Rich Hill Castle in County Armagh. **Hillsborough Fort**, built around 1650, stands beside **St Malachy's Church**.

DON'T MISS

- **Mount Stewart House and Gardens** and the Temple of the Winds: The house and famous gardens by Strangford Lough, with exotic plants, mythical beasts, and spectacular views.
- The **Ulster Folk and Transport Museum** at **Cultra**: The extensive open-air museum at Cultra gives impressions of rural and urban life over the past few hundred years and also houses transport and railway collections.
- The **Mourne Mountains**: Walk in the famous mountains along smugglers' paths and the **Silent Valley**, or climb the highest peak, **Slieve Donard**, for spectacular views.
- Visit the monastery ruins at **Grey Abbey**, where the herb garden will restore you before you tackle the antique-shops of this pleasant town.
- Take a trip out to the **Copeland Islands** to observe the many birds nesting, and stroll among the wildflowers.

ALL-WEATHER OPTIONS

- '**Exploris**' at **Portaferry**, where the teeming environment of the lough is re-created and injured marine animals are cared for.
- The **Nautilus Centre** at **Kilkeel**: a living celebration of Ireland's fishing industry at this 19th-century port.
- Sit with the ghosts of John Keats, Brendan Behan or even Peter the Great in **Grace Neill's** 17th-century inn at **Donaghadee**.

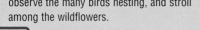

County Armagh

Armagh

Predating Canterbury in England as a Christian religious site, the town of Armagh (*Ard Mhacha*, 'Macha's height') is named after the Celtic queen *Macha*. It is the seat of both the Anglican and the Catholic Primate of Ireland. The story of Armagh can be followed in the visitor complex of **St Patrick's Trian** (deriving its name from the ancient division of the town into three districts or *trians*), which chronicles the development of the town through the ages. It offers historic Armagh, the life and work of St Patrick, and the Land of Lilliput from *Gulliver's Travels*, relating to the time *Jonathan Swift* spent in the region. For the futurist, **Armagh Observatory and Planetarium** give a different experience. The 200-year-old observatory has the largest public telescope in Ireland. The Planetarium offers star theatre, while the 'Eartharium' Gallery is designed to give visitors a 'global view of our home.'

The Georgian **Mall** is a graceful park that was the site of cock-fighting and horse-racing until the 18th-century Church of Ireland primate, *Richard Robinson*, decided they were unsuitable activities for a seat of learning. The Royal Irish Fusiliers Museum is housed in the **Sovereign's House**, damaged in an explosion in 1993, built from stone left over from the courthouse, which is under restoration. **Armagh Public Library** has a copy of *Gulliver's Travels* corrected in Swift's hand.

A church of some denomination has stood for fifteen centuries on the hill where **St Patrick's (Church of Ireland) Cathedral** now stands. Its story is told in the 9th-century Book of Armagh, housed in Trinity College, Dublin.

Around the cathedral, the narrow streets radiate in a mediaeval pattern. The twin spires of **St Patrick's (Catholic) Cathedral**, built between 1840 and 1873,

are visible across the valley. Inside it is almost Byzantine, with exuberant colour, 'Armagh marble', stained glass, and mosaics. Just beyond the gates of **Archbishop Robinson's Demesne**, where the Georgian **Palace Stables and Courtyard** are beautifully restored, are the ruins of the 13th-century **Franciscan friary**, dissolved in 1542 and subsequently further destroyed, to the point where much of the stone was quarried for use in the demesne building.

Around Armagh

The ancient capital of Ulster at *Eamhain Mhacha* or Navan Fort is associated in mythology with *Conchúr mac Neasa* and *Cú Chulainn*, who defended Ulster single-handedly against *Méabh* of Connacht. A huge circular hilltop enclosure with a mound on the top, its site was marked on *Ptolemy's* map of the known world in the year 2nd century. It offers some magnificent views on a clear day. The 'King's Stables', a 10-foot deep pond nearby, produced some Bronze Age remains. Surrounded by wild cherry trees, it stands within sight of the Bronze Age **Haughey's Fort**. **EMA** is a centre where visitors can explore early, Celtic and contemporary Navan through journeys into real and other worlds.

This is Ireland's apple region; and **Loughgall**, north of Armagh, is surrounded by orchards. It is also home to the museum of the Orange Order, which contains sashes, banners and weapons from the Battle of the Diamond in 1795 between Protestant Peep o' Day Boys and Catholic Defenders at Diamond Hill, after which Protestant farmers founded the Orange Order. The gates from the early 17th-century manor of **Rich Hill** to the south-east were moved to Hillsborough Castle in 1936. In the village of **Kilmore**, the lower half of a 3rd-century round tower stands in the present parish church, making it possibly the oldest church remains in Ireland.

Lough Neagh and north Armagh

Lough Neagh, the largest lake in Ireland, is immortalised in *Thomas Moore's* ballad 'Let Erin Remember'. Covering 150 square miles, it is bordered by five counties. According to legend, the giant *Fionn mac Cumhaill* tore a piece of earth from the ground and, flinging it into the Irish Sea, created the lough—and the Isle of Man.

The lough provides the main recreation area for north Armagh, but it is also commercially fished for freshwater herring, 'dollaghan' (lake trout), and wild eels. This is a thriving industry, and the eels are exported to the Netherlands and Germany.

The Newry Canal region

Lurgan (*an Lorgain*, 'the strip of land') was once prosperous from the manufacture of damask linen at nearby **Waringstown**. Formerly a huge industry, it influenced the development of entire communities in this area, and the small lanes off the main street recall the lives of the weavers. Nowadays the manufacture has shrunk to a small, high-quality business. William Street, Lurgan, was the birthplace of the writer *George Russell* (known by his pen-name, Æ); the town was also home to the 19th-century champion greyhound 'Master McGrath', immortalised in the town's coat of arms.

The first 'new town' was **Craigavon**, with its 'balancing' artificial lakes, offering water sports and trout fishing. The former linen town of **Portadown** (*Port an Dúnáin*) moved into synthetic manufacture in the 1950s. The construction of the now disused Newry Canal in 1740 and the arrival of the railway in 1842 ensured that Portadown remained at the hub of transport routes. The **Newry Canal Footpath** provides a beautiful walk to Newry through a corridor of willow trees and bulrushes.

Moneypenny's Lock is the last lock before

Navan Fort, Co. Armagh.

the canal joins the river, and the restored lock-keeper's house offers a glimpse of past life.

Along the Newry Canal you pass **Scarva**, the place where hospitality was offered to *King William* on his way to the Battle of the Boyne in 1690. A sham fight is held each year on 13 July. The settlement here, however, goes back to ancient times, when Ulster chieftains built huge defensive earthworks known as the Black Pig's Dyke or Dane's Cast, which extend over most of

Gulliver,
St Patrick's Trian Interpretative Centre,
Armagh.

the borders of Ulster.

Newry

The cathedral town of **Newry** (*an tIúr*, 'the yew tree'), is named after a tree said to have been planted by *St Patrick*. With a small port, it is connected to the sea at Carlingford Lough by the canal. A Cistercian monastery was established here near a 12th-century stone castle, which was repeatedly attacked throughout the centuries. The abbey was taken over by Grand Marshal *Nicholas Bagenal* in the 1570s, but no trace of it remains. The stone castle was finally destroyed by *Shane O'Neill* in 1566. In 1578 Bagenal used the rubble from the castle to construct the first Protestant church in Ireland, east of the Town Hall, which sits astride the river on a three-arched bridge, making it half in County Down and half in County Armagh. The original tower of Bagenal's church remains.

Newry is a main shopping centre, and just outside the town the market of **Jonesborough** draws big crowds at the weekends, the volume of cross-border shoppers varying according to the fluctuation of the Irish pound against sterling.

South Armagh

The Forest Park that covers the lower slopes of Slieve Gullion is situated south-west of Newry. The **Ring of Gullion** forms a circle around the peak, which features in the 4th-century prose epic *Táin Bó Chuaille* ('The Cattle Raid of Cooley'). The hills go down towards **Crossmaglen**, a village with a huge market square, a British army base, and a reputation for lacemaking.

The landscape to the north-west, studded with small lakes, reminds us of the once-thriving linen industry, and many derelict mills are still visible. **Keady** is a small village, formerly an important linen centre. The heritage centre is in a converted mill. Back towards Newry is **Bessbrook**, a town founded in 1845 by a Quaker industrialist to house workers in the huge flax mill. This model village of local granite buildings was laid out around two squares and became the inspiration for the Cadbury village of Bournville in England.

DON'T MISS
- **Armagh Cathedrals**: The mediaeval St Patrick's (Church of Ireland) Cathedral and chapter-house and the 19th-century St Patrick's (Catholic) Cathedral, with its tall spires and brilliantly coloured interior.
- Ireland's prehistoric capital, **Eamhain Mhacha**, and the visitors' centre, where you can explore early, Celtic and contemporary Navan through journeys into real worlds and otherworlds.
- See Gulliver in the Land of Lilliput and hear his story at the exhibition in **St Patrick's Trian** in **Armagh**.
- Take the 8-mile drive through the coniferous **Slieve Gullion Forest Park**, which leads to a lake and views of the Ring of Gullion, a circle of small hills around the peak (1,827 feet).
- The **Newry Town Trail** brings you around the streets and attractions of this border town at the Gap of the North.

ALL-WEATHER OPTIONS
- The **Armagh Planetarium and Observatory**, with Ireland's largest telescope, star theatre, and Astropark.
- Trace history to prehistoric times in the exhibits at the **Armagh County Museum**.
- Visit the upgraded 17th-century **Ardress House**, with its working farmyard and also the nearby gas-lit **Argory**.

Twentieth-Century Ireland

Éamon de Valera and Douglas Hyde (1920).

Parnell, the leader of Irish nationalism, fell from power in 1890. He had been cited as co-respondent in a divorce action and died, aged forty-five, the following year. Some of his oldest lieutenants ·had turned against him; a minority remained fanatically loyal to him and to his memory. It took nationalism almost a generation to fully recover from the trauma of the Parnell split.

By the first decade of the 20th century the forces that determined modern Ireland were in position. Home rule was back on the agenda after 1910, when a minority Liberal government was kept in power by the Irish Party. The Home Rule Bill of 1912 was passed by the House Commons but was not due to come into force until September 1914.

The response of the Ulster Unionists to the threat of home rule was to arm illegally and to organise a kind of rebellion of their own, all in the name of the British constitution. They did this with the open collusion of the British Conservative opposition. They formed a militia, the Ulster Volunteer Force; in response, radical southern nationalists imported arms and formed the Irish Volunteers.

The stage seemed set for civil war on the implementation of home rule. But a month before it was due to come into effect, the Great War broke out. Home rule was suspended for the duration.

The Irish Volunteers split on the issue of whether they should support the British war effort. The minority who stayed aloof from the war were in turn infiltrated by the Irish Republican Brotherhood, the most radical and uncompromising element in the nationalist tradition. It was the IRB that planned and carried out the Easter Rising of 1916, in which they held the centre of Dublin for a week. After their surrender, sixteen of the leaders were executed by the British. This, combined with the threat to conscript Irishmen to make good the horrifying British losses on the western front, drove nationalists away from the Irish Party and towards the more uncompromising Sinn Féin, under the leadership of *Éamon de Valera* and *Arthur Griffith.*

Sinn Féin swept all before it in nationalist Ireland in the post-war elections of 1918. But its republican demand for full independence was even more anathema to unionists than home rule had been. A guerrilla war began in the south in 1919 as the Irish Republican Army—very loosely the armed wing of Sinn Féin—pressed the republican demand ever more forcefully. Its leading figure was the charismatic *Michael Collins,* still only in his twenties. The British government of *David Lloyd George,* now dependent on Conservative support, partitioned Ireland, giving Ulster Unionists the six counties of the north-east, where there was an aggregate Protestant majority.

The southern war ended in a truce in 1921, followed by a treaty that gave the twenty-six counties dominion status—more than home rule and less than full independence. There followed a short but typically nasty civil war between those who accepted the treaty and those who thought it a sell-out. The pro-Treaty side won, but not before the war claimed over a thousand lives, among them that of Michael Collins.

The south settled into a forty-year period dominated first by the pro-Treaty party but later by Éamon de Valera's Fianna Fáil, the main group to emerge from the anti-Treaty side. De Valera was in power, with only two short breaks, from 1932 to 1959 and the party itself until 1973. Since then it has alternated with various coalitions and in the 1990s has even been forced to coalesce with minority parties in order to retain power.

De Valera's Ireland remained neutral during the Second World War. It attempted to build up native industry behind tariff barriers from the 1930s on— a policy that was at first successful but was reversed in the 1960s under de Valera's successor, *Seán Lemass*. The country finally left the British Commonwealth in 1949, ironically during one of de Valera's brief absences from power.

From the 1960s on, the old consensus was eroded by growing international influences, of which television and consumerism were the most important. Ireland's post-war boom came late and was nearly reversed in the late 1970s and 1980s by a period of economic mismanagement that caused the resumption of emigration—something that the 1960s had seemed to have eliminated for good. By the 1990s, however, the damage had been repaired and the Irish economy had one of the highest growth rates in the developed world.

All this was accompanied by a cultural renaissance, both at popular and elite level and by a young, well-educated population. The international success of 'Riverdance' on the one hand and the award of the 1995 Nobel Prize for Literature to *Séamus Heaney* on the other were obvious symbols of this new optimism.

That is the south. The north was a different story. It had been carved out for the convenience of the local Protestant majority but was never accepted as legitimate by the Catholic minority trapped within its borders. That minority was as much as one-third (and latterly more) of the population, too big to be absorbed in the way that the tiny Protestant minority in the south had been. Instead the local Unionist devolved government in Belfast—assured of a permanent majority—put in place a series of measures that discriminated against Catholics. Public employment, public housing and the gerrymandering of local electoral boundaries were just some of the areas in which the Unionists ensured that Catholics would remain second-class citizens. There were occasional outbursts from the IRA, especially in the later 1950s, but when the real trouble came after 1968, it took most people by surprise.

The present Northern Ireland troubles have their roots deep in history and in the opposing aspirations of two separate communities. In the late 1960s a civil rights movement protested in the streets for the removal of discriminatory legislation and practices. This met with resistance from

unionists. British troops were called in following widespread civil disorder in which nationalist working-class areas in Belfast and Derry came under attack from Protestant mobs. The situation deteriorated further following a split in the IRA, which produced the hard-line 'Provisional IRA', committed to a paramilitary campaign aimed at forcing a British withdrawal from Northern Ireland. They were matched by Protestant militias dedicated to the retention of the union and Protestant supremacy. The consequent decades saw a catalogue of atrocities, which have barely affected the underlying strategic realities. An attempt to cut the knot of civil strife in the 1970s by forming a devolved power-sharing Executive foundered on the twin rocks of loyalist and republican opposition.

Northern Ireland from the mid-70s to the mid-90s was dominated by civil disorder. Republican and loyalist paramilitaries alike were responsible for many atrocities and murders. A series of republican hunger strikes in the early 80s led to a rise in electoral support for Sinn Féin, the political wing of the IRA. Partly in order to shore up the moderate nationalists in the SDLP, the Irish Government under Garret FitzGerald negotiated the Anglo-Irish Agreement of 1985 with Margaret Thatcher's administration. This gave Dublin a formal voice in the affairs of Northern Ireland for the first time, a fact that infuriated unionists of every description. However, the violence did not stop.

By the early 90s it was clear to most people that the IRA could neither win their war nor be defeated. Gradually a peace process developed that involved the two governments, all the constitutional parties, and—crucially—representatives of paramilitaries on both sides. The eventual result was the Belfast Agreement of 1998, which—after a long wrangle over the decommissioning of paramilitary weapons—was finally implemented in December 1999 with the formation of a devolved cross-party Executive, including two Sinn Féin ministers, under the leadership of the unionist David Trimble. It was a stunning achievement and almost certainly marks the end of the troubles. Northern Ireland can face the future with real reason to hope.

Likewise the Republic. The unprecedented boom in the second half of the 90s has made it the fastest-growing economy in the developed world. Ireland north and south approaches the new millennium with renewed optimism.

Northern Ireland

Begin your journey in **Newry**, the old mercantile and border town situated between two mountain peaks. Only the tower of its Protestant parish church dates from 1578: the rest of the building was reconstructed after being burnt down by the forces of *King James II* in 1689. The 18th-century **Newry River Canal**, the first navigational canal built in Ireland, is now undergoing restoration to open it for leisure use.

Turn right from Newry centre and follow the A2 road to the picturesque resort of **Warrenpoint**, passing on your left **Narrow Water Castle**, a high, rectangular 16th-century plantation tower perched on a rocky islet. Continue through the 19th-century resort of **Rostrevor**, past the Oakwood to the village of **Kilkeel**, headquarters of Ireland's fishing industry, and on to **Annalong** marine park and working corn mill. The coast road continues at the foot of the **Mourne Mountains**, presenting spectacular seascape views. **Newcastle**, an attractive resort at the foot of the range, is the starting point for a two-hour climb of **Slieve Donard** (2,795 feet), with its stunning vistas.

Leaving the town, take the A50 road to **Castlewellan**, with its Forest Park and National Arboretum. Nearby stands **Drumena Cashel**, an Early Christian farm enclosure and souterrain. Alternatively, from **Kilkeel** you can turn left onto the B27, the only driving route through the Mourne Mountains, up 1,200 feet overlooking **Spelga Dam** before your descent. Take a right turn onto the B180 past the dense woods of **Tollymore Forest Park** to rejoin the A2 at **Dundrum**, where the castle has stood for four hundred years high among trees on the shores of Dundrum Bay. Join the A25 road for **Downpatrick** with a right turn at the village of **Clough**.

Downpatrick (*Dún Pádraig*, 'St Patrick's fort'), the county town (which gave the county its name), is an area closely connected in legend with Ireland's patron saint. Tradition held that he is buried under the main altar of **St Patrick's Cathedral**, built on the hill where he reputedly constructed his first church. **Downpatrick Museum** is situated in the former jail. Continue to **Saul** (*Sabhall*, 'barn'), about a mile away, a small village where St Patrick was reputed to have celebrated his first Mass on Irish soil, in a barn. At this point either go on to **Strangford**, a fishing village at the mouth of the lough, to take

TOURING ROUTE
Newry to Belfast

the car ferry to **Portaferry** for the scenic **Ards Peninsula**, or take the A20 road along the shores of **Strangford Lough**. Make for the antique-shoppers' haven of **Grey Abbey**, where stands one of the most complete Cistercian abbeys in Ireland, set in mature parkland. The monks practised herbal remedies in the romantic physic garden, which has been re-created.

Further on are the magnificent **Mount Stewart House and Gardens**, which feature stone dodos and mythological figures among a vast array of plants, including bamboos and palms, which flourish in this sheltered setting. Also worth seeing is the topiary garden, with its Irish harp, shamrock, and red-leaved Red Hand of Ulster. The octagonal Temple of the Winds offers great views of the lough. The next stop is **Newtownards**; then take a left for **Scrabo Country Park and Tower**, where the Somme Heritage Centre is situated, or continue on the A21 for the village of **Crawfordsburn**.

Alternative route: The coast road of the peninsula offers some spectacular views. Leaving **Portaferry**, take an immediate right turn to the National Trust's 19th-century village of **Kearney**. Rejoin the A2 near the golden beach at **Cloghy**. From the fishing village of **Portavogie** pass on through the linear coastal settlements of

Ballyhalbert and **Ballywalter** and make for the seaside town of **Millisle**, a summer holiday destination with a stone wall running out to the sea. Nearby **Donaghadee** is a mere 21 miles (34 kilometres) from Portpatrick in Scotland and merits a stop at **Grace Neill's Inn**, in business since 1611. From here the road curves around the headland, going inland slightly in the direction of **Bangor**, a holiday resort with a large marina, in considerable contrast to its 6th-century beginnings, when *St Comhghall* founded a monastery here.

At **Crawfordsburn** with its thatched Old Inn make for **Cultra**, where the **Ulster Folk and Transport Museum** is set in the beautiful parkland of Cultra Manor. This extensive open-air museum, which merits a lengthy visit, gives impressions of rural and urban life over the past few hundred years. Inside there is a modern folk gallery and a large photographic archive. It also houses a transport and railway museum.

Leaving Cultra, go back on the road past **Holywood** on the right and make for Belfast.

Belfast Parks, The Palm House.

Counties Tyrone and Fermanagh

*'I like to look across', said
Barney Horisk, leaning on his sleán,
'and think of all the people
who have bin.'*
(From 'A Severed
Head'.)

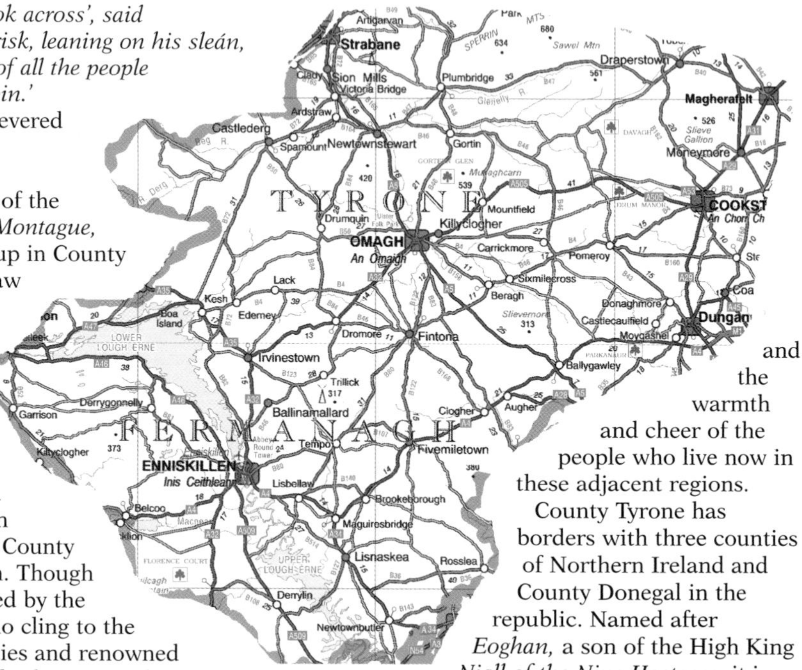

The words of the
poet *John Montague*,
who grew up in County
Tyrone, draw
us into the
distant
past
and
recent
times of
this
county and
its southern
neighbour, County
Fermanagh. Though
often missed by the
tourists who cling to the
familiar cities and renowned
coastlines, both counties have
much to offer, and their illustrious pasts
are worth seeking out.

The **Sperrin Mountains** form a rugged
border with County Derry, and the former
densely forested regions gave concealment
to those groups that resisted the invader
and settler. Emigration wore down the
population as native people left their
homes to forge different lives in the newer
worlds. In southern lakes, where the early
Celts and then Christian monks both
existed on small islands, planters later
dominated from the lough shores. More
recent struggles took their toll on these
counties, and thriving towns lost saddened
people in the name of right or wrong.
Today's peace invites visitors to recall for
themselves the great houses, ruined forts
and prehistoric sites of those who have
been—but also to experience the
revitalised waterway, the bustling towns,

and
the
warmth
and cheer of the
people who live now in
these adjacent regions.
County Tyrone has
borders with three counties
of Northern Ireland and
County Donegal in the
republic. Named after
Eoghan, a son of the High King
Niall of the Nine Hostages, it is
the largest county in Northern Ireland.
Hidden treasures of ancient stones have
been yielded by the peaty Sperrin slopes,
while gold glistens in mountain streams
and coal is buried deep near the shores of
Lough Neagh. Cutting a valley through
the foothills is the sparkling Owenkillew
River, before it makes for the sea away up
at **Lough Foyle**. From this region the
O'Neills and O'Donnells at one time ruled,
by ancient ways and Irish laws. But
submission to English control was forced
in 1603, leading to their flight and that of
many of their people. Subsequent years
saw continued dispersal as thousands left
on waiting ships for strange lands across
distant seas.

Resistance has remained in the spirit of
Tyrone people; and one of the first Civil
Rights Association marches of 1968 took
place between Coalisland and Dungannon.

A leading activist, *Bernadette Devlin*, gained renown for her election to the British House of Commons as the youngest MP ever. In succeeding years, political unrest touched many parts of the county; but in between, in the quiet pleasant towns of the Clogher Valley, a certain timelessness pervaded. Here a train once travelled, curling through the valley with the Blackwater River. Now the stations are silent, and their old red-brick walls provide office or home. Many literary voices throughout the years have told Tyrone stories, from *William Carleton* to the poets *John Montague* and *Paul Muldoon*. The county has tales to tell, and a curious visitor will seek them out 'in Tyrone among the bushes.'

Forest scene in the Cladagh Mountain, Co. Fermanagh.

When a motorway was built from **Belfast**, easy access to County Fermanagh to the south-west was made available to the tourist. In 1994 the mighty lakes of the **River Erne** were linked to the Shannon by the reopening of the old canal; the resulting waterway now offers 500 miles of cruising and fishing, all the way from Limerick in the south-west to Belleek at the north-west edge. Mariners, experienced and otherwise, navigate their way through ancient ecclesiastical sites, following routes discovered by pilgrims who paused on their way to Lough Derg in County Donegal. Where *St Molaise* guarded his relics in the tower of Devenish, 'sailors' from all over Europe moor their boats and lay out their picnics in the shadows of the ancient site. They cast their lines into the dark-blue waters, which offer up trout, perch, and bream. This was also the food of the ancient inhabitants, whose statues to their Celtic gods still stare out from lonely churchyards.

Back on land, in the far north-west corner, time has stood still in **Lough Melvin**. Here uniquely three species of brown trout inhabit the pristine lake; but there are high-tech facilities for the adventurous and the brave. **Pettigo** on the other side, adjacent to Donegal, was once a halting place for pilgrims but also for cheerful mourners bearing coffins of tea and sugar over the border during wartime rationing. In along the lough shore, ruined Plantation forts stand. Once built to guard, now only their ghostly inhabitants look out over the bay. It is the herons and swans who observe the navigators as they negotiate a way through the jigsaw puzzle that is **Upper Lough Erne**. The reedy waters brush softly against the bow as a course is gently steered through the beauty of Fermanagh, past and present.

County Tyrone

Around Strabane

County Tyrone is bordered by the rugged Sperrin Mountains and Lough Neagh. The town of **Strabane**, built along the banks of the Mourne River, looks north-west to Lifford in County Donegal. It's a busy, friendly town with a linen and printing heritage.

Recent years have seen persistent high unemployment, and political unrest has taken its toll. But new housing and a commitment to boosting tourism through exploring its common heritage with Donegal and the surrounding regions have given some new life. The American connection is celebrated in the Wilson Ancestral Home at **Dergalt**, the birthplace of *James Wilson*, grandfather of *President Woodrow Wilson* and also a former apprentice printer at Gray's. Even during boom times, Strabane experienced high emigration and now traces the steps of those who went on to better lives in the New World. The model linen village of **Sion Mills** still features half-timbered houses and workers' cottages, though more modern architecture is visible in the slate engraving on **St Teresa's Church**.

After a failed assault on Derry in 1689, *King James II of England* spent the night in **Newtownstewart**, where in rage he ordered the town and castle burnt down.

Omagh

The busy market town of **Omagh** grew around the meeting place of the Camowen and Drumragh Rivers. The town centre was bombed in 1998, with heavy casualties. Today many businesses have reopened, and plans are under way to build a community centre on the devastated site. Visitors are welcomed to explore or to fish for salmon and trout in the rivers. Omagh's most famous literary son is the playwright *Brian Friel*, whose play *Dancing at Lughnasa* was recently filmed and starred *Meryl Streep*. The songwriter *Jimmy Kennedy* of 'Teddy Bears' Picnic' and 'Hokey-Cokey' fame (among

others) was born here.

At the centre of the **Ulster-American Folk Park** is the cottage in which *Thomas Mellon* was born. He emigrated to America and later founded a vast business empire. The Mellon family and others are remembered in this marvellous museum where various aspects of emigrant life are re-created. The outdoor museum, with life-size exhibits from 19th-century streets to meeting house, emigrant ship, and dockside gallery, makes for an evocative and worthwhile visit. The **Centre for Emigration Studies** is also based here.

The Sperrins

Much older lives feature in the **Ulster History Park**, with its models of Stone Age to 17th-century settlements. A 5-mile drive goes through the conifers and wildlife of **Gortin Glen Forest Park**. As you approach the Sperrin Mountains on these quiet roads, not only the silence is golden: gold has been found in the area between Gortin and Plumbridge. You can try your luck in the streams near the **Sperrin Heritage Centre**, behind which is the highest peak of this range, **Mount Sawel**, at 2,240 feet (683 metres). Another visitors' centre is at **An Creagán**, next to the **Black Bog**, which supplies refined turf for craft-making. Several stone monuments were found in this area during turf-cutting, including the **Beaghmore Stone Circles**. This Bronze Age site is of stones of varying heights, some called the Dragon's Teeth. Found only in the 1950s and preserved in the turf, their function is still a mystery.

Cookstown and Lough Neagh

The wide main street of **Cookstown** by **Drum Manor Forest Park** points towards Slieve Gallion. This street was part of a town plan by *William Stewart* of nearby **Killymoon Castle**, now a farming area. Three linen factories used to operate along the River Ballinderry and a beetling mill at nearby **Wellbrook**.

Loughry Manor nearby was the guest residence of *Jonathan Swift* while he was writing *Gulliver's Travels*. Earlier achievement can be seen in the carved cross of **Ardboe** standing on a windswept Lough Neagh shore. This 18-foot cross has twenty-two carved panels of biblical scenes, and though it is badly weathered, scenes of Adam and Eve and others can be discerned. In the old graveyard is **Ardboe Pin Tree**, a beech tree with its trunk filled with coins and pins, inserted for cures. Ruined **Mountjoy Castle** stands guard in this area where fishermen catch eels and the tales of the Lough are told at the **Kinturk Cultural Centre**.

Clogher Valley

Forming a border with County Armagh, the River Blackwater flows down to **Benburb**, where a ruined castle still stands. The gushing river provides both electricity for the **Servite Priory** and excitement for the many canoeists and anglers. But the village history is less pastoral. Some three thousand Scots were killed by the O'Neills in 1646. There is a model of the battle in the **Benburb Valley Heritage Centre**, housed in a weaving factory.

By the appealing border village of **Aughnacloy** the ancestral home of the American president *Ulysses S. Grant*, who led the Union forces to victory in the American

Sperrin Mountains, Co. Tyrone.

Civil War, has been restored as a typical 19th-century Irish farmhouse.

Also served by the railway line were **Augher**, **Clogher**, and **Fivemiletown**. South of Augher is the childhood home of the writer *William Carleton*, the 'Irish Dickens'. He wrote many tales of peasant life but also wrote about *George Brackenridge* from Clogher, who built a tower outside the town as his own mausoleum and a reminder to the local people who had snubbed him. A different memorial is the inscribed passage grave on **Knockmany Hill**, said to be the burial chamber of *Áine*, a queen of the old Oriel kingdom. It was centred on Clogher with a seat at **Ramore**, a grassy mound behind **St Macartan's Cathedral**.

DON'T MISS

- Learn about the thousands of people who left to forge new lives in America at the **Ulster-American Folk Park**.
- Take a drive through the 1,000-acre **Gortin Glen Forest Park**, where a herd of Japanese Sika deer and other wildlife roam.
- Explore the lonely **Sperrin Mountains**, visit the heritage centre, and try your luck at gold-prospecting!
- What have beetles to do with linen? Find out at the restored **Wellbrook Beetling Mill** near Cookstown.
- See the 18-foot 10th-century **Ardboe** high cross in its bleak location at the edge of Lough Neagh, or leave a pin for a cure in the **Ardboe Tree**.

ALL-WEATHER OPTIONS

- Imagine the smell of the ink and the noise of the presses at **Gray's Printing Press** museum in Strabane.
- Watch the intricate and delicate process of glass-blowing at the **Tyrone crystal factory**.

County Fermanagh

Enniskillen and Lough Erne

The vast area of water that is **Upper and Lower Lough Erne** almost divides this border county. The town of **Enniskillen** sits on an island in the waterway that connects the two loughs. From here the ridge of the Cuilcagh Mountains can be seen rising to the south-west, where sheep and cattle graze on small farms. Enniskillen makes a good base for exploring the region, offering various cultural pursuits, such as the lakeside theatre, the **Buttermarket Craft and Design Centre**, and shopping in the town centre.

Enniskillen Castle was one of a ring of castles built to guard the lough. It now houses the **Fermanagh History and Heritage Centre**. In the turreted **Watergate** is the regimental museum of the Royal Inniskilling Fusiliers, also remembered in the Anglican cathedral and the Town Hall. The lands and 'fair castle with its shining sward' were taken from the Maguires in 1594 and later given to *Sir William Cole*. To the west is the **Cuilcagh Mountain Park** in an area of blanket bog, which aims to restore damaged peatland and its habitats, particularly for the golden plover. Topped by gritstone, the mountain offers a seven-hour climb past spectacular limestone scenery. The area includes the Marlbank Scenic Loop with the fine **Marble Arch Caves**, open to the public since 1985. Visitors can explore a fascinating natural underworld of rivers, waterfalls, and chambers.

Around Lower Lough Erne

As the larger of the two loughs, **Upper Lough Erne** has much to offer the visitor with its ancient religious sites and monuments, contemporary crafts and music. At the north end is **Belleek**, famous for over 140 years for its distinctive parian china. It marks the end of the Erne waterway, whose history is told in the **Explorerne** exhibition. The pottery began with the discovery of feldspar deposits in **Castle Caldwell** in 1857. This estate is situated on a forked peninsula and is now a nature reserve, with a forest park full of bird life. At the entrance is the **Fiddler's Stone**, a memorial to a fiddler who drunkenly fell from a boat in 1770. Undeterred, an annual fiddle festival is held each year in Belleek, where fiddlers and other musicians 'play and safely drink your fill' on dry land.

Almost cut in two by the Border, the town of **Pettigo** was the scene of considerable smuggling, particularly during the war years. It was the start and ending point for years for Lough Derg pilgrims and is a popular angling village. Just on the shore is **Castle Archdale Country Park**, site of a ruined castle and its 18th-century replacement. Now the ferry point for **White Island**, it saw different activity in 1941 when it was used by the RAF and Canadian Air Force carrying out U-boat hunts in the Atlantic. On the western loughside stands **Tully Castle**, overlooking the bay. A herb garden in 17th-century style reminds us of its former days. It is situated off the scenic **Lough Navar Forest Drive**.

The islands

Boa Island (*Inis Badhbha*, 'Badhbh's island'), named after a war goddess of the Celts, is the largest island and is joined to the mainland by a bridge. The double-sided Janus figure reminds us of these times, staring out through the centuries from **Caldragh Cemetery** and thought to date from the Iron Age. Behind, the **'Lusty Man'** is a smaller (possibly female) idol taken from **Lustymore Island**.

Seven eerie stone figures on **White Island**, reached by ferry from **Castle Archdale**, are lined up in the ruins of a small church. Their significance has been much debated: they probably date from Early Christian times, though with pre-Christian influences. The figures include a *sheela-na-gig*, a female fertility figure with a lustful grin. Many such figures were found over the years, and some were kept hidden for years because of their 'obscenity'.

Most extensive of the sites is **Devenish Island**, also accessible by ferry at **Trory**

Point. *St Molaise* founded a monastery here in the 6th century, later raided by Vikings. Various ecclesiastical ruins remain visible, as well as an accessible 12th-century round tower with elaborate cornice. Here the monks sought sanctuary when they sighted approaching enemies from the windows at the top.

Upper Lough Erne and surroundings

This reedy lake is filled with wild birds, offering the visitor solitary cruises among the maze of some sixty largely uninhabited islands. Farmhouse ruins remain as well as signs of monastic settlements. At **Inishkeen**, accessible by causeway, old carved stones are to be found in *St Fergus's Cemetery*. 12th-century **Lisgoole Abbey** was at the northern end. **Galloon Island** has a small farming community with some ghoulishly carved gravestones in the churchyard. The skull and crossbones is found on many Fermanagh gravestones, including those in **Aghalurcher Old Church** near Lisnaskea.

A splendid view of these myriad islands

Marble Arch Caves, Co. Fermanagh.

can be had from **Knockninny Hill**, north of **Derrylin**. A bridge from here travels across to **Lisnaskea**, a small town with plenty of pubs and a folk collection preserved in the local library. The market cross, put up by the *Earl of Erne* to attract dealers, was installed on the shaft of an earlier cross.

DON'T MISS

- Visit the magnificent neo-classical **Castle Coole** and take a stroll in the park, with its flock of greylag geese.
- Find your way around the fascinating underworld of rivers and winding passages that are the **Marble Arch Caves**.
- Take a boat out to the **islands of Lough Erne** and view the many Celtic and Early Christian archaeological sites.
- Observe the craftworkers at the **Belleek pottery** as they weave the intricate strands of porcelain basketware.
- Drive along the **Lough Navar Forest route** on the western shore, which leads to a viewing point a thousand feet high, offering a panoramic view.

ALL-WEATHER OPTIONS

- Mingle with the ghosts of Maguire chieftains at the **Heritage Centre** in **Enniskillen Castle**.
- Learn about the lives and times of Lough Erne—without getting your feet wet—at the **Explor Erne** exhibition.
- See the 18th-century **Florence Court** in its dramatic parkland setting, where the first Irish yew is said to have originated or the stately **Castle Coole**, just a mile south east of Enniskillen.

Myths and Legends

Children's room,
Writers' Museum, Dublin.

The myths and legends of Ireland are among the richest and most imaginative in Europe—sufficiently appealing in their diversity and grandeur to bear comparison with the exceptional materials of ancient Greece and Rome. But what's in them, and how are they organised?

The surviving material is broken down into four categories. The first of these, the **'Mythological Cycle'**, covers the gods and heroes of pre-Christian Ireland. It includes the tale of the *Children of Lir*; it also tells of the arrival of a mysterious group of invaders, *Tuatha Dé Danann* ('nation of the god Dana'), who, thanks to their magical powers, enjoy a series of great victories. However, once the Celts show up, they're forced to take refuge underground, where they've remained to this day, hiding in mounds as the *Sí,* or people of the Otherworld. Interestingly, this downgrading of Dana's people prefigures *Swift's* use of satirical scale reduction and inflation in *Gulliver's Travels.* But—as Gulliver knew better than anyone else— even diminished enemies can still prove a menace, and the idea of a revengeful return of the 'little people' is one that continues to exercise the imagination of country folk in remote parts of Ireland.

Included in the Mythological Cycle is an imaginative treatment of post-mortal existence. A happy, Hollywoodian Otherworld, exuding glamour and eternal youth, exists in the western sea. In *Tír na hÓige* ('the land of youth'), death and old age are unknown. *Oisín,* a young hero, decides to make a trip there in the company of *Niamh of the Golden Hair.* But after three days he returns home to find he's been away for three hundred years, that all his companions are dead, and that he's the last survivor. Resigned to his fate, he lives on long enough for a poet to show him chatting to *St Patrick* in what forms a delightful fictional treatment of a historical event—the meeting of pagan Ireland with the new Christian order.

The second grouping, the **'Red Branch Cycle'**, deals with Ulster heroes. Its most celebrated story, *Táin Bó Chuaille* ('the cattle-raid of Cooley'), tells how the two provinces of Connacht and Ulster go to war with one another. *Méabh,* queen of Connacht, knowing that *Dáire* of Ulster has a bull of exceptional qualities, sends her men to bargain for it; but they are overheard by the Ulstermen boasting that if they don't get the bull freely they'll take it by force. Incensed, the Ulstermen refuse to hand over the animal, and a fierce battle ensues that ends only when the white bull of Connacht and the black bull of Ulster engage in single combat. As you might expect (given that this is the Ulster version), the black bull emerges triumphant.

Chief of the Ulster heroes involved in combat is *Cú Chulainn* ('the hound of Culann'). A man of infinite valour, he is ready to die for his province. Strapped to a post, sword in hand, he defies his enemies, while a black raven, harbinger of death, perches on his shoulder. His courageous stance is immortalised in a fine bronze statue by *Oliver Sheppard* that stands today in the General Post Office in Dublin. But this statue celebrates more than Cú Chulainn's last stand: it also functions as a memorial for those heroes of 1916 who proclaimed an Irish republic in this building and who, like Cú Chulainn, were willing to lay down their lives for what they believed in.

The third mythic category, the **'Fenian Cycle'**, concerns the exploits of *Fionn* and *Oisín* and includes the great romantic story *Tóraíocht Dhiarmada agus Ghráinne* ('the pursuit of Diarmaid and Gráinne'). In this cautionary tale, Gráinne's father, *Cormac,* decides that she should marry an aging Fionn mac Cumhaill. She agrees but, frustrated in her womanly desires, casts a *geis* or spell over the handsome Diarmaid. Shortly thereafter she runs away with him, with tragic consequences. Most of the story treats of the desperate attempts of the lovers to avoid recapture, but—in contrast to the ferocity and bloodthirstiness of Cú Chulainn's world—the lovers and the pursuing Fionn are imbued with chivalric and humanitarian instincts that play off honour against love in the noblest of ways.

The fourth category of myths, the **'Cycle of the Kings'**, deals with chiefs and other historical figures invested with legendary exploits. Here the pretence of historical veracity is excessive, but the incidents and narrative development have something in common with the *Chansons de Geste.*

Ancient Irish myth persists in the memory of Irish people, thanks to the popularising skills of *Lady Gregory* and *Yeats,* but it is also blazing new paths in fantasy fiction and in films such as *Conan the Barbarian*—an unexpected Texan rerouting of the ancient Fenian Cycle that augurs well for its ability to win fresh audiences.

Our journey begins in the old printing town of **Strabane**, which looks across the Foyle to Lifford in County Donegal. You can pay a visit to the museum of **Gray's Printing Shop** before taking the A5 road to the model linen town of **Sion Mills** alongside the Strule River and peacefully through **Newtownstewart**—unlike *King James II,* who ordered the town burnt after his failed assault on Derry in 1689. The small hills of Bessy Bell and Mary Gray stand on either side of the road. On the left is the **Ulster-American Folk Park**, where the emigrant experience is explored in an extensive outdoor museum.

Where two rivers meet to form the wider River Strule is the hilly town of **Omagh**, with its courthouse and twin-spired Catholic church. Take a sharp left onto the B48 road towards **Gortin Forest Park** and pass on the left the **Ulster History Park**, which aims to cover some thousands of years of history. A tarmac road of 5 miles runs through the forest park, offering views of wildlife and conifer forest. Stopping off for a spot of gold-prospecting in the area between Gortin and Plumbridge, go right for the Sperrin Heritage Centre along the B47 road, which gives good views over the valley.

Devenish Island Tower & Cross, Co. Fermanagh

The highest peak of this gentle mountain range is Mount Sawel, at 2,040 feet (622 metres), rising up behind the centre.

The road continues through the **Goles Forest**, which commands soaring views, and turns right onto the B162 road. Slieve Gallion rises 1,737 feet (529 metres) on the east and remote Davagh Forest Park on the left. At the centre of farming country is **Cookstown**, with its broad main street, the childhood home of *Bernadette Devlin* (*Bernadette McAliskey*), civil rights activist and the youngest MP elected to the British House of Commons. At the water's edge of **Lough Neagh** (via the B181 and B73) the **Ardboe Cross** stands windswept on the site of a 6th-century monastery.

Looping back onto the road via the Diamond, by ruined **Mountjoy Castle**, commanding the lough corner, you travel inland to **Coalisland**, where old industrial features are being restored and there is a heritage centre in an old corn mill. Textile manufacturing has been replaced by fine crystal in the Tyrone Crystal glassworks at **Dungannon**, to the right off the A45, one-time chief seat of the O'Neills. South of the town are

TOURING ROUTE
Counties Tyrone and Fermanagh

Moygashel Mills, the world-famous name in linen; and a right turn onto the A4 takes you along the edge of **Parkanaur Forest Park**. You are now driving through the Clogher Valley of small farms and quiet villages, many of which were served by the Clogher Valley Railway. The American connection is further explored at the rebuilt ancestral home of President Ulysses Grant Simpson, off the A4 east of Ballygawley. A stop for a tea break at the converted railway station at **Augher** and on to **Clogher**, the oldest bishopric in Ireland, passing on the left the tall hilltop **Brackenridge Folly**, built as a reminder to the local people of *Brackenridge,* whom they would not accept in life. Five miles from here, appropriately, is **Fivemiletown**, where the railway used to run right through. A long flat mountain ridge ahead is Cuilcagh on the south-western edge of County Fermanagh, which you are now entering, passing the splendidly restored **Castle Coole** on the right.

From the busy town of **Enniskillen**, with its former **Maguire Castle**, situated where the Lower and Upper Lough Erne constrict, take the A32 to Trory and the Devenish Island ferry. The-best preserved round tower in Ireland and remarkable ecclesiastical remains are here, including the ruined 12th-century **St Molaise's Oratory**. Back along the B82 coast road to **Castle Archdale Country Park** and nature reserve, where the ruined 17th-century castle was rebuilt and later used by the RAF in 1941. There is a ferry service to **White Island**, where a ruined 12th-century church contains eight weird stone figures still causing archaeologists to argue whether all are Christian or not.

Back on land, the scenic loop to Kesh gives fine views over the lake and passes the ruined **Crevenish Castle**. **Kesh** is a pleasant fishing village on the Kesh River, where a side road leads to **Muckross Bay**

with its marina and bathing beach. There is good lake and river fishing in all directions. A bridge connects the land to **Boa Island**, said to be the last place in Ireland where druids practised. In the Caldragh graveyard is a two-headed Janus figure.

The A47 goes right across to **Castle Caldwell**, where the estate on a forked peninsula is full of wildlife. A stone at the entrance tells of a fiddler drowning from a boat. **Belleek**, on the border, is the venue for an annual fiddle festival but is best known for its 'woven' porcelain, which can be observed in the making.

From the town turn left turn onto the A46 along the western lough shore and scenic route through the coniferous Lough Navar Forest up to a viewing point. Plantation castles are many around the lough. **Tully Castle** is on the left and, further along, **Monea Castle** on the right, now in ruins. Leaving the shore, take a right turn to Springfield and follow the road via Boho to Belcoo at Lough Macnean, filled with pike, bream, and brown trout. Take the Marlbank Scenic Loop with the **Marble Arch Caves** to meet the A32 near the magnificent **Florence Court**. At Mullan take the B108 to meet the A509, and take a right to Derrylin. Head due east, and the road leaps across the lake by way of two bridges giving splendid panoramas. *Live and let live* is the wise inscription on the old market house of **Lisnaskea**, a town of much character. **Castle Balfour** is on the edge of the town. Cross again at Carrybridge, the handsome bridge across the Erne, which has seen a busy marina spring up, right to Bellanaleck, and back to Enniskillen.

Index

Index

Index

Index

Index

Index

Index